Tourism
An Exploration

Third Edition

Jan van Harssel, Ed. D.

Prentice Hall Career & Technology
Englewood Cliffs, New Jersey 07632

Library of Congress Cataloging-in-Publication Data

Van Harssel, Jan.
    Tourism : an exploration / Jan van Harssel. — 3rd ed.
        p.   cm.
    ISBN 0-13-923343-1
    1. Tourist trade.   I. Title.
    G155.A1V36   1994
    338.4'791—dc20   93-6381
                                                          CIP

Acquisitions Editor: Robin Baliszewski
Editorial/production supervision and interior design: WordCrafters Editorial Services, Inc.
Cover Design: Laura Ierardi
Manufacturing Buyer: Ed O'Dougherty
Marketing Manager: Ramona Baran

© 1994 by Prentice Hall Career & Technology
Prentice-Hall, Inc.
A Paramount Communications Company
Englewood Cliffs, New Jersey 07632

Printed in the United States of America

10   9   8   7   6   5   4   3   2   1

ISBN 0-13-923343-1

Prentice-Hall International (UK) Limited, *London*
Prentice-Hall of Australia Pty. Limited, *Sydney*
Prentice-Hall Canada, Inc., *Toronto*
Prentice-Hall Hispanoamericana, S.A., *Mexico*
Prentice-Hall of India Private Limited, *New Delhi*
Prentice-Hall of Japan, Inc., *Tokyo*
Simon & Schuster Asia Pte., Ltd., *Singapore*
Editora Prentice-Hall do Brasil, Ltda., *Rio de Janeiro*

This revised edition
is dedicated with
renewed (but unrevised) affection
to
Linda, Casey, and Lindsay

Contents

PREFACE   xi

TERM PROJECT SUGGESTIONS   xiii

INTRODUCTION   1
Growth of the Industry   1
Indications of Continued Growth   3
What Is Tourism?   3
Conclusion   9
Review Questions   9
Appendixes   10

1   THE DEVELOPMENT OF THE TOURISM INDUSTRY   19
General Overview   20
Water Transport   22
Land Transport   25
Air Transport   27
The Hotel Industry   32
The Automobile   34
Car Rental   36
Tour Operators   37
Conclusion   38
Review Questions   40

Reading: The U.S. Overseas Travel Market: A Comparison between Package Tour and Individual Travelers   41
Ady Milman

2   THE TOURISM INDUSTRY   53
Transportation   53
Accommodations   67

Travel Professionals   71
Conclusion   77
Review Questions   78

Reading: Segmenting the International Travel Market by
Activity   79
Sheauhsing Hsieh, Joseph T. O'Leary, **and** *Alastair M. Morrison*

3   THE TOURISM EXPLOSION   95
Motivations to Travel   97
Characteristics of Worldwide Travel   100
International Travel to and from the United States   104
Conclusion   110
Review Questions   110

Reading: Tourism: The World's Peace Industry   112
Louis J. D'Amore

**4   PSYCHOLOGY AND MOTIVATION
FOR TOURISM   119**
Reasons for Travel   121
Types of Travelers   122
Why People Travel   124
Choosing a Destination   126
Types of Motivation   127
Types of Travel   128
Types of Tourists   130
Barriers to Travel   131
Business Travel   132
Conclusion   135
Review Questions   136

Reading: Segmenting the Business Traveler Market   137
Pamela A. Weaver, Ken W. McCleary, **and** *Zhao Jinlin*

5   THE ECONOMIC IMPACT OF TOURISM   149
The Domestic Scene   149
Local Benefits from Tourism   151
Costs and Liabilities of Tourism   155
The International Scene   157
Relevant Economic Issues   159
Other Relevant Economic Issues   163
The Tourism Multiplier   164
Role of Tour Companies   165
Role of Government   166
Effects of Saturation   167

Importance of Government Planning   168
Tourism Activity and Economic Development   169
Alternative Tourism Development   170
Conclusion   170
Review Questions   171

Reading: Economic Impact Studies: Relating the Positive and Negative
Impacts to Tourism Development   172
William R. Fleming and *Lorin Toepper*

6   THE SOCIAL IMPACT OF TOURISM   183
Pros and Cons of Tourism Development   183
Expectations of Host and Guest   184
Result of Tourism Development   186
Changing Values and Attitudes   187
The Imitation Effect   189
Socioeconomic Impact   190
Sociocultural Impact   192
Environmental Effects of Tourism   198
Conclusion   200
Review Questions   201

Reading: Cultural Tourism: Pitfalls and Possibilities   202
Anne M. Masterton

7   COMMUNITY TOURISM PLANNING   207
What Is Tourism Planning?   208
The Planning Process   209
Conventional versus Strategic Planning   209
Why Consider Tourism Development?   210
Understanding Tourists   213
Do We Really Want Tourism   218
The Development of Tourism   219
Organization   223
The Master Plan   223
Promotion   226
The Hosting Function   228
Conclusion   231
Review Questions   231

Reading: The Social Impacts of Tourism and Their Effects on
Attitudes toward a Major Cultural Attraction   232
Laurel Reid and *Allison Boyd*

Reading: The Heritage Resource as Seen by the Tourist:
The Heritage Connection   242
Karen Ida Peterson

8   THE YEARS AHEAD   251
Trends Influencing Future Tourism Demand   251
Long-Term Predictions   254
Changes in Transportation   260
Conclusion   263
Review Questions   265

Reading: Tourism Impacts Related to EC 92:
A Look Ahead   266
Brian J. Mihalik

Reading: Environmental Ethics   276
Anne M. Masterton

**Appendix A   EMPLOYMENT OPPORTUNITIES
IN TOURISM   279**
Project   299

Appendix B   DIRECTORY OF USEFUL ADDRESSES   301

GLOSSARY   315

INDEX   333

Preface

This book is an introduction to the world's most diverse and largest industry—tourism and travel. Today, tourism is a dynamic and major industry in many regions of this country and throughout the world. The information here has been edited especially for the newcomer to this exciting field of study. A serious attempt has been made to achieve a balance between introductory and advanced concepts. *Tourism: An Exploration* provides an elementary overview of the industry without neglecting detail and accuracy.

A series of articles relevant to tourism, from a wide variety of industry resources, are included. These articles were selected for two reasons. First, they give important information from current experts in various fields of tourism. Second, they give students examples of industry information resources, useful both during their course of study and later during their careers as travel professionals. Review questions follow each chapter. Students are encouraged to think through their responses to each question and to discuss the questions with others. Students may need library resources to completely answer many of the review questions and projects.

The statistical data presented in the book are intended primarily to give students an idea of the magnitude of the tourism industry. Statistical data available in 1992 were used in this book.

Also included in this textbook is a term project. This is essential to the design of the text, and should be completed carefully and thoughtfully. The project will help the students to understand better the depth of background and the expertise that travel professionals must have. It will also help them to appreciate the complexities and excitement of careers in the tourism industry.

Many people have contributed to the final version of this textbook, and it is my pleasure, as well as my obligation, to acknowledge their contributions. My students at Niagara University helped greatly by studying the material and offering suggestions. I owe a special debt of gratitude to my editor, Robin Baliszewski, to Judy Casillo of Prentice Hall, and to the fine people at WordCrafters.

These contributions were augmented by feedback from instructors at several other colleges. Their comments, suggestions, criticism, and encouragement have all influenced this final version.

I hope that I have used these invaluable contributions from so many sources effectively and trust that this attempt to explore the many aspects of the tourism industry will contribute to the excitement of tourism education for instructors and students alike.

Dr. Jan van Harssel
Niagara Falls, New York

Term Project Suggestions

Prepare a comprehensive paper on the current status and probable future of the tourism industry in a country that will be assigned to you. Your paper should be as complete as possible. It should touch on, but not limit itself to, the following points:

1. Brief description of post–World War II history.
2. Recent developments in political climate and any implications for tourism.
3. Brief discussion of economic stability/instability.
4. Analysis of tourist flows (historic development, countries of origin, volume, why?).
5. Culture/folklore.
6. Language(s).
7. Currency/exchange rate.
8. Climate/scenic assets.
9. Listing of sights/attractions.
10. National/religious holidays–special events.
11. Listing of airports and airlines serving them.
12. Description of entry requirements.
13. Bordering countries (names, competitive analysis).
14. Ground transportation system.
15. Nature of tourism (beach, wildlife, casino, business).
16. Economic, social, and environmental impacts.
17. Describe and comment on the country's advertising and promotion strategy.
18. Discuss the country's future tourism growth opportunities/setbacks.

Give a ten-minute oral presentation to the class. This will consist of a concise summary of the paper followed by personal thoughts and opinions on whether or not you would recommend a trip to this country. This presentation should be enhanced with advertising samples, brochures, and other items relative to the country. Use the opportunity of your class presentation to show your expertise and enthusiasm.

The paper is to be typewritten, double-spaced, and range in length from ten to fifteen pages. It should include sources of information, including a complete bibliography.

Please do not use your paper during your oral presentation. You may, however, use brief notes to guide you in your speech. See Appendix B for a list of government tourist offices maintained in the United States by foreign countries. Write to the Government Tourist Office of your assigned country immediately and request information about tourism, climate, geography, and so on. You might contact a local travel agency for additional information. The local public librarian will also be able to assist you in obtaining information for this project.

About the Author

Dr. Jan van Harssel, a native of The Netherlands, is an Associate Professor at the Institute of Travel, Hotel, and Restaurant Administration at Niagara University in Niagara Falls, New York. Prior to joining the faculty of Niagara University, he was Program Director of Travel and Tourism programs at Champlain College in Burlington, Vermont and National College in Rapid City, South Dakota. He received his Master's degree in Tourism and Travel Administration from the Graduate School of Management and Urban Professions in New York City, and earned his Doctoral degree in Higher Education Administration from the University of Vermont.

Introduction

The world is a book;
he who stays at home
reads only one page.

—Augustine

Welcome to the world of travel and congratulations on your decision to plan for a professional career in the tourism industry. You will soon join an industry that employs more people worldwide than any other enterprise. In the United States, according to the Travel and Tourism Government Affairs Council, travel industry employment has grown 43 percent in the last ten years, twice the growth rate for all U.S. industries.[1]

Tourism is the largest industry in the world today in terms of economic activity and as a generator of employment. One out of every twelve workers worldwide works in the tourism and hospitality industry. The World Travel and Tourism Council concludes that travel and tourism generates more than $2.9 trillion per year, 5.3 percent of the combined gross national product of all the world's nations, and 12.3 percent of consumer spending.[2] An industry of this size obviously has a tremendous impact on the lives of individuals and the economies of nations. The explosive growth of the tourism industry has created a demand for new professionals—people just like yourself who are committed to professional careers in the hospitality industry.

GROWTH OF THE INDUSTRY

Tourism is a diverse but major industry throughout many regions of the world. It is especially significant in otherwise less-developed regions which, because of location or other reasons, have been at least partially bypassed by industrialization and other forms of economic development. Indeed, it is the lack of development that often makes such areas attractive for tourism. Tourism in these areas is based on the indigenous, distinctive, and unspoiled character of the natural, historical, or cultural environments. Unless properly planned, however, the growth of tourism in such areas can destroy the natural qualities that make tourism attractive in the first place.

---

[1]*Tourism Facts: Travel and Tourism* (Washington, D.C.: Government Affairs Council, 1991).
[2]Data from World Travel and Tourism Council's 2nd Annual Report (Brussels, Belgium, 1992).

Tourism emerged as a widely attractive alternative for economic development in the 1950s and early 1960s because of rapid post–World War II growth in population, income, leisure time, and mobility. Less-developed regions of the world were encouraged to adopt tourism as the foundation of an economic development strategy. Organizations such as the United Nations, the International Monetary Fund, the World Bank, and regional banks offered technical assistance for tourism development.

Global growth trends for the travel industry during the decades following World War II have been spectacular. In 1990, more than $2.7 trillion was spent on travel-related activities (both domestic and international). If tourism were a country, its GNP would rank fourth in the world, after the United States, Japan, and the Commonwealth of Independent States. The World Tourism Organization reports that worldwide international tourist arrivals reached 476 million in 1992. International border crossings totaled 350 million in 1980, up from 168 million in 1970, and just 71 million in 1960. In 1990, according to a report by the World Travel and Tourism Council, the travel and tourism industry employed more than 112 million people worldwide.[3]

While these figures are impressive, it is important to understand that a very high percentage of all international arrivals and expenditures occur between and within the United States and Europe. In 1990, Europe and North America received 80 percent of all tourist expenditures and 84 percent of world tourism arrivals.[4]

---

[3]See note 2 above.
[4]See note 2 above.

INDICATIONS OF CONTINUED GROWTH

Whether for pleasure or for business, travel demand is rapidly growing. Higher incomes, more leisure time, changing lifestyles, increased overseas visitation, and a growing number of people reaching retirement age—many at an earlier age—all indicate that the tourism industry will continue to expand. The industry has responded to this increased growth opportunity with new air, land, and sea transportation networks; new hotels, resort destinations, and convention centers; and growing local attractions and service industries that support the needs of the tourist.

Tourism is a service industry. Today's tourists and travelers need and expect service: service related to trip planning, reservation handling, efficiency in transportation, or the services available at their destination. Tourism is an industry of competing firms whose clients have become increasingly cost conscious. The tourist has the right to expect professional service. The quality of our leisure time is becoming increasingly important to us, and the demand for expert, professional service in planning that leisure time is growing ever more important.

In various ways, modern societies provide their citizens with the opportunity to reach their fullest potential. For many people, this opportunity is satisfied during free time rather than at work. The tourism industry, therefore, affects us not only because of its tremendous size, but because of the crucial role it plays in improving the quality of life for millions of people.

In such an important industry the potential for jobs is enormous. As the industry becomes more complex, it demands the services of well-trained, enthusiastic, responsible individuals. The future growth and competitive strength of each of the elements that make up the tourism industry depend on how well each entity cares for the safety and comfort of the traveler, on the value tourists get for their money, on how well their expectations are met, and on how well they protect and care for their resources.

WHAT IS TOURISM?

The large sums of money spent and immense volume of travel are indicative of the importance of tourism. But, what exactly is a tourist and what is tourism? The definitions are complex. Tourists travel to and from all parts of the globe seeking a variety of experiences. The tourism industry has responded and developed in ways that vary greatly in type and scale. Moreover, both tourists and the tourism industry evolve—often rapidly—in response to changing tastes and other outside influences.

Considering this diverse and dynamic nature, it is difficult, and perhaps misleading, to generalize about tourism and tourists. We lack a commonly accepted definition of tourism partially because of the complexity of tourist activity and partially because different interests are concerned with different aspects of tourist activity. For example, many data are collected for the hospitality industry. For this group, travelers not spending the night in commercial facilities are of minor interest and those using neither restaurants nor hotel/motels are of no interest. On the other hand, those interested in tourist behavior are not necessarily concerned with economic impact; hence, they may classify tourists in ways that either complicate economic analysis or make it impossible. Moreover, since tourism is part of everyone's experience and vocabulary, many people never stop to consider that they may not share common meanings or that it even makes a difference. In many parts of the U.S., the same attractions are frequently viewed differently within the community. For example, attractions or facilities that have predominantly regional attendance may be considered by those in tourism promotion to be engaged in tourism. However, one should ask whether the visitors they attract are really tourists.

Although one may define tourism for various purposes, regions that promote tourism for economic development cannot categorize any activity as a tourist attraction that does not have economic impact as tourism. The question then becomes how one can define tourism in such a way that it is possible to identify activity as having economic impact.

The common element in all definitions of tourism is that *tourist* is synonymous with *traveler*. Activity per se is irrelevant to the economist. People traveling for business or attend conferences, for health reasons, to visit friends and relatives, to study, and for vacations are tourists. Tourism, then, includes all transients who have no permanent relationship with the visited community.

Beyond the inclusion of travel in the definition of tourism, most definitions also include figures for distance traveled or distance-plus-time-spent. The most common travel distance used in defining tourism (used by both the U.S. Travel Data Center and the U.S. Census Bureau) is 100 miles—that is, 100 miles from the traveler's origin, although a minimum of 50 miles is used in some economic-impact models. Some definitions also include the specification that one night or 24 hours be spent in the place visited. This leads to the designation of a traveler who does not spend the night as an *excursionist*.

The specification of distance and time as factors that make the traveler a tourist is generally an attempt to differentiate between those who have economic impact on the area visited and those who do not. However, in certain areas, these specifications may not be appropriate. The distance that travelers must go to have an economic impact depends on both the regional level examined and geography. If one wants to attract dollars from outside the region, the

significant distance will vary according to whether the area of concern is a nation, state, region, metropolitan area, or city. In fact, distance may be irrelevant on the borders of these regions. In the northern states of the United States, proximity to the Canadian border provides an excellent source of dollars from exported tourism; yet, the traveler may only travel a few miles.

How we define a tourist depends on what we want to say about him or her, and why. To the travel agent, the tourist is a client purchasing a package tour or a business traveler seeking transportation to a meeting or convention. An international airline may distinguish between a traveler who is likely to prefer a charter package and the one who flies first class on a scheduled airline. In the eyes of an airline, the kind of ticket purchased may be the best indicator of the difference between a pleasure traveler and a business traveler.

Once the traveler disembarks, the airline's definition gives way to that of the accommodation industry. A hotel may distinguish between the convention delegate who will attend a meeting or meal function at the hotel and the visitor who is likely to use the hotel only as a place to sleep during his or her visit with friends or relatives.

A local attraction, such as an annual rodeo, will want to make all travelers, regardless of how they travel or what accommodation arrangement they have chosen, aware that the event is taking place and that they, the traveler, as well as local and area residents, are invited to participate.

To the food and beverage industry, the tourist is a source of increased sales in its year-round outlets and of economic survival in those seasonally attractive places such as beaches and the ski slopes.

Thus, the answer to the question, "Who is a tourist?" depends in large measure on which sector of the industry is answering the question. However, from the individual's point of view, one is a tourist when one seeks to get away from home for a change. The family members who spend a week in a tent at the same campground every year may not see themselves as tourists. Nor, for example, would school children on a canoe expedition in a remote part of a national park look upon themselves as tourists.

Since our purpose here is to discuss the importance of the tourism sector as a whole, we must see the traveler from the industry's point of view. It perceives the traveler as a visitor and classifies him or her according to the reason for the visit and other factors characteristic of the visit, such as the traveler's mode of transportation, point of origin, and level of spending.

The traditional tourist may represent an important proportion of the total visitor population, but we cannot equate the tourism sector with tourists or pleasure-related activities alone. The existence of a tourism industry derives primarily from the traveler's desire to experience a change and willingness to spend money in the pursuit of that experience.

The tourism industry is composed of those sectors of the economy providing services such as accommodation, food and beverages, transportation and recreation, as well as the associated distribution and sales services. It is supplemented by public and private concerns organizing and providing a broad range of events and attractions.

The management of the tourism product requires specialized skills because tourism services are uniquely different from manufactured goods. Some examples are given here to further illustrate this important concept.

When viewed as a commodity, the tourism product can not be put in storage or held in inventory. Hotel rooms that go unsold over a holiday weekend represent lost revenue. Empty seats on a departing airplane represent a lost opportunity to generate income.

In addition, customers of tourist services often pay for their transportation, accommodations, and other amenities long before they arrive at their destination. This long period between time of purchase and time of use is unique to our industry.

Brand loyalty is difficult to achieve. Most travelers seek variety in their annual vacation experience, both in the destinations and mode of transportation.

An important fourth characteristic of the tourism product is that supply is often fixed. While the supply of manufactured goods can be increased or decreased and shipped to different markets, tourist attractions are often fixed in supply and are location-specific.

Finally, the tourism experience is produced and consumed simultaneously. The creates challenges for quality control and integrity of promotional practices.

The industry operates on profit motive and its promotional efforts are aimed primarily at increasing "tourist" travel. However, it also seeks to serve those who contribute to tourism revenues who are not defined specifically as pleasure travelers. For example, the business traveler uses many of the same facilities as the "tourist;" local residents frequent recreational and cultural facilities that often serve the tourist trade as well.

The economic health of the tourism industry depends on the volume and pattern of its customers' use of a great variety of facilities and services, and it counts both local residents and all classes of visitors among its valued customers. The tourist, or pleasure traveler, is but one of the classes of visitors catered to by the hospitality industry.

Pennsylvania Bureau of Travel Marketing

Tourism, then, is the business of attracting visitors and catering to their needs and expectations. Tourists include all those who travel for either leisure, recreation, vacation, health, education, religion, sport, business, or family reasons. Following is an overview of the major components of the tourism and travel industry:

I. Tourist destinations.
    A. Government promotion offices.
    B. Regional promotion offices.
    C. Resort areas, convention centers.

II. Transportation.
    A. Airlines.
        1. Majors.
        2. Nationals.
        3. Regionals.
        4. Nonscheduled/charters.
    B. Ground transportation.
        1. Rental car.
        2. Motorcoach (intercity).
        3. Motorcoach (sightseeing).
        4. Railroad.

III. Accommodations.
    A. Hotels.
    B. Motels.
    C. Resorts.

IV. Cruise lines.

V. Tourist attractions.
    A. Attractions (natural or cultural).
    B. Theme parks.
    C. Museums.

VI. Travel brokers.
    A. Travel agents.
    B. Travel wholesalers.
    C. Tour and charter operators.
    D. Ground operators.
    E. Travel incentive companies.

VII. Travel-related services.
    A. Financial (credit cards, traveler's checks, travel insurance).
    B. Travel publications, guide books.
    C. Educational/training services.

Career opportunities in such a diverse industry are broad in scale and scope. An overview is presented in Figure 1–1. For a detailed description of employment opportunities see also Appendix A.

• Travel Agency

Travel Agency Manager, Travel Consultant, Domestic Travel Counselor, International Travel Counselor, Commercial Counselor, Group Department Manager, Receptionist-Travel Counselor, Sales Representative, Group Coordinator, Group Sales Consultant, Tour Escort, Tour Manager, Outside Sales or Commissioned Sales Representative, Agency Owner, Travel Accountant

• Airlines

Airline Operations, Airline Reservation Agents, Airline Sales Office, Airline District Sales Manager, Tour Desk Reservation Supervisors, Airline Monitoring, Rate Desk, Agency Desk, PTA Desk, Reservation Clerks/Sales Agents, Airline Station Agents, Airline Departure Services, Flight Attendant, Food Service Assistant, Accountant, Marketing Analyst, Personnel Officer, Air Freight, Public Relations Officer, Baggage Services

• Tour Operators

Tour or Ground Sales Representative, Tour Operating Companies, Reservations and Operations Employees, Group Coordinators, Reservationist, Tour Director, Ticketing Staff, Clerical positions. Operations Supervisor, Travel Scout, Corporate Travel Manager

• Cruise Lines

Cruise Line Sales, Passenger Booking Clerk, Passenger Sales Representatives, Tour Director, Purser, Station Agents, Clerical Support Positions

• Hotels

Resort Areas, Hotel Administration, Hotel and Motel Chains, Hotel Manager, General Manager, Sales Manager, Sales Representative/Manager, Director of Marketing, Reservationists, Front Desk Personnel/Manager, Front Office Clerks, Guest Services, Reservations, Concierge, Manifest Clerk, Hoteliers

• Car Rental Companies

Rental Sales Agents, General Office, Reservation Agents, Sales Representatives

• Bus Companies

Information Clerks, Ticket Agents, Tour Representatives, General Office

• Hospitality/Restaurants

Restaurant Manager, Chain Executive, Assistant Manager, Personnel Director

• Chamber of Commerce/Conventions/Conferences

Convention or Visitor's Bureaus Throughout the U.S. and Abroad, Assistant Manager, Manager, Director of Conventions, Assistant Director, Food Service Manager, Reservation, Sales and Marketing Representative, Travel Industry Service Representatives

• Government or Tourism Position

State Regional and City Tourist Offices, Tourist Board Representative, Government Tourist Offices Domestically and Internationally that Promote Travel and Tourism, Department of Commerce, Department of Transportation

• Corporate/Business

Travel Secretary, Corporate Travel Manager, Corporate Travel Department Counselor, In-house Travel Department, Corporate Travel Department

• Recreations/Theme Parks

Program Coordinators, Recreation Specialist, Purchasing Agent, Operations-Manager, Manager of Public Relations, Director of Group Sales

• Others

Journalistic Opportunities, (Travel Editors, Travel Writer), Public Relations Jobs, Recreation, Travel and Tourism Instructor, Director

Figure 1–1. Career Opportunities in the Travel Industry

CONCLUSION

Our world is diverse. It is composed of countries with a variety of cultures and customs, rural areas and urban centers each with its own distinct flavor, and so on. The activity we call tourism, with its great economic and social benefits, provides citizens of all countries with an opportunity to explore new places, to meet new people, to learn new things, and, perhaps in the process, to learn more about themselves.

Travel is a bridge between people. It makes a valuable contribution to the world's economies, employs more people than any other industry, and affects the lives of both hosts and guests in one way or another. As travel professionals, it is important that we work together to develop the potential and enjoy the fruits of this exciting industry. We hope this book contributes to that goal.

REVIEW QUESTIONS

1. Discuss what is means to be "committed to a professional career in the hospitality industry"
2. Why did tourism development emerge as a widely attractive alternative for industrial development in the 1950s and 1960s?
3. What was the growth in international tourism arrivals between 1970 and 1990 when expressed as a percentage increase?
4. Try to identify a practical definition of "a tourist" that would be relevant and practical to your region of the country.
5. Differentiate in an economic sense between the tourism product and manufactured goods.

TRENDS IN THE CAPACITY OF HOTELS AND SIMILAR ESTABLISHMENTS WORLDWIDE - 1987-1991

Number of rooms

SUB-REGIONS	1987	1988	1989	1990	1991
WORLD TOTAL	10167141	10607583	10922528	11101352	11312642
%	100%	100%	100%	100%	100%
AFRICA	280489	298824	307688	327443	334363
%	2.75%	2.81%	2.81%	2.94%	2.95%
AMERICAS	3918050	4058143	4175512	4304477	4362202
%	38.53%	38.25%	38.22%	38.77%	38.56%
EAST ASIA/PAC	943636	1035149	1110123	1196702	1276268
%	9.28%	9.75%	10.16%	10.77%	11.28%
EUROPE	4774696	4954511	5046584	4986629	5057598
%	46.96%	46.70%	46.20%	44.91%	44.70%
MIDDLE EAST	142525	147802	163278	163534	159284
%	1.40%	1.39%	1.49%	1.47%	1.40%
SOUTH ASIA	107745	113154	119343	122567	122927
%	1.05%	1.06%	1.09%	1.10%	1.08%

Source: World Tourism Organization (WTO)

TOURISM AND INTERNATIONAL TRADE WORLDWIDE - 1985-1991

(In million US$)

YEARS	EXPORTS FOB	RECEIPTS FROM INTERNATIONAL TOURISM	SHARE OF RECEIPTS IN EXPORTS (%)
1985	1933445	115426	5.97
1986	2132439	139811	6.56
1987	2494886	171577	6.88
1988	2824042	197743	7.00
1989	3024342	210837	6.97
1990	3393529	255074	7.52
1991	3482452	261070	7.50

Source: World Tourism Organization (WTO)

WORLD'S TOP TOURISM EARNERS

INTERNATIONAL TOURISM RECEIPTS

RANK 1991	COUNTRY	TOURISM RECEIPTS (MILLION US$) 1991	TOURISM RECEIPTS (MILLION US$) 1985	RANK 1985	AVERAGE ANNUAL GROWTH RATE (%) 1985/91	% SHARE OF RECEIPTS WORLDWIDE 1991	% SHARE OF RECEIPTS WORLDWIDE 1985
1	USA	45551	17937	1	16.8	17.44	15.54
2	FRANCE	21300	7942	4	17.9	8.15	6.88
3	ITALY	19668	8756	2	14.4	7.53	7.58
4	SPAIN	19004	8151	3	15.2	7.27	7.06
5	AUSTRIA	13956	5084	6	18.3	5.34	4.40
6	UK	12635	7120	5	10.0	4.83	6.16
7	GERMANY	10947	4748	7	14.9	4.19	4.11
8	SWITZERLAND	7064	3145	8	14.4	2.70	2.72
9	CANADA	5537	3103	9	10.1	2.12	2.68
10	HONG KONG	5078	1788	11	19.0	1.94	1.54
11	SINGAPORE	5020	1660	14	20.3	1.92	1.43
12	MEXICO	4355	2176	10	12.3	1.66	1.88
13	AUSTRALIA	4183	1062	18	25.7	1.60	0.92
14	NETHERLANDS	4074	1661	13	16.1	1.56	1.43
15	THAILAND	3923	1171	16	22.3	1.50	1.01
16	PORTUGAL	3700	1137	17	21.7	1.41	0.98
17	DENMARK	3475	1326	15	17.4	1.33	1.14
18	BELGIUM	3468	1663	12	13.0	1.32	1.44
19	JAPAN	3435	1137	17	20.2	1.31	0.98
20	KOREA,RP	3426	784	19	27.9	1.31	0.67
	WORLD TOTAL	261070	115424		14.6	100.00	100.00

Source: World Tourism Organization (WTO)

WORLD'S TOP TOURISM SPENDERS

INTERNATIONAL TOURISM EXPENDITURES

RANK 1991	COUNTRY	TOURISM EXPENDITURES (MILLION US$) 1991	TOURISM EXPENDITURES (MILLION US$) 1985	RANK 1985	AVERAGE ANNUAL GROWTH RATE (%) 1985/91	% SHARE OF EXPENDITURES WORLDWIDE 1991	% SHARE OF EXPENDITURES WORLDWIDE 1985
1	USA	39418	24517	1	8.2	16.05	24.33
2	GERMANY	31650	12809	2	16.3	12.89	12.71
3	JAPAN	23983	4814	4	30.7	9.76	4.77
4	UK	18850	6369	3	19.8	7.67	6.32
5	ITALY	13300	2283	10	34.1	5.41	2.26
6	FRANCE	12338	4557	5	18.1	5.02	4.52
7	CANADA	10526	4130	6	16.9	4.28	4.09
8	NETHERLANDS	7886	3448	7	14.8	3.21	3.42
9	AUSTRIA	7449	2723	8	18.3	3.03	2.70
10	SWEDEN	6104	1967	13	20.8	2.48	1.95
11	SWITZERLAND	5682	2399	9	15.5	2.31	2.38
12	TAIWAN	5678	1429	16	25.9	2.31	1.41
13	BELGIUM	5543	2050	11	18.0	2.25	2.03
14	SPAIN	4530	1010	18	28.4	1.84	1.00
15	AUSTRALIA	3940	1918	14	12.8	1.60	1.90
16	KOREA,RP	3785	606	20	35.7	1.54	0.60
17	DENMARK	3377	1410	17	15.7	1.37	1.39
18	NORWAY	3207	1722	15	10.9	1.30	1.70
19	FINLAND	2634	777	19	22.6	1.07	0.77
20	KUWAIT	2315	1988	12	2.6	0.94	1.97
	WORLD TOTAL	245480	100762	16.0		100.00	100.00

Source: World Tourism Organization (WTO)
Data available as of 15 December 1992

WORLD'S TOP TOURISM DESTINATIONS
INTERNATIONAL TOURIST ARRIVALS

RANK 1991	COUNTRY	TOURIST ARRIVALS (THOUSANDS) 1991	1985	RANK 1985	AVERAGE ANNUAL GROWTH RATE (%) 1985/91	% SHARE OF ARRIVALS WORLDWIDE 1991	1985
1	FRANCE	55731	36748	1	7.2	12.24	11.14
2	USA	42723	25417	3	9.0	9.38	7.71
3	SPAIN	35347	27477	2	4.3	7.76	8.33
4	ITALY	26840	25047	4	1.2	5.89	7.59
5	HUNGARY	21860	9724	11	14.5	4.80	2.94
6	AUSTRIA	19092	15168	5	3.9	4.19	4.60
7	UK	16664	14449	6	2.4	3.66	4.38
8	MEXICO	16560	11907	9	5.7	3.63	3.61
9	GERMANY	15648	12686	8	3.6	3.43	3.84
10	CANADA	14989	13171	7	2.2	3.29	3.99
11	SWITZERLAND	12600	11900	10	1.0	2.76	3.61
12	CHINA	12464	7133	12	9.6	2.73	2.16
13	PORTUGAL	8657	4989	14	9.6	1.90	1.51
14	CZECHOSLOV.	8200	4869	15	9.1	1.80	1.47
15	GREECE	8036	6574	13	3.4	1.76	1.99
16	HONG KONG	6032	3370	17	10.2	1.32	1.02
17	MALAYSIA	5847	2933	19	12.2	1.28	0.88
18	NETHERLANDS	5843	3329	18	9.8	1.28	1.00
19	ROMANIA	5360	4772	16	2.0	1.17	1.44
20	TURKEY	5158	2079	20	16.4	1.13	0.63
	WORLD TOTAL	455100	329636		5.5	100.00	100.00

Source: World Tourism Organization (WTO)

BREAKDOWN OF ARRIVALS BY MODE OF TRANSPORT - 1985-1991

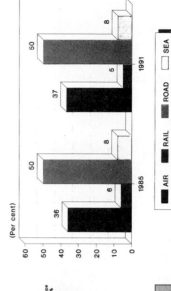

Source: World Tourism Organization (WTO)

DEVELOPMENT OF INTERNATIONAL TOURISM WORLDWIDE 1970-1992

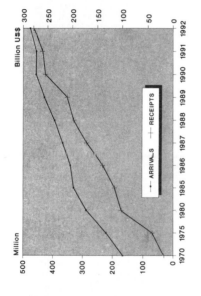

Source: World Tourism Organization (WTO)

INTERNATIONAL TOURIST ARRIVALS AND RECEIPTS WORLDWIDE 1970-1992

YEARS	ARRIVALS (THOUSANDS)	% CHANGE	RECEIPTS (MILLION US$)	% CHANGE
1970	165787	-	17900	-
1975	222290	34.08	40702	127.38
1980	287771	29.45	102008	150.62
1985	329636	14.54	115424	13.15
1986	340908	3.38	139811	21.12
1987	366758	7.61	171577	22.72
1988	393665	7.39	197743	15.25
1989	427884	8.63	210837	6.62
1990	455594	6.47	255074	20.98
1991	455100	-0.11	261070	2.35
1992	475580	4.50	278705	6.75

Source: World Tourism Organization (WTO)

Totals for 1970 to 1991 are revised figures
Totals for 1992 are preliminary estimates
Figures on receipts exclude international transport

SHARE OF EACH REGION IN TOTAL INTERNATIONAL TOURIST ARRIVALS AND RECEIPTS WORLDWIDE - 1992 (Per cent)

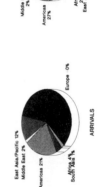

Source: World Tourism Organization (WTO)

WTO defines an **international tourist** as: " Any person who travels to a country other than that in which s/he has his/her usual residence, but outside his/her usual environment for a period of at least one night but not more than one year and whose main purpose of visit is other than the exercise of an activity remunerated from within the country visited".

INTERNATIONAL TOURIST ARRIVALS AND RECEIPTS WORLDWIDE AND BY REGION 1985-1992

REGIONS	SERIES	1985	SHARE WORLD TOTAL 1985	1992	SHARE WORLD TOTAL 1992	AVERAGE ANNUAL GROWTH RATE 1985-92
WORLD	A(1)	329636	100.00	475580	100.00	5.4
	R(2)	115424	100.00	278705	100.00	13.4
AFRICA	A(1)	9706	2.95	16988	3.57	8.3
	R(2)	2601	2.25	5167	1.86	10.3
AMERICAS	A(1)	66495	20.17	102073	21.46	6.3
	R(2)	32590	28.24	76567	27.47	13.0
EAST ASIA/ PACIFIC	A(1)	30389	9.22	58322	12.26	9.8
	R(2)	12849	11.13	43291	15.53	18.9
EUROPE	A(1)	214264	65.00	287529	60.46	4.3
	R(2)	61181	53.00	147205	52.82	13.4
MIDDLE EAST	A(1)	6242	1.89	7177	1.51	2.0
	R(2)	4803	4.16	4356	1.56	-1.4
SOUTH ASIA	A(1)	2540	0.77	3491	0.74	4.6
	R(2)	1400	1.22	2119	0.76	6.1

Source: World Tourism Organization (WTO)

Totals for 1992 are preliminary estimates
Figures on receipts exclude international transport
(1)A = Arrivals (Thousands)
(2)R = Receipts (Million US$)

INTERNATIONAL TOURIST ARRIVALS
IN EUROPE
1970-1992

| YEARS | WORLD | | EUROPE | | SHARE OF EUROPE IN WORLD TOTAL |
	THOUSANDS	% CHANGE	THOUSANDS	% CHANGE	(%)
1970	165787	-	113000	-	68.16
1975	222290	34.08	153859	36.16	69.22
1980	287771	29.45	189830	23.83	65.97
1985	329636	14.54	214264	12.87	65.00
1986	340808	3.38	218320	1.89	64.06
1987	366758	7.61	233623	7.01	63.70
1988	393865	7.39	243020	4.02	61.70
1989	427884	8.63	270548	11.33	63.23
1990	455594	6.47	284178	5.04	62.38
1991	455100	-0.11	277904	-2.21	61.06
1992	475580	4.50	287529	3.46	60.46

Source: World Tourism Organization (WTO)

Totals for 1970 to 1991 are revised figures
Totals for 1992 are provisional revised estimates

INTERNATIONAL TOURISM RECEIPTS
IN EUROPE
1970-1992

YEARS	WORLD MILLION US$	% CHANGE	EUROPE MILLION US$	% CHANGE	SHARE OF EUROPE IN WORLD TOTAL (%)
1970	17900	-	11096	-	61.99
1975	40702	127.38	26130	135.49	64.20
1980	102008	150.62	61654	135.95	60.44
1985	115424	13.15	61181	-0.77	53.01
1986	139811	21.12	77028	25.90	55.09
1987	171577	22.72	96428	25.19	56.20
1988	197743	15.25	107121	11.09	54.17
1989	210837	6.62	110021	2.71	52.18
1990	255074	20.98	139253	26.57	54.59
1991	261070	2.35	138234	-0.73	52.95
1992	278705	6.75	147205	6.49	52.82

Source: World Tourism Organization (WTO)

Figures on receipts exclude international transport
Totals for 1980 to 1991 are revised figures
Totals for 1992 are provisional revised estimates

INTERNATIONAL TOURISM IN EUROPE
1991

COUNTRY	TOURIST ARRIVALS (000)	% CHANGE OVER 1990	TOURISM RECEIPTS (MnUS$)	% CHANGE OVER 1990
EUROPE	277904	-2.21	138234	-0.73
EASTERN/CENTRAL	50115	-0.26	2893	15.44
Bulgaria	4000	-11.11	396	0.51
Czechoslovakia	8200	1.23	825	75.53
Hungary	21860	6.58	1037	3.70
Poland	3800	11.76	282	6.02
Romania	5360	-17.95	103	-2.83
USSR	6895	-4.29	250	-7.41
NORTHERN	25325	-4.99	23212	-4.84
Denmark	1429	12.08	3475	4.61
Finland	786	-9.24	1191	1.79
Iceland	143	0.70	116	-4.92
Ireland	3566	-2.73	1495	3.32
Norway	2114	8.13	1574	3.76
Sweden	623	-14.77	2726	-6.16
United Kingdom	16664	-7.53	12635	-9.17
SOUTHERN	88492	-5.56	49729	-5.14
Cyprus	1385	-11.27	1026	-18.44
Gibraltar	135	2.27	115	2.68
Greece	8036	-9.43	2566	-0.81
Italy	26840	0.60	19668	-0.37
Malta	893	2.41	528	6.45
Portugal	8657	7.94	3700	4.08
San Marino	582	-	-	-
Spain	35347	3.05	19004	2.21
Turkey	5158	7.48	2654	-19.77
Yugoslavia	1459	-81.48	468	-83.13
WESTERN	113029	0.46	61094	4.35
Austria	19092	0.43	13956	4.07
Belgium	2944	-6.92	3468	-2.99
France	55731	4.84	21300	5.52
Germany	15648	-8.20	10947	2.47
Liechtenstein	71	-8.97	-	-
Luxembourg	861	5.00	285	-1.72
Monaco	239	-2.45	-	-
Netherlands	5843	0.83	4074	12.70
Switzerland	12600	-4.55	7064	4.05
OTHER EUROPE	943	-11.29	1306	-5.50
Israel	943	-11.29	1306	-5.50

Source: World Tourism Organization (WTO)

LEADING TOURISM MARKETS FOR EUROPE 1991

RANK	ORIGIN	TOURIST ARRIVALS 1991 (Thousands)	MARKET SHARE % OF TOTAL ARRIVALS IN EUROPE	AVERAGE ANNUAL GROWTH RATE (%) 1985-91
1	GERMANY	50960	18.33	3.97
2	UK	26272	9.45	3.41
3	ITALY	17120	6.16	8.59
4	FRANCE	15717	5.65	2.73
5	NETHERLANDS	13956	5.02	2.55
6	SCANDINAVIA	12727	4.58	3.44
7	BELGIUM	12063	4.34	12.09
8	USA	11034	3.97	-8.49
9	SWITZERLAND	10054	3.61	4.42
10	SPAIN	9645	3.34	10.92
	SUB-TOTAL (1-10)	179448	64.57	3.52
	TOTAL EUROPE	277904	100.00	10.36

Source: World Tourism Organization (WTO)

DEVELOPMENT OF INTERNATIONAL TOURISM IN EUROPE 1970-1992

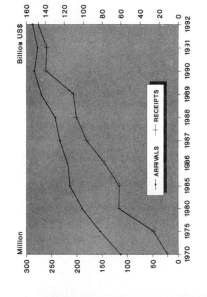

Source: World Tourism Organization (WTO)

INTERNATIONAL TOURISM ARRIVALS IN EUROPE BY REGION OF ORIGIN 1985-1991

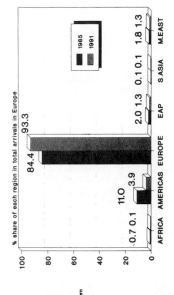

Source: World Tourism Organization (WTO)

TRENDS IN THE CAPACITY OF HOTELS AND SIMILAR ESTABLISHMENTS IN EUROPE - 1986-1991

Number of rooms

SUB-REGIONS	1987	1988	1989	1990	1991
TOTAL EUROPE	4774696	4954511	5046584	4986629	5057598
%	100%	100%	100%	100%	100%
EAST/CENTRAL	392239	414123	427439	310544	299779
%	8.21%	8.36%	8.47%	6.23%	5.93%
NORTHERN	725680	807659	810440	819149	826006
%	15.20%	16.30%	16.06%	16.43%	16.33%
SOUTHERN	1997183	2049452	2098839	2139782	2192982
%	41.83%	41.37%	41.49%	42.91%	43.36%
WESTERN	1626217	1648295	1680801	1685764	1710316
%	34.06%	33.27%	33.30%	33.80%	33.82%
ISRAEL	33377	34982	34065	31390	28515
%	0.70%	0.70%	0.68%	0.63%	0.56%

Source: World Tourism Organization (WTO)

SHARE OF EACH SUB-REGION IN TOTAL INTERNATIONAL TOURIST ARRIVALS AND RECEIPTS IN EUROPE - 1991
(Per cent)

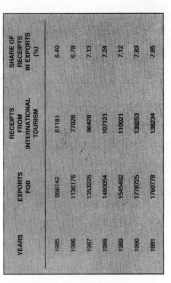

Source: World Tourism Organization (WTO)

WTO defines an international tourist as: "Any person who travels to a country other than that in which s/he has his/her usual residence, but outside his/her usual environment for a period of at least one night but not more than one year and whose main purpose of visit is other than the exercise of an activity remunerated from within the country visited"

TOURISM AND INTERNATIONAL TRADE IN EUROPE - 1985-1991

(In million US$)

YEARS	EXPORTS FOB	RECEIPTS FROM INTERNATIONAL TOURISM	SHARE OF RECEIPTS IN EXPORTS (%)
1985	956142	61181	6.40
1986	1136176	77028	6.78
1987	1353025	96428	7.13
1988	1480054	107121	7.24
1989	1545492	110021	7.12
1990	1778725	139253	7.83
1991	1760778	138234	7.85

Source: World Tourism Organization (WTO)

INTERNATIONAL TOURIST ARRIVALS
IN THE AMERICAS
1970-1992

YEARS	WORLD		AMERICAS		SHARE OF AMERICAS IN WORLD TOTAL
	THOUSANDS	% CHANGE	THOUSANDS	% CHANGE	(%)
1970	165787	-	42273	-	25.50
1975	222290	34.08	50043	18.38	22.51
1980	287771	29.45	61387	22.66	21.33
1985	329636	14.54	66495	8.32	20.17
1986	340808	3.38	71771	7.93	21.06
1987	366758	7.61	76243	6.23	20.79
1988	393865	7.39	83463	9.47	21.19
1989	427884	8.63	87462	4.79	20.44
1990	455594	6.47	93532	6.94	20.53
1991	455100	-0.11	97503	4.25	21.42
1992	475580	4.50	102073	4.68	21.46

Source: World Tourism Organization (WTO)

Totals for 1970 to 1991 are revised figures
Totals for 1992 are preliminary estimates

INTERNATIONAL TOURISM RECEIPTS
IN THE AMERICAS
1970-1992

YEARS	WORLD MILLION US$	% CHANGE	AMERICAS MILLION US$	% CHANGE	SHARE OF AMERICAS IN WORLD TOTAL (%)
1970	17900	-	4800	-	26.82
1975	40702	127.39	10219	112.90	25.11
1980	102008	150.62	24155	136.37	23.68
1985	115424	13.15	32590	34.92	28.24
1986	139811	21.12	36911	13.26	26.40
1987	171577	22.72	41394	12.15	24.13
1988	197743	15.25	48590	17.38	24.57
1989	210837	6.62	55730	14.69	26.43
1990	255074	20.98	65193	16.98	25.56
1991	261070	2.35	72021	10.47	27.59
1992	278705	6.75	76567	6.31	27.47

Source: World Tourism Organization (WTO)

Figures on receipts exclude international transport
Totals for 1980 to 1991 are revised figures
Totals for 1992 are preliminary estimates

1991 INTERNATIONAL TOURISM
IN THE AMERICAS

COUNTRY	TOURIST ARRIVALS (000)	% CHANGE OVER 1990	TOURISM RECEIPTS (MnUS$)	% CHANGE OVER 1990
AMERICAS	97503	4.25	72021	10.47
CARIBBEAN	11350	-1.16	9116	2.75
Anguilla	31	-	36	2.86
Antigua Barb	197	-	314	5.37
Aruba	501	15.70	401	13.60
Bahamas	1427	-8.64	1222	-8.33
Barbados	394	-8.80	453	-8.30
Bermuda	386	-11.26	454	-7.35
Bonaire	50	21.95	24	33.33
Br. Virgin Isl	147	-8.13	109	-17.42
Cayman Isl	237	-6.32	437	34.05
Cuba	408	24.77	300	21.95
Curaçao	206	-0.96	142	18.33
Dominica	46	2.22	28	12.00
Dominican Rp	1321	-13.83	877	-2.56
Grenada	92	12.20	42	10.53
Guadeloupe	303	5.21	284	22.94
Haiti	120	-	46	-
Jamaica	845	0.48	764	3.24
Martinique	315	11.70	255	6.25
Montserrat	19	-	11	-
Puerto Rico	2626	2.82	1445	5.71
Saba	24	9.09	5	-
St. Eustatius	19	5.56	5	-
St. Kitts Nevis	84	10.53	74	17.46
St. Lucia	165	12.24	154	6.20
St. Maarten	548	-3.01	310	-1.90
St. Vincent Grd	52	-3.70	53	-1.85
Trinidad Tobago	220	13.40	101	6.32
Turks Caicos Isl	55	30.95	43	38.71
U.S. Virgin Isl	512	-1.92	708	0.28
CENTRAL	2063	9.15	1017	12.50
Belize	223	-3.04	95	4.40
Costa Rica	505	16.09	310	12.72
El Salvador	199	2.58	157	8.28
Guatemala	513	0.79	211	14.05
Honduras	198	-1.98	31	6.90
Nicaragua	146	37.74	17	41.67
Panama	279	30.37	196	17.37
NORTHERN	74272	3.84	55423	12.65
Canada	14989	-1.76	5537	5.85
Mexico	16560	-3.59	4355	10.70
United States	42723	9.30	45551	12.25
SOUTHERN	9818	13.69	6445	13.61
Argentina	2870	5.21	2336	18.28
Bolivia	221	1.84	90	5.88
Brazil	1352	23.92	1559	7.96
Chile	1349	43.05	700	29.63
Colombia	857	5.41	410	51.85
Ecuador	365	0.83	189	0.53
Guyana	73	14.06	30	-
Paraguay	361	28.93	145	29.46
Peru	232	-26.81	277	-30.40
Suriname	30	3.45	11	-
Uruguay	1510	19.18	333	27.59
Venezuela	598	13.90	365	1.67

Source: World Tourism Organization (WTO)
Data available as of 15 December 1992

TRENDS IN THE CAPACITY OF HOTELS AND SIMILAR ESTABLISHMENTS IN THE AMERICAS - 1987-1991

Number of rooms

SUB-REGIONS %	1987	1988	1989	1990	1991
TOTAL AMERICAS	3918050	4058143	4175512	4304477	4362202
%	100%	100%	100%	100%	100%
CARIBBEAN	113107	119889	124826	129907	137027
%	2.89%	2.96%	2.99%	3.01%	3.14%
CENTRAL AMERICA	29106	30457	32137	36221	37602
%	0.74%	0.75%	0.77%	0.84%	0.86%
NORTHERN AMERICA	3329993	3436896	3545191	3651973	3710585
%	84.99%	84.69%	84.90%	84.84%	85.06%
SOUTHERN AMERICA	445844	470901	473358	486976	476988
%	11.38%	11.60%	11.34%	11.31%	10.94%

Source: World Tourism Organization (WTO)

DEVELOPMENT OF INTERNATIONAL TOURISM IN THE AMERICAS 1970-1992

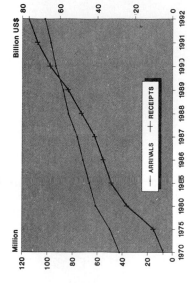

Source: World Tourism Organization (WTO)

LEADING TOURISM MARKETS FOR THE AMERICAS 1991

RANK	ORIGIN	TOURIST ARRIVALS 1991 (Thousands)	MARKET SHARE % OF TOTAL ARRIVALS IN THE AMERICAS	AVERAGE ANNUAL GROWTH RATE (%) 1985-91
1	USA	34165	35.03	8.8
2	CANADA	19926	20.43	9.2
3	MEXICO	7817	8.01	1.5
4	JAPAN	3815	3.91	19.1
5	UK	3524	3.61	12.9
6	ARGENTINA	2823	2.89	7.6
7	GERMANY	2029	2.08	11.3
8	FRANCE	1551	1.59	13.0
9	BRAZIL	1129	1.15	7.1
10	VENEZUELA	791	0.49	2.8
11	ITALY	790	0.81	10.1
12	SCANDINAVIA	663	0.67	9.9
13	NETHERLANDS	608	0.62	9.5
14	AUSTRALIA	592	0.60	11.3
15	SWITZERLAND	491	0.50	11.0
16	BAHAMAS	303	0.31	10.2
	SUB-TOTAL (1-16)	80708	82.77	8.5
	TOTAL AMERICAS	97503	100.00	6.6

Source: World Tourism Organization (WTO)

INTERNATIONAL TOURIST ARRIVALS IN THE AMERICAS BY REGION OF ORIGIN 1985-1991

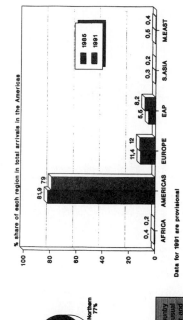

% share of each region in total arrivals in the Americas

Data for 1991 are provisional

Source: World Tourism Organization (WTO)

SHARE OF EACH SUB-REGION IN TOTAL INTERNATIONAL TOURIST ARRIVALS AND RECEIPTS IN THE AMERICAS - 1991 (Per cent)

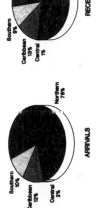

ARRIVALS — Northern 76%, Southern 10%, Caribbean 12%, Central 2%

RECEIPTS — Northern 77%, Southern 9%, Caribbean 13%, Central 1%

Source: World Tourism Organization (WTO)

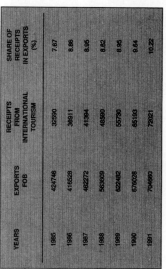

WTO defines an international tourist as: "Any person who travels to a country other than that in which s/he has his/her usual residence, but outside his/her usual environment for a period of at least one night but not more than one year and whose main purpose of visit is other than the exercise of an activity remunerated from within the country visited."

TOURISM AND INTERNATIONAL TRADE IN THE AMERICAS 1985-1991

(In million US$)

YEARS	EXPORTS FOB	RECEIPTS FROM INTERNATIONAL TOURISM	SHARE OF RECEIPTS IN EXPORTS (%)
1985	424746	32590	7.67
1986	416528	36911	8.86
1987	462272	41384	8.95
1988	563909	48580	8.62
1989	622482	55780	8.96
1990	676028	65193	9.64
1991	704660	72021	10.22

Source: World Tourism Organization (WTO)

TRENDS IN THE CAPACITY OF HOTELS AND SIMILAR ESTABLISHMENTS IN EAST ASIA AND THE PACIFIC (EAP) 1987-1991

Number of rooms

SUB-REGIONS	1987	1988	1989	1990	1991
TOTAL EAP	943636	1035149	1110123	1196702	1276268
%	100%	100%	100%	100%	100%
NORTHEASTERN ASIA	456610	502850	561146	604548	641258
%	48.39%	48.57%	50.55%	50.52%	50.24%
SOUTHEASTERN ASIA	305435	334879	344108	374221	411672
%	32.37%	32.35%	30.99%	31.27%	32.25%
AUSTRALIA/N.ZEALAND	163611	178646	185244	196486	201243
%	17.34%	17.26%	16.69%	16.42%	15.77%
MELANESIA	8152	8394	8521	9345	9897
%	0.86%	0.81%	0.77%	0.78%	0.78%
MICRONESIA	5166	5850	6475	7305	7268
%	0.55%	0.57%	0.58%	0.61%	0.57%
POLYNESIA	4662	4530	4629	4797	4930
%	0.49%	0.44%	0.42%	0.40%	0.39%

Source: World Tourism Organization (WTO)

TOURISM AND INTERNATIONAL TRADE IN EAST ASIA AND THE PACIFIC (EAP) 1985-1991

(In million US$)

YEARS	EXPORTS FOB	RECEIPTS FROM INTERNATIONAL TOURISM	SHARE OF RECEIPTS IN EXPORTS (%)
1985	393785	12849	3.26
1986	439239	17200	3.92
1987	524344	22784	4.35
1988	626264	30380	4.85
1989	676958	33806	4.99
1990	733067	38542	5.26
1991	813015	40291	4.96

Source: World Tourism Organization (WTO)

1991 INTERNATIONAL TOURISM IN EAST ASIA AND THE PACIFIC (EAP)

COUNTRY	TOURIST ARRIVALS (000)	% CHANGE OVER 1990	TOURISM RECEIPTS (MnUS$)	% CHANGE OVER 1990
EAP	53892	3.14	40291	4.54
NORTHEASTERN ASIA	28845	53.00	18445	45.00
China	12464	8.89	2845	28.27
Hong Kong	6032	1.67	5078	0.91
Japan	2104	11.97	3435	-4.00
Korea Rp.	3196	8.01	3426	-3.74
Macau	3047	21.25	1643	19.84
Mongolia	147	-	-	-
Taiwan (Prov.of China)	1855	-4.08	2018	15.98
SOUTHEASTERN ASIA	19848	37.00	14396	36.00
Brunei	377	-	35	-
Indonesia	2570	18.00	2518	19.62
Lao P.Dem.R.	25	-	4	33.33
Malaysia	5847	-21.47	1530	-8.22
Philippines	849	-5.46	1281	-1.91
Singapore	4913	1.47	5020	6.38
Thailand	5087	-4.00	3923	-9.32
Viet Nam	180	-	85	-
AUSTRALIA/NEW ZEALAND	3333	6.00	5253	13.00
Australia	2370	7.00	4183	14.29
New Zealand	963	-1.33	1070	-0.19
MELANESIA	428	1.00	443	1.00
Fiji	259	-7.17	211	-7.05
New Caledonia	81	-7.00	150	-
Papua New Guinea	37	-9.76	47	14.63
Solomon Islands	11	22.22	5	25.00
Vanuatu	40	14.29	30	20.00
MICRONESIA	1177	2.00	1545	4.00
Guam	729	-6.54	1093	16.77
Kiribati	3	-	2	-
Mariana Islands	430	-1.15	450	-1.10
Marshall Islands	7	-	-	-
Pohnpei State	3	-	-	-
Truk State	4	-	-	-
Yap State	1	-	-	-
POLYNESIA	261	1.00	209	1.00
American Samoa	37	-21.28	10	-
Cook Islands	40	17.65	2845	28.27
French Polynesia	121	-8.33	150	-12.28
Niue	1	-	-	-
Samoa	39	-18.75	18	-10.00
Tonga	22	4.76	10	11.11
Tuvalu	1	-	-	-

Source: World Tourism Organization (WTO)
Data available as of 15 December 1992

INTERNATIONAL TOURIST ARRIVALS IN EAST ASIA AND THE PACIFIC (EAP) 1970-1992

YEARS	WORLD THOUSANDS	% CHANGE	EAST ASIA AND THE PACIFIC THOUSANDS	% CHANGE	SHARE OF EAP IN WORLD TOTAL (%)
1970	165787	-	5331	-	3.22
1975	222290	34.08	8657	62.39	3.89
1980	287771	29.45	20945	168.39	7.28
1985	329636	14.54	30389	45.09	9.22
1986	340808	3.38	33505	10.25	9.83
1987	366756	7.61	38905	16.12	10.61
1988	393865	7.39	45077	15.86	11.44
1989	427884	8.63	45549	1.05	10.65
1990	455594	6.47	52253	14.72	11.47
1991	465100	-0.11	53882	3.14	11.84
1992	475680	4.50	58322	8.22	12.26

Source: World Tourism Organization (WTO)

Totals for 1970 to 1991 are revised figures
Totals for 1992 are preliminary estimates

DEVELOPMENT OF INTERNATIONAL TOURISM IN EAST ASIA AND THE PACIFIC (EAP) 1970-1992

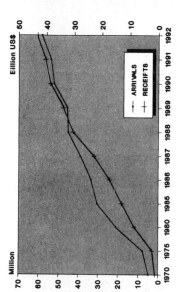

Source: World Tourism Organization (WTO)

LEADING TOURISM MARKETS FOR EAST ASIA AND THE PACIFIC (EAP) 1991

RANK	ORIGIN	TOURIST ARRIVALS 1991 (Thousands)	MARKET SHARE % OF TOTAL ARRIVALS IN IN EAP	AVERAGE ANNUAL GROWTH RATE (%) 1985-91
1	JAPAN	8268	15.34	25.0
2	SINGAPORE	4804	8.91	9.4
3	USA	3568	6.62	2.2
4	TAIWAN	3528	6.54	27.4
5	HONG KONG	2248	4.17	10.2
6	MALAYSIA	2010	3.72	7.5
7	UK	1968	3.65	5.4
8	AUSTRALIA	1833	3.40	2.9
9	KOREA RP	1689	3.13	28.6
10	THAILAND	1138	2.11	14.9
11	GERMANY	1093	2.02	12.6
12	NEW ZEALAND	792	1.46	9.8
13	PHILIPPINES	731	1.35	11.8
14	FRANCE	709	1.31	10.8
15	INDONESIA	478	0.88	7.4
16	ITALY	428	0.79	11.6
	SUB-TOTAL (1-16)	35385	65.65	10.4
	TOTAL EAP	53892	100.00	10.0

Source: World Tourism Organization (WTO)

INTERNATIONAL TOURISM RECEIPTS IN EAST ASIA AND THE PACIFIC (EAP) 1970-1992

YEARS	WORLD MILLION US$	% CHANGE	EAST ASIA AND THE PACIFIC MILLION US$	% CHANGE	SHARE OF EAP IN WORLD TOTAL (%)
1970	17900	-	1100	-	6.15
1975	40702	127.38	2164	96.73	5.32
1980	102008	150.62	8469	291.36	8.30
1985	115424	13.15	12849	51.72	11.13
1986	138811	21.12	17200	33.88	12.30
1987	171577	22.72	22784	32.47	13.28
1988	197743	15.25	30380	33.34	15.36
1989	210837	6.62	33806	11.28	16.03
1990	255074	20.98	38542	14.01	15.11
1991	261070	2.35	40291	4.54	15.43
1992	278705	6.75	43291	7.45	15.53

Source: World Tourism Organization (WTO)

Figures on receipts exclude international transport
Totals for 1980 to 1991 are revised figures
Totals for 1992 are preliminary estimates

SHARE OF EACH SUB-REGION IN TOTAL INTERNATIONAL TOURIST ARRIVALS AND RECEIPTS IN EAST ASIA AND THE PACIFIC - 1991 (Per cent)

Source: World Tourism Organization (WTO)

WTO defines an international tourist as: "Any person who travels to a country other than that in which s/he has his/her usual residence, but outside his/her usual environment for a period of at least one night but not more than one year and whose main purpose of visit is other than the exercise of an activity remunerated from within the country visited".

INTERNATIONAL TOURIST ARRIVALS IN EAST ASIA AND THE PACIFIC (EAP) BY REGION OF ORIGIN - 1985-1991

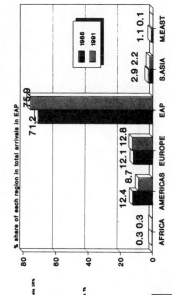

Data for 1991 are provisional
Source: World Tourism Organization (WTO)

TOURISM DESTINATIONS

INTERNATIONAL TOURIST ARRIVALS (Day visitors excluded)

RANK 1991	COUNTRY	TOURIST ARRIVALS (THOUSANDS)		RANK 1985	AVERAGE ANNUAL GROWTH RATE (%)	% SHARE OF ARRIVALS WORLDWIDE	
		1991	1985		1985/91	1991	1985
1	FRANCE	55 731	36 748	1	7.19	12.25	11.15
2	UNITED STATES	42 723	25 417	3	9.04	9.39	7.71
3	SPAIN	35 347	27 477	2	4.29	7.77	8.34
4	ITALY	26 840	25 047	4	1.16	5.90	7.60
5	HUNGARY	21 860	9 724	11	14.45	4.80	2.95
6	AUSTRIA	19 092	15 168	5	3.91	4.20	4.60
7	UNITED KINGDOM	16 664	14 449	6	2.41	3.66	4.38
8	MEXICO	16 560	11 907	9	5.65	3.64	3.61
9	GERMANY	15 648	12 686	8	3.56	3.44	3.85
10	CANADA	14 989	13 171	7	2.18	3.29	4.00
11	SWITZERLAND	12 600	11 900	10	0.96	2.77	3.61
12	CHINA	12 464	7 133	12	9.75	2.74	2.16
13	PORTUGAL	8 657	4 989	14	9.62	1.90	1.51
14	CZECHOSLOVAKIA	8 200	4 869	15	9.08	1.80	1.48
15	GREECE	8 036	6 574	13	3.40	1.77	1.99
	WORLD	**455 100**	**329 636**		**5.52**	**100.00**	**100.00**

TOURISM SPENDERS

INTERNATIONAL TOURISM EXPENDITURE (International transport excluded)

RANK 1991	COUNTRY	TOURISM EXPENDITURE (Million US$)		RANK 1985	AVERAGE ANNUAL GROWTH RATE (%)	% SHARE OF EXPENDITURE WORLDWIDE	
		1991	1985		1985/91	1991	1985
1	UNITED STATES	39 418	24 517	1	8.24	16.06	24.01
2	GERMANY	31 650	12 809	2	16.27	12.89	12.54
3	JAPAN	23 983	4 814	4	30.69	9.77	4.71
4	UNITED KINGDOM	18 850	6 369	3	19.82	7.66	6.24
5	ITALY	13 300	2 283	10	34.14	5.42	2.24
6	FRANCE	12 338	4 557	5	18.06	5.03	4.46
7	CANADA	10 526	4 130	6	16.87	4.29	4.04
8	NETHERLANDS	7 886	3 448	7	14.78	3.21	3.38
9	AUSTRIA	7 449	2 723	8	18.26	3.03	2.67
10	SWEDEN	6 104	1 967	12	20.77	2.49	1.93
11	SWITZERLAND	5 682	2 399	9	15.45	2.31	2.35
12	TAIWAN (Pr. China)	5 678	1 429*	14	25.85	2.31	1.40
13	BELGIUM	5 543	2 050	11	18.03	2.26	2.01
14	SPAIN	4 530	1 010	15	28.42	1.85	0.99
15	AUSTRALIA	3 940	1 918	13	12.75	1.61	1.88
	WORLD	**345 480**	**102 121**		**15.74**	**100.00**	**100.00**

TOURISM EARNERS

INTERNATIONAL TOURISM RECEIPTS (International transport excluded)

RANK 1991	COUNTRY	TOURISM RECEIPTS (Million US$)		RANK 1985	AVERAGE ANNUAL GROWTH RATE (%)	% SHARE OF RECEIPTS WORLDWIDE	
		1991	1985		1985/91	1991	1985
1	UNITED STATES	45 551	17 937	1	16.80	17.45	15.54
2	FRANCE	21 300	7 942	4	17.87	8.16	6.88
3	ITALY	19 668	8 756	2	14.44	7.53	7.59
4	SPAIN	19 004	8 151	3	15.15	7.28	7.06
5	AUSTRIA	13 956	5 084	6	18.33	5.35	4.40
6	UNITED KINGDOM	12 635	7 120	5	10.03	4.48	6.17
7	GERMANY	10 947	4 748	7	14.94	4.19	4.11
8	SWITZERLAND	7 064	3 145	8	14.44	2.71	2.72
9	CANADA	5 537	3 103	9	10.13	2.12	2.69
10	HONG KONG	5 078	1 788	11	19.00	1.95	1.55
11	SINGAPORE	5 020	1 660	13	20.25	1.92	1.44
12	MEXICO	4 355	2 176	10	12.26	1.67	1.89
13	AUSTRALIA	4 183	1 062	15	25.67	1.60	0.92
14	NETHERLANDS	4 074	1 661	12	16.13	1.56	1.44
15	THAILAND	3 923	1 171	14	22.32	1.50	1.01
	WORLD	**261 070**	**115 424**		**14.57**	**100.00**	**100.00**

CHAPTER 1 The Development of the Tourism Industry

Today, the terms *tourism* and *travel* have become almost interchangeable. However, when we look at the history of transporting people, we see that in the early days, travel was an activity that was far from pleasurable. The word *tourism* is a relatively new addition to the English language, introduced only in the nineteenth century. It connotes the act of traveling and refers as well to that industry that developed to service that activity.

Tourism also connotes the ability of people to escape from familiar surroundings and everyday routine. It is no wonder, then, that the history of tourism is the history of those who broadened the horizons of transportation.

It was those who dreamed and those who dared, including Henry Ford and the Wright brothers, who gave us our present-day transportation system which harmoniously links speed, safety, comfort, and economy. While travel has been a human passion since the dawn of history, tourism only became possible as technological improvements provided comfortable, safe, and, above all, enjoyable ways to travel.

The modern tourism industry is composed of numerous separate industry segments. Sometimes competing, yet more often providing services supplementary in nature, each segment of the industry developed as a result of different historical forces.

A study of the tourism industry—its development, current issues, and future opportunities—can best be introduced by a closer look at the major historical developments.

GENERAL OVERVIEW

The history of early travel parallels the development of transportation. A definition of *transportation* goes far beyond the meaning of providing a means to travel. Transportation is a personal activity, a social and economic service, and an industry.

Prior to the Industrial Revolution, transport was only possible through human power (walking), animal power (on camel or horseback or, later, animal-drawn vehicles, for example), and the use of wind power (sailing ships). The Industrial Revolution brought steam, electricity, and the modern-day engine. These technological innovations changed the scale and scope of tourism development. Increased productivity, steady employment and the growth of urban centers would provide for the emergence of a middle class with the income and desire to travel in the years to come.

The use of animals for transport was the first great advance. Although the dog was probably the first animal to be used in transport, the ox quickly became the most widely used of transport animals. The domestic ox was common in Europe and Asia throughout the Stone Age, and is still in use today in countries around the Mediterranean, Africa, and South America.

The domestication of the horse altered the history of Europe. Stray horses, running wild over the plains of North America, influenced the lives of the Indians. It is surprising that the horse was never domesticated by the people of Sub-Saharan Africa, except among those in close contact with the Arabs.

Various other animals played a role in the history of transportation. The reindeer not only provided transport, but also milk, meat, and skins to communities in Siberia and the extreme northwestern parts of Europe. The camel brought wealth and prosperity to people living in areas surrounding the Sahara desert. A good camel will cover 150 miles in one day, and the two-humped camel can carry well over 1,000 pounds. The elephant also contributed to the

Missouri Division of Tourism

growth of civilization. Its strength and intelligence were used in construction projects throughout India and, later, in Africa.

Early in human history it became apparent that it was easier to drag heavy objects than to carry them. The wheeled cart was preceded by sledge-type carriages or by a V-shaped framework dragged by a dog or, later, a horse. There were no wheeled vehicles in the Americas before Columbus's arrival.

The first step toward more efficient overland transport was the use of tree trunks as rollers placed under a load to move it over short distances. Eventually, these rollers evolved into wheels, and special tracks (roads) were needed to make efficient transport over long distances possible.

Perhaps the first tourists were those who traveled for the purpose of trade and commerce. This type of tourism reached its pinnacle in Roman times with development of an extensive empire and an early transportation network. In fact, the first roadbuilders in Europe were the Romans, who built a network of paved roads throughout their empire. Looking at the history of many countries, we find that the existence of roads can be attributed to a strong central government interested in transport for military purposes. Even in the nineteenth century, the most spectacular roads were developed in France under Napoleon; and, in the twentieth century, in Italy and Germany under the Nazi regime. When the Roman Empire collapsed, the road network in Europe declined. The movement of people and goods was restricted, and travel was conducted only by knights, priests, and a few merchants.

Tourism in the Middle Ages was dominated by religious motivations as long pilgrimages were often undertaken to sacred places. The church assumed responsibility for the construction and maintenance of bridges and short stretches of road. It was not until the sixteenth century that a system of local governments or "parishes" began to develop. These parishes charged taxes for road upkeep. This system often led to disputes, which still persist, regarding how far roads are used by local people, and to what extent they are used by through traffic. Should the expense for road upkeep be paid for by the local community, the nation as a whole, or by the users of the road? The question persists today.

Among European countries, France led in developing a modern inland transport system. By the early eighteenth century, France had a network of surfaced roads exceeding 15,000 miles. It was a Scotsman, however, who first built roads according to scientific methods. John Loudon McAdam laid a base of large stones onto which smaller stones were placed. The final surface consisted of finely broken rock. This method continued to be used into the twentieth century. Reference is still made to a "McAdam road" (commonly spelled, macadam) when people talk about a surface of asphalt or concrete.

By the early 1600s, the "grand tour" was emerging as a means of finishing the education of the young aristocracy. The elder son of well-to-do families was sent abroad for a year or more to experience the great cultures of the world.

It was the emergence of a wealthy middle class and a reasonably good road system that led to the introduction of the carriage in the seventeenth century. Horseback, however, remained the most common form of transportation through the late eighteenth and early nineteenth centuries. As roads continued to develop, the stage carriage (or stagecoach) appeared on a large scale. Their full development, however, had to await the construction of a more modern road network which allowed the coaches to maintain adequate average speeds. The rapid development of the stagecoach was followed by an even more rapid decline. As the railroads came into operation, the coaches quickly disappeared. The stagecoach era had lasted only three decades.

The period between 1830 and 1870 saw the rapid growth of railroads in both Europe and America. Roads, as a serious rival for transporting people and goods over long distances, became dominant again only after World War I.

Rapid increases in transportation technology, leisure time, and economic prosperity over the past century have contributed to the phenomenon of modern mass tourism, which can be summarized as increasingly large numbers of people traveling for diverse reasons. Further developments in the twentieth century are discussed in more detail on the following pages when we look more closely at the historical background of several components of the industry.

WATER TRANSPORT

Transport by water required less effort than overland transport, and, thus, became highly developed among early civilizations. The earliest type of boat was the raft, made of grasses, logs, and bundles of reeds or other light materials tied together. Floating rafts, of varying materials, were used by the Egyptians on the Nile and by the Incas in South America. Similarities in boat construction led the Scandinavian anthropologist Thor Heyerdahl to develop his theory that South American civilizations originated in the Mediterranean region.

Egyptian boats were made from bundles of papyrus, which grew on the banks of the Nile river. The skin covered canoe, used by the natives of North America, is another type of early boat. A fine example is the Eskimo kayak. Another development was a boat made from a solid tree trunk. Remnants of early dugout canoes, sometimes fifty to sixty feet long, have been found all over the world. The finest and most varied boats are found among the islands of Polynesia. The natives of the South Pacific undertook voyages, sometimes hundreds of miles long, from island to island. Polynesian ships explored the Pacific, colonizing hundreds of islands in an area extending from New Zealand to the west, Easter Island to the east, and Hawaii to the north.

Early ocean shipping originated in the Mediterranean. Phoenicians, Greeks, and Romans navigated the waters in vessels equipped with sails and with one to three banks of oars. By means of these crafts, they established trade and maintained colonies. The Phoenicians, who were highly skilled navigators and very proficient in the use of the sail, traveled as far as England, their source of tin. Later, the Greeks ruled the Mediterranean. They introduced the geographical terms latitude and longitude and built a 460-foot tall lighthouse in the harbor of Alexandria. The largest ships of ancient times were built by the Romans. Rome exported oil, wine, pottery, metal goods, and marble. They imported silks from China, spices from India, cosmetics from Arabia, ivory from Africa, copper and silver from Spain, and slaves from everywhere. Grain, however, was the item imported in the greatest quantity. Rome imported 150,000 tons of grain each year from Egypt alone. One Roman ship, the Isis, was 180 feet long and had a crew of 1,000 men.

The most (in)famous sailors of Western Europe were the Vikings. Their oaken vessels were powered by up to twenty-five pairs of oars. They traveled as far south as the Mediterranean, established settlements on Iceland and Greenland (still part of Denmark) and reached the coast of North America around 900 A.D.

The compass, long known in China and India, was introduced in Europe in the fourteenth century. It allowed explorers to sail beyond the horizon, and, by the end of the fifteenth century, the sailing vessel had carried man to America and around Africa to India. Columbus reached the Americas in 1492. The Cape of Good Hope was discovered in 1487, but it was not until 1498 that Vasco da Gama reached India by sea. Ferdinand Magellan sailed around South America into the Pacific and discovered the Philippine Islands in 1520. Sixty years later, in 1580, the first around-the-world "cruise" was completed by Sir Francis Drake.

The Netherlands began to develop its fleet in the seventeenth century. By the middle of the century, the Dutch merchant fleet had twice as many ships as England and France combined.

The principal shipping routes were concentrated in the Mediterranean until colonies became established in the New World, West and South Africa, and the Far East.

Explorers were followed by colonists. The British founded colonies in the New World during the sixteenth century. As early as 1500, the Spanish had started settlements in Latin America. By the mid-sixteenth century, the French had colonies in Canada, and the Dutch had colonies from Brazil to New York. In 1620, the Pilgrims on board the small ship, Mayflower, reached the coast of America.

Ocean shipping flourished since the colonies depended on their motherlands for supplies and export opportunities. During the seventeenth century, it was common for a merchant to own his ships. Each voyage became a single trading venture. As a result of the industrial revolution, worldwide shipping became more specialized, and it became less common for a merchant also to be a shipowner. It was during this period that two main trends in worldwide shipping developed. Some ships carried both goods and passengers on a scheduled service, charging fixed rates. At the same time, tramp freighters, with no fixed rates, sailed to any port in the world where a profitable cargo could be obtained. (An interesting parallel would occur with the growth of air transportation in modern times.)

The wooden vessels gradually were replaced by the steel steamship during the first three-fourths of the nineteenth century. England dominated international shipping during this era. In 1840, 50 percent of all ships sailing the oceans of the world were of British registry, resulting in the reference to that country as "Great" Britain.

In ship design, however, the Americans became the leaders. The discovery of gold in California, in 1848, created a demand for passenger service from the east coast to the Pacific coast around Cape Horn. Superior to all contemporary sailing ships, the clippers were built to meet this demand by combining speed with strength.

Following the Civil War, the westward expansion across the continent disrupted the growth in American shipping, resulting in the decline of the country's role in ocean shipping. On the inland waterways, however, the steamship flourished. In 1807, Robert Fulton constructed the first commercially successful steamship, and this mode of transportation was widely used from the Hudson River to the Mississippi River.

The first regular mail and passenger service by steamship on the North Atlantic market was inaugurated in 1840. The company was called the British and North American Royal Mail Steam Packet Company, but in the history of tourism, the founder's name would become more important: Samuel Cunard.

The opening of the Suez Canal in 1869 advanced the development of the steamship. And, the replacement of coal by oil made overseas transport quicker, safer, and cheaper than it had ever been.

The development of the large passenger steamship brought Europe within five or six days of America. In the years prior to World War I, 150,000 Americans crossed the Atlantic to Europe annually, many on their own version of the "grand tour." The Titanic, designed as the fastest and safest ship of its day, could accommodate 2,500 passengers. On her maiden voyage in 1912, the "unsinkable" luxury liner hit an iceberg south of Newfoundland, resulting in the loss of 1,513 lives.

The period following World War I witnessed the rivalry among the express luxury liners on the North Atlantic shipping market. German, American, French, Dutch, and British liners competed for the Blue Ribbon, an honor given to the ship that crossed the Atlantic at the greatest speed.

The French launched the Ile de France in 1926. The Queen Mary, nearly twice its size, was launched in 1934 by the Cunard Line, followed, in 1938, by the Queen Elizabeth by the same company.

The decade following World War II was the most successful period the shipping industry had ever known. It was not unusual for fifteen or more ships to leave the docks of Manhattan daily for the ports of Europe. Many of the ships carried well over 1,000 passengers, and business was booming as never before.

Then, after the first jetliners flew the Atlantic route in 1958, the entire pattern suddenly changed. By 1959, the airlines had secured more than 60 percent of all transatlantic passenger traffic; 1,539,934 by air versus 881,896 by sea. The trend would never reverse. By the early 1960s, the liners began to leave service, one by one. As an alternative to the scrapyards, company executives sought new uses for their ships. Entire passenger lines disappeared; some concentrated on freight service, while others went bankrupt. Finally, some former transatlantic liners found new lives in the cruise trade. It proved the perfect answer to the problems of many firms.

The story of the passenger cruise lines is a tribute to the flexibility and marketing ingenuity of the industry. During the decade of the 1980s, the cruise industry experienced explosive growth. In 1984, 1.7 million people took a cruise vacation. Annual growth rates of 10 percent to 13 percent caused this number to increase to 3.5 million passengers annually by the end of the decade. Still, nearly 80 percent of the U.S. population has never taken a cruise, and this untapped market will provide continued growth opportunities in the future.

Hawaii Visitors Bureau Photo by Anthony Anjo

LAND TRANSPORT

The Railroads

The story of the railroads is the story of America—always exciting and highlighting man's courage and ingenuity. The railroads opened the West, tied the country together with a web of rails that criss-crossed the land, and literally hauled the United States into the twentieth century. Wherever rails were laid, new towns sprang up. Industry and commerce developed, and agricultural production increased as new markets opened up. For three full generations the railroad was a dominant factor in American life.

The beginning of what eventually became a railroad can be dated back to the sixteenth century when flanked wheels (with guide trains along rails) were used on mining carts. Horse-drawn railways came into use in English mines in the eighteenth century. The next development, and probably the most direct ancestor of the modern railroad, was a somewhat strange-looking contraption resembling a wheelbarrow with a heavy kettle on its prow, which was developed in France in 1769. It was used primarily to haul cannons and was driven through the streets of Paris at a speed of 2 miles per hour.

The world's first working locomotive was built in England in 1804. It moved along a 9-mile track, hauling five cars, with a total weight of 25 tons, at a speed of 4 to 5 miles per hour. Many innovations and improvements were made in the next few years, and, in 1830, the first railroad was built in the United States. The Baltimore & Ohio began business was horse-drawn traffic over a 13-mile stretch, and it was to be two more years before the famous locomotive, Tom Thumb, was to go into service.

By the end of 1830, the United States had 23 miles of railroad track in operation. By 1840, the figure had jumped to 2,808; by 1850, to 9,021; and, by 1860, to 30,626.

A railway journey across the entire American continent was made possible in 1869, when the Union Pacific, starting from the Missouri River at Omaha, Nebraska, met at Promontory Point, Utah, with the Central Pacific, which had started from Sacramento, California. Active construction had been started by both lines in 1864. Many hardships and difficulties were encountered by the workers on both lines. The completion of the transcontinental connection made it possible to travel from New York to San Francisco in six days, a trip that had previously taken several months by river or wagon and several weeks by even the fastest clipper ships rounding South America.

George Mortimer Pullman designed the first passenger railroad car, and the term "first class" was added to the vocabulary of the travel industry. There were plush sleeping cars with cherrywood seats, disappearing beds, curtains to ensure privacy, and washrooms. Next came cars that contained both eating and sleeping facilities, and, soon thereafter, separate dining cars which offered the ultimate in mobile gracious living.

Railroad construction boomed throughout the world. In 1891, construction began on the Trans-Siberian Railway, which linked Europe with the Pacific. By 1900, the world's rail mileage totaled over .5 million miles. Railroads had brought trade and helped improve the standard of living everywhere.

Innovations and modifications, in both improvements and equipment, followed rapidly as the industry moved into the twentieth century. Safety, especially, was an industry concern. During the 1870s, it was estimated that 30,000 people died in railroad-related accidents each year.

As the twentieth century progressed, the railroads in Europe continued to flourish, but in the United States the railroads found they couldn't compete (as movers of people) with automobiles and planes.

In 1929, the railroads, operating some 20,000 passenger trains, carried 77 percent of intercity public transportation traffic in the United States. Buses carried 15 percent, and the airlines served an unmeasurable, small number.

By 1950, more than half the passenger trains had disappeared, and the railroads' share of intercity passenger traffic had declined to 46 percent. In the meantime, traffic on buses increased to 37 percent, and the airlines' share had grown to 14 percent.

Twenty years later, in 1970, railroad passenger traffic dropped to just over 7 percent of the commercial share, and there were fewer than 450 trains still operating. Of these, about 100 would be discontinued. Airlines dominated the public carrier market with 73 percent, while buses, still in second place, held on to barely 16 percent. If we include the private automobile as an important mode of intercity passenger transportation, the railroad's share for all passenger miles in this country dropped below 1 percent by 1990.

Through efforts by the Department of Transportation, the Congress, in 1970, passed legislation that set up a semipublic corporation—the National Railroad Passenger Corporation—to run the country's intercity passenger trains. Amtrak was founded as an experiment to free the nation's freight railroads from their obligation to provide passenger service and to see if a national corporation could reverse the long-term erosion in rail passenger travel. The formation of Amtrak resulted also from the realization that the United States could not rely soley upon further massive construction of highways and airports to meet its transportation needs. Creation of a national rail passenger system was viewed as a method of saving an alternate form of transportation that possessed a priceless asset: existing tracks and rights-of-way into the major population centers of the nation. These rail facilities could be upgraded quite economically when compared to the costs for constructing new highways and airports.

Amtrak's objective was to gradually revitalize public confidence in rail passenger service through service improvements, thereby attracting the traveling public back to the trains. The fuel shortage of the mid-1970's helped railroad passenger service establish itself as the most energy-efficient form of transportation.

Beginning May 1, 1971, Amtrak assumed responsibility for managing intercity passenger train service over 23,000 route-miles, connecting twenty-one pairs of cities. Amtrak inherited a declining business. Not one railroad operated a computerized reservations system. The majority of the passenger cars were old, and many were in disrepair; stations and maintenance facilities had been neglected; and there was not one manufacturer in the United States who could provide intercity rail passenger equipment, because no such equipment had been purchased for years.

Amtrak supporters were in disagreement about what Amtrak should become. Some wanted 150-mile-per-hour corridor "bullet-trains;" others called for restoration of the great long-distance trains of the past. The first few years were rocky for the newly formed corporation, which was called a "for-profit" company but which no knowledgeable person believed would ever turn a profit. Despite a difficult start, there were rapid improvements.

New locomotives were ordered in 1972, a nationwide reservation system was installed, and travel agents were offered a 10 percent commission on all sales. Today, travel agents have access to Amtrak information and ticketing through their computerized reservation system.

Amtrak increased frequency on some of its routes, resulting in increased passenger usage. By the early 1990s, Amtrak was carrying over 22 million passengers annually and was setting records in both ridership and revenues. The company moved from a "short-term crisis management" situation to a second decade that has allowed the company to concentrate on long-term objectives. The company is now looking at new technology to move people as efficiently on the ground from city to city as the airplane does through the airways and, perhaps one day, nearly as quickly. Recent improvements include the renovation of stations (including Washington D.C.'s Union Station), the enhancement of service (including on-board movies and telephone service), improvements in dining service and tableware, and the introduction of the Viewliner, Amtrak's new sleeping and dining car.

AIR TRANSPORT

Greek mythology tells us how Icarus, equipped with wings made of bird feathers held together with wax, failed in his attempt to escape imprisonment on Crete. He flew too close to the sun, which melted the wax, and gravity pulled him into the sea.

The desire to escape gravity—to fly—has been an ancient dream. The sight of a bird's miraculous movements through the skies, seemingly free of gravity's limitations, must have inspired Leonardo da Vinci to draw up sketches of devices that, at least in theory, would help man escape from earth.

The earliest pursuit of this dream focused on the hot air balloon. The first successful launching took place outside Paris in 1783. The Montgolfier brothers, with the knowledge that smoke rises, filled a balloon made of paper with hot air. The balloon stayed up until the air inside cooled and gravity brought it down again. Military uses for balloons soon developed. In 1870, Gambetta, who directed the defense of France during the Franco-Prussian war, escaped the occupied city of Paris in a balloon to establish himself in Tours where he continued efforts to organize and defend his country. Napoleon used anchored observation balloons in some battles, as did both sides in the U.S. Civil War during the 1860s.

The second half of the nineteenth century witnessed the invention of the gasoline engine, which, when used to power a balloon, developed into the Zeppelin-type airship. In 1926, the Norge airship flew across the North Pole, and, by 1929, the passenger carrying Graf Zeppelin blimp had made two transatlantic round trips and a flight around the world.

Two brothers in Dayton, Ohio were captivated by the success of the first airship experiments in Europe. Wilbur and Orville Wright operated a bicycle shop and, in their spare time, enjoyed the hobby of gliding. By 1902, they had built a glider with moveable fins and wingtip controls. On a trip to the dunes at Kitty Hawk, North Carolina that summer, they made hundreds of perfectly controlled runs, and, encouraged by their success, were ready to build a powered "heavier-than-air" craft. Unable to find a manufacturer that could supply a small engine, they built one in their shop, and, in December, 1903, the Wright brothers assembled their machine on the beach at Kitty Hawk. A four cylinder, 13-horsepower engine lifted the aircraft four times that day at a speed of about 10 miles per hour. On its first run, the craft was in the air 12 seconds and covered a distance of 120 feet. Later in the day, after making adjustments and repairs, Wilbur flew over 850 feet and kept the plane up for nearly one minute.

N.C. Travel and Tourism Division/Photo by Clay Nolen

During the ensuing years, many flight records were set and broken. In 1909, the English Channel was successfully crossed; in 1911, a pilot flew his little plane under Niagara Falls' Rainbow Bridge; and, in 1913, the first successful voluntary airloop was performed.

World War I stimulated research that resulted in the rapid development of the aircraft industry. Scheduled passenger service started in Europe on the London-Paris route as early as 1919. After nineteen months of operation, this service was stopped because the number of passengers per trip averaged only 1.5. Fear of flying as well as the absence of restrooms were the major causes of this lack of passengers. In the early days of air travel, flying was obviously far from comfortable. It was not until the late 1920s that larger, safer, planes made flying more attractive.

The first successful solo crossing of the Atlantic by Charles Lindbergh in 1927 sparked interest in aviation. Lindbergh, an accomplished pilot, conceived the idea of flying nonstop between New York and Paris. He had logged 2,000 flying hours when he convinced a few wealthy St. Louis businessmen to back his plan to be the first pilot to fly more than 3,000 miles across the Atlantic. Fully aware that others were about to try the same stunt, his plane, The Spirit of St. Louis, was built in San Diego in less than sixty days. Lindbergh, in a hurry not to let anyone succeed first, broke the transcontinental record by five hours when he flew his new plane from San Diego to Long Island. Finally, on May 21, 1927, carrying 450 gallons of gasoline, the tanks blocking forward visibility, the plane lifted off.

The flight, as Lindbergh would recall later, was rather uneventful. His most difficult problem was staying awake. After 28 hours, the southwestern coast of Ireland appeared. As he touched down, a large crowd was on hand to welcome him at Le Bourget Airport outside Paris. Lindbergh's solo flight was celebrated the world over, and he became an American hero. The "Air Age" had arrived. His flight convinced investors of the value of air travel, and nearly $1 billion worth of shares in the aviation industry were sold within two years following the historic flight.

Scheduled passenger service had been introduced in the United States in 1925 on the Los Angeles—San Diego route. By 1930, passenger travel in the United States equaled total passenger airline travel in the rest of the world. This growth in air travel led to the rapid development of larger and faster aircraft. Initially, Europe maintained the lead in aircraft development, but, by 1930, the Douglas Company in California began manufacturing the DC-2 model, which carried fourteen passengers. It reached a speed of 213 miles per hour and climbed to an altitude of 12,000 feet. The most celebrated plane of all time, the DC-3, was introduced in 1936. By the end of World War II, more than 11,000 of these planes, often called Dakotas, had been built. As late as 1990, 3,500 of them were still flying.

World War II interrupted international commercial aviation but accelerated technological progress. New aircraft, such as the DC-4 and the Lockheed Constellation, were introduced. These aircraft had higher load capacity and greater range and speed than the DC-3.

By the end of the war, the United States had a surplus of equipment and trained personnel. Europe's airline industry, on the other hand, was virtually nonexistent. Civil airports had been destroyed, together with aircraft and operational equipment.

In 1944, at the invitation of the United States, forty-four nations sent delegates to a conference in Chicago to arrange for the establishment of world air routes and services. At the conference, a serious difference emerged between the United States and the European countries (under the leadership of Great Britain). The United States wanted relatively unrestricted competition while the European countries failed to reach agreement.

Representatives from Great Britain and the United States met again in Bermuda in 1946. The objective of this meeting was to develop a compromise between their opposing positions. An agreement was reached based upon an exchange of international traffic rights. The Bermuda Agreement, in which countries exchanged benefit for benefit, became a model for all bilateral negotiations in later years.

The "six freedoms of the air" formulated in Bermuda included:

1. The right to fly across another nation's territory.
2. The right to land in another country for noncommercial purposes.
3. The right to disembark passengers and cargo that originated in the carrier's home country in a foreign country.
4. The right to pick up passengers and cargo destined for the carrier's home country from a foreign country.
5. The right to transport passengers and cargo from one foreign country to another foreign country.
6. The right of an airplane to carry traffic from a foreign country to the home nation of that airline and beyond to another foreign country.

At the Chicago conference, airlines established the principle of agreed rates for transportation of passengers on the various airlines. Seventy airlines, representing forty nations, created the International Air Transport Association

(IATA). The association's functions were divided among four committees, responsible for financial affairs, legal matters, technical exchange, and traffic. The traffic committee was responsible for rate fixing by means of twice-yearly traffic conferences. IATA became the major trade association of the world's airlines. It operates as a supranational organization, proposing rates (subject to approval of the governments concerned), conditions of service, and safety standards. It provides the machinery which makes the worldwide system of air transportation possible.

In 1946, the number of passengers carried by U.S. scheduled airlines totaled well over 13 million, compared to slightly over 1 million in 1938. By the end of 1955, this number had risen to 41 million.

A permanent body, the International Civil Aviation Organization (ICAO), charged with the coordination and development of all aspects of civil aviation, was established in 1957. The organization is concerned with the formulation of international standards and recommended practices. It collects data on international air traffic, government subsidies, and operating costs. It provides assistance in the preparation of multilateral agreements on commercial air rights and makes studies on various economic aspects of air transportation. Both IATA and ICAO are headquartered in Montreal, Canada.

The introduction of jet aircraft in the late 1950s contributed more to the growth of the tourism industry than any other development since World War II. The first American jet airliner, the Boeing 707, was put into operation in 1958. The DC-8 started service a year later. The jet airliner changed the nature of air travel. Cruise speed went from less than 350 miles per hour to nearly 600 miles per hour, reducing travel time over long distances by 40 percent. The efficiency of this new airplane, combined with higher load capacities, produced lower airfares and made air travel a reality for larger segments of the population. In 1971, only 49 percent of the population had ever flown. By 1974, the percentage was up to 55 percent. Today, more than 74 percent of all adult Americans have traveled by plane.

In 1958, the anticipated growth of the industry resulted in the creation of two new federal agencies to regulate air activities in the United States. The Federal Aviation Administration (FAA) handled the safety aspects of the industry, while the Civil Aeronautics Board (CAB) assumed responsibility for the regulation of airline economics.

An important chapter in the history of aviation was written by the wide-body aircraft, which were added to the world's fleet during the early and mid-1970s. They include the Boeing 747 (jumbo jet), as tall as a five-story building and carrying up to 480 passengers; the DC-10; the Lockheed L-1011; and the European-built Airbus A-300.

The dramatic development in aircraft production is perhaps best illustrated by this comparison: the fuselage of a DC-3 would fit comfortably into the tail engine of a modern day DC-10. Or this amazing comparison: man's first powered flight, covering 120 feet, could easily be repeated inside the cabin of a modern jetliner.

Aviation's achievements are impressive, but they are even more remarkable when we consider their brief time-span: nine decades is but a mere heartbeat in history. There are more than 6 million Americans today who were living when Orville and Wilbur Wright launched not just an airplane, but a technological embryo.

The latest chapter in the history of aviation in the United States was written by deregulation. It removed many of the regulations governing air carriers routes and fares. Prior to deregulation, all airlines charged the same price for the same trip, and there were only a few choices of fares. With deregulation, the airline industry became involved in the concepts of market segmentation and marketing by price.

When the Airline Deregulation Act of 1978 was passed, the expectation of those voting for it was that it would result in improved service to the public, offer lower fares, allow airlines to become more profitable, and increase competition.

The results have been mixed. Many travelers are benefiting from lower fares, but others are paying considerably more. Few still say that service has improved. In fact, service levels have been among the greatest problems created by deregulation in many instances and the public has even become concerned about safety.

Airlines have had some very unprofitable years, but the final results are still unknown. Competition has definitely not increased in terms of the number of carriers and the market share of the largest ones.

The hub-and-spoke system was born from deregulation. Although it has given many travelers more choices from their home airport, it has vastly decreased the chance of having a nonstop flight. Connections are the rule for most travelers today. One of the reasons for the great statistical increase in passenger boardings is that many former nonstop and direct flights have been replaced by connections.

Airlines have passed through several phases during the process of deregulation. The first, occurring right after the act was passed, was expansion. New airlines entered service faster than you could count; most of them did not survive.

The next phase was consolidation. Mergers and consolidations abounded. Several airlines went bankrupt.

Concentration was the third phase. The large airlines realized that, in this era of deregulation, they had to control their own markets. Interlining,

connecting passengers using different airlines, became the exception as the hub-and-spoke systems allowed an airline to feed itself.

The final phase, in which we are now, is globalization. This can be seen in the international route expansions of American, Delta, and United in the 1990s.

THE HOTEL INDUSTRY

The lodging industry developed along with the need to provide accommodation for travelers. As soon as people started to travel, boarding houses of some kind must have existed. There are several mentions in both the Old and New Testaments of early roadside inns. Excavations in Pompeii reveal that the Romans had developed the concept of hospitality into a trade.

In France and Italy alike, during the centuries that followed the fall of the Roman Empire, monasteries provided shelter and rest for pilgrims, merchants, and strangers. Later, the Crusaders, traveling between Europe and the Levant, stimulated travel for nonmilitary purposes.

The history of the hotel in its present form goes back to the Middle Ages. German and English literature of the thirteenth and fourteenth centuries made frequent reference to the "inn." An early description of an English inn is preserved in the work of William Harrison. In 1577, in his *Description of England*, he writes:

> Those townes that we call thorowfaires have great and sumptuous innes builded in them... verie well furnished with naperie.. ech commer is sure to lie in cleane sheete, wherien no man hath beene lodge since they came from the laundresse . . . . There is no greater securitie anie where for travellers than in the gretest innes of England.

The development of the inn in the late medieval period must have been related to the improvements in security in many European societies; it had become safe to travel. Also, the end of the Middle Ages was an era that gave rise to an emerging middle class.

The rising bourgeoisie could afford accommodations when traveling away from home. Innkeepers profited from catering to the needs of growing numbers of travelers, and, by the sixteenth century, the hospitality concept had developed a form it would retain until the coming of the "jet age."

America's first hotels were seaport inns. Manhattan's Fraunces Tavern is an outstanding example of an early American inn, and other prerevolutionary boarding houses are preserved in Guilford, Connecticut; Colonial Williamsburg, Virginia; and elsewhere.

By the mid-seventeenth century, the beginning of the public stagecoach system had appeared. For the next 200 years, the hospitality industry was closely influenced by the development of road transport. Often, coach service was established by enterprising innkeepers in an attempt to attract business.

Throughout the age of coaching, end terminals and "stages" were usually at inns. The inn served not only as a boarding house, but also as a booking office, waiting place, eating establishment, and, often, as the center of the town's social activities.

With the rapid development of the railways in the 1820s and 1830s, traffic almost vanished from some roads. By 1840, coach service had virtually disappeared in Europe. The railroads' effect on the older, established hotels was disastrous. Not only did this new form of transportation alter traditional travel routes, but travel by train reduced the time that travelers spent on their journeys. Many hotels went out of business, and the roadside hotels did not flourish again until the automobile brought large numbers of customers back to the roads.

With the growth of the railroad industry, and the concomitant increase in long distance travel, a different kind of hotel developed. In Europe, large hotels were constructed next to or across from the new downtown railroad station; in the United States, the hotel industry flourished in communities along the westward route and elsewhere along the expanding railroad network.

The railroad's speed resulted in the popularity of the day trip, which, in turn, stimulated hotel development in seaside and mountain resort areas. Numerous resorts were built in New York's Catskill Mountains and along New Jersey's Atlantic coast. The Chesapeake & Ohio Railway developed the Greenbrier resort in West Virginia into one of the world's finest. Other early American resorts include Hotel del Coronade in San Diego, built in 1887; the Ponce de Leon, built in St. Augustine, Florida, in 1888; and the French Lick Hotel in Indiana, south of Chicago, built in 1892. Denver's magnificently restored Brown Palace Hotel was begun in 1888, while Colorado Springs' pride, the Broadmoor, was built in 1891.

In nineteenth-century Europe, the rise of the famous spas and sea resorts throughout England and continental Europe illustrated health as another major motivating force for tourism and hotel development.

The introduction and further development of the automobile industry eventually led to a renaissance of the roadside hotel. The nature of tourism and travel changed dramatically between the two world wars, as fewer people traveled by rail, choosing the private automobile instead. With the construction of highways, thruways, expressways, and beltways, the lodging industry responded to the specific needs of the motorist, and the motor hotel (or motel) was born. At the same time, as cities grew, and in response to the needs of the business traveler, new hotels providing luxurious accommodations arose in downtown areas. In America, a standard of comfort and convenience, unknown to the rest of the world, developed.

Post–World War II development of the hotel industry is best characterized by the words "growth" and "change." The increased number of travelers, spurred by advances in air transportation, created a need for more and more hotel space. Widespread use of the car led hoteliers to build more roadside motels, and business travelers demanded specialized accommodations, including meeting and convention facilities. The completion of the interstate highway system induced Americans to "take to the roads" in record numbers; travel by rail was no long an attractive alternative for many people, and airfares remained high.

Although the hotel industry was booming, many small, family-owned properties could not compete with the fast-growing chains. There were nearly 20,000 more hotels and motels in the United States in 1960 than there are today. However, room inventory has nearly doubled because of the increased size of the modern hotel.

Ellsworth Statler was America's first hotel chain pioneer. By the 1920s, hotels bearing his name had been built in Buffalo, Cleveland, St. Louis, Detroit, Boston, and New York. The most famous name in the history of the deluxe hotel is that of the Hilton corporation. Conrad Hilton built an empire that included the world's most acclaimed hotel, New York's Waldorf Astoria, and Americas largest hotel, the 3,000-room Conrad Hilton Hotel in Chicago. The fastest growing group of first-class hotels during the 1960s was the Sheraton chain, founded, in 1941, by Ernest Henderson.

Surprisingly, the most important name in the history of the worldwide hospitality industry is unknown to most people. Yet, his impact on the tourism industry equals that of the Wright brothers, Thomas Cook, and Henry Ford. Kemmons Wilson, in 1952, built the first hotel of what would, in just three decades, grow into a chain of 1,600 properties. He called his new company Holiday Inn, and its concept of clean, comfortable, reasonably priced, "no surprise" hotels would become a model and standard for hotel construction and service.

With the popularity of the sun vacation in the 1960s came the development of the resort hotel. It primarily catered to the vacationing traveler who stayed for a number of days. Resorts differ from the traditional hotel in that they provide a wide range of special services, often targeted to a special interest group such as sun enthusiasts, golfers, tennis players, scuba divers, and honeymooners. Resorts, traditionally, offer a wide range of price packages.

As the function of the hotel changed, so did its architecture. Owners spent large sums to renovate older, downtown properties, adapting them to the changing needs of the modern-day traveler. Hotel properties initially were simple in design to serve the basic need (and budget) of the one-night transient traveler. They changed in appearance as extra features were added in response to competition and changing travel demographics. The traditional role of a hotel, providing overnight accommodations for the person away from home, was given a new meaning by the hospitality industry during the 1970s.

Staying at a hotel had become "an experience" and marketing became the most important management tool for the industry. The interiors of modern hotels have made them into fantasy lands—glass covered elevators, atrium lobbies, a variety of restaurants and bars, functional meeting rooms, and a full array of recreational opportunities are all designed to enhance the visitors' experience.

Another development was the overseas expansion of the American chains. As international airlines linked the business centers and vacation destinations of the world during the 1960s, the hotel industry responded to the specific and often discriminatory needs of the new international traveler. Hotels that met international standards became an American export item. Hilton International, which opened its first hotel in 1949 in San Juan, Puerto Rico, opened a hotel in Berlin in 1958, followed by several properties in other European countries. Intercontinental Hotels, formed by Pan Am in 1946, opened several hotels in Latin America prior to 1960. Sheraton, another giant on the international scene, opened its first hotel outside the United States in 1949 in Canada. Holiday Inn, a relative newcomer, opened its first foreign property in Montreal in 1960. That chain's first European hotel opened in 1968 in the Netherlands.

During the past decade, developments in the lodging industry have been characterized by market segmentation. New entrants and many of the larger chains now offer facilities at various price levels, ranging from full-service luxury hotels to economy and budget facilities.

THE AUTOMOBILE

The first self-propelled passenger vehicle, a forerunner of the modern automobile, was designed by Nicolas Cugnot, a Frenchman, who, in 1769, built a three-wheeled vehicle equipped with a steam power plant. His vehicle was never put to practical use because it had to stop approximately every 200 feet to generate steam, and it ran at only 2.5 miles per hour. Cugnot's original creation can be seen in the National Museum of Arts and Trade in Paris. During the second half of the eighteenth century, other attempts were made to build steam-powered carriages, but none of them were able to operate under their own power for any length of time. The nineteenth century saw further development of steam vehicles, but their practical use was hindered by the fact that these vehicles enjoyed little public acceptance. The British Parliament passed legislation that practically removed the steam coaches from the roads. In 1832, a law was enacted—popularly known as the Red Flag law—that required that a man precede the horseless carriage on foot, carrying a red flag during the day and a red lantern by night. Toll roads and bridges raised charges for steam-powered vehicles. Restrictive laws such as these stayed in effect in England until 1896.

German and French interests turned toward the internal combustion engine to replace the cumbersome power plant of the early steam vehicles. It is difficult to trace definite dates for events in the early days of the automobile industry. Many people were working on the same problems in different countries, and the complex machine that we now know as the automobile was never the sole invention of a single individual.

Gottlieb Daimler patented his first high-speed, internal combustion engine in Germany in 1885 and is generally credited with revolutionizing automotive transportation. Developments continued rapidly in Germany, France, England, and the United States during the last decade of the nineteenth century. The new cars varied greatly in design, and pioneers on both sides of the Atlantic were, in general, primarily concerned with developing a product that would operate, be reliable, and, despite the road conditions of the time, be durable. Among the early pioneers were Gottlieb Daimler, Karl Benz, René Panhard, Sir Henry Royce, R. E. Olds, and Henry Ford.

During this experimental period, cars of every description were produced, with varying gear and steering mechanisms. Public acceptance, as with the steam-powered vehicles a century earlier, was slow in coming. Poor road conditions, a high investment, the cost of maintenance, and the unreliability of this new radical invention hampered acceptance of the motor vehicle. It is amusing now that the first recognition of the car came as a sporting commodity at racetracks in Europe and America. The resulting publicity led to its appreciation as a means of reliable, economical, comfortable, and functional individual transportation.

After 1910, the demand for cars grew substantially, and the industry became concerned with the development of marketing and distribution facilities. More than any other car built, Henry Ford's Model T made car ownership possible for millions of Americans. Because of his assembly-line production methods, Ford was able to reduce the price of the Model T to $500. Bankers facilitated the purchase of a car on an installment-payment basis, and, by 1927, more than 15 million Model T cars had left the factory.

The mass-produced automobile created a revolution in transportation and travel. Travel was no longer a privilege reserved for the wealthy. Now workers, as well as the growing middle class, could afford a private means of transportation. The popularity of the automobile grew steadily. In 1920, close to 2 million were sold in the United States. By 1929, the number had increased to 4.5 million. More than 23 million cars were on the roads of the United States by the end of that year (one automobile for every five Americans).

The growth of car ownership necessitated road improvements. Early drivers had to contend with unmarked, often unpaved, roads. In 1916, President Wilson signed the first federal law establishing a countrywide network of interstate highways. By 1920, nearly 300,000 miles of surfaced roads were completed. During the 1930s, the Germans constructed their network of auto-

N.C. Travel and Tourism Division/Photo by Clay Nolen

bahnen. These four-lane, divided highways were the world's first high-speed roads.

Tourism planners soon realized the importance of the family car as a means of transportation for millions of Americans. In turn, the National Park Service improved access and parking facilities at major parks, and Walt Disney, in planning the opening of an 83-acre amusement park near Anaheim, California, in 1955, included a 110-acre parking area.

The automobile continues to be the most important mode of transportation for both the business and pleasure traveler. It is estimated that automobile travel accounts for over 85 percent of all trips.

CAR RENTAL

The car rental industry has a history that began in 1918 when a Chicago Ford dealer started to rent secondhand Model Ts. In 1924, the company was bought by the owner of a local cab company, a gentleman named John D. Hertz. General Motors, impressed by the success of this new company, bought the company in 1925. Hertz biggest competitor, Avis, was founded in 1946 by a retired U.S. Air Force officer, Warren E. Avis. Initially, Avis pioneered downtown rental locations. It was during the same time period that National Car Rental was organized. By the late 1950s, car rental company locations were found at all major airports.

The success and growth of the business is closely linked to increases in the number of people traveling by air. As people started to travel for business by air, they rented cars wherever they landed. The car rental industry over the past twenty years is best characterized as highly competitive. Individual companies claim to be first at various innovations, such as the rent-it-here, leave-it-there service. As each company provides a new service, the others add it, and each company, through its advertising, claims to be the first or the best in that service. In this fiercely competitive environment, car rental companies have battled for decades, vying for the patronage of both the business and pleasure traveler. During the 1960s, Hertz and Avis battled for the number-one position in the industry. Hertz launched its famous "We're #1" campaign, while Avis attacked with its highly successful "We try harder" concept. The 1970s witnessed the entrance of many aggressive newcomers into the market, among them Budget, Dollar, Thrifty, and Alamo, in addition to many other smaller companies.

The growth in the 1970s and 1980s can be directly attributed to the introduction of the fly-drive concept. It encouraged travelers not to use their personal car to get to their destination (whether for pleasure or business), but to travel by plane and to rent a car on arrival. The fly-drive concept became extremely popular in the Florida market, birthplace of many new car rental companies. The tourism industry was adversely affected during the periodic oil shortages of the 1970s, which impacted both road and air travel. However, the car rental industry did not suffer as badly as was initially expected. The prospect of renting a car with a full tank of gas soon became a major selling point.

Historically, the car rental business has been a strong growth industry, and indications are that this trend will continue. The leisure market is the future growth area for the industry. At the moment, 70 percent of all cars rented are used for business-related purposes, but only one in four American adults has ever rented a car.

TOUR OPERATORS

With the progression of the industrial revolution, recreation and environmental tourism expanded as a release from the effects of urbanization. During this period the foundations were laid for mass participation in tourism. In 1841, Thomas Cook conducted the first package tour, marking the beginning or organized, economical travel marketed to the middle class.

The further development of the present-day tour operator dates to the turn of the century when individuals coordinated ship tours and rail packages. During its early years, Cartan Tours, founded in 1899, offered Mississippi River excursions. Around the turn of the century, Thomas Cook's rail packages grew in popularity, and, in North America, American Express began wholesaling tours in the 1920s. However, it was not until the arrival of the "jet age" that the package tour business created a revolution. In 1960, fewer than 700,000 Americans visited Europe annually. By 1964, the number had grown to 1 million. The number doubled to 2 million by 1969. The introduction of the wide-body aircraft that year helped realize an astonishing growth, resulting in 3.7 million Americans visiting Europe in 1972. The story of Frommer Tours' early days is typical of how many pioneer tour operators got started. Arthur Frommer's book, "Europe on $5 a Day," achieved a spot on the nation's bestsellers list for years. Frommer realized the potential of mass market travel to Europe. In the early 1960s, he started his tour company, and, in 1963, sold 2,000 packages. This number grew to more than 5,000 in 1964.

Airfares continued to drop during these tumultuous times. In 1948, it cost $600 to fly from New York to Europe; or, expressed in 1990 dollars, $3,100. By 1964, the fare came down to about $300, or just over $1,000 in 1990 terms. In other words, Americans paid three times as much to fly to Europe in 1948 as they did in 1964.

CONCLUSION

As we have seen, the development of the modern tourism industry has a relatively short history. During the 1950s, highway building programs were implemented in the United States, Canada, and Europe. The jet age was in the making, and the economies in the industrialized nations showed year-to-year increases in both productivity and personal income. Improvements in communications, the introduction of television, and revolutionary developments in transportation technology changed lifestyles more dramatically in one decade than they ever had in centuries before. It was in this environment that industry leaders began to perceive that tourism was, in fact, an industry, and not a collection of separate transportation companies and service organizations.

The period from 1960 until the first Arab oil embargo in 1973 was truly the golden age of the tourism trade. U.S. citizen departures by air increased from slightly over 1 million in 1958 to well over 5.5 million in 1970. Many companies, now giants in the industry, can trace their origins back to those pioneer days of the 1950s and early 1960s.

Since then, travel industry achievements have been spectacular. The growth of our industry is a dynamic story. These are the highlights:

1958   The jet age begins. Pan Am becomes the world's first airline to introduce the jet aircraft on its New York–to–Paris route.

1960   The cruise era begins. Holland America Lines, Norwegian Caribbean Lines, and Italian Lines introduce their ships to America's travel agents.

1961   President Kennedy signs a bill that allocates money for the development of an agency responsible for promoting overseas tourism to the United States.

1964   National organizations of travel agents join together in the first international association, the International Organization of Travel Agency Associations.

1966   The forerunner of the first computerized airline reservation system, American Airlines' SABRE, is introduced. The system displays schedules and seat availability.

1967   The Boeing 747 (jumbo-jet), is introduced to the world's airline fleet.

1968   Niagara University is the first institution of higher education in the United States to introduce a four-year degree program in Tourism and Hospitality Management.

1969   Neil Armstrong becomes the first man to set foot on the moon. Technological progress, achieved as a by-product of the space program, would continue to revolutionize the world of transportation.

1970   Amtrak is created by Congress in an effort to revitalize passenger rail transportation in the United States

1972   The Mediterranean region enjoys one of its best tourist seasons. Visitor arrivals to Greece are up 30 percent over 1971; Israel's figures are up 47 percent.

1973   The number of travel agency locations in the United States exceeds 10,000.

1974   The World Tourism Organization is formed. The new organization chooses Madrid, Spain, for its headquarters.

1976   British Airways and Air France inaugurate service on the supersonic Concorde. Travel time between New York and London is reduced to three and one-half hours.

1978   President Carter signs the Airline Deregulation Act. The airline industry celebrates its seventy-fifth anniversary.

1979   The number of international tourist arrivals tops 270 million, compared to 154 million in 1969, a decade earlier.

1980   Travel and tourism generates more new jobs in the United States than any other private industry except health services.

1981   For the first time, foreign visitors to the United States outnumber Americans travelers to foreign countries.

1982   Congress passes the National Tourism Policy Act and the U.S. Travel and Tourism Administration receives a 60 percent increase in its budget, from $7.5 million to $12 million.

1983   European airlines, hotels, and tour operators report that arrivals on the continent from the United States reach record levels.

1984   The number of travel agency locations in the United States passes the 25,000 mark. Just two years earlier, there were 20,000 agency locations, and only 8,000 locations in 1972.

1985   International arrivals in Europe by Americans break all records. Six million Americans visited Europe this year.

1986   Terrorist attacks in Europe cause millions of Americans to vacation in North America. Vancouver's World Exposition is the most popular world's fair ever.

1987   Carnival Cruises, already the largest cruise line, goes public with a stock offering, the first such offering of a major cruise line. The company announces the addition of three new ships to its fleet over a five-year period.

1988   International arrivals to the United States rise a dramatic 20 percent over 1987. Thirty-three million international visitors come to the United States—half of them from Canada.

1989   Dramatic changes in the Communist world cause havoc with world-wide travel patterns. The Soviet Union, Poland, and Hungary ease travel restrictions; travel to the People's Republic of China comes to a virtual standstill after a violent government reaction to student protests in Beijing.

1990   West and East Germany unite and dramatic changes in the Soviet Union signal the end of the cold war, spurring renewed interest in travel to Eastern Europe and the former Soviet Union.

1991   The Persian Gulf War and a nationwide recession slow demand for domestic and international travel. It was also the year of airline bankruptcies. Pan Am, Eastern, and Midway Airlines ceased operations.

1992   The place to be was Europe! Major events included the Winter Olympics and the opening of EuroDisney in France. Spain was the setting for the World Expo in Seville, the Summer Olympics in Barcelona, and celebrations commemorating the five-hundredth anniversary of Columbus' sailing to the new world.

1993   The Boeing aircraft company, positioning itself to meet the air transportation needs of the twenty-first century, unveils plans for the world's newest airliner, the Boeing 777.

REVIEW QUESTIONS

1. Explain why the word "tourism" is a relatively new addition to the English language.

2. What was the industrial revolution and what was its impact on travel?

3. Explain why water transport systems developed earlier than overland transportation.

4. Explain how the expansion of the railroads helped develop the growth of industry, commerce, urban development, and agricultural production.

5. Write a short biography on an early transportation pioneer. Use library reference sources.

6. How did the railroads influence the growth of the hospitality industry?

7. Who is considered the architect of modern tourism?

8. During what year was the first commercial jet airliner introduced?

9. What is IATA?

10. How did the creation of the "package tour" contribute to the growth of our industry?

The U.S. Overseas Travel Market: A Comparison between Package Tour and Individual Travelers

Ady Milman

Research Director
The Dick Pope, Sr. Institute for Tourism Studies
University of Central Florida

INTRODUCTION

The main objective of this study was to compare demographic characteristics, travel behavior, and attitudes of U.S. travelers who prefer to travel on a package tour versus those who prefer to travel individually.

The package tour market has long been recognized, and a large proportion of the literature is concerned with market segmentation. Kale, McIntyre, and Weir (1987) examined travel preferences of the eighteen to thirty-five age group and compared their preferences to representative tour offerings targeted at this group. Sheldon (1986) differentiated between basic package tours (accommodation and transportation) and inclusive package tours. Thompson (1986) compared travel habits and demographic characteristics of "inquirers" and "purchasers" of bus tours. Roger, Thomason, and Pearce (1980) investigated characteristics of coach tours, camping tours, and fly-drive travelers, and Woodside and Ronkainen (1980) differentiated between self-planners, motor club users, and travel agent users. Cunningham and Abbey (1979) studied the relevance of lifestyle and demographic information in the design of package tours.

Satisfaction with motorcoach tours was measured by Whipple and Thatch (1988), while Lopez

(1980) investigated the effect of tour leadership style on tour members' level of satisfaction. Holloway (1981) offered a sociological approach in his study of the relationships between guides, drivers, and their passengers.

Travelers' tour selection criteria was reported by Meidan (1979), while Kent, Meyer, and Reddam (1987) assessed tour wholesalers marketing strategies to travel agents.

The demand for package tours in Europe was investigated by Pearce (1987). Askari (1971) also developed a macro demand model but did not include an analysis of why some travelers choose to travel on a package tour.

A recent significant study was conducted by Sheldon and Mak (1987), who presented a model that explained a traveler's choice of independent travel vis-à-vis travel on package tours to the Hawaiian Islands. The results indicated that purchasers of package tours were likely to be elderly, intended to visit multiple destinations, had fewer people in their party, intended to make short visits, and were first-time visitors to the destination.

The increased capacity of U.S. and foreign carriers to international destinations (as a response to the increased demand), may suggest an examination of some of Sheldon and Mak's findings for the potential U.S. market to overseas destinations. While many official studies have been commissioned by federal and state tourism and travel organizations, no recent analysis have been published regarding international traveler's choice of vacation arrangements.

This article was presented at the twenty-first Annual Conference of the Travel and Tourism Research Association, New Orleans, Louisiana, June 10–14, 1990.

Since this study was exploratory in nature, no formal hypotheses were developed.

METHODOLOGY

Instrument

The study was conducted in two phases: first, three focus groups of U.S. residents who traveled to foreign destinations were held in three major metropolitan areas that had exhibited a high propensity to travel overseas (Princeton, NJ, Houston, TX, and Chicago, IL).

The purpose of the focus group discussions was to identify the main subject matters that were of importance to travelers to overseas destinations. In particular, the discussions focused on the choice between package tours and individual travel.

Each of the focus groups consisted of ten to twelve participants who had traveled extensively to international destinations. They also represented different age groups and an array of ethnic, educational, occupational, and economic backgrounds. The groups also consisted of equal representation of men and women.

In the second phase, a sixty-four-item telephone questionnaire was developed based on the focus groups' findings. The questionnaire included variables that were mentioned in the research objectives.

For the purpose of this study, package tour was defined as "a tour that included such things as lodging, ground transportation, meals or sightseeing." This definition did not distinguish between "basic" and "inclusive" tours (Sheldon, 1986).

Sampling

Telephone interviews were conducted among a representative sample of U.S. residents who resided in geographical areas that had the highest propensity to travel to overseas destinations. The selection of these areas was based on data collected by the United States Tourism and Travel Administration 1988 *"Inflight Survey Outbound."* The respondents also had visited at least one overseas destination (excluding Mexico and Canada) in the past five years.

To achieve a net sample of 2,000 respondents residing in sixteen Standard Metropolitan Statistical Areas (SMSAs) in ten states, 45,000 telephone calls were made. Out of these, 18,900 were business phones or disconnected numbers, and 23,229 were disqualified respondents (did not take any overseas trip in the past five years), leaving a net of 2,871 eligible. The remaining 871 calls were refusals or call-backs, making the net response rate 69.7 percent.

The number of interviews completed in each SMSA was proportional to the number of residents in each of these clusters (Table 1). Interviews were conducted with male or female heads of household during a period of twelve days between 5:00 P.M. AND 9:00 P.M.

FINDINGS

Vacation Preference: Package Tours versus Individual Travel

The majority of the sampled U.S. overseas travelers (71.1 percent) preferred to plan and take their overseas vacation individually, and 18.4 percent preferred to go on a package tour. The remaining 10.5 percent preferred to utilize both package and their own plans when vacationing overseas. Please note that the respondents were asked to report on their *preferences* rather than their actual *practice*. This distribution is fairly consistent

TABLE 1   SMSAs in Which Interviews Were Conducted

SMSA	NUMBER OF INTERVIEWS	PERCENT
New York, NY	435	21.7%
Los Angeles, CA	258	12.9
Chicago, IL	200	10.0
Boston, MA	197	9.8
Newark, NJ	108	5.4
Miami, FL	97	4.9
Atlanta, GA	87	4.4
Houston, TX	89	4.4
Dallas, TX	79	4.0
Tampa, FL	77	3.9
San Francisco, CA	74	3.7
Seattle, WA	74	3.7
Middlesex/Somerset, NJ	66	3.3
Monmouth/Ocean, NJ	67	3.3
Hartford, CT	43	2.2
Ft. Worth/Arlington, TX	30	1.5
Subtotal	1,981	99.1
Missing values	19	0.9
Total	2,000	100.0%

TABLE 2   Preference of Overseas
Travel Arrangement

TYPE OF TRAVEL ARRANGEMENT	PERCENT
1. Individual planning	71.1%
2. Organized tour	18.4
3. Both	10.5
Total	100.0%

with Sheldon's (1986) findings of visitors to the Hawaiian Islands.

The analysis of this paper will be limited to the comparison between the former two segments of the travel market.

Demographic Profile of the U.S. Adult Overseas Vacationer

The findings revealed that among the package tour potential market, more men (69.9 percent) preferred this vacation mode than women (30.1 percent) (Table 3). While there are no empirical studies to justify this trend, it is possible that men, who are concerned with the expenditure aspect of family-travel decision making (Jenkins, 1978), may perceive package tours to be a better value for money than individual travel arrangements.

Marital status may also suggest different segments for the package tour and individual traveler markets. While more single travelers (never married) preferred to go on individual tours than on package tours (26.6 percent versus 19.2 percent), a larger proportion of widowed travelers preferred package tours over individual travel (15.1 versus 4.6 percent). Singles' preference for individual travel may also be attributed to the age of this group. Over one-half (53.3 percent) of the single respondents were between the ages of 18 and 29, and over one-fourth (25.8 percent) were between the ages of 30 and 39.

A further investigation of this group revealed that of the widowed traveler group who preferred to take package tours, 94.5 percent of the sample were widowers and 5.5 percent were widows (N=55). We may extend Sheldon and Mak (1987) suggestion—that single female travelers prefer package tours—to include single male travelers as well. Please note that the proportion of men and women in the divorced/separated segment had almost similar preferences to both choices of vacation mode (Table 4).

TABLE 3   Gender of the Respondents

GENDER	ALL RESPONDENTS PERCENT	PREFER TO TRAVEL . . . BY PACKAGE TOUR PERCENT	PREFER TO TRAVEL . . . INDIVIDUALLY PERCENT
Female	41.5%	30.1%	45.1%
Male	58.5	69.9	54.9
Total	100.0%	100.0%	100.0%

TABLE 4   Marital Status of the Respondents

MARITAL STATUS	ALL RESPONDENTS PERCENT	PREFER TO TRAVEL . . . BY PACKAGE TOUR PERCENT	PREFER TO TRAVEL . . . INDIVIDUALLY PERCENT
1. Single (never married)	24.8%	19.2%	26.6%
2. Married	59.7	56.6	60.3
3. Divorced/separated	8.4	9.1	8.4
4. Widowed	7.1	15.1	4.6
Total	100.0%	100.0%	100.0%

TABLE 5   Respondents' Level of Education

		PREFER TO TRAVEL . . .	
LEVEL OF EDUCATION	ALL RESPONDENTS PERCENT	BY PACKAGE TOUR PERCENT	INDIVIDUALLY PERCENT
1. Grade school .	.8% .	.8% .	.6%
2. Some high school	3.8	3.1	3.8
3. High school diploma	33.5	45.2	31.5
4. College degree	44.7	41.3	45.4
5. Advanced degree	17.4	9.6	18.6
Total	100.0%	100.0%	100.0%

Note: [a]Mann-Whitney U T.est revealed that the two populations are different from one another.

The level of education may also be a predictor for the choice between a package tour or individual travel. Mann-Whitney U Test revealed that the two groups were different from one another (Table 5).

The large proportion of educated respondents who prefer to make their own travel arrangements and travel individually may be explained by the assumption that highly educated people may be more involved with research and information gathering prior to their trip and also may not be interested in the "generic" sightseeing usually offered by the tour companies.

Fluency in foreign languages appeared to be an important factor when choosing the type of vacation mode. Of those respondents who spoke English only, a larger proportion (47.3 percent) preferred to go on a package tour than to make their own travel arrangements (34.4 percent) (Table 6).

In addition, different frequency distributions illustrated the relationships between age and travel arrangements. While 53.4 percent of the respondents who preferred to go on package tours were over 50, almost the same proportion (53.6 percent) were respondents under 39 who preferred to make their own travel arrangements (Table 7). These findings are consistent with Sheldon and Mak's (1987) study of visitors to Hawaii.

Finally, respondents who preferred package tours had, in general, a lower income than respondents who preferred to make their own travel arrangements (Table 8). For example, 61.7 percent of the respondents who preferred to go on package tours had an annual income of less than $40,000, compared to 46.6% of the respondents in the same income category who preferred to make their own travel arrangements. Sheldon and Mak (1987) justified this trend and suggested that wealthy travelers may demand luxury services that are not available in package tours.

Foreign Vacation Travel Behavior

The respondents took an average of 2.9 trips to overseas destinations in the past five years. Further analysis revealed an inverse correlation

TABLE 6   Respondents' Fluency in Foreign Languages

		PREFER TO TRAVEL . . .	
FLUENCY	ALL RESPONDENTS PERCENT	BY PACKAGE TOUR PERCENT	INDIVIDUALLY PERCENT
1. Speak English only	36.0%	47.3%	34.4%
2. Speak foreign language(s)	64.0	52.7	65.6
Total	100.0%	100.0%	100.0%

TABLE 7   Age of the Respondents

| AGE GROUPS | ALL RESPONDENTS PERCENT | PREFER TO TRAVEL. . .[a] | |
		BY PACKAGE TOUR PERCENT	INDIVIDUALLY PERCENT
1. 18–29	23.2%	18.8%	25.8%
2. 30–39	24.7	14.3	28.8
3. 40–49	20.3	13.4	22.4
4. 50–59	13.4	17.6	11.4
5. 60–69	12.3	20.7	8.7
6. Over 70	6.1	15.1	2.6
Total	100.0%	100.0%	100.0%

Note: [a]Mann-Whitney U Test revealed that the two populations are different from one another.

between frequency of overseas travel and the propensity to choose a package tour. A t-test revealed that respondents who preferred package tours took significantly fewer foreign trips in the past five years (mean=2.5) than respondents who traveled individually (mean=3.0) (Table 9).

While individual travelers preferred to take their trip mainly during the summer or in any season (37.1 percent and 19.3 percent respectively), package tour travelers preferred to travel overseas during the summer and spring (32.8 percent and 24.7 percent respectively) (Table 10).

Travel Information and Family Decision Making

The majority of the respondents said that they use travel agencies (61 percent) as their major source of information. Other important sources of information included friends and relatives, travel guide books, and newspaper articles. Note that radio and TV advertising were not reported as major information sources for overseas trip planning (Table 11).

Respondents who preferred to take a package tour relied more on *travel agencies* and *travel clubs* (69.3 percent and 10.4 percent, respectively) than respondents who preferred to make their own travel arrangements (57.0 percent and 5.1 percent respectively). On the other hand, overseas travelers who preferred to go on individual trips relied more on *travel guide books, airlines, magazine articles, and their previous experience at the destination* (12.4 percent, 10.4 percent, 7.9 percent, and 8.3 percent, respectively) than overseas travelers who preferred to go on package tours

TABLE 8   Respondents' Level of Income

| LEVEL OF INCOME | ALL RESPONDENTS PERCENT | PREFER TO TRAVEL . . . [a] | |
		BY PACKAGE TOUR PERCENT	INDIVIDUALLY PERCENT
1. Under $10,000	2.9%	4.8%	2.4%
2. $10–20,000	9.8	12.7	9.6
3. $20–30,000	18.1	23.3	17.1
4. $30–40,000	18.0	20.9	17.5
5. $40–50,000	13.8	14.4	13.2
6. $50–60,000	11.1	8.9	11.9
7. $60–70,000	5.7	4.1	6.3
8. Over $70,000	20.6	11.0	22.0
Total	100.0%	100.0%	100.0%

Note: [a] Mann-Whitney U Test revealed that the two populations are different from one another.

TABLE 9   Number of Overseas Trips Taken by the Respondents

| | | PREFER TO TRAVEL... | |
NUMBER OF TRIPS	ALL RESPONDENTS PERCENT	BY PACKAGE TOUR PERCENT	INDIVIDUALLY PERCENT
1	41.0%	50.1%	40.3%
2	23.3	18.4	23.9
3	13.8	15.1	13.0
4	5.8	4.9	5.8
5	7.2	4.7	7.2
6	2.3	1.9	2.5
7	1.2	0.5	1.1
8	.6	0.5	0.5
9	.2	0.5	0.1
10	2.4	1.9	2.4
Over 10 trips	2.2	1.4	3.3
Total	100.0%	100.0%	100.0%
Mean:	2.9	2.5[a]	3.0[a]
Standard deviation:	4.0	3.3	4.4
Median:	2.0	1.0	2.0

Note: [a] Statistically significant at the 0.05 level.

(6.8 percent, 5.5 percent, 4.7 percent, and 1.1 percent, respectively).

We may conclude that individual travelers may prefer to apply their own "research skills" to find travel information, while package tours travelers prefer to go to a professional travel source.

In over one-third of the households, both spouses decided where to go on vacation (34.8 percent). However, in a large proportion of the sampled households, women (32.6 percent) were more dominant than men (24.7 percent) in choosing the vacation destination. Please note that the role of children was almost insignificant with regard to overseas destination choice. In less than one-tenth of the households (7.4 percent), all family members participated in the destination selection decision (Table 12).

Further analysis reveals that in households in which women were dominant in choosing the vacation destination, a larger proportion preferred to go on a package tour (44.9 percent) than to make their own travel arrangements (28.4 percent). In households in which men were the dominant decision makers, a larger proportion preferred to make their own travel arrangements (28.1 percent) than go on a package tour (16.1 percent) (Table 12).

TABLE 10   Season When Foreign Vacation Is Usually Taken

| | | PREFER TO TRAVEL... | |
SEASON	ALL RESPONDENTS PERCENT	BY PACKAGE TOUR PERCENT	INDIVIDUALLY PERCENT
1. Winter	14.2%	8.6%	15.8%
2. Spring	17.9	24.7	16.2
3. Summer	35.4	32.8	37.1
4. Fall	12.8	17.8	11.5
5. Any season	19.7	16.1	19.3
Total	100.0%	100.0%	100.0%

TABLE 11   Travel Information Sources(*)

INFORMATION SOURCES	ALL RESPONDENTS PERCENT	PREFER TO TRAVEL. . .	
		BY PACKAGE TOUR PERCENT	INDIVIDUALLY PERCENT
1. Travel agency	61.0%	69.3%	57.0%
2. Friends and relatives	26.2	22.2	27.2
3. Travel guide books	11.9	6.8	12.4
4. Brochures of destinations	11.1	14.0	10.2
5. Newspaper articles	9.6	10.1	9.2
6. Airline	8.6	5.5	10.4
7. Magazine articles	7.7	4.7	7.9
8. Previous experience at the destination	6.4	1.1	8.3
9. Travel club	6.2	10.4	5.1
10. Newspaper advertising	3.4	3.3	3.3
11. Magazine advertising	3.1	2.7	2.8
12. Tour operator	1.6	2.7	0.9
13. TV advertising	0.7	1.1	0.6
14. Radio advertising	0.3	0.8	0.1
15. Other	11.2	10.4	10.9

(*) Percentages exceed 100% due to multiple responses.

Foreign Vacation Travel Behavior

Respondents were asked to express their opinion regarding a sixteen-statement description of their foreign travel behavior. The statements were developed from the dominant themes that emerged in the focus group discussions.

A five-point scale was used to evaluate these statements, in which "1" represented total disagreement with the statement and "5" represented total agreement. Overall means and standard deviations were computed for each of the statements and are summarized in Table 13.

In general, the respondents liked to return to a destination where they had a good time, liked to mix with the local people and experience local customs, and thought that one of the best parts of overseas traveling was to visit new cultures and a new way of living. A good value for money was also an important aspect of a foreign vacation as well as the role of accommodation and restaurants in the enjoyment of a vacation trip. Less important aspects of foreign vacations included vacationing in big cities and nightlife activities (Table 13).

A series of t-tests were conducted in order to find whether overseas travelers who preferred to

TABLE 12   Family Member That Chooses Vacation Destination

FAMILY MEMBER	ALL RESPONDENTS PERCENT	PREFER TO TRAVEL. . .	
		BY PACKAGE TOUR PERCENT	INDIVIDUALLY PERCENT
1. Man	24.7%	16.1%	28.1%
2. Woman	32.6	44.9	28.4
3. Children	0.5	-	0.6
4. Man and Woman equally	34.8	32.1	35.4
5. All equally	7.4	6.9	7.5
Total	100.0%	100.0%	100.0%

TABLE 13   Agreement/Disagreement with Vacation Travel Statements

| | ALL RESPONDENTS | | PREFER TO TRAVEL . . . | | | | |
| | | | BY PACKAGE TOUR | | INDIVIDUALLY | | T-TEST RESULTS |
STATEMENT	MEAN	SD	MEAN	SD	MEAN	SD	
1. I would return to a destination where I had good time.	4.2	0.7	4.2	0.8	4.2	0.7	N/S
2. I always like to mix with the local people and experience the local customs.	4.1	0.8	4.0	0.8	4.1	0.8	N/S
3. One of the best parts of traveling is to visit new cultures and new ways of living.	4.1	0.8	4.1	0.8	4.1	0.8	N/S
4. The most important thing to me when I go on vacation is to get a good value for money.	4.1	0.9	4.3	0.8	4.1	0.9	*
5. Accommodations and good restaurants are important to the success of any vacation trip.	4.1	0.9	4.2	0.8	4.1	1.0	*
6. I enjoy traveling to historical places.	4.0	0.8	4.1	0.8	3.9	0.8	*
7. I would go on foreign vacations only to countries that are friendly to the U.S.A.	3.8	1.2	4.1	1.1	3.7	1.2	*
8. I like to go on vacation to places where there are a lot of activities to do.	3.6	1.0	3.7	1.0	3.6	1.0	N/S
9. Crossing an international border is exciting.	3.5	1.0	3.5	1.0	3.5	1.0	N/S
10. I like to vacation destinations where there are beaches.	3.5	1.2	3.3	1.2	3.6	1.1	*
11. Every vacation destination should have shopping facilities.	3.4	1.1	3.6	1.0	3.3	1.1	*

TABLE 13 (CONTINUED)

STATEMENT	ALL RESPONDENTS		PREFER TO TRAVEL...				
			BY PACKAGE TOUR		INDIVIDUALLY		T-TEST RESULTS
	MEAN	SD	MEAN	SD	MEAN	SD	
12. I take pride in traveling to places where my friends have never been.	3.2	1.0	3.1	1.0	3.2	1.0	*
13. The nicest vacation is one where I can just relax and do nothing.	3.1	1.2	2.9	1.2	3.2	1.2	*
14. Children are important when deciding where to go on vacation.	3.0	1.2	2.9	1.2	3.1	1.2	*
15. The best vacations are those that have a lot of nightlife.	2.7	1.0	2.7	1.0	2.7	1.0	N/S
16. On vacations, big cities are more fun than places tucked away from metropolitan areas.	2.4	1.0	2.6	1.0	2.4	1.0	*

Key:

Strongly disagree	Disagree	Neither agree nor disagree	Agree	Strongly agree
1	2	3	4	5

Note: (N/S) Not significant at the 0.05 level.
(*)Significant differences at the 0.05 level were found between the means of travelers who preferred to take package tours and travelers who preferred to make their own travel arrangements.

take a package tour had significantly different attitudes toward vacation travel than overseas travelers who preferred to make their own arrangements.

The findings revealed that in ten out of the sixteen statements, significant differences were found between the two groups of travelers. Respondents who preferred to go on a package tour attributed higher importance to *good value for money, the role of accommodations and restaurants to the success of their vacation,* and *shopping availability at the destination* (means= 4.3, 4.2, and 3.6, respectively) than respondents who preferred to make their own arrangements (means= 4.1, 4.1, and 3.3, respectively).

Furthermore, respondents who preferred to go on a package tour enjoyed more *traveling to historical places* (mean=4.1) than respondents who preferred to make their own arrangements (mean=3.0). Tour package seekers also preferred to visit *countries that were friendly to the U.S.* (mean=4.1) than individual travelers (mean=3.7).

Individual travelers preferred more to take *relaxing* vacations where *beaches* were an important component of their vacation (means=3.2 and 3.6, respectively) than travelers who preferred to take package tours (means=3.1 and 3.3, respectively). They were also more likely to disagree that *"large metropolitan cities are more fun than isolated locations"* (mean=2.4) than respondents who preferred package tours (mean=2.4).

Individual travelers were also more concerned with the *impact of their travel experiences on their social network* (mean=3.2) than were travelers who preferred to take package tours (mean=3.1). Finally, individual travelers agreed more that *children were important* when deciding where to go on vacation (mean=3.1) than did package tour travelers (mean=2.9).

We may also conclude that the two groups varied in regard to their interests, perceptions, values, and needs of international vacation. The variation was exhibited with regard to various *dimensions* like perception of value for money, activities at the destination (for example, shopping, relaxation, visiting large cities), as well as comfort (accommodation and restaurants), security, and social and family considerations.

SUMMARY AND CONCLUSIONS

The study examined U.S. overseas travelers and compared the characteristics of the two segments of that market: travelers who preferred to go on package tours and travelers who preferred to make their own travel arrangements. The empirical results indicated significant differences between these two groups with regard to their demographics, vacation travel behavior, and attitudes and needs when traveling internationally.

Package tour companies may consider attracting men, widows and widowers, older age groups, and moderate-income groups. Package tour companies should also realize that members of their potential market usually like to take their vacations in the spring and summer but do not tend to be frequent travelers to overseas destinations.

Potential package tour customers also gather their travel information from travel agencies and travel clubs and consequently their contribution as intermediaries or as a "middleman" should be considered. Our empirical results also indicated that women were more dominant in choosing the vacation destination.

As far as vacation activities, those interested in package tours were more concerned with a good value for money and believed that accommodations and restaurants, shopping, and large metropolitan areas were major components of a successful vacation. They also preferred to travel to destinations that were friendly to the U.S. and to visit historical places.

On the other hand, international tourist destinations, attractions, and facilities should study carefully the "individual travelers" who preferred to plan their trips individually. These were young, affluent, highly educated and multilingual travelers.

Individual travelers were quite frequent travelers and usually traveled year-round, with some peak travel during the summer months. They relied on their research skills and read about the destinations in travel guide books and magazines. They also used the airlines and their previous experience at the destination as a source of information.

As far as their vacation needs, this group was more interested in relaxation and beaches and had a "self-esteem" need to talk in their social network about where they went. They also valued the impact of children on deciding where to go.

While the study referred to overseas travel (excluding Canada and Mexico), it did not treat specific destinations that may generate additional demand for package tours such as China, the Soviet Union, and some parts of Africa.

Furthermore, interviewing occurred during a period when the U.S. dollar was relatively weak compared to many European currencies. This might have affected responses to some of the questions.

It is clear that additional studies of this kind should be conducted to allow development of comprehensive models across origin-destination pairs that will reveal the characteristics of potential markets for both choices of vacation mode and to target promotional campaigns accordingly.

BIBLIOGRAPHY

Abbey, James R., "Does Life-Style Profiling Work?" *Journal of Travel Research*, (Summer 1979), 8–14.

Askari, Hossein, "Demand for Package Tours," *Journal of Transport Economics and Policy*, (January 1971), 40–51.

Cunningham, Lawrence F., and Kenneth N. Thompson "The Intercity Bus Tour Market: A Comparison Between Inquirers and Purchasers," *Journal of Travel Research*, (Fall 1986), 8–12.

Jenkins, Roger L., "Family Vacation Decision Making" *Journal of Travel Research*, (Spring 1978), 2–7.

Holloway, Christopher J., "The Guided Tour: A Sociological Approach," *Annals of Tourism Research*, (8) (1981) 377–402.

Kale, Sudhir H., Roger McIntyre, and Katherine M. Weir, "Marketing Overseas Tour Packages to the Youth Segment: An empirical Analysis," *Journal of Travel Research*, (Spring 1987), 20–24.

Kent, William E., Robert A. Meyer, and Thomas M. Reddam, "Reassessing Wholesaler Marketing Strategies: The Role of Travel Research," *Journal of Travel Research*, (Winter 1987), 31–33.

Lopez, Elsa M., "The Effect of Leadership Style of Satisfaction Level of Tour Quality," *Journal of Travel Research*, (Spring 1980), 20–23.

Meidan, Arthur, "Travel Agency Selection Criteria," *Journal of Travel Research*, (Summer 1979), 26–32.

Pearce, Douglas G., "Spatial Patterns of Package Tourism in Europe," *Annals of Tourism Research*, (14) (1987), 183–201.

Sheldon, Pauline J., and James Mak, "The Demand for Package Tours: A Mode Choice Model," *Journal of Travel Research*, (Winter 1987), 13–17.

Sheldon, Pauline J., "The Tour Operator Industry—An Analysis," *Annals of Tourism Research*, (13) (1986), 349–365.

Thomson, Christine M., and Douglas G. Pearce, "Market Segmentation of New Zealand Package Tours," *Journal of Travel Research*, (Fall 1980), 3–6.

Whipple, Thomas W., and Sharon V. Thatch, "Group Tour Management: Does Good Service Produce Satisfied Customers?" *Journal of Travel Research*, (Fall 1988), 16–21.

Woodside Arch, G., and Ilkka Ronkainen, "Vacation Travel Planning Segments: Self Planning vs. Users of Motor Club and Travel Agents," *Annals of Tourism Research*, (7) (1980), 385–394.

CHAPTER 2 The Tourism Industry

PROJECT

Select a component of the tourism industry in which you have a particular interest. What is the future outlook for this industry segment? Develop a job description outlining the specific tasks you might be asked to do within this organization. What particular skills would be required? What are the job opportunities in your geographic area? Do you think you might have to relocate? Are there opportunities for an internship, part-time work, or volunteer work? Are there any trade papers you can subscribe to now? Is there a professional association you may join as a student member? Could you establish professional contacts there? Summarize your findings in a three-page report.

The industry we call tourism has three major components: transportation, accommodations, and the professional services furnished by the wholesaler and retail travel agent. The would-be traveler needs a way to travel, a place to stay at the destination, and—for the most satisfying travel experience—the services of professionals experienced in making these arrangements.

TRANSPORTATION

The Airlines

Scheduled air-mail service was inaugurated in 1918, but regular air passenger service was not offered in the United States until 1925. The first mail was carried on the New York–Philadelphia–Washington route. This service was operated by the U.S. Post Office, using a fleet of World War I surplus aircraft. Mail was still transported by rail from New York to San Francisco. As better engines, new navigational aids, and improved radio communication reduced transcontinental flight time and increased safety, other air routes were added. Night service was introduced in 1924.

In 1925, passenger service was introduced first on the Los Angeles–San Diego route. The flight time for the 125-mile trip was one and one-half hours; a one-way ticket cost $17.50. Passenger traffic grew rapidly, and aircraft manufacturers developed new aircraft to meet the demand for faster and larger

53

planes. In 1935, the DC-3 was introduced. It had a capacity of twenty-one passengers and flew at nearly 200 miles per hour.

CAB and IATA

The development, regulation, and control of the rapidly expanding airline industry was administered by the Civil Aeronautics Board (CAB). The CAB, formed in 1918 as an independent agency of the federal government, was to design an air transportation system adaptable to the present and future needs of foreign and domestic commerce, the postal service, and national defense. Domestic airlines had to obtain a Certificate of Public Convenience and Necessity before being authorized to provide air service between two points. Air fares, too, were subject to CAB approval.

The International Air Transport Association (IATA) formulates standards for air travel between countries. Initially, this association of international airlines was concerned with such issues as the transfer of passengers, baggage, and cargo from country to country and carrier to carrier, and establishing standard conditions of services. Today, IATA is concerned with both the economic and noneconomic regulation of international air transportation, but its most important role is in setting international rates and fares. Through IATA, the airlines enter into agreements concerning rates, conditions of service, and routes to be awarded to each airline. These agreements are subject to the approval of the respective governments. Until recently, agreements in the United States had to be submitted to the Civil Aeronautics Board for its approval. Since deregulation and the demise of the CAB, they are now handled by the U.S. Department of Transportation.

The Airlines and World War II

World War II greatly influenced the development of the airline industry. The war disrupted virtually all civil air transportation. In the United States, the civilian fleet was taken over by the armed forces, and an additional 200 aircraft were held in the United States for use in emergency military air transportation. The demands of war led to the rapid technical and operational improvements of aircraft. New aircraft, such as the DC-4 and the Lockheed Constellation, were introduced. These aircraft had increased load capacities, range, and speed. By the end of the war, the United States had a surplus of both equipment and trained personnel, which, combined with increased demand for air travel during the years following World War II, created a healthy environment in which the airline industry could further develop.

The Post-War Years

The tremendous time-saving aspects of air travel and its cost effectiveness when compared to other modes of transportation, such as rail or automobile, aided the growth of the airline industry during the post–World War II years.

Introduction of larger aircraft resulted in lower airfares, making air travel more affordable. Between 1950 and 1970, the number of people traveling between the United States and foreign countries increased from a little over 1 million to well over 80 million. Since the introduction of the DC-7 in 1953, new aircraft types have appeared approximately every five years. Each one has been larger and more efficient than its predecessor, lowering the cost per seat and the fare per passenger. The impetus for the tremendous growth in air travel among people traveling for business is its time-saving advantage; for the pleasure traveler, it is the affordable price that has had the greatest impact.

One of the most important years for aviation in the United States was 1958. First, the National Aeronautics and Space Administration (NASA) was established, launching America on its tremendously popular mission to put a person on the moon and to build a permanent station in space. Second, legislation passed establishing the Federal Aviation Administration (FAA), which provided the safety guidelines that allowed the industry's spectacular growth. Third, in October 1958, Pan American World Airways initiated the age of commercial jet travel in the United States when it launched a Boeing 707 on the transatlantic route to London. Jet technology created a revolution in the world of transportation. In particular, it caused the demise of most passenger rail travel in the United States and most point-to-point ocean-going passenger ship transportation. The jet made the world a smaller place. Until 1958, the fastest commercial airplane in the United States was the DC-7, which had an average cruising speed of 350 miles per hour and took nearly an entire day to fly from New York to San Francisco. The introduction of Boeing 707 and the DC-8 changed that. Cruise speed went to 590 miles per hour and travel time over long distances went down 40 percent.

The early years of passenger jet service were not without problems. The British inaugurated London–New York service on October 4, 1958 with a Comet aircraft, beating the United States by three weeks. But three crashes brought things to a halt, and the Comet was grounded. Millions of inexperienced travelers were uneasy about the jet. Still, this new form of transportation stirred excitement, and those able to afford frequent air travel soon became known as "jet-setters."

By the end of 1958, less than 10 percent of the U.S. population had flown. Flying was still expensive, but the efficiency of jets, combined with much higher load capacities, produced lower fares, making air travel more available to millions of people.

In the United States, more than twenty-five airlines were transporting over 450 million passengers annually by the early 1990s. United Airlines, the largest airline in the United States and in the western world, carried nearly 60 million passengers in 1990. Aeroflot, the airline of the Commonwealth of Independent States, carried more than 100 million people in that same year, making it the largest airline in the world.

Deregulation

In 1978, Congress passed legislation that removed many of the regulations governing air carrier routes and fares. Before then, the Civil Aeronautics Board would set airline fares according to route distances and the industry's average. By the end of 1982, all official controls on domestic U.S. air fares were abandoned. Today, no airline holds exclusive rights to any market in the United States.

The Airline Deregulation Act of 1978 began a revolution in commercial aviation in the United States. Airlines, developed under the framework of government regulations, had to learn to operate successfully in a competitive environment. Deregulation has fascinated economists, enraged airline executives, bewildered travel agents, and dismayed trade unionists. The early years were unsettling to many. The act was passed in a year when the airlines had record operating profits of $1.4 billion. But in 1979 and 1980, the price of fuel more than doubled. In 1981, when the nation's air traffic controllers went on strike, aircraft movement was curtailed in the cause of safety and, meanwhile, the country was undergoing its worst recession in fifty years. The airlines suffered. Many airlines reduced their size, both labor force and number of aircraft; restructured their organization; controlled costs; and realigned routes in an effort to become more efficient. Nevertheless, the early 1980s were difficult for many United States airlines. To attract customers, they were forced to cut fares. The operating profit of 1978 became a loss of $222 million in 1980, $438 million in 1981, and $700 million in 1982. It was not until the mid-1980s that the airline industry again operated profitably. Coincidental with the early years of deregulation was the continuing decline in fuel prices which positively affected the airlines' profitability.

In the turbulent industry climate of the early to mid-1980s, there were casualties. Braniff, hit by rising fuel costs just after a major route expansion, ceased operations in 1982. Continental Airlines ceased operations in 1983 after it clashed with its unions. Eastern Airlines experienced a similar situation in 1989, followed by Pan Am and Midway.

Deregulation resulted in profound structural changes in air travel, and it is still difficult to predict what the industry will look like in the future. The airline industry continues to be extremely competitive. It is probable that only the most efficient airlines—large or small—will survive.

The most noticeable result of deregulation has been in the area of routes. By keeping connecting times to a minimum, airlines are serving different kinds of markets through nontraditional airports. The popularity of the nonstop flight yielded to the operating philosophy of hubs. Airlines convinced the traveling public that changing planes onto the same airline was a reasonable alternative. The "hub-and-spoke" system is not entirely a postderegulation phenomenon. Atlanta had been the hub for Delta's route system for years, and it has been largely credited for that airlines's consistent performance and financial success throughout the turbulent years of deregulation. In the new competitive environment of airline operations, companies have learned that hubs are essential to survival, since they allow airlines to control their own traffic. Hubs tend to be most successful when set up to serve the travel needs of the short-haul traveler, especially when connecting times are kept to a minimum.

Pricing, too, has changed radically since deregulation. Before deregulation, pricing policies related to the elasticity of demand. Since the demand for most business travel is inelastic, fares on routes carrying a large percentage of business travelers (like New York–Chicago) were high. Pleasure travel is more likely to have an elastic demand. A substantially lower fare on a route popular with tourists will result in more demand. While the principle of elasticity of demand is still applicable, current pricing policy is affected by many complex factors. Many fares are set by new entrants; others by airlines that are desperately trying to stay alive. The ability of an airline to offer a lower fare than its competitors relates directly to the airline's cost of operations.

The larger airlines—United, American, Northwest, and Delta—have a high cost of operations and, therefore, they tend not to lower fares until forced to do so by competition. Smaller carriers may have lower costs and can sell their product at a lower price. They have introduced low fares in several markets, giving the larger carriers no choice but to match these discounted fares. This resulted in fare wars, which became common occurrences since the early 1980s. Fare wars result in passenger increases, but cause the profit picture for the airlines to be negative. Today, airlines initiating lower fares are often the one(s) in the worst financial fix who engage in a desparate attempt to hold on to market share and to stay alive. An example is Continental in 1992. Airline executives refer to $99 transcontinental fares as "bankruptcy fares."

Netherlands Board of Tourism

On January 1, 1985, deregulation entered its last phase with the official dissolution of the Civil Aeronautics Board. Initially, many airlines were seeing improved financial results; others continued their struggle to achieve profitability and overcome financial problems resulting from market erosion and heavy debt payments. For some larger airlines, impressive progress was made during the decade of the 1980s, despite the well-publicized difficulties of some. The stable economy during much of the 1980s allowed for the introduction of firmer fare structures and better controls by the airlines over management of operating costs. Perhaps the most positive element in the financial picture for the airlines was their ability to increase their average fares after one or two years of discounted fares. Labor costs stabilized; some airlines hired new workers at lower wage scales, while others received wage reduction in exchange for profit sharing and stock payment plans. However, some carriers, such as Continental Airlines and Eastern Air Lines, made national headlines as management had to make unpopular decisions to keep the companies in business. Eventually, both fell victim to changing realities. Another approach was that of Frontier Holdings: it started a wholly new airline, which operated with a lower labor scale than did its existing carrier. However, it too would soon stop operations.

During the decade of the 1980s, the number of airline passengers has nearly doubled to more than 486 million per year. Airlines were challenged to rebuild their fares to a level that permitted profitable operations. The major airlines also improved their cost structures to compete against the many low-cost airlines that had expanded into their route systems.

Airlines routes also have changed since deregulation. Companies have changed strategies as they eliminated marginal segments of their systems that did not support the desired traffic flow. Airlines took instant advantage of sudden opportunities, such as the failure of a competing carrier.

In general, the airlines have been concerned with the development and expansion of hub-and-spoke networks. This method enables the airline to collect passengers from feeder flights, transfer them on the same carrier through the hub, and carry them to their ultimate destination. In addition to establishing new hubs and strengthening old hubs, airlines pursue a variety of other strategies, including improving the seasonal balance of passenger flow, penetrating new areas, changing the balance between business and pleasure traffic, and encouraging brand loyalty among passengers through special incentive programs such as the immensely popular frequent flyer programs.

During the 1980s, there was a shift into the West and South as airlines penetrated new areas where the number of new routes available is greater than those in the North and East. Majors created new hubs, resulting in increased competition among the airlines. United Airlines, long the leading airline in Chicago, has developed a new center of operations in Denver, where it is now the leading carrier. American Airlines kept Dallas/Fort Worth as its major hub, while TWA has focused its attention on St. Louis.

Although airlines are no longer classified by the size of their route structure (majors and minors), most of the smaller companies are concentrated in particular regions of the country. They tend to operate shorter hauls and serve smaller cities than do larger companies. The fleet of regional airlines consists largely of smaller two-engine aircraft which prove more efficient during times of rising costs. In general, small airlines have been more successful in adapting to the deregulated environment than the larger ones. Regional airlines have extended their territories well beyond former boundaries. Most national carriers, in fact, are former local service airlines, such as USAir and Piedmont which merged in 1989; or they began as intrastate carriers, like PSA, Southwest, and Air Cal. Southwest is the only survivor. Most, if not all regionals, except Southwest, which is now a national, have become "—— Express"—that is, United Express or Continental Express. While many regional airlines, especially USAir, outperformed even the expectations of experts, others, such as Air Florida, Frontier, and Midway were unable to adjust to the deregulated environment.

New Entrants and Commuters

Since 1982, major airlines have suspended service to nearly seventy cities. This provided the opportunity for regional or commuter airlines to fill the void. In the early years since deregulation, the commuters were the fastest-growing segment of the airline industry. Operating small aircraft, they achieved high load factors on routes that were unattractive to the larger airlines. Unaffected by the complex network of routes offered by the full-service airlines, commuters were able to offer lower fares, as their own cost structures were well below the industry's average. Dozens of new airlines were formed since 1978, most on small budgets with used planes. Their success was almost entirely a function of price and decreased services, since they did not offer complex baggage handling and on-board service. They often enjoyed a competitive advantage on labor costs; commuters tended to be nonunionized and tended to utilize their employees more effectively.

Future Trends

The United States airlines industry currently employs more than 300,000 people, 32 percent of whom are directly involved with servicing customers and aircraft at the airports. In addition, reservations, sales, and administrative personnel account for 30 percent; mechanics, 15 percent; flight attendants, 14 percent; and pilots, copilots, and flight engineers, 9 percent of the airlines' personnel.

Within the United States, nearly 60,000 city-pairs (nonstop service between two cities) have scheduled air service. The top 1,000 city-pairs account for about 70 percent of all passenger traffic. One might conclude from this that the airlines operate many thousand aircraft. Not so. The fleet of commercial aircraft in the United States numbers about 2,500. Through effective scheduling, these aircraft provide service on a network of routes.

Of major concern to the airline industry in recent years is the substantial increase in operational costs. In 1973, airlines paid an average of $.12 per gallon for aviation fuel, representing under 15 percent of their operations budget. Today, fuel accounts for over 30 percent of total operating expenses for the airlines.

Despite increasing operating costs, the growth of the scheduled airline industry has been substantial, and the trend continues. For example, since 1960, the number of passengers flying on scheduled carriers has increased fourfold. The population of the United States, by comparison, has increased approximately 25 percent.

Today, 145 million Americans, or nearly 80 percent of the adult population, has traveled in an airplane. In 1990, more than one in three adult Americans took a trip by air.

Three key factors account for the success of many of the surviving airlines: operations, capital accumulation, and marketing.

Operations. Research has shown that the main reason many travelers choose one carrier over another is convenience or time of departure. Scheduling, therefore, is critical to an airline's success. For most travelers, when a flight departs or arrives is more important than any brand preference that might have been established.

Cost control is also of major importance to scheduled carriers. During the past two decades, airline unit costs increased nearly 200 percent, mainly in the areas of fuel, commissions, landing fees, and labor; while the average airline fares, based on revenue per passenger-mile, increased only 45 percent. As is the case for most business ventures, costs for airlines can be divided into those that are *fixed* and those that are *variable*. Fixed costs are those that go on regardless of the amount of business and are costs that are incurred regardless of volume, regardless of sales. Examples of fixed costs are those for the amortization or lease of airplanes, interest costs on borrowed money, insurance costs, pensions for retired employees, and for the operation of airport terminals owned or leased by airlines. Examples of variable costs are wages and salaries, advertising and promotion costs, fuel costs, passenger meals, and landing fees. These costs tend to rise and fall with the volume of sales or number of flights. Perhaps the most important variable in cost control is *aircraft utilization*; that is, the rate at which an airplane is in the air producing the greatest amount of revenue for the greatest possible number of hours in a day. Labor relations is another important aspect of air carrier operations. Most employees of major airlines belong to labor unions. When a strike occurs, it can cripple a carrier.

Another vital aspect of operations is the utilization of gate space at airports. Except for Denver and Pittsburgh, no new airports have been built in the United States since the late 1970s despite the enormous increase in the number of flight operations. Airlines are responding to a limited availability of airport gate space by flying larger aircraft, which is leading to a increased demand for new and used aircraft. By the mid-1980s, the worldwide shortage of larger aircraft was so acute that used planes (when available) were demanding a higher price than new aircraft.

Capital Accumulation. The approximate cost of a middle-size airplane (160 to 210 passengers) is $20 to $25 million, depending on the type purchased. There are no obvious answers for airlines, manufacturers, and governments in choosing planes to handle traffic growth, replace inefficient fleets, and meet noise abatement regulations. One fact is certain: an airline's ability to accumulate capital and arrange for favorable financing will have tremendous impact on future profitability.

Marketing. Brand loyalty among travelers is extremely low, because domestic carriers offer essentially a similar product at a competitive price. Scheduling and route structure, as mentioned earlier, are all important. It is often said that an airline is only as good as the last flight a passenger flew on it. Because of this, the larger carriers (American and United) spend $50 to $70 million annually in advertising to create an impression of superiority. A spilled cup of coffee or a dinner poorly served by a flight attendant, however, can negate all the advertising expenditure for any given passenger.

The key statistic in analyzing an airline's profitability is the *load factor*, defined as the number of seats filled on every flight expressed as a percentage of total seats available on all flights. The load factor, like the occupancy rate in the hotel, indicates the efficiency of the operator. Prior to deregulation, airline marketing was not very sophisticated compared to that used for most packaged goods. In the future, the successful carriers will have to focus their efforts on three elements of marketing: advertising slogans, primary passengers (vacation and/or frequent flyers), and distribution channels. In today's deregulated environment, airline seats are considered a commodity to be sold to customers rather than a public service that must be offered to the public. Slogans such as "Number One," "The Friendly Skies," and "Ready When You Are" are important in marketing commercial airlines' services. They encourage use and repeat business from vacation customers. However, vacationers are not usually frequent travelers. Airlines report that a small number of loyal riders (3 percent of the airline total) contribute 26 percent of passengers revenues. These passengers, primarily business people, are a group for which special programs must be created since their brand loyalties are much higher than those of the average traveler. Advertising campaigns directed at this group emphasize the special treatment they may expect, the convenience of a certain airline's schedules for the business traveler, or special frequent-flyer incentives.

Over 75 percent of a scheduled carrier's business is booked through travel agents. This percentage has been increasing each year, and it underscores the importance of travel agents to airlines. Airline programs designed to influence travel agents, to offer competitive commission incentives, and to provide the agents with up-to-date information, can have a major impact on an agent's choice of carrier for a client.

Conclusion

Today's financial results of U.S. airlines show a strengthening of performance on the part of some carriers, while others struggle to hold on. Some airlines, often those with sizeable financial reserves, have evolved into very successful mega-carriers, such as Delta, United, and American, each reporting continued growth and expansion into overseas markets. Some of the traditionally very successful airlines, such as Eastern and Pan Am, did not survive.

The biggest setback for both domestic and international carriers came in 1991. Both the war in the Persian Gulf and a worldwide recession caused a dramatic drop in demand for air travel. With fewer people flying, some carriers made it through the crisis and became stronger; others cut service or ceased operations. Some carriers, often those in or close to bankruptcy, dropped fares to levels sufficient to meet short-term cash expenses. This, in turn, forced competing carriers to match these lower prices, resulting in a dramatic drop in overall yield for the entire industry.

While it seems likely that fuel costs will continue to stabilize (or even decrease) during the decade of the 1990s, it no longer serves as a barometer of the industry's chances for success or failure. Other factors, including the economy, competition with foreign and supplemental carriers, overcapacity, and cost management are all factors that contribute to pricing policies. Simply put, the airline industry will not recover until it can charge higher fares, and to do that, price wars must end and consumer demand for both domestic and international air travel must increase. It is important to remember that the airline industry achieves a profit of only $2 for each $100 of sales, while the average U.S. industry achieves $5 profit for each $100 of sales.

Airline officials must continue to focus attention on marketing, the task of further streamlining operations, and containing costs. Population growth, liberalized outbound travel policies in many countries, more and longer vacations, increased globalization of industry, international education, lifting of international trade restrictions, and higher incomes are all forces that will increase travel. Recessions, political instabilities, and rising costs will tend to force travel down. On balance, and over a period of time, business and pleasure travel, especially by air, will continue their now-familiar growth patterns.

The Railroads

As airlines began to take over the market for surface transportation of travelers in the United States, the railroad industry faced serious problems. By 1970, less than 1 percent of all passenger miles in this country were traveled by rail. One year later, the federal government created the National Railroad Passenger Corporation, better known as Amtrak. This corporation was created to free the nation's freight railroads from their obligation to provide passenger service and to preserve and restore passenger railroad transportation throughout the country.

Amtrak's Early Years

Amtrak faced many challenges during its first decade. Competition with the private automobile, buses, and the airlines was intense. In many cases, Amtrak's equipment was outdated. In addition, the poor condition of the roadbeds meant that even newly installed equipment was unable to operate efficiently. Despite this, Amtrak succeeded, for the most part, in meeting its passengers' needs. New equipment (including the enhancement of the Superliner and introduction of the Viewliner cars) was designed and put into service, and roadbed improvements was undertaken in the northeast corridor between Boston and Washington. During its early years, Amtrak introduced computerized reservations and renewed its commitment to the travel agency industry. Moves were also made toward intermodal travel—the coordination of services and ticket sales with some bus, air, and steamship lines. Other recent initiatives on the part of Amtrak include the commitment to restoring some of this country's grand railroad stations, including Union Station in Washington, D.C.

Current Challenges

While Amtrak has succeeded in preserving passenger railroad transportation in this country, it has been unable to do so profitably. Despite this, Amtrak has consistently improved its performance and efficiency. By 1990, total revenues covered nearly 70 percent of cost. It requires millions of dollars in subsidies each year. This need, coupled with changes in government priorities, has led to the suspension of some routes and reduction of service on others.

In the future, perhaps the railroads in the United States need to look to the cruise business for new ideas. The cruise lines faced a similar situation three decades ago, when air travel made inroads into the transatlantic passenger market. At that point, the operators of the cruise lines realized that they were no longer in the business of transportation, but in that of entertainment. They adjusted their routes and the services they offered accordingly.

Given the increasing sense of sameness in air travel, perhaps railroad transportation in the future will have to be sold as an entertaining experience, rather than merely a mode of transportation. For long trips, train travel becomes an undesirable alternative to air travel for many people. In those instances, train travel is only attractive to those who are afraid to fly, those who enjoy train travel as an experience, and those who happen to live in or near towns that have railroad stations. Because of the travel time required to get from downtown to the airport or because of congested skies, trains can link the population corridors of both east and west coasts and provide new travel experiences for those who enjoy longer trips by train.

Railroads in Europe and Japan

While the future of the railroads in North America is uncertain, railroads continue to play a vital role in the transportation network of European countries and Japan. Factors that have helped the railroads survive overseas include the relative closeness of major urban centers and the always-high cost of gasoline. Parking facilities in European cities have become increasingly scarce as car ownership has increased sharply. This, in turn, has caused more people to choose the train over the private automobile for their home/work commute. In many countries, public transportation is subsidized in an attempt to discourage people from driving their cars to and from work. In Holland, for example, all college and university students receive a pass that provides for unlimited travel on the nation's railroad system.

It is important to remember that many cities in the United States developed around the automobile, whereas the downtown areas of European cities took shape centuries ago, and are thus less adapted to heavy automobile traffic. The convenience of boarding a train in downtown Paris to arrive two hours later in downtown Brussels is something that neither the airplane nor the private automobile can match. Furthermore, air fares have traditionally been very high within Europe and this has also encouraged railroad ridership. However, perhaps the most important reason that railroad travel is so popular among Europeans is its record of reliability. Delays are rare, cancellations unheard of, and virtually all trains arrive at their destination within minutes of the scheduled arrival time.

Train travel provides convenient transportation over mountain passes in the Alps and the Pyrenees, making it a favorite among winter sport enthusiasts. Special charter trains leave northern Europe in the winter for the ski resorts in Switzerland, Austria, Italy, and France. Special auto trains follow these same routes during the summer. Travelers may use the special open cargo cars in back of the passenger train to carry the family car along with them to their final vacation destination.

Long-distance international rail travel in Europe is provided by the TEE (Trans-European Express) trains. These standardized, deluxe trains are managed and operated under a joint agreement by the individual government-run railroads in each of the European countries. TEE trains are equipped with first-class restaurants, lounges, running water, and special sleeping compartments (couchets). In 1981, it was announced that one of Europe's most famous trains, the Orient Express, would once again provide weekly service between London and Istanbul. In that same year, the French national railroad system started service with a so-called TGV train between Paris and Lyon. This train travels at speeds exceeding 200 miles per hour, making it the fastest train in the world. In Japan, the high-speed Tokaido and Hikari "bullet" trains have been a resounding success for many years. In the United States, the "super-trains" might have promise only for relatively short-run routes in highly congested areas such as between Boston, New York, and Washington, D.C., or along the Pacific coast.

The European railroads, in their effort to promote train travel in Europe by North Americans, introduced the Eurailpass. This pass, for sale only outside Europe to non-European residents, provides unlimited train travel on the railroads of sixteen participating countries.

Cruise Lines

By the end of the 1950s, the world's major passenger ship lines resembled the dinosaurs that had failed to adapt to the changes around them. We have identified 1958 as an important year for the airline industry because in that year the first commercial jetliner flew the Atlantic. It also heralded an era that altered the face of transatlantic shipping forever. A new generation of travelers, seeking time and cost efficient travel, was no longer attracted to the six-day journey by ship when they could take a eight-hour flight by plane. The passenger ship, however, escaped extinction through one of our industry's most amazing examples of market adaptation. Carving out a new niche in the tourism industry, passenger lines have established the concept of cruising not as a means of transportation but as a total vacation experience. The story of the passenger cruise line over the past thirty years is a tribute to flexibility and marketing expertise and ingenuity. Today, scheduled overseas passenger service is provided by airlines. The only vessels presently offering passenger service between Western Europe and North America (and then only during the summer) are the Queen Elizabeth II, owned by Cunard Lines, and Poland's Stefan Batory, which sails out of Montreal.

By the early 1970s, the cruise line industry established itself as a permanent force in the tourism industry. That growth would continue. In fact, the number of cruise passengers has increased fivefold between 1970 and 1990 to a total of 3.5 million. This growth might have been even more dramatic if more space had been available in the early decades. In the mid-1970s, hardly a cruise ship sailed with an empty berth. Travel agents who did not reserve space three

or four months ahead could not be certain of available cabin space. These were golden years for cruise companies, and it stimulated new construction orders that increased the capacity of the fleet in North America. An innovative approach to the capacity problem involved midsectioning, whereby a vessel is cut in half, additional facilities inserted, and the whole put back together again. This method was used by Royal Caribbean Lines with the Song of Norway in 1979 and the Nordic Prince in 1980. Total berths offered by the cruise industry tripled during the 1980s. In the 1989, Royal Caribbean Cruise Line introduced the 2,282-passenger Sovereign of the Seas, the largest cruise ship ever built. A year later, Carnival Cruises introduced the first of three larger ships. The Fantasy, carrying 2,600 passengers and costing $200 million, started service in 1990. In 1990 alone, no less than 15 new ships entered the cruise market.

The challenge for the industry is to maintain high occupancy levels by realizing an overall increase in the number of passengers during this period of major new construction.

Initially, it was expected that supply might exceed demand, and that there would be a period characterized by price competition and creative promotional and advertising campaigns to attract new customers. While sales have been up in recent years, yields have dwindled because of fare reductions. Marketing experts, however, point out that less than 10 percent of the U.S. population has ever taken a cruise, making the long-term outlook a bright one for this industry. Recent years have been very successful for the industry. Even during the unsettling situation in the Persian Gulf and an unprecedented recession in the United States, cruise bookings continued to break all previous records. In fact, during the early years of the 1990s, the cruise industry represented one of the few tourism industry components that was actually thriving.

Traditionally popular cruise destinations, such as the Caribbean and Mediterranean, will continue to satisfy the demands of cruise passengers, but as the industry expands its fleet, it is seeking new destinations to explore new markets and appeal to both first-time and repeat cruise passengers. Mexico has been an area of continuous expansion for the industry. By 1985, regular departures to Mexico's west coast were offered by not less than eight major lines. With that many ships concentrated on the west coast, cruise lines aggressively developed an additional market to the north. Many of the ships that begin their Mexican season in the fall spend their summers along the British Columbian and Alaskan coasts. Westours Holland America Cruises, a firm believer in the growth potential of the west coast market, moved its headquarters from New York to Seattle.

Fly-Cruise

The fly-cruise concept, introduced in the early 1970s, increased the number of cruise passengers originating in the Midwest and Canadian markets and also resulted in a dramatically lower average age of participants. The customer is offered a substantial discount on the round-trip air fare to the departure point. In most promotions, air transportation is provided free or is included in the total cruise package.

Miami, Fort Lauderdale, and the nearby harbor of Port Everglades are popular departure points for Caribbean cruises. During the winter months, many vessels make San Juan, Puerto Rico their home port. Other important ports are Los Angeles, San Francisco, and, during the summer season, New York City. Interestingly, the Port of Miami embarks/disembarks more cruise passengers than all the port cities in the rest of the world.

Repeat Business

A key factor in the success of the cruise line industry is the ability to attract repeat business. A significant number of cruise passengers are repeat customers, and this percentage increases as the duration of a cruise gets longer. For example, a one-week cruise may have one-third of its passengers as repeat cruisers, while on a recent around-the-world cruise, more than 90 percent of the passengers had cruised before.

As pointed out earlier, cruise lines are more in the entertainment business than in the transportation business. The single most important factor for success is the quality of the product; that is, the provision of entertainment, exciting destinations, and a courteous staff. Excellent entertainment and happy employees can create an ambience on board that will please the passengers, and result in repeat voyages and referrals.

Marketing

Public relations departments of large companies, such as Royal Caribbean Cruise Line, Carnival, Holland America Lines, Princess, and Norwegian Caribbean Lines maintain lists of passengers names. Several times each year promotional material is sent to keep past customers informed about new itineraries. Strong, targeted marketing programs are needed to get people to take their first cruise. This includes advertising and promotion aimed at potential cruise passengers. The composition of the market for cruises has changed dramatically during the past few years. Passengers are younger, the average length of cruises has been getting shorter, and fierce competition has produced heavy discounting of fares. The fastest-growing segments of the market are the short duration cruises (three to four days).

Importance of Travel Agents

Cruise lines are more dependent on travel agents for the sale of their product than are other segments of the industry. More than 90 percent of people taking their first cruise purchase their tickets from travel agents. It is, therefore,

vital for the cruise line companies to offer attractive travel agent commissions and incentives.

The Motorcoach Industry

The motorcoach industry experienced a period of economic growth during the 1970s, as automobile and airline travel were plagued by rapidly increasing fuel costs. The intercity bus industry transports nearly 400 million passengers annually. However, scheduled ridership on U.S. bus lines has been on the decline each year since 1979. Bus lines, however, have been carrying increasing number of passengers on tours and charter service.

Commuter/Intercity Uses

Buses are used for many purposes. In large metropolitan areas such as New York City and Chicago, thousands of people use buses to commute to work. During the rush-hour periods, special lanes facilitate the movement of buses in and out of the city.

Naturally, buses are used widely in intercity transportation. For several years, Greyhound and Trailways were the country's largest intercity bus operators. In 1990, the two companies merged under the name Greyhound, and together they operate well over 10,000 buses and have a route network of over 150,000 miles. While the new company is large and a highly visible component of this industry, there are also close to 1,100 smaller companies operating buses in the United States, which transport a total of 300 million people yearly.

In addition to intercity transportation, many bus companies offer an airport transfer, hotel pick-ups, and convention services.

Recreational Uses

Buses are widely used in sight-seeing programs. The world's largest sight-seeing organization, Gray Lines, offers more than 1,500 sight-seeing excursions daily. The company has offices in all major cities throughout the United States, Canada, Mexico, Africa, Asia, Europe, the Orient, Caribbean, Middle East, South Pacific, and Central and South America.

Vacation Tours. Escorted bus vacation tours are another fast-growing area. These tours range from day trips to thirty-one day tours and depart from major cities across the United States and Canada. Spring, summer, and fall are the most popular seasons. The client knows in advance the exact itinerary and the cost involved. Itineraries vary from very busy, on-the-go schedules to more leisurely paced agendas. Escorted vacation tours are popular in areas such as our national parks, New England, Pennsylvania Dutch communities, Rocky Mountains, Florida, and the California and Canadian coastlines. These tours have become very popular with travelers for whom overseas travel is too expensive, people who like to vacation closer to home, and people who prefer not to travel by automobile.

Charter Tours. The charter tour differs from the escorted vacation tour in that it is comprised of a preformed group. Such tours might include trips to casinos, flower shows, ball games, theaters, and other special events. Charter tours are especially popular with senior-citizen groups, for whom they provide a relatively unhurried and inexpensive mode of travel.

The modern bus provides a high standard of service and comfort for the passengers. It offers a quiet ride, and seating comfort compares favorably with that found in modern airplanes. All intercity buses are equipped with restrooms and air conditioning, and many have panoramic view windows. Since the bus passenger is usually economy-minded, bus companies do not serve food on board, nor do they employ attendants.

Future of the Industry

The bus is currently the most fuel-efficient mode of intercity travel and is likely to play an important role in the growth of the travel industry. At the moment, the bus industry is the nation's second-largest form of public transportation. Busses carry 400 million passengers annually; airlines carry 486 million; the railroads carry 25 million. The bus industry provides service to 14,600 communities; the airlines serve 700 communities; and the railroads serve 550 communities. As a result of deregulation in the 1980s, bus companies now may select the routes they travel, choose their pick-up points, and set fares independently.

ACCOMMODATIONS _____

Of all the segments that make up the tourism and travel business, none has a longer history than accommodations—what we now call the hospitality industry. During the stagecoach era, most modern major roads in both the United States and western Europe had boarding houses where travelers were, for the most part, wealthy. Once at their final destinations, travelers expected to stay at private homes.

Development of Resorts and Hotels

Modern resort-type accommodations originated in the health spas of Britain and Germany. Originally operated as accommodations for patients receiving medical treatment, these spas became popular leisure destinations as facilities for pleasure and entertainment were added to alleviate the boredom associated with spa treatment.

In the cities, the expansion of the railway system in the middle of the nineteenth century created an environment in which the large downtown hotel could develop. The great number of travelers carried by the railroads, and the resulting rapid growth of many towns, increased demand for accommodations for transients. By the late nineteenth century, every city in Europe and the United States offered a variety of hotel accommodations, from simple bed-and-breakfast pensions to luxury hotels such as the Ritz in Paris and the Savoy in London. The Savoy opened in 1889, and was the first hotel having private bathrooms. More importantly, it was the first hotel in London to pioneer the use of electric light not only in the sitting room, but in all bedrooms.

The development of the luxury hotel spurred the growth of the food and beverage industry. The growth of cities in the nineteenth century led to the practice of eating out since workers could no longer easily return home for lunch. The number of restaurants, therefore, increased sharply, and new hotels included restaurants and tea rooms as part of their facilities.

Hotels also developed rapidly in coastal and scenic mountain areas, usually in locations not too far from major urban centers. In Britain, Brighton became Europe's first real seaside resort. On the east coast of the United States, hotels were built along the Hudson River, in the Catskill Mountains, and along the New Jersey shoreline, where Atlantic City became this country's most popular summer resort.

Influence of the Automobile

The period between the two world wars changed the nature of tourism and travel dramatically, as fewer people traveled by rail, choosing the private automobile instead. With the construction of highways, throughways, expressways, and beltways, the lodging industry responded to the specific needs of the motorist, and the motor hotel, or motel, was born. Development of the nationwide highway system in the 1950s opened up the entire country to the average person. The national highways made business travel a common way of doing business. It became possible to go from New York City to Albany in three hours instead of nine hours and to reach Buffalo in eight hours instead of two days.

Numerous hotel companies got their start at this time. Westin Hotels, founded as Western Hotels, began operating hotels in the northwest corner of the United States in 1930. Quality Inns began in 1939 as Quality Courts. Another arrival on the scene was Sheraton, founded in Boston and taking its name from the sign on the Hotel Sheraton acquired by the founders in 1939.

Postwar Growth

After World War II, travel and tourism quickly became one of the world's largest and fastest-growing activities, and the construction of hotels kept pace with this development. Several influences caused the lodging industry to prosper. After the war, many Americans resumed their business and personal lives with a more global perspective. It influenced their interest in travel and dictated their needs and desires. Changes in transportation, technology, and lifestyle sowed the seeds for mass travel in the years that followed. The airplane made it possible for resorts to develop, and enabled thousands, rather than hundreds of visitors to visit places like Florida and Hawaii.

During the 1950s and 1960s, thousands of hotels were built in the Mediterranean, the Caribbean, and in Florida. By the late 1960s, the entire coastline from Spain to Italy served as a resort for the population of northern Europe. Today, the world's inventory of hotel rooms is estimated at more than 10 million. Global revenue exceeds $35 billion annually.

The United States, with well over 2 million rooms, is by far the world's leader in the hospitality industry. Italy, with about 1.5 million rooms, ranks second, and Germany, Great Britain, France, and Spain each have inventories of close to 800,000 rooms.

International statistics on the lodging industry are difficult to compile. Some countries keep statistics on the number of rooms, while others count the number of beds. Statistics from many countries include small family-home-type guest houses (pensions) and youth-hostel-style accommodations, whereas other countries limit their figures to tourist, first-class, and deluxe hotels. Regardless of the statistical methods used, there has been substantial growth in number of rooms, occupancy rates, and operating revenues.

In 1990, the U.S. hotel industry added about 120,000 more rooms to its inventory. About 85,000 of these rooms were introduced by the major chains. Average occupancy rates for 1990 were established at 67 percent, a slight increase over previous years.

Accommodation Classification

Various attempts have been made to develop an international classification system, through which the quality of accommodation, in terms of facilities and

services, can be rated. Great differences in the characteristics of hotels in different countries have hindered these efforts. Many countries have their own internal classification codes, using either a star system or a system that puts hotels into one of four classes: deluxe, first-class, moderate first-class, and tourist class.

The Chains

Prior to the advent of large hotels, the accommodation industry was made up of a large number of small, privately owned facilities. As the capital required for the operation of a large hotel grew, individual owner-management was replaced by some form of corporate organization. While most hotels are still individually owned and operated, most of the world's first-class and deluxe hotels operate under a lease, franchise system, or under a management contract. The international hotel scene is dominated by American corporations. Of the world's thirty largest hotel chains, nineteen are American-owned.

Role of the Airlines

The airlines have likewise played an important role in the development of the hotel industry. As routes opened up to new destinations, first-class accommodations were often lacking. The airlines had both a need and an opportunity to become actively involved in the construction and management of hotels. In 1946, Pan American created Intercontinental Hotels. TWA became the parent company of Hilton International. Westin Hotels, formerly Western International, is affiliated with United Airlines.

KLM, the national carrier of The Netherlands, has a major interest in the worldwide network of Golden Tulip Hotels; and Aer Lingus, the airline of the Republic of Ireland, was the parent corporation of the Dunfey Hotel chain. Most airlines use their sophisticated reservation systems to sell hotel rooms as well as airplane seats.

Meetings and Conventions

During the 1970s, the hospitality industry entered an era in which function and location became of foremost importance. The tremendous increase in the number of meetings, conventions, trade shows, and seminars conducted each year is especially important to the hotel industry. If the development of the airplane boosted leisure travel, it revolutionized business travel. Since the emergence of the jet airplane as a form of mass transportation, there was a proliferation of business hotels. Now, travelers could go to five or six cities per month, rather than one city a month by train.

Before long, many hotels relied almost exclusively on the convention business. Many hotels, such as Sheraton Washington and the Hyatt-O'Hare Hotel outside Chicago have been designed to serve as convention centers. The occupancy rates of these hotels depend heavily on the number and size of conventions and meetings the hotel books.

Fragmentation

The lodging industry is highly fragmented. It is estimated that more than 50,000 establishments operate in the U.S., ranging from small roadside motels to resort hotels with more than 3,000 rooms each. Operators of these facilities may often be single individuals or a large corporation with diversified worldwide interests. Lodging chains may have full or partial ownership of properties bearing their names, or they may operate through management contracts or franchises.

Franchises

Franchised properties are neither owned nor managed by the lodging company. Rather, the company receives an initial fee and a percentage of gross receipts in exchange for use of the company's name, national advertising support, reservations services, and other considerations. Most national and worldwide lodging chains are franchise operations. The largest, Holiday Inns, with a total of 1,740 properties containing 312,426 rooms, had franchisees operating 1,514 of the facilities with a total of 255,726 rooms.

The Holiday Inns licensing agreement is typical of those in the industry. A franchisee obtaining a domestic license is required to make an initial payment of $300 per room (minimum $30,000), plus royalties of 4 percent of gross room revenues. In addition, all franchisees are required to pay for marketing and reservation services at a rate of 2 percent of gross room revenues, with a minimum of $.14 per room per night. As with any franchise operation, the franchisees must meet certain standards (such as service and quality of accommodations) to retain the franchise.

Although licensing operations account for a small percentage of industry revenues, they are extremely profitable, since related costs are minimal. Licensing fees are an attractive source of income to the hotel chains during inflationary periods; since they are computed as a percentage of revenues, they rise in response to inflationary price increases without being affected by rising costs.

Challenges to the Industry

The world's lodging industry continues to expand as global travel continues to increase. A hotel shortage is evident in many cities, including New York (despite the city's 70,000-room inventory), Beijing, and Hong Kong. New construction is expected to relieve these shortages by the end of the decade.

An immediate challenge faced by the entire tourism industry is the lack of lower-priced hotels. The various components of the world tourism industry grew at different rates and in different rates and in different areas: the airlines arranged their rates so that flying became affordable for more people, but the hotel industry, in an attempt to accommodate the larger numbers of travelers, built hotels that often proved too expensive for this new group of tourists.

Future Outlook

By the early 1990s, the hotel industry in the U.S. was recovering from the slump of the mid-1980s. Occupancies, rates, and revenue increased. Part of this success is the result of the expansion of many hotel chains into specialized facilities. Hotels began to realize that some people want a lot more room in which to live and to work; they wanted more amenities, and they wanted more components to be included in the room rate. At the same time, however, other travelers were unhappy at paying for hotel services and facilities they never used. As a result, more hotels are targeted to specific markets: luxury, limited-service, all-suite, and so on. Holiday Inn, for example, renamed its no-frills facilities Hampton Inns and its luxurious properties Crowne Plazas. Similar repositioning strategies were attempted by Quality Inn, Howard Johnson's, Ramada, and Marriott hotels.

The long-term outlook for the hospitality industry is excellent. A recovering economy means that leisure and business travel is increasing, resulting in more hotel use. The relative value of the dollar against other foreign currencies has created a boom in overseas visitors to this country in recent years. The increase in leisure travel and hotel occupancy rates can be tied to another industry that is enjoying a renaissance—automobiles. Weekend car trips and minivacations are on the rise, in part because of the increase in two-income households. It is not surprising that hotel executives are sensitive to car-sales statistics; they know that historically the hotel business has enjoyed a very good year following a good year for auto sales.

In recent years, both business travelers and leisure vacationers have become more cost-conscious and appreciate being well-looked-after. A general rule for the decade of the 1990s is that hotels must provide a product of value in order to do well. Segmentation, then, can be viewed as an effort on the part of the hotel industry to reach as wide an audience as possible by offering as diverse a product line as possible. The entry of more women into the workforce made the hospitality industry aware of the unique needs and desires of this important market. Women business travelers started to demand additional amenities in the rooms, lighter meals in the restaurants, and different architectural design features. Today, women account for well over 35 percent of all business travelers. Product segmentation will be the most significant influence on the marketing direction of hotels in the near future. Client satisfaction will continue to be the key word in the hospitality industry and, increasingly, product segmentation will be the way to ensure continued growth.

TRAVEL PROFESSIONALS

Tour Operators

A *tour operator* (or *travel wholesaler*) is a company that creates package tours and markets them directly to the public or through retail travel agents. A *package tour* is a travel product that offers, at a set price, several travel elements that would otherwise be purchased separately by a traveler. A tour package can include, in varying degrees, any or all of the following components: transportation by air, bus, and/or rail; lodging; meals; sight-seeing; entertainment; and car rental.

Package tours are now produced and sold by independent tour wholesalers, a tour unit of an airline, an operator of motor coach tours or a retail travel agent. Three types of wholesalers actually plan and create tour products:

• Wholesalers, who combine air and ground elements into a package and contract out the ground portion;

• Tour operators, who provide ground services for wholesalers, travel agents, and airlines;

• Wholesalers/operators, who not only package and sell tours but operate the ground portions as well.

Although there are a few large wholesalers, wholesale travel is extremely fragmented, with over 2,000 companies currently operating in the United States. Most wholesalers fit into a category of market specialization, such as:

• Special markets—religious, ethnic, sporting groups, and senior citizens. A recent phenomenon is a specialization in serving the cultural and language needs of incoming ethnic groups, such as Germans, South Koreans, and Japanese tourists who are traveling in the United States.

• Mass market—standard tours to popular destinations, incentive market, or travel club tours.

• Destinations—many wholesalers specialize in only one or two destination areas.

• Special interest—some wholesalers cater to customers interested in specialty vacations, such as yachting, rafting, or gourmet tours.

• Incentive travel—an increasingly important part of the travel market. Such wholesalers supply travel packages to corporations to be offered as rewards to productive employees.

It is critical for a wholesaler to stay attuned to popular destinations and to provide services that customers want and need. One characteristic of a tour package is that it requires lengthy planning (up to three years) and has a relatively short selling period. Anticipating future changes in preferred vacation destinations is an important aspect of the wholesale industry.

Different skills are required to reach the various buyers a wholesaler needs to reach. The buyers are travel agents, airlines (who can promote the tours in their advertising and brochures), and consumers. Essential skills include effective use of direct mail, negotiation, advertising, and sales promotion.

There are several advantages for hotels, airlines, motorcoach companies, and restaurants in return for being part of a package tour. Each will benefit from the marketing expertise and selling effort that the tour package operator can offer. A successfully marketed tour can be promoted and sold through the highly organized network of more than 40,000 United States' travel agencies coast-to-coast, as well as by travel agencies throughout the world.

A package tour can be designed and priced to bring business to a destination when it is needed most—during the off-season or during "shoulder" periods. There is generally no cost to the supplier for being included in a package tour, unless the tour packager requires a financial contribution toward advertising and promotion.

Pricing is an important factor in designing a successful package tour. The consumer expects a tour to cost less than the total of all tour elements if they were purchased individually. Each package participant, therefore, must provide the tour operator with the lowest possible rate at which the facility or service still can make a reasonable profit.

After adding each of the net rates together, the tour operator must then mark up the package by an optional percentage that includes retail commissions; the expenses of printing, advertising, selling, and reservations; and a reasonable profit.

The growth of package travel has been spectacular over the past two decades. As more and more consumers discover the savings that these tours provide, and as the industry becomes aware of the expanded sales opportunities, this growth is expected to continue. Wholesalers who provide a consistent, quality product, who fulfill their contractual commitments, and who are financially stable are generally quite successful.

Retail Travel Agencies

A *travel agent* can be defined as one who acts on behalf of, or as a representative for, any segment of the travel industry, providing travel service on behalf of airlines, cruise lines, hotels, tour operators, or car rental agencies. The travel agent sells the services of these companies, and is compensated by a commission each time a sale is made.

The travel agent is often the first person with whom a prospective traveler comes into contact. Travel agents assist their clients by helping them find economical, comfortable, reliable, and enjoyable transportation and accommodations. The average travel agent has traveled widely and is well informed. Travel agents are very important to the travel business because they act as sales agents for the airlines, hotel companies, cruise lines, car rental companies, and tourist attractions.

History

Thomas Cook has been credited with organizing the first group tour. In 1841, he chartered a train to carry 500 people to a convention site. In 1867, Cook introduced the hotel coupon and, by 1880, had expanded into banking. By the end of the century, he had moved into the retail travel business. Today, Thomas Cook's company (after a recent merger with Crimson/Heritage) has more than 330 locations and more than 2,500 employees in the United States alone.

In the same year that Cook chartered his first train, a young man began a simple freight-forwarding business in the United States. In 1841, Henry Wells founded Wells Fargo, which was to become the world's foremost travel and financial conglomerate, the American Express Company. Today, American Express remains the largest travel retailer in the United States.

While some travel agencies have a history dating from 1841, the modern-day agent really emerged with the growth of the airline industry. Previously, the activities of travel agents were limited to organizing group tours that traveled by train or steamship. Traditionally, the railways and shipping companies had no need for a network of sales outlets; tickets were sold at the railroad station and at the shipping company's office.

On the other hand, airlines had their offices at airports, far from downtown areas that were more easily accessible to their customers. Independent travel agents provided the solution to the problem of ticket sales. During the 1950s and 1960s, 75 percent of a travel agency's business came from the sale of airline tickets.

Many entrepreneurs opened travel agencies following World War II. During those years, starting a travel agency required relatively limited capital; the industry was not licensed, and the airlines were eager to help new agents get started in their venture.

The growth of the travel agency industry has been phenomenal. Since 1970, the annual dollar volume increased by an incredible 800 percent. What are some of the reasons for this enormous growth? To begin with, the American public's outlook has changed. They are more educated, sophisticated, affluent, and more interested in the world around them, and thus more able and willing to travel. Since jet travel has made distant locations more accessible, there has been a shift away from the family car toward a much greater use of air travel.

What's more, a new attitude has developed. People place a greater value on vacations. Pleasure travel had become an essential element in people's lives and they are willing to pay for it. Concurrently, the trend in corporate growth and expansion increased the volume of business and convention travel.

In addition, new markets have been created. Senior citizens are living longer and are in better health. They have more free time and money to spend, and are traveling more frequently. Single adults, too, are traveling far more frequently than in the past.

As these socioeconomic changes have occurred, the travel industry has responded in a variety of ways. To serve the growing needs of pleasure and business travelers, the number of conference appointed agencies increased from 6,700 in 1970 to nearly 40,000 today. Travel agents in the United States handle more than $80 billion in travel sales (1990) and it is estimated that they account for more than 75 percent of all U.S. air travel; 95 percent of all cruises booked; 100 percent of all package tours, and 60 percent of the booking volume handled by hotel chains' central reservations systems.

The retail travel business reflects the changes in society. Take, for example, the move to the suburbs: more people who live outside the city and work in industrial parks and offices have caused an increase in the number of suburban agencies. Almost one-half of all travel agencies are located in suburbs. Yet, urban travel retailers have survived. More than half the dollar volume is earned in the city, a ratio that has fluctuated very little over the years.

Business and Pleasure Travel

One of the most dramatic changes in travel retailing in the past decade is the increase in business-related bookings. This occurred for several reasons. First, the travel industry itself is expanding. A host of airlines, hotels, and other suppliers have entered the business. The airline deregulation process has accelerated the advent of new carriers, increasing the complexity of travel options for frequent business travelers. At the same time, industry, in general, has expanded to new locations around the world and throughout the country, and business people have traveled with increasing frequency, domestically and internationally.

These factors have intensified the business traveler's need for objective counseling and advice, for help in making sense out of the bewildering number of options available, and finding the best values. As a result, business-related bookings in agencies have skyrocketed, becoming a majority of all agency sales.

Conversely, the share of agency bookings for personal and pleasure travel has moved down to just under half of total bookings. The types of travel arrangements made by agencies, however, have remained relatively unchanged. Almost 60 percent of revenues are derived from air travel, and the balance from hotels, cruises, car rentals, and other land arrangements.

Travel agents report that almost half of all vacation and pleasure travelers seek a travel agent's advice and guidance on the choice of a destination. It is estimated that half of all business travelers consult with their travel agent on the selection of airlines, hotels, car rentals, and itineraries.

Corporate versus Individual Accounts

Almost all agents handle corporate accounts, but the bigger, more automated agencies handle a higher proportion of these clients. With corporate bookings showing a gradual increase over the years, travel agents are providing an even broader range of services to their corporate customers. This is important business to travel agents, and they must work hard to obtain it. Sometimes it comes through recommendations by existing accounts, but for the most part, agents must actively seek it. They must often make formal face-to-face presentations to prospective clients. Two techniques that are growing in importance are telephone solicitations and direct-mail campaigns.

Although booking individual travel for companies is important, six out of ten agencies book conventions with an average attendance of eighty people. For business meetings, forty-three is a typical size, and incentive trips average forty-nine winners per trip. As this type of travel increases, more and more agencies are working hard to obtain these groups.

The backbone of the business traveler account is the repeat customer. Seventy-eight percent of these bookings come from clients with whom the agent has previously worked. Generally speaking, corporate clients are more likely to know what they want, yet some still look to their travel agent for assistance. Even the most seasoned traveler needs guidance occasionally, and the travel agent is happy to provide it.

The use of a travel agent is advantageous to a business or corporation. The travel agent is able to handle travel arrangements more efficiently, since the agent is more experienced and has a greater knowledge of the travel industry. Using a travel agent can also dramatically reduce administrative employees for a corporation, and thereby save the corporation money.

The most important services travel agents provide to corporate accounts are planning and booking business trips and delivering the travel documents to the client. It is very important that the travel agent maintains an excellent relationship with business clients. To a corporate account, the cost of a trip is as important as the departure times of flights and locations of hotels. In dealing with corporate clients, travel agents must be continually efficient, creative, and, above all, knowledgeable. A side benefit to the agency may be the planning of pleasure trips for the corporate employees and their families, since more than half of all travel agents report doing such business.

For the pleasure traveler and vacationer, the picture is different. Whereas business travelers have a predetermined and definite itinerary, many vacationers have only a general idea of their destination. They may say, "We've pinned it down to somewhere in the Caribbean, or Mexico, or maybe Florida for sometime next year." Actually, only 40 percent of vacation travelers know exactly where they want to go when they contact a travel agent, and that is why agents are able to play a key role in influencing vacation plans. Just over half of these customers seek help in deciding where to go, and over half of all travel agents report that their guidance is being sought more often. Vacationers also tend to ask advice on more than just destinations. Travel retailers are consulted on where to stay, which package tours to take, the selection of carriers, choosing side trips, and picking car rental options. Moreover, agents can suggest alternative arrangements when the client's first choice is unavailable. Agents can also make clients aware of discounts and special values, and so quite naturally, clients call their travel agent for help in choosing carriers, arranging itineraries, and renting cars.

A satisfied customer often becomes a repeat customer, so agents make a strong effort to get that repeat business. Most agents do this by follow-up calls to vacationers on their return.

Even before the vacationer returns home, agents may send gifts to the customer's room, providing emergency telephone numbers, and so on. Many agents keep in touch with their customers between trips to announce new offerings or promote agency services. Needless to say, those who promote their services, rather than wait for someone to drop in or call, are the most successful agents.

Automation

Computers are used for a variety of functions throughout the world, providing instant information, answering the need for greater productivity. Today computers are an integral and essential part of travel agency business.

Nearly all agencies use on-line automated reservation systems (often with interfacing accounting systems). Their use has increased productivity dramatically. These computer systems are designed to make an agency's operation more productive and more efficient. A trained agent using a CRT produces 50 percent more volume than the same agent produces without it. Thus, automation has become an increasingly important tool in the successful operation of any travel agency.

Small versus Large Agencies.   The retail travel industry is also extremely fragmented. Key factors for the successful operation of a small agency are somewhat different than they are for a large, multibranch operation. A small agency will try to obtain the business of local commercial clients and secure the repeat business of annual vacation travelers. The owners will deal with clients on a personal basis, and will themselves book these clients.

Making reservations, writing tickets, recordkeeping, and accounting are very time consuming in the travel agency business. A high premium must be placed on developing administrative procedures to streamline these non-revenue producing activities

The larger agency will have specialized employees in certain areas, such as commercial airline ticketing, the Caribbean, Europe, meetings and conventions, and group tours. A larger agency will try to streamline the administrative function. Currently, most agencies have automated ticket writing and computer hook-up to the various airline reservation systems. Large agencies may integrate into the wholesale business.

Depending on their location, most travel agencies tend to specialize in either personal or commercial accounts. Further specialization can occur between domestic versus international, and individuals versus groups. Marketing strategy is of prime importance. Sales techniques are also critical, and it is important for an agent to know the expected returns of direct selling, referrals, advertising, and direct-mail efforts. Many agencies fail or remain small because they are not aggressive enough or do not apply basic business skills and techniques.

Whether the agency is small or large, however, staff management is an extremely important aspect of financial planning. On the average, 60 percent of all travel agency expenses are salary and benefit costs. Having the right number of qualified employees and keeping them highly motivated is a prime concern of the successful travel agency manager.

CONCLUSION

Tourism is a highly diversified business with over 1 million component companies, ranging from small travel agencies to large airlines and hotel chains. The opportunities for employment in such an industry are enormous. Travel and tourism is the largest business activity in the world. It is also an important part of the lifestyle of most Americans, as well as those in other industrialized countries.

Worldwide tourism is an activity of considerable economic significance. Worldwide domestic and international travel expenditures have reached a level larger than the gross national product of all but three countries. The industry has met the challenges of economic uncertainties, political upheaval, deregulation, and shifts in levels of consumer confidence with a remarkable degree of ingenuity, management flexibility, marketing skill, commitment to service quality, and a sense of responsibility to the traveling public. Tourism continues to be a growth industry, and it appears that the factors that have been responsible for this growth during the past decades will continue to be with us for the duration of this century.

REVIEW QUESTIONS

1. Describe why 1958 was an important year for American aviation.
2. How has deregulation affected air travel in your city?
3. Identify the three key factors that account for the successful operation of an airline company.
4. Why did the "fly-cruise" concept result in a lower age of the average cruise passenger?
5. What are some of the major difficulties that hinder attempts to develop a uniform international hotel classification system?
6. What are some of the incentives offered to travel agents by industry suppliers?
7. What is meant by "hotel occupancy rate?"
8. What is a "wholesaler?"
9. Discuss the future outlook for the motorcoach industry in this country.
10. Why is it advantageous for a business to use the services of a travel agent?

Segmenting the International Travel Market by Activity

Sheauhsing Hsieh

Graduate Research Assistant
Department of Forestry and Natural Resources
Purdue University

Joseph T. O'Leary

Professor
Department of Forestry and Natural Resources
Purdue University

Alastair M. Morrison

Associate Professor
Department of Restaurant, Hotel, and Institutional Management
Purdue University

In June 1986 a five-year agreement was assigned between Canada and the U.S. Travel and Tourism Administration to undertake join travel market research in overseas countries. Three years later, twelve overseas countries have been examined. Through this research, market strategies and activities can be conceptualized for overseas trips and the marketing plans and promotional strategies can also be developed.

Hong Kong, which borders the Chinese province of Guangdong on the southeastern coast of the Chinese mainland, is one of the countries examined. Hong Kong's population is over 5.7 million and comprises about 98 percent ethnic Chinese and 2 percent other ethnic groups.[1] From an economic perspective, rapid economic and trade growth has helped Hong Kong become one of the "Four Asian Dragons" (including Taiwan, South Korea, Singapore, and Hong Kong). People in Hong Kong have a great capacity to spend money on travel. In addition, concern about political stability (Hong Kong will return to Chinese control on July 1, 1997) has caused many people to travel and move to overseas countries. Political and economic factors may cause these people to have more travel opportunities than before. The territory of Hong Kong is only 411 squares miles, and this limited space causes extreme crowding. The population of nearly 6 million in such a small area limits people's activity opportunities. The lack of natural scenery and historic places also restricts opportunity for outdoor experiences. There are numerous man-made entertainment facilities, but opportunities for active pastimes (sports) are limited and expensive.[2]

This article was originally published in *Tourism Management*, (June 1992).

[1]United States Department of State, Bureau of Public Affairs, *Background Note for Hong Kong*, (Washington, D.C.: U.S. Government Printing Office, 1988).

[2]United States Department of State, Bureau of Public Affairs, *Hong Kong Post Report*, Department of State Publication 9165, Foreign Affairs Information Management Center Publishing Services Division. (Washington, D.C.: U.S. Government Printing Office, 1986).

Many people therefore seek recreation and activity opportunities overseas. It is interesting to note that the most popular form of entertainment in Hong Kong is eating. About 1.5 million people eat out daily, the highest per capita rate in the world.[3] The Chinese pay a lot of attention to the art of eating and food. For this reason, famous food operations and restaurants may be a primary motivation for overseas travel. Sociodemographic, geographic, and cultural characteristics may entice different types of travellers. With this potential, it is important to conduct travel market research in Hong Kong.

MARKET SEGMENTATION

Travel and tourism marketing is different from the marketing of manufactured products. Travel is an experience, an intangible product. It is produced and consumed at the same time on site.[4] It is very important for travel and tourism industries to understand that they are marketing an experience. Travelers who have had good experiences will generate more travelers. Any organization, whether public or private, profit or nonprofit, has to understand the make-up of its market in order to provide products and services which meet client needs and wants. Most recreation and tourism businesses service a wide variety of clientele groups.[5] These businesses can be more effective if they target their marketing efforts towards a limited number of well-defined market segments.[6]

Market segmentation is a management strategy based upon assumptions about the behavior of population subgroups. Therefore, this becomes one of the ways to decide the target market.[7] This strategy will adjust a product or service and its price, promotion, and distribution to meet the needs and wants of discrete target segments. Segmentation leads to a more efficient allocation of marketing resources and a more precise setting of market objectives. It can offer significant advan-

tages as a competitive strategy and as a guide to market planning and promotional strategies.

ACTIVITY AS A SEGMENTATION BASE

Many variables have been suggested as useful segmentation bases, including sociodemographic, psychographic, geographic, and product-related items.[8] An important research question relates to which segmentation base is appropriate for travel and tourism activity. Many travel and tourism industries have paid attention to travelers' needs, wants, and preferences by supplying a much greater inventory of facilities, packages, and services.[9] Certain travelers may prefer sight-seeing, visiting landmarks, or visiting historic places, while others may focus on different activities such as swimming, water sports, or sun-bathing. In this case, the different packages of preferred activities participated in can be considered sub-aggregates of the total travel market. The creation of activity packages can provide advantages to both travelers and travel industries. For travelers, activity packages can provide greater convenience in planning, offer more economic travel, and increase the desire for specialized activities and experiences. For travel industries, they can improve profitability by increasing customer volumes in off-peak periods, by enhancing appeal for special target markets, or by attracting new target markets.[10] Travelers pursuing different sets of activities may be significant and distinctive. Many studies identify the socioeconomic-demographic factors associated with recreation/leisure participation.[11] Other researchers have focused on the interaction between the social group and sets of recreation participation.[12] Romsa and McCool, fi-

[3]Ibid.

[4]A. M. Morrison, *Hospitality and Travel Marketing* (Albany, NY: Delmar Publishers, 1989).

[5]E. M. Mahoney, "Marketing Parks and Recreation: The Need for a New Approach," *Visions in Leisure and Business*, Vol. 5, no. 4 (Winter 1987), 53–69.

[6]P. R. Dickson and J. L. Ginter, "Market Segmentation, Product Differentiation, and Marketing Strategy," *Journal of Marketing*, (April 1987), 1–10; and D. J. Stynes, "Marketing Tourism," *Journal of Physical Education and Dance*, vol. 54, no. 4, (1983), 21–23.

[7]Ibid.

[8]Ibid.; Morrison, *Hospitality.*

[9]Morrison, *Hospitality.*

[10]Morrison, *Hospitality.*

[11]S. F. McCool, "Recreation Activity Packages at Water-Based Resources," in Carlton S. Van Doren, George B. Priddle, and John E. Lewis (eds.) *Land and Leisure* (Chicago: Maaroufa Press, 1979); G. H. Romsa and S. Girling, "The Identification of Outdoor Recreation Market Segments on the Basis of Frequency of Participation," *Journal of Leisure Research*, vol. 8, no. 4, (1976), 247–255; G. H. Romsa, "A Method of Deriving Outdoor Recreational Activity Packages," *Journal of Leisure Research*, vol. 5, no. 3 (1973), 34–46.

[12]J. T. O'Leary, D. R. Field, and G. Schreuder, "Social Groups and Water Activity Clusters: An Exploration of Interchange Ability and Substation," in D. R. Field, J. C. Barron, and B. F. Long (eds.), *Water Community Development: Social and Economic Perspectives* 195–215; W. R. Burch Jr. (Ann Arbor, MI: Ann Arbor Sciences, 1974), "Two Concepts for Guiding Recreation Management Decisions," *Journal of Forestry*, vol. 62, no. 10 (1964), 707–712.

nally, have suggested that grouping activities into packages can help managers and planners to market, plan, and manage their target markets.[13]

From a broad view, cultural, social, economic, and political conditions, and geographic restraints may cause Hong Kong travelers to participate in different sets of activities when visiting overseas countries. Moreover, the make-up in the different sets of activities may not be the same as found for a Western population. It is therefore important that planners and managers of host countries have a better knowledge base of the preferred activity packages and characteristics (media habits, socioeconomics, travel types) of Hong Kong travelers in order to target their potential customers and develop efficient market mixes.

OBJECTIVES

The more we understand the traveling public in different sets of activities, the more potential tourists will be generated by efficient market planning and promotional strategies. This study attempts to analyse the Hong Kong pleasure travel market by activity segmentation base. The primary objectives of this study are: to provide a description of the Hong Kong travel market; to segment the Hong Kong travel market using activity segmentation to identify those variables for which there are significant differences between activity sets; and, finally, to provide recommendations for public and private travel/tourism groups interested in the Hong Kong travel market.

LITERATURE REVIEW

Market segmentation has become one of the most valuable concepts in developing promotional strategies to better reach the market.[14] Market segmentation is the process of portioning markets into segments of potential customers with similar characteristics who are likely to exhibit similar purchasing or travel behavior. Mahoney has suggested the process of market segmentation is to group existing and/or potential customer/travelers with similar preferences into groups referred to as market segments; to se-

lect the most promising segments as target markets; and to design market mixes that satisfy the special needs, desires and behavior of the target markets.[15] As a result, marketing programs will be more effective and active.

A number of market segmentation approaches such as product-oriented, sociodemographic, psychographic, and geographical segments have been developed in travel and tourism marketing. Gordon segmented the U.S. travel market based on the type of trips which were chosen: visiting friends and relatives, close-to-home leisure, touring city, resort, outdoor, cruise, and theme parks, special events, etc.[16] A major report on the Hong Kong pleasure travel market used the three segmentation bases—travel philosophy, benefit pursued, and product preference—to segment the travel market.[17] In addition, a number of studies have segmented the travel market by sociodemographic variables.[18] Many of these variables can be subsumed under a new variable such as family lifecycle which is based on age, marital status, and the number and ages of children living at home.[19] Different approaches to travel and tourism market segmentation do help travel/tourism industries to understand their traveling public better, and to target their customers more professionally.

Early work in leisure types was presented by de Grazia.[20] He classified activities into active–passive, participant–spectator, solitary–social, indoor–outdoor, in the home–outside the home and sedentary–on the feet. Burch later identified four types of auxiliary activities such as "family fishing camps," "nature study camps," "family water-skiing camps" and "overnight transient tourist groups" at forested campgrounds in the Pacific Northwest.[21] Bishop used a factor analytic

[13]Romsa, "Deriving Outdoor Packages," and McCool, "Recreation Activity Packages."

[14]Stynes, "Marketing Tourism;" J. L. Crompton, "Selecting Target Markets—A Key to Effective Marketing," *Journal of Park and Recreation Administration*, vol. 1, no. 1 (1983), 7–26.

[15]Mahoney, "Marketing Parks."

[16]D. T. Gordon, "Foreign Pleasure Travel by Americans, *Journal of Travel Research*, vol. 25, no. 3 (1987), 5–7.

[17]United States Department of Commerce, United States Travel and Tourism Administration, *Pleasure Travel Markets to North America: Hong Kong, Singapore, Switzerland* (Toronto: Market Facts of Canada, 1988).

[18]B. Anderson and L. Langmeyer, "The Under-50 and Over-50 Travelers: A Profile of Similarities and Differences," *Journal of Travel Research*, vol. 20, no. 4 (1982), 20–24; J. E. J. Graham and G. Wall, "American Visitors to Canada: A Study in Market Segmentation," *Journal of Travel Research*, vol. 16, no. 3 (1978), 21–24.

[19]D. J. Stynes and E. M. Mahoney, *Michigan Commercial Campground Marketing Study* (East Lansing, MI, Michigan State University, Park and Recreation Resources Department, 1986).

[20]S. de Grazia, *Of Time, Work, and Leisure* (New York: Anchor Books, 1964).

[21]Burch, "Two Concepts."

technique to cluster leisure activities which included indoor and outdoor recreation.[22] Tatham and Dornoff showed that distinct sets of activities are pursued by different groups who have similar patterns of socioeconomic characteristics.[23] Further, Romsa used cluster analysis to identify activity types with associated profile variables such as income, education, age, marital, and socioeconomic status.[24]

Hendee and others suggested a typology of recreation activities based on stated preferences of recreationists rather than on observed recreation activities.[25] Their categories and definitions of activity types are "appreciative–symbolic," "extractive–symbolic," "passive–free play" and sociable–learning." McCool applied this typology to develop activity packages at water-based resource centers since it is based on the similarity in meanings of activities and useful in describing the visitor's definition of the recreation place.[26] He further suggested that the set of activities in which the visiting group engaged at a water-based recreation area might be termed an activity package.

Romsa also suggested that sets of activities are significant in themselves if analyzing them leads a better knowledge of recreational demand for recreation planning.[27] McCool mentioned that grouping activities into packages by their meaning might thus help managers and planners to:

- better understand the kinds of opportunities visitors are seeking, and their consequent behavior;
- develop facilities and visitor contact programs to enhance those opportunities; and
- identify those packages that might conflict with other packages in the use of a recreation site.[28]

Therefore, segmenting the market by means of packages can provide a plethora of insights into planning, management, and marketing strategies for private and public recreation sectors.

However, little of the travel literature applied the concept of activity packages to travel and tourism. Bryant and Morrison segmented Michigan recreation activities and opportunities into four distinct groups—young sports activities, outdoorsman/hunters, winter/water types, and resort types.[29] In earlier international travel and tourism research carried out by the U.S. Travel and Tourism Administration and Tourism Canada, the travel markets of Japan, the U.K., FR Germany, and France have been segmented by products for travelers to North American trips.[30] Product segments were created based on the importance rating of a list of fifty-two activities, features, and amenities that might be found at a vacation destination. Japanese travelers were segmented into six segments—"culture and comfort travelers," "sports and entertainment travelers," "rural beach travelers," "culture and nature travelers," "developed resort travelers," and "amenities travelers." Seven segments were identified in the U.K. They were "developed resort travelers," "beach culture and comfort travelers," "sports and entertainment travelers," "culture adventure travelers," "big city travelers," and "outdoor sports travelers." West Germany travelers were segmented as "sports and entertainment travelers," "developed resort travelers," "big city travelers," "culture and nature travelers," "rural beach travelers," and "outdoor sports travelers." Finally, five segments were distinguished in France—"sports and entertainment travelers," "culture and comfort travelers," "outdoor and subculture travelers," "rural beach travelers," and "developed resort travelers." In the 1988 report, Hong Kong travelers were segmented into three traveller segments by product preferences. They were "high roller travelers," "outdoor sports travelers," and "foreign experience travelers."

The literature reviews thus far has focused on recreation activities on sites such as campgrounds, parks, and recreation sites rather than on long-distance travel. Researchers have also identified the activity packages that are based on frequency of participation or the similarity in meanings of activities, revealing relationships with socioeconomic and demographic variables. However, with regards to international travel

[22]D. W. Bishop, "Stability of the Factor Structure of Leisure Behavior: Analysis of Four Communities," *Journal of Leisure Research*, vol. 2, no. 3 (1970), 160–170.

[23]R. L. Tatham and R. J. Dornoff, "Market Segmentation for Outdoor Recreation," *Journal of Leisure Research*, vol. 3, no. 1 (1971), 5–16.

[24]Romsa, "A Method."

[25]J. C. Hendee, R. R. Gale, and W. R. Catton Jr., "A typology of Outdoor Recreation Activity Preferences," *The Journal of Environmental Education*, vol. 3, no. 1 (1971), 28–34.

[26]McCool, "Recreation."

[27]Romsa, "A Method."

[28]McCool, "Recreation."

[29]B. E. Bryant and A. J. Morrison, "Travel Market Segmentation and the Implementation of Market Strategies," *Journal of Travel Research*, vol. 18, no. 3, 2–8.

[30]United States Department of Commerce, United States Travel and Tourism Administration, *Pleasure Travel Markets to North America: Japan, United Kingdom, West Germany, France* (Toronto: Market Facts of Canada, 1987).

markets, activity packages may interact with a greater variety of variables such as language capacity, information sources, travel types, and so on. These all need to be considered. It is hoped that this study can demonstrate the application of activity packages as a segmentation base for Hong Kong pleasure travel markets and provide useful insights for host countries.

METHODS

Data from the Pleasure Travel Markets Survey for Hong Kong was collected during September and October of 1987. Over 1,200 personal, in-home interviews averaging fifty minutes in length were conducted. All respondents were eighteen years of age or older and had taken an overseas vacation in the past three years or intended to take such a trip in the next two years. Finally, over 807 observations were chosen from all respondents who had taken a four-night or longer trip by plane.

The sample was selected by using a random probability cluster sampling procedure. Geographic areas were selected at random in which households at specified skip intervals were approached, and eligible respondents within households were randomly chosen to participate in the personal interview. However, higher-income areas were disproportionately sampled in relation to squatter and multifamily household neighborhoods to increase the chance of reaching qualified respondents.[31]

The survey collected information on:

- Socioeconomic and demographic variables—age, gender, income, education, occupation and lifecycle;
- Travel characteristics—party size, length of stay, and travel type;
- Activities engaged in on the most recent trip;
- Information sources used to plan a trip;
- Travel philosophy, benefit and product preference;
- Places visited on most recent trip.

DATA ANALYSIS

Cluster Analysis

Segmentation methods in tourism may be generally described as being either a priori or as factor clustering.[32] A priori segmentation is a procedure in which the analyst selects at the outset the basis for defining the segments. This basis may be the use of one objective variable the researcher believes is critical for understanding travelers' behavior. Cluster analysis is a useful method of separating objects or respondents into groups so that homogeneity is maximized within the groups and heterogeneity is maximized between the groups. Myers and Tauber found that cluster analysis was an effective segmentation technique.[34] They divided cluster analysis into hierarchical clustering and partition clustering. Hierarchical clustering is more often used for segmentation projects. One of the unique characteristics of cluster analysis is that there is no preassignment of respondents into categories as there is with a priori segmentation. Several articles have been written on the subjects of the leisure pattern and activity package. Tatham and Dornoff identified outdoor recreation market segments.[35] Romsa then indicated that eight activity packages existed in Quebec recreational data and tested them to ascertain whether or not socioeconomic characteristics were associated with them.[36] Ditton and others used cluster analysis to cluster water-based recreation patterns in northeastern Wisconsin.[37] All these studies suggested that cluster analysis is useful to market segmentation based on relatively homogeneous characteristics within the groups and heterogeneous characteristics between the groups.

Variable Indentification

Dependent Variables. The dependent variables were the activity participation during the trips. Respondents were asked to indicate whether they had participated in each of thirty-six activities during their trips in the past three years (Table 1). These activities included traditional, sight-seeing, outdoor recreation, consumptive recreation, entertainment, and water-based and safety-based activities. The participation rates by percentages on each of the clusters are presented in Table 2.

[31]Tourism Canada, *Pleasure Travel Markets to North America: Hong Kong, Toronto* (Toronto: Market Facts of Canada, 1988).

[32]S. Smith, *Tourism Analysis* (New York: Wiley, 1989).
[33]Ibid.
[34]J. J. Myers and E. Tauber, *Market Structure Analysis* (Chicago, IL: American Marketing Association, 1977), 68–90.
[35]Tatham and Dornoff, "Market Segmentation."
[36]Romsa, "A Method."
[37]R. B. Ditton, T. L. Goodale, and P. K. Johnsen, "A Cluster Analysis of Activity, Frequency, and Environment Variables to Identify Water-Based Recreation Types," *Journal of Leisure Research*, vol. 7, no. 4 (1975), 282–295.

TABLE 1   Variables Utilized

SOCIOECONOMIC AND TRAVEL CHARACTERISTICS	ACTIVITY
1 Age	13 Taking pictures/films
2 Income	14 Visit places of historic significance
3 Education	15 Restaurants/dining out
4 Gender	16 Sampling local foods
5 Marital status	17 Shopping
6 Occupation	18 Visit scenic landmarks
7 Life cycle	19 Sightseeing/cities
8 Information sources	20 Visit commemorative places
9 Frequency of language	21 Tour countryside
10 Party size	22 Visit national parks/forests
11 Length of trip	23 Observing wildlife
12 Travel type	24 Contacting local inhabitants
	25 Visit amusement/theme parks
	26 Guided excursions
	27 Visit entertainment places
	28 Visit archaeological places
	29 Visit galleries/museums
	30 Attending festivals/events
	31 Attending concerts/live theatre
	32 Visit seaside
	33 Visit mountains
	34 Visit military history
	35 Swimming
	36 Visit friends/relatives
	37 Visit wilderness areas
	38 Water sports
	39 Visit casinos/gambling
	40 Sunbathing/beach activities
	41 Attending sporting events
	42 Visit health spas
	43 Climbing/hiking
	44 Horse-riding
	45 Fishing
	46 Hunting
	47 Snow skiing
	48 Golfing/tennis

Clusters were established for the same 807 respondents, but respondents were compared on the basis of thirty-six activity variables. The respondents were cluster-analyzed into five groups. The first group of Hong Kong travelers was labeled "visiting friends and relatives." The second cluster was called "outdoor sports activities." The third cluster was "sight-seeing activities," the fourth was called "full-house activities," and the fifth was labeled "entertainment activities."

Independent Variables.   The independent variables selected to describe the activity types were as follows: travel characteristics such as length of trip, party size, travel type; socioeconomic and demographic characteristics, such as house-hold income per year, age, education, occupation, marital status, and lifecycle; information sources; and language capacity in English.

Statistical Analysis

Once segments were formed, the customers or travelers comprising each segment were examined. A profile which included all independent variables for each activity segment was developed.

TABLE 2   Participation Rates for Clusters by Percentage

ACTIVITY	CLUSTER[a]				
	1	2	3	4	5
Visit places of historic significance	74.6	64.3	96.6	97.1	92.3
Visit commemorative places	44.6	32.2	89.3	100.0	61.3
Visit archaeological places	22.1	13.9	79.2	89.7	34.5
Visit galleries/museums	20.0	22.6	51.7	75.0	38.7
Visit military history	16.7	7.8	53.7	64.7	23.0
Restaurants/dining	81.7	44.3	96.6	98.5	89.4
Sampling local goods	72.5	42.6	97.3	100.0	89.4
Visit seaside	18.3	8.7	16.8	86.8	52.3
Swimming	10.4	11.3	3.4	77.9	48.9
Water sports	9.2	4.3	6.0	57.4	35.3
Sunbathing/beach activity	3.8	5.2	4.7	66.2	27.7
Fishing	5.0	7.8	4.0	20.6	9.4
Hunting	3.8	2.6	1.3	19.1	6.0
Taking pictures/films	81.3	60.9	99.3	98.5	94.0
Shopping	65.8	52.2	87.9	100.0	94.5
Visit scenic landmarks	74.6	47.0	96.0	91.2	84.3
Sightseeing/cities	61.7	17.4	100.0	100.0	80.0
Tour countryside	39.2	11.3	89.9	95.6	60.4
Visit national parks/forests	44.2	13.0	73.8	95.6	58.7
Observing wildlife	41.3	7.8	74.5	88.2	60.9
Contacting local inhabitants	34.2	30.4	71.1	83.8	54.5
Visit amusement/theme parks	28.8	8.7	61.7	92.6	58.7
Guided excursions	25.8	17.4	66.4	67.6	57.9
Visit entertainment places	27.9	14.8	32.2	86.8	70.2
Festivals/special events	20.8	9.6	59.1	76.5	32.3
Concerts/live theatre	10.4	20.0	51.0	94.1	35.7
Visit mountains	16.3	7.0	47.0	64.7	28.5
Visit friends/relatives	31.7	9.6	20.8	27.9	23.4
Visit wilderness areas	10.8	4.3	29.5	55.9	23.8
Visit casinos/gambling	17.9	5.2	6.0	26.5	30.6
Attending sporting events	8.8	3.5	22.8	50.0	12.8
Visit health spas	11.7	11.3	7.4	45.6	17.0
Climbing/hiking	8.3	6.1	12.1	39.7	10.6
Horse-riding	4.6	8.7	7.4	33.8	15.7
Snow skiing	2.1	0.0	5.4	11.8	5.1
Golfing/tennis	2.9	3.5	0.0	7.4	4.3

Note:
[a]Cluster 1: visiting friends/relatives activity set.
Cluster 2: outdoor sports activity set.
Cluster 3: sight-seeing activity set.
Cluster 4: full-house activity set.
Cluster 5: entertainment activity set.

Finally, this study also used chi-squared tests of homogeneity of proportions for categorical variables and one-way analysis of variance (ANOVA) for continuous variables to examine whether difference existed across different activity groups.

RESULTS

Results are presented in four parts: activity participation for the general population; the definition of each activity package; marketing profiles between sociodemographic, travel characteristics, language capacity, information sources, and activity clusters; and summary of the Hong Kong travel market.

Activity Participation for General Population

Taking pictures/films were the most popular activities, followed by visiting places of historic

TABLE 3   Activity Participation Rate

ACTIVITY	FREQUENCY	PERCENT
Taking pictures/films	701	86.9
Visit places of historic significance	680	84.3
Restaurants/dining out	668	82.8
Sampling local foods	646	80.0
Shopping	639	79.2
Visit scenic landmarks	636	78.8
Sight-seeing/cities	573	71.0
Visit commemorative places	489	60.6
Tour countryside	448	55.5
Visit national parks/forests	434	53.8
Observing wildlife	422	52.3
Contacting local inhabitants	408	50.6
Visit amusement/theme parks	372	46.1
Guided excursions	363	45.0
Visit entertainment places	356	44.1
Visit archaeological places	329	40.8
Visit galleries/museums	293	36.3
Attending festivals/special events	277	33.6
Attending concerts/live theatre	272	33.7
Visit seaside	261	32.3
Visit mountains	228	28.3
Visit military history	227	28.1
Swimming	211	26.1
Visit friends/relatives	192	23.8
Visit wilderness areas	169	20.9
Water sports	158	19.6
Visit casinos/gambling	148	18.3
Sunbathing/beach activities	132	16.4
Attending sporting events	123	15.2
Visit health spas	123	15.2
Climbing/hiking	97	12.0
Horse-riding	92	11.4
Fishing	63	7.8
Hunting	41	5.1
Snow-skiing	33	4.1
Golfing/tennis	26	3.2

significance (Table 3). Both dining out and sampling local food attracted over 80 percent of the travelers. Shopping, which was the fifth most popular activity, represented an almost 80 percent participation rate. In general, Hong Kong travelers preferred sight-seeing, visiting historic places, and good food dining to outdoor recreation and sports activities. Horse-riding, fishing, hunting, snow-skiing and golfing/tennis attracted fewer travelers from the Hong Kong travel market.

Description of Activity Set Clusters

For clarity and purposes of identification, each of the five clusters was given a name. Each name rep-

resents the activity packages/sets. They were: Cluster 1—visiting friends/relatives; Cluster 2—outdoor sports; Cluster 3—sight-seeing; Cluster 4—the full-house activity, and Cluster 5—entertainment activity (Table 4).

Visit Friends/Relatives.   (Cluster 1, n = 240, 29.7 percent of the Hong Kong travel market.) Visiting friends/relatives (31.7 percent) was characterized as the major activity in this cluster, and a larger proportion of people were involved than in any other clusters. Visiting places of historic significance (74.6 percent), restaurants/dining (81.7 percent), sampling local food (72.5 percent), taking pictures/films (81.3 percent), and visiting scenic

TABLE 4   Definition of Activity Clusters

CLUSTER/ACTIVITY PACKAGE	FREQUENCY	PERCENT
Visiting friends/relatives (Cluster 1)	240	29.7
Visiting places of historic significance	179	74.6
Restaurant/dining out	196	81.7
Sampling local food	174	72.5
Taking pictures/films	195	81.3
Visit scenic landmarks	179	74.6
Visit friends/relatives	76	31.7
Outdoor sports (Cluster 2)	115	14.3
Visiting places of historic significance	74	64.3
Restaurants/dining out	51	44.3
Taking pictures/films	70	60.9
Shopping	60	52.2
Visit scenic landmarks	54	47.0
Swimming	13	11.3
Sunbathing/beach activity	6	5.2
Fishing	9	7.8
Horse-riding	10	8.7
Golf/tennis	4	3.5
Sight-seeing (Cluster 3)	149	18.5
Visiting places of historic significance	144	96.6
Restaurants/dining out	144	96.6
Sample local foods	145	97.3
Taking pictures/films	148	99.3
Sight-seeing	149	100.0
Visit scenic landmarks	143	96.0
Full-house activity set (Cluster 4)	68	8.4
Visiting places of historic significance	66	97.1
Visit commemorative places	68	100.0
Visit archaeological places	61	89.7
Visit galleries/museums	51	75.0
Visit military history	44	64.7
Restaurants/dining out	67	98.5
Sampling local foods	68	100.0
Visit seaside	59	86.8
Swimming	53	77.9
Water sports	39	57.4
Sun-bathing/beach activity	45	66.2
Fishing	14	20.6
Hunting	13	19.1
Shopping	68	100.0
Sight-seeing/cities	68	100.0
Tour countryside	65	95.6
Visit national parks/forests	65	95.6
Observing wildlife	60	88.2
Contacting local inhabitants	57	83.8
Visit amusement/theme parks	63	92.6
Guided excursions	46	67.6
Visit entertainment places	59	86.8
Festivals/special events	52	76.5
Concerts/live theater	64	94.1

TABLE 4 (Continued)

CLUSTER/ACTIVITY PACKAGE	FREQUENCY	PERCENT
Visit mountains	44	64.7
Visit wilderness areas	38	55.9
Attending sporting events	34	50.0
Visit health spas	31	45.6
Climbing/hiking	27	39.7
Horse-riding	23	33.8
Snow-skiing	8	11.8
Golfing/tennis	5	7.4
Entertainment (Cluster 5)	235	29.1
Visiting places of historic significance	217	92.3
Restaurants/dining out	210	89.4
Sampling local foods	210	89.4
Taking pictures/films	221	94.0
Shopping	222	94.5
Visit casinos/gambling	72	30.6

landmarks (74.6 percent) also presented high participation rates (Tables 2, 4).

Outdoor Sports. (Cluster 2, n = 115, 14.3 percent of the Hong Kong travel market.) People in this cluster liked to participate in outdoor sports such as swimming, sun-bathing/beach activity, fishing, horse-riding and golf/tennis, but also chose visiting historic places, scenic landmarks, dining, shopping, and taking pictures/films (Tables 2, 4).

Sight-Seeing. (Cluster 3, n = 149, 18.5 percent of the Hong Kong market.) Sight-seeing (100 percent), visiting scenic landmarks (96 percent), and taking pictures/films (99.3 percent) represented the major activities in this cluster. Within this group, travelers also participated in visiting historic places, restaurants/dining, and sampling local foods (Tables 2, 4).

The Full-House Activity. (Cluster 4, n = 68, 8.4 percent of the Hong Kong travel market.) Travelers in this cluster participated in most activities during their trips (Tables 2, 4).

Entertainment. (Cluster 5, n = 235, 29.1 percent of the Hong Kong travel market.) Travelers in this cluster liked to visit casinos/gambling (30.6 percent) as well as visiting historic places (92.3 percent), restaurant/dining (89.4 percent), sampling local foods (89.4 percent), taking pictures/films (94 percent), and shopping (94.5 percent) (Tables 2, 4).

Hong Kong Travel Market Profile by Activity Segment

The profile of Hong Kong travel markets is represented by socioeconomic/demographics, travel characteristics, language capacity, and information sources (Table 5).

Market Share. The visiting friends/relatives activity set represented the largest market share (29.7 percent). The entertainment activity set accounting for over 29 percent, ranked second. Over 18 percent made up the sight-seeing activity set followed by the outdoor sports activity set (14.3 percent). The full-house activity set consisted of only 8.4 percent of the Hong Kong market.

Socioeconomic and Demographic Variables. Age composition varied among the different clusters. Young people represented the highest percentage of the Hong Kong market. The full-house activity set attracted more young people (64.8 percent) in the 18–34 age group. The sight-seeing activity set tended to have more people (20.8 percent) over 55 participating. Over 57 percent of the travelers participating in the entertainment activity set were young people. The chi-square test for age groups between activity clusters was significant at 0.05 level (chi-square = 52.92, $P < = 0.00$, DF = 28).

Travelers participating in the outdoor sports activity set tended to have higher percentages

TABLE 5   Socioeconomic and Travel Characteristics of Each Cluster

			CLUSTER[a]			
ITEM	1	2	3	4	5	TOTAL
% of HK market	29.7	14.3	18.5	8.4	29.1	100.0
Party size (number of people)	2.4	2.5	2.6	3.0	2.7	
F = 2.16 P < = 0.0282						
Length of trip (number of nights)	13.2	15.3	12.5	16.5	13.5	
F = 1.20 P < = 0.1970						
Age group (chi-square = 52.92 P < 0.00)			Percentage			
18–24	7.5	14.8	10.1	17.7	19.2	
25–34	38.3	40.0	33.6	47.1	38.3	
35–44	33.8	20.0	21.5	25.0	20.4	
45–54	13.3	11.3	14.1	7.4	12.8	
55–64	5.4	10.4	16.8	2.9	6.8	
65+	1.7	3.5	4.0	0.0	2.6	
Total	100.0	100.0	100.0	100.0	100.0	
Income (household per year, HK$)[b]						
(chi-square = 51.87 P < = 0.194)						
<48,000	5.4	5.0	5.8	5.7	2.4	
48–59,999	4.4	8.3	7.3	3.8	8.3	
60–71,999	9.5	10.0	3.7	6.2	3.6	
72–77,999	5.4	3.3	7.3	8.1	14.3	
78–83,999	6.4	1.7	10.2	4.7	4.8	
84–89,999	7.3	5.0	7.3	7.1	9.5	
90–119,999	11.8	10.0	11.0	10.0	14.3	
120–179,999	16.8	18.3	19.0	21.8	21.4	
180–239,999	10.8	15.0	8.7	11.9	2.4	
240–359,999	7.9	13.3	8.8	9.5	7.1	
360,000 and over	11.1	5.0	5.8	7.1	4.8	
Not stated	3.2	5.0	5.1	4.3	7.1	
Total	100.0	100.0	100.0	100.0	100.0	
Education (chi-square = 44.27 P < = 0.026)						
Some/completed primary school	5.4	3.5	3.4	0.0	3.0	
Some/completed junior college	5.0	7.8	11.4	0.0	3.0	
Some/completed technical/commercial	9.6	10.4	16.1	10.3	7.7	
Some/completed high school	13.3	20.9	18.1	19.1	17.0	
Some/finish university	34.2	30.4	25.5	32.4	35.7	
Post-secondary/polytechnic	17.1	15.7	16.1	20.6	17.0	
University	15.0	10.4	8.1	17.7	16.2	
Postgraduate	0.4	0.9	1.3	0.0	0.4	
Total	100.0	100.0	100.0	100.0	100.0	
Gender (chi-square = 4.54 P < = 0.337)						
Male	47.1	51.3	46.3	35.3	46.8	
Female	52.9	48.7	53.7	64.7	53.2	
Total	100.0	100.0	100.0	100.0	100.0	
Marital status (chi-square = 13.24 P < = 0.655)						
Single	25.4	28.7	28.2	32.4	36.2	
Married	70.4	67.8	68.5	64.7	61.7	
Divorced/separated/widowed	0.0	0.0	0.7	0.0	0.4	
Cohabiting	3.8	3.5	2.7	2.9	1.7	
Other	0.4	0.0	0.0	0.0	0.0	
Total	100.0	100.0	100.0	100.0	100.0	
Life cycle (chi-square = 36.27 P < = 0.052)						
Living alone/under 55	5.0	5.2	3.4	4.4	3.8	
Living alone/55+	1.3	1.7	0.0	0.0	1.3	
Live with 1 adult/55	12.9	9.6	14.8	16.2	14.0	

TABLE 5 (Continued)

ITEM	CLUSTER[a]					TOTAL
	1	2	3	4	5	
Live with one adult/55+	0.8	1.7	5.4	1.5	0.4	
Single with children	9.2	7.8	7.4	5.9	8.5	
Couple with children	50.4	42.6	35.6	41.2	39.2	
Other	20.4	31.3	33.6	30.9	32.8	
Total	100.0	100.0	100.0	100.0	100.0	
Occupation (chi-square = 52.91 P < = 0.011)						
Owner	10.8	3.3	6.6	7.2	11.1	
Manager/executive	9.5	11.7	2.9	7.2	7.4	
Professional/technical	8.5	6.7	16.2	13.9	8.6	
Clerical sales	17.7	28.3	14.7	25.8	19.8	
Skilled worker	9.5	6.7	6.6	8.1	14.8	
Unskilled worker	11.1	11.7	11.0	12.9	8.6	
Student	0.7	5.0	2.2	2.4	0.0	
Retired	4.3	3.3	5.2	3.8	1.2	
Homemaker	28.1	23.3	34.6	18.7	28.4	
Total	100.0	100.0	100.0	100.0	100.0	
Travel type[c]						
Travel alone	24.2	20.9	17.5	11.8	13.6	
Spouse/"significant other"	45.4	36.5	40.9	51.5	47.2	
Child(ren)	12.1	5.2	12.8	8.8	10.6	
Father/mother	2.1	3.5	2.7	1.5	3.4	
Other relatives	4.2	8.7	5.4	1.5	7.2	
Friends	19.6	27.8	25.5	32.4	28.5	
Organized group/club/etc.	0.0	1.7	0.7	2.9	0.4	
Business associates/colleague	3.3	4.4	2.7	1.5	3.8	
Information source[c]						
Travel agent	45.4	51.3	46.3	45.6	51.9	
Brochures/pamphlets	9.6	12.2	14.8	13.2	11.1	
Friends/family	27.9	19.1	30.2	23.5	20.9	
Airline?	8.8	11.3	2.0	7.4	6.8	
Tour operator/company	0.0	0.0	0.0	0.0	0.0	
Newspapers/magazines/article	3.3	0.9	1.3	4.4	1.3	
Book/library	0.0	0.0	0.7	0.0	0.4	
Automobile association	0.0	0.0	0.0	0.0	0.0	
Government tourism office	0.0	0.0	0.7	0.0	0.0	
Embassy/consulate	0.8	0.9	0.0	1.5	0.9	
Clubs/association	0.4	0.0	0.0	1.5	0.0	
Advertisements	1.3	0.0	2.7	2.9	3.8	
Others	0.8	1.7	0.0	0.0	0.0	
None	1.7	2.6	1.3	0.0	3.0	
Facility with language[c]						
English-reading	72.1	61.7	61.7	80.9	80.4	
English-writing	69.6	60.0	61.1	76.5	76.2	
English-speaking	69.6	64.4	54.4	72.1	76.2	

Note:
[a] Cluster 1: visiting friends/relatives activity set.
 Cluster 2: outdoor sports activity set.
 Cluster 3: sight-seeing activity set.
 Cluster 4: full-house activity set.
 Cluster 5: entertainment activity set.
[b] 1US$ = 7.74 HK$
[c] Percentages on multiple responses.

(33.3 percent) in the higher-income brackets over HK$180,000 per year. Almost 30 percent of people in the visiting friends and relatives activity set, as well as 29 percent of travelers in the full-house activity set were also in the high-income brackets (HK$180,000). Household income differences between activity clusters were not significant (chi-square = 51.87, $P <= 0.194$, DF = 44).

Over 70 percent of the full-house activity set and 69 percent of the entertainment activity sets contained respondents with a college education. Only half of the travelers in the sight-seeing activity set had a college education. A test of the relationship between education differences and activity clusters indicated a significant association (chi-square = 44.7, $P < = 0.026$, DF = 28).

Females represented a higher percentage (64.7 percent) in the full-house activity set. Males (51.3 percent) participated at higher levels in the outdoor sports activity set. Visiting friends/relatives, sight-seeing and entertainment activity sets exhibited a similar gender distribution. The chi-square test for gender difference between activity cluster was not significant (chi-square = 4.54, $P < = 0.337$, DF = 8).

Over 70 percent of respondents who were married liked to participated in the visiting friends/relatives activity set. The entertainment activity set attracted more single travelers (36.2 percent). Marital status between activity clusters was not significant (chi-square = 13.24, $P < = 0.665$, DF = 23).

More than half of the respondents in the visitings friends/relatives activity set were families with children. The category "other" represented high percentages in each activity cluster. This may result from a high percentage of intergenerational families in Chinese society. No respondents were found to be living alone or over 55 years old in the sight-seeing and the full-house activity sets. Statistically significant differences between the life-cycle and activity cluster were not found (chi-square = 36.27, $P < = 0.052$, DF = 33). Of travelers in the sight-seeing activity set, 34 percent were homemakers. The outdoor sports activity set (28.3 percent) and full-house activity set (25.8 percent) had more travelers working in clerical sales. The occupation differences between activity clusters was significant (chi-square = 52.90, $P < = 0.011$, DF = 32).

Travel Characteristics. Those who participated in the full-house activity set averaged three people per party. They also took longer trips, averaging 16.5 days (compared to 13.7 days on average). Travelers participating in outdoor sports traveled with an average of 2.5 people and spent 15 days on the trip. The sight-seeing activity set attracted parties averaging two persons. They spent only 12.5 days on a trip. A statistically significant difference between party sizes by activity clusters was found (F = 2.16, $P = 0.028$). Travelers participating in the visiting friends/relatives activity set liked to travel with their spouse, "significant other," or travel alone. Travelers in the full-house activity set tended to travel with friends and a spouse/"significant other."

Information Sources. All of the travelers in the activity clusters relied most on information from travel agents to plan their trips. Friends and families were also important sources for most travelers. Travelers participating in the sight-seeing activity set referred more to information from brochures/pamphlets.

Language Capacity. Most people in the activity clusters felt comfortable in speaking, reading, and writing English. Travelers participating in the full-house and entertainment activity sets showed a greater capacity for use of the English language.

Summary of the Hong Kong Travel Market

Visiting Friends/Relatives Activity Set (29.7 percent). Travelers in this cluster were found to be young, college-educated people. Most of them (70.4 percent) were married and liked to travel with a spouse or "significant other." Over half of them were from the family couples with children group. They travelled over thirteen days and sought travel information from travel agents and friends/relatives (Table 6).

Outdoor Sports Activity Set (14.3 percent). Young, college-educated travelers tended to participate in outdoor sports activity. They traveled more than fifteen days and liked to travel with a spouse and/or "significant other." Most of them were in clerical sales (28.3 percent) or were homemakers (23.3 percent). Finally, over 33 percent of them had household incomes more than HK$180,000 per year (Table 6).

Sight-seeing Activity Set (18.5 percent). More older people liked to participate in the sight-seeing activity set. They took shorter trips, and liked to travel with a spouse/"significant other." Over 34 percent of them were homemakers (Table 6).

Full-House Activity Set (8.4 percent). Travelers in this set were younger, colleged-educated and had higher incomes. Over 25 percent of them were clerical sales. About 65 percent of travelers in this cluster were female. They took longer trips—over sixteen days—and traveled with an average of three people per party, and were very proficient in the English language (Table 6).

Entertainment Activity Set (29.1 percent). Young, highly educated people liked to engage in entertainment activities during their trips. Over 28 percent of them were homemakers. Most of them obtained travel information from travel agents and took over thirteen day trips with two or more people in their travel parties (Table 6).

CONCLUSIONS AND IMPLICATIONS

The results of this study provide a profile of Hong Kong travelers by activity segment which is one of the product-oriented segments. Socioeconomic characteristics, travel patterns, information sources, and language capacity of travelers can be effectively used in designing market strategies for Hong Kong travel markets.

Travelers seem to like engaging in a set of activities rather than one particular pursuit. Cluster analysis is one method of reducing and clarifying the number of activities for the purpose of assigning Hong Kong travelers to different activity sets. The results yielded clusters of activities which could be described by several predictor variables such as sociodemographic, travel pattern, information sources, and language capacities. Five activity sets were produced: visiting friends/relatives, outdoor sports, sight-seeing, the full-house activity set, and the entertainment activity set.

There is no doubt that, given the diversity of characteristics, preference and travel patterns, it is more effective to segment and target the travelers' market than to use a shotgun approach. The results suggest that visiting friends/relatives and participation in entertainment were major activity sets engaged in by Hong Kong travelers. Travelers who participated in the full-house activity set are also worth attention because they traveled for more days than members of any other segment and had high income levels, al-

though their market share was small. Variables such as party size, age, education, and occupation were tested for significant differences between activity sets.

Most Hong Kong travelers were young, had a high education level, and had good English language proficiency. They relied most on information from travel agents and friends/families and liked to travel with a spouse or "significant other." Generally, young people tended to participate in the full-house activity set and older people chose sight-seeing activities. The full-house activity set attracted more female travelers.

Activity packages were also found to have distinct socioeconomic and travel characteristics indicating unique submarkets of demand. Travel agents and tourist offices of host countries need to pay attention to this uniqueness in designing efficient marketing and planning strategies.

Implications

The Activity Packages. Most travelers do not have the time, experience, or resources to engage in a combination of favorite activities during their trips. Travel organizations representing both public and private groups of host countries might consider providing a menu of activity packages for their target markets in order to satisfy needs. For example, host countries could place more emphasis on new or improved product development with the design of activity packages such as entertainment or full-house activity packages for younger people, a sight-seeing activity set for older people, and traditional activities like shopping, taking pictures, and dining for most potential travelers. In addition, host countries also need to emphasize their unique travel characteristics within activity packages. Thailand might focus on the outdoor sport activity set and water-based activities; China, on the other hand, could emphasize sight-seeing and visiting historic places.

Activity Packages and Programming. Packaging and programming are interrelated. Packaging is the combination of related and complementary services into a single-price offering. Programming is a technique developing special activities, events, or programs to increase customer spending, or to give added appeal to a package or other hospitality/travel service.[38] Many packages include some programming. Thus, host countries

---

[38]Morrison, *Hospitality.*

TABLE 6   Summary of Activity Clusters

ACTIVITY CLUSTER	SOCIODEMOGRAPHIC	TRAVEL CHARACTERISTICS

Visiting friends and relatives	Age: 38.3% from 25–34
	Income: 29.8% make more
	  than HK$ 180 000 pa
	College educated
	Female: 52.9%
	Married: 70.4%
	Couple with children: 50.4%
	Homemakers
		Length of stay over 13 days
		Travel parties of 2 or more
		Travel with spouse/significant other
		Information sources from travel agents
		  and friends/relatives
		Good English

Outdoor sports activity	Age 25–34 (40%) Income: 33.3% make more than HK$ 180 000 pa College educated Male: 51.3% Married: 67.8% Couple with children Clerical/sales/homemakers	Length of stay over 15 days Travel size: 2 or more people Travel with spouse/significant other Good English
Sight-seeing	More people 55 + :20.8% Fewer college education Female: 53.7% Homemakers and professional/ technical	Length of stay no more than 13 days Travel parties with 2 or more Travel with spouse/significant other Information from travel agents Good English
Full-house activity	Age: 25–34 (47.1%) Income: 28.5% make more than HK$ 180 000 pa College education: 70.7% Female: 64.7% Married: 64.7% Clerical sales	Length of stay over 16 days Travel size: 3 people Information sources from travel agents Good English
Entertainment	Age: 25–34 (38.3%) College education Female: 53.2% Homemakers	Length of stay over 13 days Travel parties of 2 or more Information sources from travel agents Good English

could develop special programmes and events to attract travelers. For example, lower prices could be used to create demand at off-peak periods. Retired people are usually less tied to a peak travel period and special packages can be designed for them.

Information Channels.   Most Hong Kong travelers relied on travel agents, families, and friends for receiving important travel information. Cooperation with the carriers and travel trade intermediaries, either in host countries or in Hong Kong, may be helpful to host countries. The establishment and availability of convenient communication channels with local agents from Hong Kong, plenty of brochures/pamphlets, and videos for potential travellers should always be considered. Since travelers also relied on word of mouth chan-

nels, host countries should aim to improve travelers' satisfaction by conducting special training for domestic travel agents, or employees in popular destinations.

Language.   Most Hong Kong travelers felt comfortable speaking, reading, and writing English. After Chinese, English is the major language of Hong Kong. Brochures and pamphlets should be written in English and Chinese. English speaking countries have a promotional advantage. They provide the customer with a feeling of greater comfort and security. However, the value of activity segmentation points out that while the majority in each cluster appears to be able to use English, the analysis still points toward substantive differences between groups.

CHAPTER 3
The Tourism Explosion

PROJECT _____

Integrate the material covered in this chapter with your personal travel experiences and those of your classmates. Each student should talk about a place he or she has visited. Include travel experiences of family members. The mode of transportation should be identified. Mark each spot a student (or family member) has visited on a world map on the classroom wall. Contribute to this group experiment by talking about interesting people you met while traveling or at a destination. Share the impact that travel has had on your personal values and outlook. Tell the group where you'd like to visit next and how you will plan your next trip.

Although contemporary mass tourism is a relatively recent phenomenon, tourism has existed in a variety of forms over a long history. Anthropologists conclude that travel and tourism in some form has been a part of nearly all cultures. People have always traveled over long distances and across international borders.

International travel, however, achieved its current magnitude as a result of the rapid development of transportation technology, which affected all aspects of travel—speed, cost, comfort, and so on. In my family, my grandparents never traveled by air. My parents have boarded a plane only a dozen or so times. I fly several times each year (but did not make my first flight until I was nineteen). My young children now fly regularly (including trips to Europe). These trends, indicating enormous growth in travel, are reflected in the annual reports of the World Tourism Organization (Table 3–1).

Over the past twenty years, tourism has become the world's fastest-growing industry. In 1950, 25 million people crossed an international border. In 1960, nearly 70 million international arrivals were recorded. By 1970, this figure had grown to 160 million. In 1980, international arrivals totaled well over 280 million. By 1992, the figure had climbed to 476 million. This growth was achieved despite periodic recessions, political upheavals, wars, and uncertainties about the price and availability of fuel. Despite these setbacks, international tourism is now the largest single item in the world's foreign trade budget (three times bigger than world expenditures on defense), and, for some countries, the

TABLE 3–1   World Tourism Statistics, 1950–1992

YEARS	INTERNATIONAL TOURIST ARRIVALS (THOUSANDS)	INTERNATIONAL TOURIST RECEIPTS (THOUSANDS)
1950	25,300	2,100
1960	69,300	6,900
1961	75,300	7,300
1962	81,300	8,000
1963	90,000	8,900
1964	104,500	10,100
1965	112,800	11,600
1966	120,000	13,300
1967	130,000	14,500
1968	131,000	15,000
1969	143,100	16,800
1970	160,000	17,900
1971	172,250	20,900
1972	181,900	24,600
1973	190,600	31,000
1974	197,000	33,800
1975	214,300	40,700
1976	220,700	44,400
1977	240,000	55,600
1978	260,000	68,800
1979	274,000	83,300
1980	284,800	102,300
1981	288,800	104,300
1982	286,700	98,600
1983	284,400	98,400
1984	312,400	110,000
1985	326,400	115,000
1986	334,000	138,700
1987	360,000	169,500
1988	392,000	194,200
1989	420,000	211,700
1990	450,800	255,000
1991	448,500	260,000
1992	476,000	279,000

Source: World Tourism Organization.

most important export industry and source of foreign exchange.[1] For other countries, tourism represents a promising area for economic development, and its significance for stimulating investment, earning foreign exchange, and creating employment opportunities is widely recognized.

Between 1975 and 1990, international travel and tourism grew at a steady rate, and this growth in worldwide tourism shows no sign of diminishing. If anything, its most explosive growth lies ahead. Tourism is no longer an activity

---

[1] World Tourism Organization *International Tourism Statistics* series. (Madrid, Spain, 1992).

reserved only for the privileged few. It is now engaged in by millions of people who enjoy new places, seek a change in their environment, and look for meaningful experiences. Indications are that, by the year 2000, over 3 billion people will travel each year, making tourism an even larger industry at the start of the twenty-first century than it is today.

MOTIVATIONS TO TRAVEL

It is no accident that tourism is growing at the same pace as new technologies such as computers, robots, and satellite communications, which are transforming the way that people live, work, and play. These technologies spur the development of tourism in two major ways: they increase leisure time for millions of people, and they greatly speed up communications throughout the tourism industry. Together these advances make travel more possible, appealing, and commonplace occurrences. It was the combination of desire, ability, and mobility that made tourism and travel possible after World War II.

Throughout many industrial countries, the current work week is fewer than forty hours, and it is estimated that, by 2000, the majority of people will have jobs that call for thirty-five or fewer hours a week—a decrease, since 1945, of more than 40 percent in the lengthy of the average work week. Equally important from the standpoint of tourism is the gradual increase of routine annual vacation periods from two to three or even four weeks.

People increasingly live and work in an "information environment" which favors travel, recreation, and personal improvement. In the United States, more than 50 percent of the work force is involved in the information economy; that is, doing jobs and using skills related to the processing and transmission of information. In their homes, these people have increasing access to information that expands their awareness of opportunities for enjoyment and self-improvement at home and abroad. This information-filled environment encourages people to travel, to participate in recreation and entertainment in ways that could only have been a dream two decades ago. Persuasive advertising, the conditions of employment, and the experience of peers all convince people to

Japan National Tourist Organization

become "global citizens." Extensive domestic and foreign travel are considered an essential aspect of personal growth and improvement.

Increased Industrial Activity

Dramatic growth in industrial activity occurred in the decades following World War II. As a result, the disposable income of the average family in the developed world nearly doubled during this forty-year period. One consequence was an expanding middle class able and willing to travel. However, a correlation between per capita gross national product and the frequency of vacation travel is not always clear. Although the United States has the highest per capita income, the proportion of the population traveling on vacation is considerably lower than that of some European countries. Overseas travel was once restricted to those with not only the financial means but also sufficient time to make the journey. Today's trend toward longer vacations combined with a more efficient transport system have made the time factor less inhibiting. An increase in available leisure time, a result of shorter work weeks, and paid vacations permitted the annual family vacation to become a reality for many Americans. In terms of extended vacation time, however, Americans lag far behind European countries; Germans, for example, on average, enjoy six weeks of paid vacation time annually.

Jet Aircraft

The advent of the jetliner drastically reduced travel time to distant countries, had pronounced effects on overseas travel, and made travel by air the most popular means of transportation. In 1958, Pan Am used the first jetliner on its New York–Paris route. The Boeing 707 was followed later that year by the DC-8, introduced by McDonnell Douglas. Jet aircraft had larger load capacities, which, in turn, resulted in lower fares for the individual traveler. Because of improvements in travel facilities of all kinds, the cost of foreign travel, relative to the cost of other goods and services, has been falling steadily. United States airlines carried 49 million passengers on their domestic and international routes in 1958. Twenty years later, in 1978—the seventy-fifty anniversary of powered flight—United States airlines provided transportation for nearly 275 million passengers.

Liberalized International Relations

Intricate formalities, once part of crossing international borders, in some cases disappeared as relations between countries improved. A United Nations conference on international travel and tourism, held in 1963 in Rome, greatly contributed to worldwide efforts to streamline international travel requirements. In Europe, travelers can now journey between most countries without any border-crossing formalities.

Streamlined Tourism Product

Perhaps one of the major factors contributing to the enormous growth of tourism is the degree of professionalism achieved by the industry. Package tours became widely available during the 1960s. They enabled people to buy all the components of a trip—transportation, lodging, sight-seeing, meals, and entertainment—at a single, all-inclusive price. These tours, offering a combination of services that otherwise would be purchased separately by the traveler at a greater cost, soon became one of the most popular ways to travel.

The creation of the "package" tour was one of the most striking developments in the postwar period. The main reason for its success was its price competitiveness. By providing occupancy guarantees, tour operators were able to book large numbers of hotel rooms on favorable terms and to purchase seats in bulk on aircraft at prices below the normal individual rates on schedule airlines. As a result, Mexico, the Caribbean, and East African countries, traditionally the holiday destinations of wealthy international travelers, and even the Far Eastern countries, attracted completely different types of visitors.

Other Factors

Many other factors motivate people to travel. For one, television constantly brings the world into our living rooms. It shows us new destinations and helps create a desire to see different sights and experience other cultures. The popular television series "Love Boat," for instance, glamorized the cruise ship business and the jobs of cruise ship employees.

Credit cards added further stimulus. They enable travelers to visit almost any destination with little or no cash. (Not surprisingly, travelers who pay for their lodging, food, and entertainment with credit cards tend to spend more than those who pay cash).

Tourism is a major source of foreign exchange. Countries such as Switzerland, Italy, and Spain view tourism as their biggest income-producing export item. All major countries have their own ministries of tourism, responsible for the development and promotion of their own tourism industries.

It is known that the propensity to travel increases with education, since education stimulates curiosity and the desire to broaden one's perspective.

International tourism is also heavily dependent on the size of a country and its geographic location. A European vacationer is more likely to cross an international frontier than a North American vacationer, although the latter may travel a longer distance.

Business travel has grown enormously, adding to the growth of tourism. Statistically, it is difficult—often impossible—to separate pleasure travel from business travel, since the economic impact is the same. As a result, domestic and international tourism statistics include a substantial amount of business travel.

The popularity of travel is a direct result of what we regard as the "right to leisure." More than 600 million people worldwide now enjoy a paid vacation. The growth of international leisure travel reflects a relevant attitude on the part of the customer who demonstrates a greater interest in intangible benefits and the quality of life.

CHARACTERISTICS OF WORLDWIDE TRAVEL

The Importance of Short-Haul Travel

Statistics on worldwide tourism arrivals are dominated by a high proportion of interregional and domestic traffic. Most international tourist travel takes place over relatively short distances. More than three-fourths of international travel takes the form of short-haul travel. It is estimated that 80 percent of all travel in Europe is interregional in nature. Holland, for example, receives 85 percent of its visitors from other Western European countries. Over 90 percent of the visitors to Spain are other Europeans. Renewed promotional efforts to attract nearby markets, improvements in the tourism infrastructure in many of the tourist-generating and tourist-destination countries, and the ease of border-crossing between European countries are all factors favoring short-haul travel.

Few Major Generating Countries

It is important to note that an extremely high portion of travel is generated by relatively few countries. Most international travel takes place within and between the developed nations of Europe, Asia, and North America. Two-thirds of all international tourism arrivals are attributed to nationals of only twelve countries. They are, in alphabetical order: Austria, Belgium, Canada, France, Germany, Italy, Japan, the Netherlands, Sweden, Switzerland, United Kingdom, and the United States. More than 50 percent of the world's total international travel expenditures is accounted for by the nationals of just five countries: the U.S., Germany, Britain, France, and Japan.

Until 1967, foreign travel from Japan was limited. With the easing of currency restrictions following the build-up of a strong foreign exchange position, tourism has grown very fast. Japan has shown the highest average increase in number of tourists registered in other countries. The Japanese outbound market reached 10 million travelers by the 1990s. More than 3 million visited the United States, including 1.7 million who visited Hawaii.[2]

---

[2]Data from World Travel and Tourism Council's 2nd Annual Report (Brussels, Belgium, 1992).

Germany has long been the country generating the highest number of international tourist arrivals; 15 percent of the world total is attributed to its residents. Of all international arrivals from the twelve main generating countries, over 22 percent are from Germany. The next highest numbers came from the United States, Japan, and France.

Countries having small geographic areas, high standards of living, liberal vacation policies, and high population density are prime tourist-generating countries. Larger countries generate fewer tourists, even when they have high standards of living. Canada and the United States are prime examples. Citizens of Canada and the United States do not travel less; rather, a lower percentage of their total travel will be to foreign countries. United States citizens, for example, make over 1.3 billion trips away from home each year while remaining within U.S. borders; had they been European, these travelers would have crossed several international borders. Geographic isolation, even if favorable economic conditions are present, acts as a damper on international tourism departures. A prime example is Australia.

The observation that only twelve countries generate nearly 70 percent of all international arrivals raises some long term challenges for the world's tourism infrastructure. For example, what will happen when income rises in the densely populated but relatively poor areas of the world such as India and the People's Republic of China? What will happen to international tourist arrivals when the Commonwealth of Independent States and Eastern European countries develop strong economies and do away with remaining international travel restrictions currently in effect?

Tourism Statistics

Gathering statistics on incoming tourists is difficult. Not all persons arriving in a country are visitors. A large percentage of travelers arriving at international airports are returning residents. Others arrive intending to become permanent residents. Often, travelers arrive at an international airport only to catch the next plane out to their final destination (transfer passengers).

Some countries try to develop statistics through passenger surveys. Passengers arriving in the United States, for example, complete a questionnaire prior to arrival. The completed form is given to an official when going through customs procedures. Other countries, like Mexico, require travelers to fill out a tourist card, which provides valuable information such as the tourist's point of origin, final destination, length of stay, and reasons for travel. While these methods give an overview of arrivals at specific entry points, they are insufficient to give a complete picture of overall tourism arrivals for a particular country. This method is most accurate when there are a limited number of entry points. For example, island destinations like Iceland, Hawaii, Majorca, and the Caribbean Islands can make almost exclusive use of this method and obtain accurate numbers. However, not all countries can gather accurate information based on actual border crossings. Millions of tourists travel by car between countries each year.

Another method of tabulation, therefore, is of total registration at hotels and motels. It provides data on place of origin, length of stay, and total numbers. But, this method is far from foolproof. Not only is it difficult to enforce but it is also virtually impossible to include all types of accommodations (for example campgrounds or private homes) in a survey of this nature. And, special care must be taken to avoid double counting as arrivals those tourists who change their accommodations.

Despite the seemingly insurmountable challenge of compiling international tourist arrival statistics, the World Tourism Organization publishes a report in which it attempts to reflect annual trends. It collects information from over 120 countries and publishes the results each year in a publication entitled *Tourism Compendium*. While these figures aren't always precise, the overview they present each year is important. Most countries have developed a system that is based on the United Nations definition of tourism. In 1937, the United Nations, then known as the League of Nations, proposed the first definition of the term *international tourist:* "Any person visiting a country other than that in which he usually resides, for a period of a least twenty-four hours." Within this definition, tourists include those pursuing special interests that might be scientific, diplomatic, religious, or athletic in nature. Nontourists are persons relocating with the purpose of establishing a residence in the country, student, persons living in one country and working in a bordering country, and transfer passengers.

Current statistics reflect that France is the world's top tourism destination with 55 million arrivals, followed by the United States (42 million arrivals), and Spain (35 million arrivals). The world's major international tourism spenders are the United States ($39 billion), Germany ($31 billion) and Japan ($23 billion).[3]

Tourism Flows

While there are many more countries of destination than countries of origin, international tourism movements are not always easy to interpret. Certain patterns, however, seem to be regular, and enable tourism marketers to predict

Italian Government Travel Office

---

[3]See note 2 above.

growth rates. Most prominent among major tourist flows in the world is the phenomenon of summer mass migration by northern Europeans to the Mediterranean region. The unpredictable summer weather in northern Europe seems to be responsible for this annual exodus by millions of Britons, Dutch, Germans, and Scandinavians.

A similar flow can be identified in North America; however, these numbers are smaller, and the migration primarily takes place in the winter months. In Canada and the United States, a trip south by people from such heavily populated areas as the northeast and the midwest is motivated by the cold, harsh, winter weather. A vacation in Mexico or Florida provides a welcome escape from the elements at home.

The trends in international tourism can shift rapidly depending on economic factors (most notably changes in currency exchanges), political developments (as was the case after the invasion of Kuwait by Iraq), or changes in public taste and fashion (the Caribbean versus Europe or Mexico).

Tourism As an Export Industry

Tourism, in reality, is an invisible export with the unique characteristic that the purchaser of its products have to travel to a (foreign) destination in person to become customers. International tourism is an export industry, where what is actually exported is the country's image. If exported successfully, tourists will be attracted and will spend money on lodging, transportation, meals, admission fees, souvenirs, and the like. For many countries, it is the most important export industry, source of foreign exchange, and employer. As a by-product of tourism, the income of more affluent countries may be redistributed to developing and economically weaker countries. Today, one-fifth of all worldwide tourism expenditures occur in developing countries, and their share of tourist arrivals is approximately 14 percent.

Worldwide Travel Trends

World Tourism Organization statistics indicate that global travel volume reached 450 million annually by the decade of the 1990s.[4] These numbers represent nearly 200 million people, or just under 4 percent of the world population. Some 40 percent of all international travel is connected with holidays and leisure activities. International tourism generates $100 billion in spending at destinations, excluding transportation fares. Measured in current dollars, international tourism receipts represent about 5 percent of world trade. Despite these remarkable figures, the tourist boom has not yet begun, particularly since, in 1990, over 80 percent of the world's population never crossed an international border.

Regional Distribution

The distribution of domestic tourism is highest in developed areas. Europe accounts for over 50 percent of all domestic arrivals, and the Americas, nearly 40 percent. European countries account for about 70 percent of all international travel, or nearly 280 million arrivals in 1990.

---

[4]See note 1 above.

In other areas of the world, international travel volume increased marginally, with the biggest increase recorded from Asia and the Pacific. Receipts from international tourism generally followed the pattern of arrivals. In European countries, 1990 expenditures amounted to $115 billion, which represents about 60 percent of the global total. Another 25 percent of the worldwide receipts was spent in the Americas.

World's Leading Markets and Destinations

The 1992 statistics indicate that the United States is both the top tourism-generating country and a leading destination. U.S. nationals spent $39 billion in other countries in 1992, compared to a monetary outflow of $31 billion from Germany, $23 billion from Japan, and $18 billion from the United Kingdom. In tourism receipts, the top earner was the United States, where citizens from other countries spent $45 billion. Second-place France earned $21 billion from tourism; Spain just under $20 billion; Italy, $19 billion; and the United Kingdom, $12 billion.

The two most frequented destinations are France and the United States, which registered, respectively, 55 and 42 million international arrivals in 1992. Spain is in third place with 35 million visitors, and Italy is fourth with 27 million. Other leaders include Hungary (21 million), Austria (19 million), the United Kingdom (17 million), Canada (15 million), Germany (15 million), and Switzerland (12 million).

As might be expected, the large majority of travel occurs between neighboring countries. The best customers for Italy are Germany, Switzerland, and France, in that order. France produces most arrivals in Spain, followed by the United Kingdom and Germany. In turn, France is most popular with neighboring Germany, Belgium, the United Kingdom, and the Netherlands. In other areas, nationals of Canada, the United States, and Mexico visit each other more than they do other countries of the world; and the Japanese come to the United States (primarily the Pacific Islands, Alaska, and Hawaii) more frequently than to the other leading destinations, which are much further removed from Japan.

INTERNATIONAL TRAVEL TO AND FROM THE UNITED STATES

U.S. International Travel

Just a few years ago, in 1985, the strength of the economy and the gathering strength of the U.S. dollar in foreign exchange markets was a boon to Americans traveling abroad. But those same factors made travel to the United States expensive for most foreign visitors. Statistics in that year reflected a sharp rise in the volume and expenditures of American travelers to foreign countries, and the continuing softness in the number and expenditures of visitors to the United States from other countries.

During the decade of the 1980s, Americans left the United States in record numbers. More than 25 million of them traveled to foreign countries in 1985. Foreign visitors to the United States in that year totaled 22 million. By the mid-1980s, Americans spent $20 billion annually on overseas travel. Travel payments received by the United States from foreign visitors totaled $14 billion in 1985.

Toward the end of the 1980s, this picture began to change dramatically, and by 1989, for the first time in history, the U.S. registered a travel surplus. In 1992, foreign visitors spent $45.5 billion in the U.S., compared with $39 billion spent by Americans traveling outside the country. Since the late 1980s, travel to the U.S. has been growing twice as fast as the travel of U.S. nationals to foreign countries. In just five years (1985 to 1990) this differential growth has pulled the U.S. from an all-time record travel deficit of nearly $10 billion to a $1.5 billion surplus.[5]

By 1990, tourism became the largest U.S. export industry in terms of export receipts. To call attention to the economic significance of travel and tourism and its impact on the U.S. economy, the Travel and Tourism Government Affairs Council published the results of a research study entitled *Tourism Facts.*[6] Highlights of this 1991 report include:

Size of the U.S. travel industry

- The travel industry is the third-largest retail industry in the United States (after automobile dealers and food stores).
- International travel services rank as the largest U.S. export industry.
- Travel receipts make up 6.5 percent of the U.S. GNP.

Travel's economic contributions

- $328 billion was spent on travel and tourism related activities in the United States in 1990.
- Travel and tourism generated $83.7 billion in payroll receipts.
- The travel and tourism activity generated 5.9 million jobs directly (an additional 6.4 million indirectly).
- The tourism activity was responsible for $43.6 billion in total tax receipts ($24.5 billion in federal taxes, $12.6 billion in state taxes, and $6.6 billion in local taxes).

Receipts from tourism

- Americans spent $893 million a day on travel and tourism in 1990.
- Travel receipts grew 9.4 percent in 1990 and have more than doubled over the past ten years.
- Tourism expenditures increased by over 43 percent in just five years, rising from $229 billion in 1985 to $328 billion in 1990.
- Expenditures in the United States by international visitors has increased by over 247 percent in five years, growing from $11.7 billion in 1985 to $40.6 billion in 1990.

Travel industry employment

- Direct employment generated by travel in the United States in 1990 exceeded the population of 80 countries in the world.
- The wage and salary income from tourism was four times that of the nation's steel and auto manufacturing industries combined in 1990.

---

[5]See note 2 above.
[6]*Tourism Facts: Travel and Tourism* (Washington, D.C.: Government Affairs Council, 1991).

- Travel industry employment has grown 43 percent in the last ten years, twice the growth rate for all U.S. industries.

Tourism export revenue (international visitor spending).

- Tourism is the largest U.S. export industry in terms of export receipts.
- International visitors spend $1,046 each while in the United States.
- International visitors spend $77,245 every minute while in the United States.
- International visitors spend $1,287 every second while in the United States.
- In 1990, an estimated 38.8 million international visitors spent $40.6 billion in the United States directly supporting 870,000 jobs.
- International visitors spend more on gifts, souvenirs, and other retail purchases than they do on lodging while in the United States.

Tax receipts from international visitors

- The government collected enough tax revenues from international visitors in 1990 to fund the entire federal tourism effort for 163 years—through the year 2153.
- The federal government receives more money in tax revenue from international visitors in three days then it spends on overseas promotions in one year.
- Federal tax revenues from international visitor spending in the United States has increased by nearly 300 percent over a five-year period, increasing from $812 million in 1985 to $3.1 billion in 1990.
- The federal government receives an average of $80 in federal taxes from each international visitor.

International visitors to the United States.

- As estimated 37 million international visitors traveled to the United States in 1990.
- The number of international visitors to the United States has increased by nearly 53 percent over a five-year period, growing by over 13 million from 25.4 million visitors in 1985 to 38.8 million in 1990.
- Seventy-four international visitors arrive in the United States every minute.
- The number of visitors from Asia has increased from 1.96 million in 1980 to 4.36 million in 1990, an increase of 122 percent over a ten-year period.
- The number of visitors from Western Europe has increased from 3.4 million in 1980 to 6.46 million in 1990, an increase of 90 percent over a ten-year period.

Characteristics of Visitors to and from the United States

A recent survey launched by the United States Tourism and Travel Administration (USTTA) provides a wealth of information, not previously available from any source, on the characteristics of visitors to the United States and of travelers from the United States to overseas destinations.[7] The population sur-

---

[7]In-flight survey of international air travelers profile of visitors traveling to U.S.A. and overseas destinations (Washington, D.C.: United States Travel and Tourism Administration, 1992).

veyed consists of all international air passengers who are traveling on participating airlines and whose trips originate in the United States or include the United States in their itineraries. Below are some significant findings.

- U.S. travel abroad is split roughly between Canada, Mexico, and overseas destinations.

- About 22 percent of U.S. travelers overseas reside in the Far West (principally California, but also Washington, Oregon, Nevada, Idaho, and Alaska). Eastern gateway states (New York and New Jersey) generated 20 percent of travelers. Another 14 percent of travelers were from the South (principally Florida, but also Alabama, Arkansas, Georgia, Kentucky, Louisiana, Mississippi, North Carolina, and Tennessee); and 12 percent were from the Great Lakes region (principally Illinois, Ohio, and Michigan; but also Indiana, Iowa, Minnesota, and Wisconsin).

- U.S. travelers to Mexico were primarily from the Far West (35 percent) or the Frontier West (22 percent). Texans generated the most travel from the Frontier West, which also encompasses Arizona, Kansas, Missouri, New Mexico, and Oklahoma.

- The purpose of trip was vacation or holiday for over half of overseas travelers (62 percent) and the vast majority of travelers to Mexico (70 percent). A significant amount of overseas travel was for business reasons (30 percent) or visiting relatives (21 percent).

- U.S. travelers to either overseas destinations or Mexico most frequently list their occupations as professional/technical (31 and 35 percent, respectively), manager/executive (23 and 17 percent, respectively) or homemaker (13 percent for both).

- Annual family income of overseas travelers to all countries was $58,000.

- Slightly over half of the adult overseas travelers were male (53 percent), averaging slightly less than forty-five years old. Forty-seven percent were female adults, averaging forty-four years old. Travelers to Mexico were also evenly split between sexes (roughly 50 percent each) and were significantly younger, averaging forty years for males and thirty-eight years for females. Children under eighteen represented only about 10 percent of each group.

- The travel party was most frequently a family group for both overseas travelers (46 percent) and travelers to Mexico (55 percent). Nearly one-third of overseas travelers were alone, compared to 15 percent of travelers to Mexico. Party size averaged slightly larger for overseas travelers (4.7 persons) than for travelers to Mexico (3.7 persons).

- The vast majority of both groups had extensive foreign travel experience. The average overseas traveler had made more than seventeen previous air trips to foreign destinations; the average traveler to Mexico, nearly twelve.

- Length of stay averaged nearly forty nights outside the United States for overseas travelers compared to less than ten nights for travelers to Mexico. The vast majority stay in hotels and motels, but one-third of overseas travelers reside in private homes.

- About 60 percent of overseas travelers visited one country; 21 percent, two countries; and 18 percent, three countries or more. Almost all travelers to Mexico (98 percent) were visiting that single destination.

- Planned non–U.S. expenditures (it should be noted that respondents were surveyed at the outset of their trips) averaged $975 per traveler, or $48 per day.

Principal characteristics of foreign travelers to the United States include:

- Forty-five percent of visitors were from Europe (13 percent from the United Kingdom); 26 percent from the Far East (20 percent from Japan); and 14 percent from South America. Other areas were under 10 percent each.

- The primary purpose of trip was vacation and holiday (48 percent). Business brought 31 percent of visitors and conventions another 8 percent, for a total of 39 percent. About 20 percent visited relatives and 11 percent visited friends.

- Visitors were managers or executives (26 percent) or professional/technical (28 percent).
- Annual family income averaged about $46,000.
- About 60 percent of overseas visitors were male adults averaging forty years old. Another 30 percent were female adults averaging thirty-eight years old. Only 10 percent of visitors were children under eighteen.
- About 40 percent of visitors were traveling in a family group. Another 38 percent were alone and 10 percent were with a business party. The average party size was 3.7 persons.
- Seventy-eight percent of visitors had been to the United States before.
- Principal ports of entry were New York (30 percent), Miami (20 percent), Honolulu (12 percent), and Los Angeles (13 percent).
- The average visitor was away from home for thirty nights, spending about twenty-five nights in the United States. Most stayed in a hotel or motel (78 percent); traveled in the U.S. by air (50 percent); rented auto (39 percent) or private auto (38 percent); and visited one state (53 percent).
- For most visitors, the peak months of arrival are July and August, coinciding with summer vacations. However, spring and fall are also popular with Canadians and Western Europeans. And there is a fairly even year round distribution of arrivals from Asia, eastern Europe, and Oceania.
- Median age is highest for Eastern Europeans (49.4) and lowest for those from Asia (31.1). Median age for other visitors ranges through the thirties.
- The top four destinations (first intended address) in the United States are Florida, California, New York, and Hawaii for Asians; California for residents of Oceania; and Florida for those from South and Central America and the Caribbean.
- Although average length of stay is long (19.2 nights), most visitors stay between four and fourteen nights. Those from Eastern Europe and the Middle East stay longest; those from Asia and the Caribbean register the shortest stays.

Recent economic indicators continue to signal a steady economic recovery from the post–Gulf War recession. The remainder of this decade promises to be good for the American tourism industry. Overseas travel to the United States will reach record highs of well over 40 million arrivals annually until the year 2000.

Recent improvements in consumer confidence and buying attitudes among Americans are strong indications that the personal financial situation of the American family will improve rather than worsen in the years ahead.

Boeing Aircraft company predicts that worldwide traffic will grow at an annual rate of about 6 percent. As a result of this growth, the world's fleet of commercial aircraft will nearly double over the next twenty-five years.

Tourism is a multifaceted business that involves millions of people on a local, state, national, and international level. It includes suppliers and sellers in a variety of travel related services, from transportation to accommodations to sight-seeing. Possible areas of employment includes the hotel industry. A typical 300-room hotel employs approximately 300 people in such diverse areas as guest relations, food and beverages, sales, housekeeping, maintenance, and meetings and conventions management.

Most cities, every state, and the U.S. government have agencies that promote tourism. A small town may have a Chamber of Commerce staffed by a few individuals: a large city, like Denver, functions with a large staff, an advertising agency, and a large budget.

The attractions and amusement component of the tourism industry is another fast-growing area. It includes theme parks, scenic sites, museums, fairs, outdoor recreation facilities, and the like. Last year, this industry segment realized a 9 percent employment growth.

The domestic airline industry, despite a temporary setback, is expected to make a strong comeback. With the early turbulent years of deregulation behind us, stable fuel prices, and newly introduced equipment, the airlines are optimistic that, with recently revised fare structures and the emergence of strong mega carriers, the industry will recover.

Cruises have become increasingly popular and are now taken by people who had never done so before. Shorter cruises and more aggressive competition have lowered the cost of a cruise and enhanced its value. This, in turn, has created growth. A dozen or so new ships are expected to join the existing fleet during the next few years.

The number of travel agencies in the United States has doubled in less than ten years, providing new employment for more than 70,000 people.

Numerous related industries also will benefit from this growth. Job opportunities are expected in travel journalism, travel insurance, incentive travel, travel education, advertising, and with related trade associations.

CONCLUSION

In many states, increased spending for tourism continues to outpace the growth of the economy. The U.S. Travel Data Center reports that travel and tourism directly generates more jobs than any other private industry. Travel is the leading source of jobs in thirteen states and among the top three employers in thirty-nine states. One person in eight in the United States is working in travel, transportation, or tourism. Projections for the remainder of the decade indicate continued stability and growth, making tourism a large and expanding industry. To accommodate the enormous volume of future domestic and international vacation and business travelers, more jobs will become available at travel agencies, hotels, airlines, bus companies, attractions, and recreation facilities.

REVIEW QUESTIONS

1. What have been the major factors contributing to the explosive growth of the tourism industry?

2. Explain how currency exchange rates impact on international travel trends.

3. Why is Australia not among the list of twelve top tourist-generating countries?

4. Describe the difficulties in obtaining correct tourism statistics.

5. What is the major difference in north-south tourism flows between Europe and the Western Hemisphere?

6. Explain why tourism is often referred to as a export industry.

7. What are the world's top five tourist destinations?

   What are the world's top five tourism-generating countries?

8. South Americans have the biggest per person expenditures in the United States. How would you explain this?

9. This chapter contained the results of a survey done by USTTA. What is USTTA and what does it do?

10. What were some of the more interesting findings of the USTTA survey? Give examples of how these findings might change USTTA activities in the future.

Tourism:
The World's Peace Industry

Louis J. D'Amore

L. J. D'Amore and Associates Ltd.
Montreal, Quebec

"In short, both the United States and its allies, and the Soviet Union and its allies, have a mutually deep interest in a just and genuine peace and in halting the arms race. . .

So let us not be blind to our differences—but let us also direct attention to our common interests and the means by which those differences can be resolved. . .

For, in the final analysis, our most basic common link is that we all inhabit the same small planet. We all breathe the same air. We all cherish our children's future. And we are all mortal."

John F. Kennedy

The accelerated pace of events in Eastern Europe over the past few years and the spread of glasnost and perestroika throughout Eastern Bloc countries have brought new meaning and significance to Kennedy's prophetic words, spoken more than 25 years ago.

Disarmament has begun. The "Iron Curtain," which for forty years separated East and West Europe, had come tumbling down.

Clearly, we are living at a historic time. A time when events now occurring will give shape and direction to the decade and century ahead. A time when the philosophers of leisure might come again to examine the ageless question of what is the ultimate purpose in life? Why am I here? What is really worthwhile? Not so much within a concept of leisure as time free of work, but within an Aristolian-based philosophy of leisure as the freedom to do what is really worth doing.

This article was originally published in *Recreation Canada*, Canadian Parks/Recreation Association, Gloucester, Ontario, Canada.

Within this more integrated concept of leisure, what one chooses to do with his/her "work life," also becomes a choice and a choice which may well become available to greater numbers of people.

In a real sense, the trend of global events will broaden the choices available to governments, institutions and corporations as well. Reductions in world expenditures for the military, which now exceed U.S. $1 trillion, will open new vistas for constructive and collaborative enterprise which can "choose" for example to address major issues on the global agenda such as environmental determination and Third World development.

"NEL MEZZO CAMIN DI NOSTRO VITA"—AT THE MIDPOINT IN THE PATH OF OUR LIVES . . . DANTE

For the first time in history, we embark on a segment of the human journey with a global perspective—an awareness of the inter-connectedness of all people and all life on earth. We recognize for the first time that there are no "foreign countries" or "foreign people"; rather we are all neighbors living interdependently as members of a "Global Family" in Marshall McCluhan's "Global Village." We recognize as well that the same life support systems of air, land, and water sustain us all.

Historians may well conclude that this vision of planet earth will have as great an impact on the future direction of human thinking as the Copernican Revolution of the 16th century which revealed that the earth was not the center of the universe.

TOWARDS A POSITIVE CONCEPT OF PEACE

The months and years ahead offer several opportunities and challenges. One of these challenges is conceptual in nature—it is to move from the historic notion of peace as the absence of war, to a positive concept of peace.

From space, we view the world as one living organism where the health of the total organism is necessary for the health of each component part, and the health of each component part, in turn, contributes to the health of the total organism. Once we accept the perspective of an organic and interconnected world as described above, we can begin to think in terms of a *positive* concept of peace.

To achieve this, we must first have a vision of what peace in positive terms can be. Once we have created that vision, we have already set the forces in motion to bring about the actualization of that vision. We must be armed with new insights rather than new weapons. Insights which harness the resources of nature and the intelligence of humans for the common good of all. New visions will be required from fields other than politics—from fields such as anthropology, psychology, sociology and geography; from the scientific community with visions for the constructive use of scienπce and technology; from the environmental and ecological sciences with visions of ecological harmony; from the cultural community and the full range of creative art forms for a spirit of celebration in cultural diversity; from the fields of sport, recreation, and education with a view towards self-fulfilment and the pursuit of excellence; and from the business community for a vision of the benefits from in-

ternational trade and the free flow of goods, people and ideas.

Most importantly, we must as individuals and ordinary people work towards and contribute to a positive vision of our common destiny. President Dwight D. Eisenhower said some forty years ago, "I'd like to believe that people in the long run are going to do more to promote peace than are governments. Indeed, I think that people want peace so much that one of these days, governments had better get out of their way and let them have it."

GLOBALLY RESPONSIBLE ENTERPRISE

A parallel challenge at this juncture in world history is a redeployment of the massive human, scientific and capital resources currently engaged in military enterprise, or the economic enterprise of destruction—to constructive economic enterprise; from *national* security based on the principles of "Mutually Assured Destruction"—to *global* security based on the principles of "Mutually Assured Development."

In the words of Buckminster Fuller, a shift from "weaponry to livingry" clearly would provide the resources needed to meet the full range of human needs. It would also provide the resources necessary to gradually bring about a balanced restoration of the world's major ecosystems and the prospect of global security within the context of sustainable development.

The "window of opportunity" in current world events comes as we approach the start of a new century—a new millenium. The decade of the 1990s offers an opportunity for visionary thinking—creative visionary thinking which will in turn determine the manner in which we relate to one another as a global family with our environment, and the constructive manner in which we engage our human, natural, and capital to create a better world for all in the 21st century.

This "window of opportunity" also comes at a time when we are witnessing the globalization and concentration of business enterprise. As corporations grow in scale and scope, the manner in which they define their missions, their philosophical base and policies, their concept of stakeholders, and the manner in which they conduct their operations, all will be increasingly instrumental in shaping the quality of life and quality of the environment in the world of the 21st century.

THE GLOBAL SIGNIFICANCE OF TOURISM

Tourism is now the world's largest industry with revenues (including both domestic and international travel) approaching US $2.5 trillion (an amount two times greater than world military expenditures). Tourism is the world's second largest export industry after oil and represents 25 percent of international trade in service. Domestic and international travel combined account for 10–12 percent of the gross world product. More than 100 million persons are employed by the world tourism industry either directly or indirectly.

Prospects for the continued growth of world tourism appear to be most promising. Societal trends are favourable to the continued growth of demand, and low-cost air travel is becoming increasingly available. As well, the governments of the world are playing a stronger role in encouraging the growth of both domestic and international tourism as a means of job creation, economic diversification, and a source of foreign exchange.

Beyond its economic significance, there is a growing realization of the role of international travel in promoting understanding and trust among people of different cultures. This is not only a pre-condition for additional trade in goods and services, particularly with newly emerging trading partners, but also a foundation on which to build improved relationships among nations towards the goal of world peace and prosperity.

TOURISM—THE WORLD'S PEACE INDUSTRY

As we travel and communicate in ever-increasing numbers, we are discovering that most people, regardless of their political or religious orientation, race, or socio-economic status, want a world in which all are fed, sheltered, productive, and fulfilled.

Tourism, properly designed and developed, has the potential to help bridge the psychological and cultural distances that separate people of diverse races, colors, religions and stages of social and economic development. Through tourism, we can come to an appreciation of the rich human, cultural and ecological diversity that our world mosaic offers; to evolve a mutual trust and respect for one another and the dignity of all life on earth.

The 8,000 international conferences held each year increasingly draw on people of all nations to share their concerns, propose solutions to problems, exchange ideas, and create "opportunity networks." The growth in student exchanges, cultural exchanges, twinning of cities, and international sporting events not only give us an appreciation of our differences, but also show us the commonality of our goals and aspirations as a human family. The collective outcomes of these travel and tourism experiences help humankind to appreciate the full meaning of the "Global Village" and the bonds that people everywhere have with one another.

Approximately 450 million persons travelled to another country in 1988. This number is growing by 5–7 percent each year. Millions more will act as "hosts" to these travelers as part of their daily job and/or as interested residents of the host country. These millions of daily person-to-person encounters are potentially a powerful force for improved relations among the people and nations of the world; relations which emphasize a sharing and appreciation of cultures rather than the lack of trust bred by isolation.

GLOBALLY RESPONSIBLE TRAVEL

Many new forms of what might be called "Globally Responsible Travel" have evolved over the past several years including people to people travel, education and study travel, work camp travel, and special interest travel, to name a few. These types of programs are currently one of the most accelerated growth segments of the travel industry and will continue to be in the 1990s as people become more globally aware and oriented.

Earthwatch is a noteworthy example of an organization whose members use their vacations to assist in research projects around the world. Since its inception in 1971, Earthwatch has mobilized 67 projects in 79 countries providing researchers with 20,000 volunteers and more than $12 million in funds and equipment.

Also noteworthy are work camp vacations which offer a mini version of a "Peace Corps" type experience. Funded by more than 100 U.N.-affiliated organizations, individuals and groups are able to spend their two or three week vacations at one of 800 socially significant projects in 36 countries.

A particularly interesting form of tourism which gradually emerged in the 1980s is "Ecotourism." Ecotourism is a form of culturally and environmentally sensitive travel which fosters an environmental ethic among travelers and also contributes to the conservation and management of natural areas for long term, sustainable economic development.

Ecotourism is increasingly being seen as a model of nonconsumptive economic development, emphasizing the long term protection of biological resources and ecological processes. Costa Rica, for example, welcomes nature enthusiasts with the slogan "Costa Rica—It's Only Natural." With tourism now the number three earner of foreign exchange for Costa Rica, government officials and private industry have been motivated to protect their rain forests.

Journeys International is an excellent example of Ecotourism. Working within the concept of an "extended global family," Journeys invites and facilitates participation in a kinship that extends beyond the temporal bonds of a trip. Through the nonprofit Earth Preservation Fund, the Journeys' staff and travellers have volunteered time and resources in small-scale local projects: forest restoration in Nepal and Costa Rica; wildlife conservation in Africa; monastery restoration in the Himalayas, restoration of Peru's Inca Trail, to name a few.

Ecotourism is particularly advantageous to developing countries. It attracts persons who are tolerant—even interested in experiencing—small scale, locally operated accommodations, built by local people with local materials. Ecotourism emphasizes the employment of local people as managers, interpreters and custodians of protected areas because of their experience and knowledge accumulated and handed down over centuries. Ecotourism also directs economic activity to rural communities thereby spreading the economic benefits into the interior of a country.

TOURISM AS A MODEL OF GLOBALLY RESPONSIBLE ENTERPRISE

The tourism industry, perhaps more than any other, is well positioned to be a 21st century model of globally responsible enterprise.

The tourism industry, combined with our world park systems, can make a contribution to living in harmony with our environment. Tourism makes possible the setting aside and preservation of vast tracts of land as national parks and wilderness areas. More than 3,000 protected areas in 120 countries and covering more than 4 million square miles are now preserved in their natural state Visitors to these areas experience the beauty and majesty of the world's finest natural features and come away with a heightened appreciation of environmental values. In national parks townsites such as Banff and Jasper, we have the opportunity for "Man" to be co-creators with nature, bringing the best of human design in juxtaposition with the best of nature.

Kenya provides an excellent example of how the establishment of parks and the development of a tourism industry have evolved. In that country, tourism is now second only to the export of tea and coffee as an earner of foreign exchange. Since independence, Kenya has enjoyed an internal peace and stability uncommon in the Third World. The Kenyans have astutely avoided military action on their frontiers and have acted as mediators for peace in the region.

Tourism contributes to both the preservation and development of the world's cultural heritage. It provides governments with the rationale for the preservation of historical sites and monuments and the motivation for indigenous groups to preserve unique dimensions of heritage in the form of dance, music and artifacts.

Tourism provides both the audience and the economic engine for museums, the performing and visual arts and the restoration of historical areas. It has also been a major factor in the rebirth of urban centers.

By providing new opportunities and creating new jobs, travel and tourism serve as a catalyst for positive change. Through public/private partnerships and other initiatives, many decaying cities around the world are being transformed from areas of urban blight to places of culture and beauty. Warehouses become boutiques, restaurants and hotels; old hospitals and factories are transformed into museums; communities that formerly were shunned create needed jobs for area workers and infuse additional dollars into their economies.

J. Willard Marriot
First Global Conference
Tourism—A Vital Force for Peace

It also contributes to Third World Development. The tourism industry is a human resource-intensive industry and has the capacity to generate foreign exchange and a high ratio of government revenues as a proportion of total expenditures. As well, it has a capacity for both forward and backward linkages with other sectors of the economy. Properly designed, it can contribute to social and cultural enrichment as well as economic development. For these reasons, it is increasingly attractive as an industry among developing nations. Tourism earned developing countries $55 billion in foreign currency in 1988, second only to oil revenues.

The greatest economic impact of tourism is its ability to create employment in hotels, restaurants, parks, recreation facilities, gift shops and so on. Each job created directly by the tourism industry in turn creates economic spinoff activity which creates a second job.

In the Caribbean, for example, tourism is the major industry of each of the more than 30 states in the region. The tourism industry contributes further to the economy of each state through its linkages to other economic sectors such as fishing, agriculture, and manufacturing. Tourism has, in fact, been the only industry in the Caribbean that has shown steady growth over the past 15 years.

In Egypt, as well, the one Arab country at peace with Israel, tourism now accounts for 30 percent of trade in goods and services and is Egypt's single, most important industry. Tourism is also bringing Egyptians in closer personal contact with their Israeli neighbors thereby helping to secure a long term peaceful relationship. In 1988, 77,000 Israelis visited Egypt as tourists.

Tourism has contributed in some destinations to the preservation and even the rebirth of local customs such as dance, festivals and crafts. In several Third World destinations, tourism allows traditional artists to survive and provides funding for the restoration of historic sites.

FIRST GLOBAL CONFERENCE: TOURISM—A VITAL FORCE FOR PEACE

The first major international conference, totally dedicated to discussing the concept of "Tourism as a Vital Force for Peace" was held in Vancouver, Canada in October 1988. Sponsors were Air Canada, en Route Card, the Financial Post, and the Governments of Canada, British Columbia and Alberta.

The Conference attracted 800 motivated participants from 67 countries and featured 20 keynote addresses from prominent international leaders including videotaped messages from President Reagan and Pope John Paul II. Two hundred other presenters were involved in a stimulating series of concurrent sessions and work shops.

The Conference served to broaden awareness of the potential for tourism, the world's largest industry, to contribute to:

- Greater mutual understanding, trust and good-will among people of the world;
- An improved quality of environment, both built and natural;
- The World Conservation Strategy of "Sustainable Development."

Delegates reached consensus on a broad range of recommendations related to the environment, planning and development of tourism, "Places for Peace," exchange programs, education, and the social cultural and economic aspects of tourism.

The International Institute for Peace through Tourism has been established as a legacy of the Conference. The Institute, located in Montreal, will serve to orchestrate the implementation of key conference recommendations.

PLACES FOR PEACE—AN INVITATION TO THE PARKS AND RECREATION COMMUNITY

A central recommendation of the Vancouver Conference was that the tourism industry join with the Parks and Recreation community, environmental groups and peace groups as catalysts in creating PLACES FOR PEACE throughout the world. From the local community level (Peace Gardens, Peace Memorials, Peace Parks) to the national and international level (International Peace Parks, World Heritage Parks and sites, International Friendship trails), Places For Peace will serve as places of ceremony and celebration and as crossroads for both domestic and international travelers.

Municipal Peace Parks might serve as the site for Visitor Information Centres which might also serve as "Network Centers" facilitating people-to-people contact for those visitors and local residents desiring such an experience.

Some recent noteworthy examples of Places for Peace are the Toronto Peace Gardens in Nathan Phillip's Square; a Peace Park in Tashkent, a USSR sister city of Seattle, built by 200 volunteers from Seattle working with local residents; and the National Peace Garden in Washington D.C. which has recently been announced and is expected to draw more than 2,000 entries in its design competition. The National Peace Garden has already generated interest around the world and has resulted in the building of several peace parks elsewhere in the United States.

Mayor Doré in Montreal has announced intentions to dedicate a Peace Park, and in Vancouver, steps have been taken to dedicate a Peace Park at the site of the Vancouver Conference Peace Tree Planting Ceremony.

CONCLUSION

In the mid 1980s, Buckminster Fuller stated that humankind would be taking its final exam in the remaining years of the Twentieth Century. Events of the past year give some hope that we will pass that final exam.

The decade of the 1990s may well be a transitional decade. A decade in which relations among people in the global village and their governments are based on mutual understanding, trust, respect and love—rather than fear bred from isolation. A decade which is based on international cooperation in adressing major issues, such as a deteriorated environment; as well as the challenges before us, such as space exploration.

The nature of such a transition in confluence with new vistas in science and technology, global communications, and new perspectives on the global interrelatedness of all life on earth, can truly make the 1990s a decade in which we start the BUILDING OF A NEW WORLD as declared by the cover of *Time* Magazine following the weekend of summitry in Malta and the Vatican.

The travel and tourism industry is well positioned to play a lead role in such a global agenda. Through encouraging each traveler, each host, each front-line person in the industry to extend a hand in friendship as an Ambassador for Peace, by advocating and contributing to an improved quality of environment, both built and natural, and by future development which enhances the social values and cultural traditions of host countries, the tourism industry can become a model of globally responsible enterprise.

The concept of Places for Peace provides an appropriate link with the parks and recreation community. Perhaps we can launch a decade of collaboration by joining together in communities across Canada for the design and development of Places for Peace.

CHAPTER 4

Psychology and Motivation for Tourism

PROJECT ———————————————————————————

Look at a recent Sunday newspaper (preferably of a large metropolitan area) and pull out the travel section. (1) What destinations are most frequently advertised? Why? (2) Select five different ads that appeal to distinctly different audiences. Describe the consumer profile that each ad is trying to address. (3) Find one that emphasizes the "pull" factor and another that stresses the "push" factor in its advertising message. (4) Are there any ads you particularly liked? Why? (5) Are there any ads you particularly disliked? Why?

Remember, answer these questions in terms of how well advertisers understand consumer motivation.

When we look at world travel statistics, we learn that the largest number of tourists is generated by countries that have relatively high standards of living. The three most important tourism-generating regions in the world are Europe, North America, and Japan. High standards of living in these areas have created a rapid growth in disposable income, a reduction in hours of work, increased vacation time, and, in many instances, vacations with pay or, in some cases, paid-for vacations.

In the United States, 80 percent of all workers now receive paid vacations. In 1960, there were 87 million vacation weeks available in this country. By 1970, this figure had increased to 130 million. In 1990, the working population in America enjoyed 200 million vacation weeks. This growth reflects, of course, an increase in the size of the labor force. More importantly, it reflects the fact that more workers were granted vacations and that the length of vacation time granted increased tremendously. In 1960, the average vacation time available to a full-time worker was 1.8 weeks. By the end of the 1970s, this had lengthened to 2.6 weeks. People use this free time in different ways. What they decide to do with their vacation time depends on many factors, including money, time available, and past experiences. But *why* they do what they do—their motivation— is the primary interest of the tourism researcher.

The decision to travel is a complex process based on motivations, attitudes, needs and values. A *motive* can best be defined as "the need or desire of an individual to do a particular thing." Once we understand a person's expectations, we can predict his or her behavior in a given situation. A person's expectations are influenced by personal preferences, past travel experiences, and hearsay.

Before we analyze what motivates people to travel, we can make some general correlations between travel behavior and demographic characteristics. Recent studies in both North America and Europe show a strong relationship between age and travel. Nearly two-thirds (64 percent) of the sixteen to twenty-four-year-old age group traveled on vacation during 1990; 40 percent of the fifty-to-sixty-four age groups took a trip; only 25 percent of the sixty-five-and-over age group traveled regularly.

Young people travel for entirely different reasons than other age groups. Relaxation is not a primary reason for the young to travel. Excitement and the opportunity to experience a different environment seem to be the primary motivations. Travel provides an opportunity to be independent, even if only for a short time.

In general, individuals in the fifty-to-sixty age group, just before retirement, are at the peak of their personal income. This group represents the most active travelers. With paid up mortgages and smaller family units, travel participation in this and older age groups is far above the average of the general population. Some older people travel less, at least in part, because they grew up in a time when frequent travel was not a tradition. For some in this age group, such travel is simply not a part of their lifestyle. Mental or physical handicaps can also hinder travel participation. If one of the spouses has died, lack of companionship acts as a further deterrent. However, it is important to point out that today's and tomorrow's retirees will be very different from yesterday's retirees. Today's older persons are lifestyle pioneers with many new and exciting choices not available to previous generations of senior travelers.

Education is regarded as a prime determinant for the likelihood of a person to travel. An individual with more education will be more likely to travel than someone in the same income bracket who is less educated. Travel research shows that people with advanced degrees tend to take vacations more frequently and to travel greater distances that those with less education. Basically, people who are more educated are likely to want to learn about different people and unfamiliar cultures and experience less difficulty with encountering unfamiliar cultures and unexpected situations.

A similar correlation exists regarding income. Simply stated, the higher one's income level, the more likely it is that one will travel. Those people in high-income professions often have a greater desire to get away from routine. Also, a higher income level often correlates with greater amounts of free time.

In addition to age, education, and income levels, there is another important factor that greatly influences an individual's desire to travel. People who live in large urban areas tend to travel more than those living in rural areas. Opportunities for city dwellers to enjoy the outdoors and breathe fresh air are limited. The desire for elbow room is strong. Cities often provide employment that attracts specialized and highly qualified personnel. Hospitals, universities, banks, and corporate headquarters attract professionals whose education and income make them prime candidates for travel. Contact between neighbors is often less intense in cities and living conditions may be crowded and noisy. Easy accessibility to airports and other transportation terminals makes travel easier. The volume of travel generated by a large city results in bargain fares on certain routes (a two-hour flight from New York to Florida may cost only half that of a flight from Rapid City to Sioux Falls, both in South Dakota). For these reasons, city dwellers are more strongly motivated to travel. In rural areas travel is less important since recreational opportunities often abound, and those employed in farming or ranching often have year-round responsibilities.

REASONS FOR TRAVEL

As already noted, tourists travel for a wide variety of reasons. For some, traveling itself can be the most rewarding experience; for others, the activities at the destination are most important. While most people travel for relaxation, a number of other motives can be identified. Tourists like to learn how people in other countries live. They like to see popular or interesting sights such as the Eiffel Tower, Machu Picchu, Mount Rushmore, or the Taj Mahal. Tourists like to attend special events. For many, a trip to Spain or Mexico is not complete without visiting a bullfight. When visiting the western United States, most tourists want to experience a rodeo. Thousands of people from all over the world travel to Munich in the fall to participate in the famous Oktoberfest.

An executive might choose a weekend fishing trip as a means of getting away from daily stress. The college student spending two weeks in Fort Myers simply wants to have a good time. Young people taking a one week cruise out of Miami are lured by romance. Many Americans travel overseas to learn more about the country where their parents or grandparents were born, others visit places to meet family members or old school friends. Thousands of American Christians and Jews make pilgrimages to Israel each year. People travel great distances in search of sunshine and warm weather. Within Europe, millions of Germans, Dutch, Swedes, and Britons travel to the beaches of Italy and Spain during July and August to escape the unpredictable summers in their home countries. Spain alone receives more than 40 million visitors annually.

People in many Western societies are becoming increasingly health conscious. As a result, exercise and active sport vacations have gained popularity. Travel agents now sell fishing vacations to Ireland, bicycle tours through Europe, and whitewater rafting trips to Colorado, Pennsylvania, and Arizona. Ski vacations have become very popular, and many winter sport enthusiasts take an extra vacation each year during the winter season.

Often a destination is chosen because of the relatively low cost in the host country. Until recently, Portugal was an attractive destination, and many

Americans took advantage of low-priced package tours to this country. Sudden changes in currency exchange rates can either stimulate tourism or cause it to decline.

As we examine the motivations which induce people to travel, our list would be incomplete without mentioning that travel is the "in" thing to do. Having has become synonymous with going on vacation. Taking a trip and being able to talk about it with friends and neighbors is important to many, if not most, people. As travel becomes an important part of everyone's life, it is treated in the same way that people treat their houses, cars, or the labels on their clothing. Travel provides an opportunity to be surrounded by glamour, and serves as an escape from daily troubles and normal societal restrictions.

Perhaps the most widely noted classification of tourists is Plog's[1] continuum, which ranges from the *allocentric* to the *psychocentric* tourist. Allocentrics are adventurous people whose travel is an expression of their inquisitiveness and curiosity. They prefer nontouristlike destinations that offer a sense of adventure. Psychocentrics are more inwardly oriented and inhibited. They prefer the familiar in travel destinations and accommodations. Somewhere along this continuum between these two extremes lie the vast majority of tourists.

TYPES OF TRAVELERS

In an effort to develop targeted promotions to important types of travelers, the tourism industry segments its markets into smaller categories of people with

Norwegian National Tourist Office

---

[1]Stanley C. Plog, "Why Destination Areas Rise and Fall in Popularity," *Cornell Hotel and Restaurant Administration Quarterly* (Ithaca, NY), 1973.

certain common characteristics. An example follows. These categories were defined some years ago by the Division of Tourism in New York state and became the foundation for the highly successful "I love NY" campaign.

Outdoor Enthusiasts

The outdoor enthusiasts are usually married with children. In age and income, they represent a cross-section of vacationers, but fewer are college educated. In general, they live in smaller metropolitan and rural areas. They look for a country vacation, beautiful scenery, mountains, lakes, seashores, and parks. They seek peaceful and quiet places, uncrowded and away from big cities. They prefer wilderness and unspoiled beauty over well-developed resorts. The vast majority of outdoor enthusiasts (81 percent) take their vacations during the six warm months. Regarding vacation facilities, they are not preoccupied with quality and have little interest in luxury, extras, or frills. Many take a camping vacation. They show little interest in nightlife or urban sports such as golf, tennis, and skiing. In the United States, the majority take their vacations in the north and west, favoring New England, New York state, and the Rocky Mountain states. This group is the least likely to take city vacations or go overseas.

Young Fun Lovers

The young fun lovers tend to be single and well educated. They tend to live in large metropolitan areas and have a wide range of interests. They like the beaches and the sun but are also interested in outdoor recreation in a country atmosphere.

Quite a few take vacations in hot climates during the winter months. This group is most often identified as "Club Med" customers.

They look for good-quality motels and hotels that are sensibly priced, comfortable, and modern. They show some interest in places where they can meet other singles. They spend less money per trip than other vacationers, but this is because the travel party is smaller rather than as a result of efforts to economize.

Young fun lovers enjoy swimming and other sports, such as sailing, horseback riding, and tennis. They also show above-average interest in spectator sports. To them, a good vacation includes many things to do, good nightlife, dining out, "partying," and going to discoteques. Therefore, a city vacation with cultural activities—theater, museums, or opera—also appeals to them.

When vacationing in the northern United States, they favor New England and New York state. Almost half take their vacations in the "sun" states of Florida, Arizona, California, and Hawaii. They show above-average interest in California and city vacations, as well as in overseas vacations, especially in Europe.

Sun Resorters

The sun resorters are usually married and have young children. They have the highest incomes, but fewer are college educated. They tend to come from large metropolitan areas. They seek resorts on the seashore and look for well-known, exciting, and "in" places. Almost half (40 percent) take vacations during the colder part of the year, traveling to warmer climates when possible. They look for modern, top-quality motels or hotels that offer comfort, luxury, and extras. They prefer resorts with top name entertainers and show some interest in planned activities. They spend more than the average vacationer, but they want to get good value for their money and like to take advantage of vacation packages.

Their preferred activities center around the beach, swimming, and sunbathing. They want to have fun and many things to do. Good nightlife is an important part of their vacation. Their favorite sports are golf and tennis. They show some interest in spectator sports. Almost half of this group vacation in the "sun" states, especially Florida. When going overseas they favor the Caribbean.

Culture-Oriented Vacationers

The culture-oriented vacationers are older and well educated. A high proportion of these travelers are women. They seek destinations with opportunities for cultural and urban activities and sight-seeing. They are least interested in outdoor recreation.

They look for hotels or motels of good quality that are modern and comfortable, but without extras and frills. They show some interest in vacation packages and spend more money per trip than those in the other three categories of pleasure travelers.

The culture-oriented vacationers like to go sight-seeing and are especially interested in historical sites. They enjoy urban cultural activities, including theater, opera, ballet, concerts, museums, and art galleries. They like to dine in fine restaurants and go shopping on their trips. They show moderate interest in the beach, but are the group least inclined to engage in sports or other physical activities. Although almost half of these tourists vacation in "sun" states, they are the least interested in Florida. They favor California and big-city vacations. Among the four travel groups, they are the most likely to travel overseas, especially favoring Europe.

WHY PEOPLE TRAVEL

Recent research into travel motivation has concentrated on the concept of "push and pull." The "push" factors for a vacation emanate exclusively from within the traveler. They are often a reaction to the living or working environment and are related to the social and psychological conditions unique to a particular individual. The vacationer is looking for a change of pace from his or her everyday work and leisure routines. The "pull" factors for a vacation are aroused by the destination itself. Push motives help explain why people develop the desire to go on vacation; pull motives help explain the choice of destination.

Tourism researchers are divided over the answer to the question, "What makes tourists travel?" Some feel the answer lies primarily in the push motives, which include self-fulfillment, break from routine, the need for social interaction, and the opportunity for self-recognition that travel provides. Other researchers conclude that pull factors are at least equally important. They believe that people would not travel if the unique attractions and opportunities offered away from home did not exist. Most writers on this subject agree that the primary motive for taking a pleasure vacation is the desire for personal enrichment of one kind or another. (Of course, personal enrichment may be achieved through ways that are not travel-related. Some people might seek to relieve tension by remodeling the home or expanding a garden.) In general, though, a pleasure vacation is regarded by most people as more or less essential period of refreshment.

In studying motives for pleasure vacations, John Crompton[2] found that almost every respondent described the essence of a vacation as being a break from routine. This term did not necessarily mean doing different things or a change in lifestyle. Indeed, for many respondents, it meant a continuation of doing the same kinds of things but in a different physical or social context. The essence of a break from routine was, in most cases, either going to a different place or changing the dominant social context (from the work milieu, usually to that of the family group) or doing both of these things. In general, persons engaged in their usual daily activities, although these activities were sometimes more concentrated. The respondents' lifestyles did not change. A break from routine often involved emphasizing particularly desired elements of the lifestyle rather than changing the lifestyle to incorporate different activities.

Travelers are motivated by the general ability of the destination to meet their psychological needs and support their values. Tourists' psychological needs are categorized in many ways, but most can be combined to fit the categories developed by Crompton, who suggests that one might imagine vacation centers that predominantly provide for either self-exploration, social interaction, or excitement. Promotion and marketing for tourism also focuses on these needs.

Self-Exploration

Tourists learn about themselves by learning about the world around them. Travel connects them to a world that they would not know and understand strictly on the basis of their work and daily activities. Rather than having the world brought to them through books and television, they are free to explore the unexpected and have immediate experiences "unedited by other minds." Although, in this process, the tourist can show habitual behavior and stereotypical understanding, the basic motivation to explore himself and his relationship to the world remains.

---

[2]John Cromptom, "Why People Go on a Pleasure Vacation," *Annals of Tourism Research*, vol. 6, no. 4.

Social Interaction

In addition, rather than "what" people do with their leisure, "how" they do it may be more relevant to the quality of the experience, and the social context is an important part of the "how." It is important to point to the importance of social interaction in any experience. Sport has been identified as primarily a social and not an athletic activity. Visitors to the wilderness rarely go alone. The high-tech world of the future will increase the importance of social interaction. The more technology we introduce into society, the more people will aggregate, will want to be with other people: movies, concerts, shopping. Shopping malls, for example, are now the third most frequented space in our lives following home and workplace. People want to be with people.

Excitement

One of the common requirements of the experience of the pleasure traveler is that it brings a change from the routine and commonplace, providing something that is strange, unusual, or novel, an experience not commonly present in the daily life of the traveler. For some, this can be achieved in a different but conventional setting. For others, it requires elements of fantasy and the ability to free oneself from the inhibiting mores of home to enjoy a more permissive environment. Those escaping the conventions of the real world may be sold experiences in which they replace reality with a dream world.

Ego Enhancement

Ego enhancement is not a completely separate category from those above, since each of the previously mentioned motivations can contribute to ego enhancement. However, there is an additional factor in ego enhancement that needs to be mentioned. For many travelers, the need for prestige, or "keeping up with the Joneses," influences trip choice. Going to a known and admired destination is important. One wants to be able to have others respond knowingly, with admiration, or even with a touch of jealously when a destination is mentioned. The taste of one group will set the standards that others try to emulate. Changing taste and fashion can destroy tourist destinations or, at least, change their clientele to those with less money. The problem of image faced by many places can be a hindrance to successful tourism development. A traveler gets little secondary gain from friends' responses—even when a holiday has been pleasurable—if he or she has traveled to a place with no positive recognition value.

Perceptions of Tourist Experiences

Various types of tourists settings and experiences meet the motivational needs of travelers. Moreover, some have different meanings to different people. For example, skiing may be a way of having a social interaction, providing excitement and romance, or even making business contacts. The degree to which motivational needs are met may also relate to the depth of involvement of the tourist in his/her experience.

CHOOSING A DESTINATION

Once a desire to go on a pleasure vacation has been established, the concern shifts from push dimensions of motivation to its directive dimensions which serve to guide the tourist toward the selection of a particular type of vacation or destination.

The data suggest that respondents' motives could be described as being either cultural or sociopsychological in nature. Much of the tourist industry's marketing activities are based upon the assumption that tourists are attracted to a destination by the particular cultural opportunities or special attributes that it offers. However, the findings of Crompton's study suggested that, for some respondents, the destination itself was relatively unimportant. Respondents did not go to particular locations to seek cultural insight or artifacts; rather, they went for sociopsychological reasons unrelated to any specific destination. The destination served merely as a medium through which these motives could be satisfied.

In *The Psychology of Leisure Travel*[3] Mayo and Jarvis explore travel motivation and conclude that all leisure travelers are driven by curiosity combined with a utilitarian ethic influencing them to be productive rather than resort to idle pleasures. They, too, point to the need for variety as the underlying common denominator for all forms of leisure travel.

TYPES OF MOTIVATION

McIntosh and Goeldner[4] have grouped travel motivations into four categories:

- *Physical Motivators* include those related to physical rest, sports participation, beach recreation, relaxing entertainment, and other motivations directly connected with health. Additional reasons might be doctor's orders or recommendations and the use of health spas, curative baths, medical examinations, and similar health treatment activities. These motivations all have one feature in common, which is the reduction of tension through physical activities.

- *Interpersonal Motivators* include a desire to meet new people, visit friends or relatives, escape from routine, from family and neighbors, or make new friendships.

- *Status and Prestige Motivators* concern ego needs and personal development. Within this category are trips related to business, conventions, study, and pursuit of hobbies and education. The desire for recognition, attention, appreciation, knowledge, and good reputation can be fulfilled through travel.

Marinus Kosters, a Dutch tourism researcher and scholar, in his book *Focus on Tourism*,[5] explores three major motives that overlap all areas we have discussed and serve to further explain travel behavior.

The Need to Compensate.   Daily responsibilities prevent many of us from doing the things we'd like to do. People in high-pressure careers need time off to reenergize. Some need to get away from the hustle and bustle of urban life, while others need some time in a different place to become refreshed in body and mind. In this situation, the annual holiday serves as an energizer which enables the vacationer to get through another year. A vacation is viewed as a

---

[3]Edward J. Mayo and Lance P. Jarvis, *The Psychology of Leisure Travel* (Boston: CBI Publishing, 1981).

[4]Robert McIntosh and Charles Goeldner, *Tourism, Principles, Practices, Philosophies* (Columbus, OH: Grid Publishing, 1984).

[5]Marinus Kosters, *Focus on Tourism* (The Hague, the Netherlands: VUGA Publishing, 1981).

change from daily pressure at work and/or at home. Being on vacation provides an element of freedom. Travelers engage in new activities such as sports, gambling, sun-bathing, and enjoying the company of others. These activities may be explained as resulting from motives that serve to compensate for limited freedom (few choices) enjoyed in the daily routine.

The Need to Explore. By nature, the human being is a curious creature whose desire to see, experience, and learn new things is never ending. Rising educational levels have broadened people's horizons. As people learn more about countries, cultures, and attractions, a desire develops to travel and explore. Some might travel long distances, while others have learned to appreciate new discoveries closer to home. The desire to participate in new activities, to sample different foods, to mingle with foreigners, and to adjust to new customs, all combine the element of learning; the desire to explore.

The Need for Status Recognition. The decades following World War II witnessed an era of increased prosperity for larger segments of our population. Greater disposable income provides an opportunity for individuals to purchase consumer articles that enhance their social status in the eyes of others. The way we spend our money and use our leisure time becomes a means by which we express our success and well-being. Vacations are an essential part of this consumerism.

TYPES OF TRAVEL

Contemporary studies, particularly those aimed at assessing the effects of tourism, have tended to classify tourists on the extent to which they seek novel experiences and are willing to immerse themselves in different environments and cultures without extensive reliance on the trappings of familiarity. Now that we have (with the aid of learned colleagues) established a variety of motives that help explain why people engage in travel, let's take a closer look at

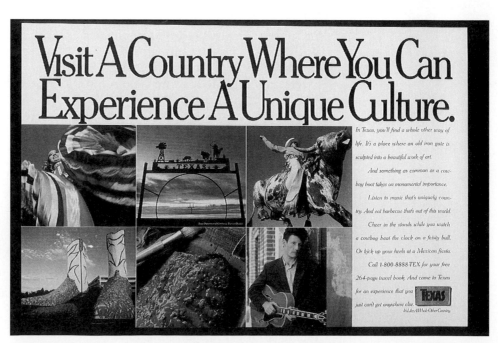

Texas Department of Commerce, Tourism Division

different forms of tourism and draw some conclusions of our own. All travelers are not the same. Some prefer the security of an escorted group tour with a tightly organized itinerary, while others prefer to explore on their own. Choosing the type of vacation depends greatly on an individual's expectations. What follows is an overview of ten different classifications organized by type of tourist orientation.

- *Nature Tourism* attracts the individual who enjoys the outdoors, beautiful scenery, and wildlife. Vacationers in this group will seek the beauty of the national parks, the foliage of New England, or the excitement of an African safari.

- *Cultural Tourism* attracts the individual whose primary interest lies with the history and folklore of the destination. This traveler will visit museums, stay at country inns, and attend wine festivals and cultural events of local significance.

- *Social Tourism* attracts the person for whom contact with people is most important. The primary satisfaction for some might be derived from the companionship with other tour group members, as is often the case on a bus tour. For others, it is the opportunity to mingle with the indigenous population at the destination. Family visits could be included in this category.

- *Active Tourism* attracts the tourist with a challenge to accomplish a predetermined activity on his vacation. A traveler might set out to learn more about his or her ancestry, improve on a foreign language skill, or explore the geology of a certain area.

- *Recreation Tourism* attracts the individual whose primary reason for a trip lies in the enjoyment of participating in activities like camping, organized games, and learning new skills. This type of tourism challenges the participant to be active while on vacation, without giving way to the element of relaxation.

- *Sport Tourism* attracts the serious sport participant. Tennis camps, ski vacations, whitewater excursions, and bicycle marathons are all examples of activities that fit this category.

- *Specialized Tourism* is unique. A small group of people travel together with purpose and interest particular only to them. Car dealers visiting a manufacturer overseas or a school group on a study tour are examples of this type of tourism.

- *Religious Tourism* attracts individuals for whom a destination has spiritual significance. It manifests itself in pilgrimages to sacred religious sites. Mecca and Medina in Saudi Arabia, Lourdes in France, the shrine of Guadeloupe (outside Mexico City), Rome, and Israel are among the world's major pilgrim destinations.

- *Health Tourism* attracts the individual who seeks to improve a physical condition. Weight-loss camps, high-altitude resorts, and European spas come to mind.

- *Ethnic Tourism* is characterized by the tourism that returns to the homeland of his or her ancestors. Often, the serious tourist in search of indigenous cultural traditions among the host country's people is also referred to as an ethnic tourist.

TYPES OF TOURISTS

Another method of grouping different types of tourists is used by Valene Smith, an anthropologist associated with the University of Pennsylvania. In her classification,[6] she is concerned with the different impact (both economic and social) tourists have on the residents of the host country. There are a number of important variables: the extent to which the tourist is interested in immersing himself in the host country's environment; the time spent by tourist in the host country; and the type of host-country resident that the tourist meets (and the purpose of the meeting). In an attempt to measure the impact that tourists have on a destination, its people, and local norms, she identifies seven types of tourists.

Explorer-Type Tourists. These tourists look for discovery and knowledge. Their numbers are limited. They don't consider themselves tourists and would rather be identified as anthropologists, living as active participants-observers among the local people. They easily accommodate themselves to local norms in housing, food, and lifestyles. Explorer-type tourists have very different expectations from other travelers. They are often intent on leaving familiarity behind and experiencing other cultures fully. They seek to achieve a much higher level of contact with the societies of the countries they visit than any of the other types of vacation tourist. The "alternative tourist" often shuns air transport, instead using road or rail on overland tours of Asia or Africa. Visits tend to be of long duration (several weeks), enabling more contact with and (at least as a general rule) more understanding of the host community.

Elite Tourists. These tourists are few in number and usually include individuals who have been "almost everywhere" and who now, for example, choose to spend $1,500 for one week of travel by dugout canoe, with a guide, on the inland rivers of Panama. They differ from explorers because they are tourists; they use facilities that could be prearranged at home by any travel agent. However, they adapt easily, often with the attitude that "if they (the natives) can live that way all their lives, we can, for a week." Their experience of host countries is often deep, but generally it is gained in the role of spectators not willing to adapt permanently to any of the host country's characteristic lifestyles. Their visits will be largely unstructured and of longer duration than those of the mass tourist.

Off-Beat Tourists. These tourists include those who currently visit Nepal or participate on a hunting safari in Zimbabwe. They seek either to (1) get away from the tourist crowds, or (2) heighten the excitement of their vacation by doing something beyond the norm. In general, they adapt well and "put up with" the simple accommodations and services provided for the occasional tourist.

Unusual Tourists. These tourists are those who visit South America on an organized tour and buy an optional one-day package tour to visit the Cuna Indians rather than spend the day shopping in duty-free Panama. This tourist tends to be interested in the "primitive" culture, but is much happier with his "safe" box lunch and bottled soda rather than a native feast.

Incipient Mass Tourism. This category consists of a steady flow of people who usually travel as individuals or in small groups. This group is increasing in size. They seek destinations such as Peru, or, in summer, Alaska, secure in

[6]Valene Smith, *Hosts and Guests.* (Philadelphia: University of Pennsylvania Press, 1977).

their guided tour, heated or air conditioned buses, and modern hotels. They seek Western amenities and assume that the hotel room in the Arctic has a private bath. They pay dearly for this comfort. (This type of tourist might complain about the "ring around the bathtub.")

Mass Tourism.   This type of tourism consists of a continuous influx of visitors, such as those who inundate Hawaii and European resorts most of the year. This type of tourism is built upon middle-class income and values and the impact of high numbers. With a "you get what you pay for" attitude, they fill up hotels of every category, but, as a common denominator, they expect trained, multilingual hotel and tourist staffs to be alert and solicitous to their wants as well as their needs.

Charter Tourism.   This category consists of groups that arrive in mass to resorts like Waikiki, Acapulco, and Palma de Majorca. While the mass tourist expects Western amenities, the charter tourists are characterized by minimal involvement with the people of the country visited to their culture. The emphasis is on the hotel and other facilities which have been developed specifically for this type of tourist. These tourists do not expect to forgo many of the leisure features to which they are accustomed; they want to experience "the novelty of a strange place with the security of a familiar environment." Visits will be structured and generally of short duration, ranging from a long weekend to two weeks.

BARRIERS TO TRAVEL

Most of what we discussed in this chapter concentrated on the active traveler. Experts believe that, even in major tourist-generating countries, over 30 percent of the population does not actively participate in an annual vacation. This group, in any given year, consists of people that never vacation or that vacation less than annually.

Some of the reasons are obvious. Travel is an expensive item in any family budget, and some simply can't consider it a priority. Even when cost is not a factor, many people hesitate to give up their annual vacation trip or fishing outing for an overseas vacation.

For ranchers, farmers, and owners of small businesses, it is often difficult to take time off for a vacation. Although I hesitate to draw the conclusion that people residing in more rural areas are less likely to travel than other groups, it is true that they make less frequent use of the services of travel professionals. Often this segment of our population explores the unique sites and enjoys the recreational opportunities that are close to their homes. The popularity of recreational vehicles, especially in the Midwest, supports this notion.

To many, the thought of overseas travel creates anxiety or fear over what the new experience will bring. They take to heart the old American adage, "There's no place like home."

While tourism is a growth industry, we should not overlook the large segment of our population that has not yet discovered that there are places or things of interest outside their familiar surroundings. All of you, as future tourism professionals, will need to remind these potential customers that "The world is a book. Those who stay home read only one page."

A person has two very strong drives: the need for safety and the desire for exploration. Travel can reduce this conflict. It satisfies the anticipation of the unknown, yet we all know how sweet it is to return home.

In several studies, the reasons why people don't vacation have been explored. They indicate the following:

- *Economic Limitations.* We all have limited budget and have to set priorities. For some, travel is a desire to work toward.
- *Time Limitations.* Many cannot leave their daily routine for any length of time.
- *Health.* While progress is being made in this area, for many, physical limitations prohibit participation in travel. Physical limitations, poor health, and advanced age can be barriers to travel.
- *Family.* Young couples with small children often don't travel because of family priorities and the inconvenience of travel at this stage of their lives.
- *Unawareness.* As discussed before, travel has not been a part of everyone's lifestyle. Unfamiliarity with travel destinations and the activities of traveling in general, reinforced by fear of the unknown, is a major barrier to enjoying the excitement of new experiences.

BUSINESS TRAVEL

Long before the concept of traveling for pleasure became widespread, people traveled on business trips. Business travel includes sales, conventions, corporate meetings, and training, as well as other activities. Today, more than half of all air passengers on domestic routes travel for job-related reasons; business travel represents one-fourth of all travel. Some travel to meet prospective clients, while others travel to attend meetings or conventions. Meetings and conventions in the United States attract over 100 million attendees annually.

Business travel has become a very important market for the accommodation industry, to the point where many deluxe hotels cater exclusively to the specific needs of these travelers. The enormous increase in business travel can be attributed to many different factors. The multinational corporation, a post–World War II phenomenon, has opened world markets. Shoppers all over the world, be it Los Angeles or Amsterdam, can find the same brand names on the shelves of supermarkets. Panasonic television sets are put together in Taiwan, while many brand-name blue jeans, identified with the American West, are manufactured in Hong Kong. Domestically, many companies expand into other states to take advantage of reduced taxes and a cheaper labor force.

Business travel, with the exception of convention travel, is generally unrelated to the perceived qualities of the region or its promotion. Business needs rather than tourist attractions dictate trips. Convention travel, in contrast, is more likely to be influenced by characteristics of an area. Unless size of convention facilities is a limiting factor, the competitiveness of convention sites reflects what the area can offer, and attendance may be related to holiday potential. Indeed, both convention and business travel can bring additional dollars to an area if vacation time is added to business and convention trips. It is believed that one-fourth of business/convention travelers combine their business trips with some pleasure travel, and one in three take other household members with them on these type trips. Numerous meeting and convention facilities are currently being constructed. Almost any city with a population of more than 50,000 people either has a civic center or convention facility, is building one, or has one planned. Meetings and conventions in the United States generated $36 billion annually, and everyone wants of piece of this fast-growing and lucrative market. Business travelers are younger, better-educated, and more affluent than pleasure travelers or the U.S. population as a whole. Their travel patterns also differ from pleasure travel in that parties are smaller, distances traveled are longer, and nights stayed away from home are fewer. Moreover, business travelers are more likely to use the services of travel-related industries than are pleasure travelers.

Regions produce business travel in about the same proportion as their population, but destinations vary in the amount of business travel that they receive. The highest percentage of business travel is to the South Atlantic states.

Traditionally, large cities were hosts for conventions. The purpose and selling point was based strictly on business. Because of the boom in convention business in the 1970s and 1980s, many regions built convention centers to capture this type of travel business. The market is now crowded and very competitive (fully half of the 245 convention bureaus in the United States have been established since 1980), and many cities have experienced annual operating deficits and have been disappointed that predicted benefits have not been forthcoming. A major justification put forward for public expenditures for convention centers is that they extend the season, providing year-round tourism. However, even in very successful convention cities, off-season demand cannot be guaranteed. Winter convention business seems to belong to warm climate locations.

More recently, many smaller cities, where they can incorporate recreational activities into the business routine, have become hosts of conventions. Corporations are beginning to realize that it is less expensive to hold a meeting outside large metropolitan areas, and they are moving their convention sites to suburban areas or smaller towns. A hotel near or in a convention facility in a major city can cost over $200 per night. Smaller cities can provide less-expensive accommodations as well as a wealth of recreational opportunities. In

Missouri Division of Tourism

addition, facilities in smaller cities often have the feasibility of multipurpose options as a means of spreading the operating and capital cost of the facility. Strategies have included incorporating office, trade, or exhibit halls into the centers as well as adding community cultural and recreational facilities (cinemas, libraries, art galleries, and restaurants).

The average business trip takes from one to three days; convention and sales trips take between six and ten days. Most often, people attending conventions will do so in the company of one or two colleagues. Many airlines, if designated the host carrier, will offer reduced fares for all attendees.

Cities throughout the country have accelerated their efforts to attract convention business. The average convention delegate currently generates an average of just under $1,000 in income for the host community. Often, city convention bureaus will justifiably operate with a larger budget and staff than do their state tourism office counterparts.

The volume of business travel seems to be unaffected by economic recession. While attendance at some nonbusiness conventions will be down, a recession appears to encourage business travel as businesses feel the need to stay in close contact during economically lean years.

Frequently, more business transactions can be facilitated in a convention setting than by individual trips. Business travel occurs for many different reasons, but it is about equally divided among the following four: trips to visit clients, trips to attend company meetings, trips to attend noncompany meetings, and trips to another company office.

The outlook for business travel in the United States remains positive, and the volume of the business travel is expected to continue to increase. Employment opportunities should be excellent as a result, since hotels will feel the need to hire convention specialists and coordinators for meetings. Larger corporations often employ full-time meeting planners, who have the responsibility of selecting future sites and coordinating the necessary meeting arrangements.

Travel agencies also have become increasingly involved in meeting the specific needs of the business traveler. Generating a larger percentage of commercial accounts has become important in the overall operation of the average travel agency. Airline companies operate entire departments that devote their service to the promotion and administration of meeting and convention traffic.

CONCLUSION

Tourism in not new. Names like Herodotus, Augustine, Marco Polo, and Columbus remind us that people have always traveled. However, mass tourism is a product of the post–World War II air age which has dramatically shortened world travel distances to hours instead of weeks. Simultaneous advances in industrial technology have provided large segments of our population with longer vacations, earlier retirement, and more surplus income to spend away from home. The brokers of tourism have translated the expanding economy into marketable tour packages and have "psyched" millions of people into believing that "taking a vacation" means going somewhere new, and that to "stay home and do nothing" is unacceptable and/or an admission of low economic status. To "do something," it must be away from home. Within the present framework of tourism, those who do not travel are at a disadvantage. As more nations industrialize, a continuing expansion of tourism is bound to occur. Mass tourism from Japan and extensive touristic mobility in Eastern Europe are indications of growth and geographic expansion.

Tourism is generally conceived as being "play," not work. It is supposed to renew us for the regular "workaday" world. We attach a symbolism to the link between staying (working) and traveling (playing).

In our society, very strong moral feelings are attached to the concepts of work and play, including an idea of what is "proper" in time and place. Serious compulsory activities "properly" take place at home; travel is voluntary, does not involve routine work, and is therefore "good for you." These are now viewed as alternating necessities: living at home and working for longer periods, followed by vacations (playing) away from home for shorter periods.

Tourism is but one of a range of choices for vacation or recreation, which may include renting a house at the shore or visiting relatives. Furthermore, it is not merely a matter of money that separates the stay-at-homes from the travelers. Many very wealthy people never become tourists, while many "youthful" travelers are relatively poor.

In this chapter we looked at the many factors that induce people to become tourists. It is important that tourism professionals are familiar with the motives and characterizations of vacation travelers. It is a combination of product knowledge and understanding our clients' way of thinking that allows us to recommend the type of vacation that will be most beneficial to the tourist-to-be. The tourism industry is a very competitive one. In order for any component of this industry to reach its fullest potential, its leaders must understand what motivates people to travel, how they travel, and the patterns they follow. Knowing these will help in the planning for development of goods and services. Also, knowing what causes these patterns to change allows contingency plans to be established that can be implemented when conditions call for such change. Managers also need to understand the complementary role of attractions and services and the linkages that must be provided for a total and positive tourism experience. Finally, because the world is shrinking into a global community of business and pleasure travelers, local tourism managers and promoters must be appreciative of the special motivations and needs of international visitors.

REVIEW QUESTIONS

1. Explain why people with college degrees tend to be more active travelers.
2. What are some of the likely motives for visiting a destination such as Hawaii? How would these be different from the motives of people traveling to Rome?
3. Identify at least twenty-five reasons why people might travel. (For example, (1) honeymoon, (2) business, (3) pleasure, and so on.
4. What type destination might appeal to an allocentric traveler.
   What type destination might appeal to a psychocentric traveler?
5. Name the ten different classifications by which tourists' orientations can be organized.
6. Name the reason that a person might never become an active traveler.
7. Comment on the appropriateness of including a section on business travel in a chapter on "The Psychology and Motivation for Tourism."
8. Why is it important for a travel professional to understand the different motives people have to travel?
9. How could the market categories developed by New York state have helped the state in its advertising efforts?
10. Why do people who live in urban areas tend to travel more than those living in rural areas?

Segmenting the Business Traveler Market

Pamela A. Weaver

Department of Hotel, Restaurant & Institutional Management
College of Human Resources
Virginia Polytechnic Institute
and State University

Ken W. McCleary

Professor

Department of Hotel, Restaurant & Institutional Management
College of Human Resources
Virginia Polytechnic Institute
and State University

Zhao Jinlin

Department of Hotel, Restaurant & Institutional Management
College of Human Resources
Virginia Polytechnic Institute
and State University

INTRODUCTION

Business travelers are important customers for the hotel industry. Understanding what business travelers want and need is vital for the success of the hotels that target business travelers. However, it is often a difficult task for hotel managers to identify what is important to potential guests (Weaver and McCleary, 1991).

The Study of Business Travelers

Lewis and Nightingale (1991) argued that in order to develop a service strategy, hoteliers need to

This article was originally published in *The Journal of Travel and Tourism Marketing*, vol. 1, no. 4, pp. 53–76, Haworth Press, Inc., Binghampton, NY, 1993.

identify what the customers want and expect, and choose the optimal mix and level of service to attract a target market. A number of studies have been done relative to general business travelers. Niles (1988) reported that 36 million business travelers took 158 million business trips in 1987. He indicated that 73 percent of the business travelers would use hotel facilities while they are on the road. Knutson (1988) identified five important factors that a frequent business traveler uses to originally select a hotel and for repeat visits. The five factors that frequent business travelers were interested in were room conditions (clean and comfortable); location (convenient); service (prompt and courteous); safety; and employees (friendly). Weaver and McCleary (1991) profiled the business traveler, identifying the twenty most important choice criteria for hotels and examining business travelers' usage of hotel amenities and services.

A number of researchers have been interested in hotel frequent guest programs (FGPs). McCleary and Weaver (1991, 1992) studied business travelers in terms of whether they belonged to FGPs. They determined that it would be difficult for a hotel chain to drop FGPs due to industry competition. Toh, Rivers, and Withiam (1991) used eight factors to test frequent business travelers' perception of hotel selection. They found location, overall service, and readiness of rooms were the most important factors. In a related article, Rivers, Toh, and Alaoui (1991) reported that out of the respondents in their sample who were members of frequent guest programs, 93 percent considered themselves to be business travelers. Weaver and Oh (1992) compared perceptions of the importance of hotel services to frequent and infrequent business travelers. They found little difference in service usage by the two groups.

Multivariate Techniques in Hospitality Research

Lewis (1983) argued the importance of utilizing more sophisticated marketing research techniques in the hospitality industry. In his six-part series of articles, "Getting the Most from Marketing Research," which appeared in *The Cornell Hotel & Restaurant Administration Quarterly* (1983–1985), he introduced several multivariate analysis techniques: factor analysis, MANOVA, regression, discriminant analysis, and cluster analysis. He used these techniques to analyze a study of 1,314 patrons of six hotels. By using factor analysis, he extracted seventeen component factors from sixty-six attributes of hotel choice. This technique helped the researcher to reduce the data to obtain a smaller number of variables. By employing discriminant analysis he identified six composite attributes of hotel choice that had power to differentiate among guests in their perceptions of the hotels. He utilized a clustering technique to gather individuals into three groups based on their similarities.

McCleary and Weaver (1992) used multivariate analysis of variance and factor analysis in their study of business travelers and their membership in FGPs. They factor-analyzed hotel selection and usage criteria. With the factor-analysis technique, they extracted thirteen factors from fifty-six hotel selection criteria and six factors of hotel-usage criteria. By using MANOVA, they determined seventeen out of the fifty-six services and amenities listed under hotel selection and six of the twenty-five items listed under usage were significantly different (at the .05 level) between members and nonmembers of frequent guest programs.

Weaver and Oh (1991) utilized MANOVA to identify significant differences between frequent and infrequent business travelers. There were significant differences between the frequent and infrequent business travelers with regards to only a few hotel selection criteria. There were also demographic differences in gender and annual income between the two groups of business travelers at an alpha level of .05.

Other studies in the hospitality industry have also used applications of multivariate analysis to identify market segments. For example, Schaffer (1987) utilized factor and cluster analyses to extract factors from strategic components and cluster strategic groups. Hawes (1988) applied factor and cluster analysis to profile travel-related lifestyles of older women.

The purpose of the study reported here was to segment the business traveler market on the basis of responses to fifty-five hotel selection criteria. These segments are interpreted and profiled according to the selection criteria and various demographic variables.

METHODOLOGY

The present study used the data obtained from the responses of 350 business travelers who participated in a 1991 national survey of business travelers commissioned by *Hotel and Motel Management*. The survey was mailed along with a cover letter and postage-paid return envelope to a random sample of 3,000 subscribers to *Travel Smart* magazine. This mailing list was purchased from a mailing list broker. The usable respondent rate was 11.7 percent. A six-page questionnaire consisted of questions covering individual travel patterns, hotel selection criteria, importance and usage of hotel facilities, demographic data, and other related information.

While the response rate was lower than is desired, it was not unexpected. The use of bulk mailing and a lengthy questionnaire are likely to contribute to a low response rate. For example, Shoemaker (1989), using bulk mail and a six-page questionnaire, received only an 8 percent response rate on a mailing to 5,000 people in a study of the senior pleasure travel market.

The study reported here focused on fifty-five attributes that may be deemed important to business travelers in the selection of hotels. The fifty-five attributes were originally used in a 1990 study of the business travel market (Taninecz, 1990). The questionnaire used in the 1990 study contained fifty-six items relating to hotel selection (one was dropped for the 1991 study due to a low importance rating). This original questionnaire was based on items included in studies by Lewis (1984) and Knutson (1989). The items generated from those two sources were added to and pretested on a group of hospitality faculty and industry professionals. After discussions with this group, some items were added and a few deleted from the questionnaire. Items deleted were viewed by members of the pretest group as being insignificant in site selection. In a further attempt to ensure that no important items were missing, respondents to the 1991 survey were asked to write in any other services or features that were considered important. Response to this request was negligible.

Nonresponse Bias

Funding for this study did not allow for a major check of nonrespondents through follow-up mailings. However, two checks were made to address the issue of nonresponse bias. First, a comparison of the demographics of the last 50 respondents was made with the demographics of the first 300 respondents. Oppenheim (1966) contends that late respondents are similar to nonrespondents when comparing them to the total sample. Using chi-square analysis on the demographic variables, no significant differences were found between late respondents and the rest of sample.

A second check was made by comparing the responses to the 1991 survey with the responses to the 1990 survey. Even though the demographics of the two samples were quite different, the responses to the hotel selection items were similar.

Statistical Analysis

Several statistical techniques were utilized to analyze the data relating to the fifty-five attributes:

1. Factor analysis was utilized to extract factors from the fifty-five attributes of hotel selection.
2. Surrogate variables obtained from the factor analysis were used in cluster analysis (10 percent of the respondents randomly selected) to determine the number of homogeneous groups represented by the data.
3. Quick cluster analysis was then employed on the total of respondents (n = 350).
4. Discriminant analysis was employed to profile the groups obtained in the quick cluster technique according to demographic and other related data.
5. Frequency distributions and cross-tabulations were also used to analyze the results in the study.

The Statistical Package for the Social Sciences (SPSS, Inc., 1990) was used to tabulate the data.

RESULTS

Factor Analysis

Respondents were asked to respond to fifty-five attributes related to hotel selection on a five-point scale (1 = very unimportant, 5 = very important). In order to reduce the fifty-five attributes into a more workable number of composites, the items were factor-analyzed by collapsing related original variables into single correlated component factors. Two-hundred-seventy-two cases were utilized in a Principal Component Factor Analysis with Varimax (orthogonal) rotation. (Only 272 cases were used because respondents with missing data on any of the fifty-five items were eliminated). The factor analysis procedure grouped the fifty-five attributes of hotel selection into fourteen factors as selected by the latent root criteria or Eigenvalue greater than one. The results of the factor analysis are displayed in Figure 1 together with the Eigenvalues, percentage of variance, and cumulative percentage of variance explained by each of fourteen resulting factors. For example, the first factor has an Eigenvalue of 13.128 and explains 23.9 percent of variance. Sixty-seven percent of the variance was explained by the fourteen factors.

Based on the similarities and characteristics of items in each factor, the authors titled the factors as follows:

Factor	1	Business and personal services.
Factor	2	Room/hotel basics.
Factor	3	Special in-room facilities.
Factor	4	Free extras.
Factor	5	Easy check-in/room service.
Factor	6	Frequent travel program/ advertising.
Factor	7	Low rate.

FIGURE 1   Factors and Factor Loadings from Importance of Hotel Selection (N = 272)

FACTORS	FACTOR LOADING
Factor 1 (E = 13.128, % of Var = 23.9, c% = 23.9)*	
Copy machine	**.86589**
Fax machine	**.84612**
Computer	**.81462**
Secretarial service	**.78069**
Audio-visual equipments	**.73883**
Valet service	**.51522**
Laundry service	.46678
Iron and Ironing board	.41601
Fitness and recreational facilities	.35907
Suite rooms	.34164
Factor 2 (E = 4.900, % of Var = 8.9, c% = 32.8)	
Comfortable mattress and pillows	**.82411**
Good quality bath towels and wash towels	**.79919**
Cleanliness of the hotel	**.77955**
Well maintained furnishings	**.75325**
Friendly service of the hotel staff	**.69588**
Safety and security facilities	**.61794**
Good reputation of the hotel	**.61147**
Personal-care amenities in bathroom	.45361
No-surcharge long-distance telephone calls	.38930
Factor 3 (E = 2.594, % of Var = 4.7, c% = 37.5)	
In-room whirlpool tub	**.72564**
In-room VCR	**.71200**
In-room mini bar	**.68937**
Bathrobes	.43579
Game room	.42871
In-room safe	.39723
Factor 4 (E = 2.367, % of Var= 4.3, c% = 41.8)	
Free newspaper	**.83106**
Free continental breakfast	**.79721**
In-room coffee	**.58816**
Free cable TV	.41565
Factor 5 (E = 2.031, % of Var = 3.7, c% = 45.5)	
In-room check out	**.75359**
Pre-arranged check in	**.74361**
Room service (Meals only)	.47527
Factor 6 (E = 1.743, % of Var = 3.2, c% = 48.7)	
Airline frequent travel program	**.86757**
Hotel frequent traveler program	**.83749**
Impressive advertising	.34733
Factor 7 (E = 1.582, % of Var = 2.9, c% = 51.6)	
Low price	**–.74444**
Concierge floor	**.50275**
Gourmet restaurant	.45611
Factor 8 (E = 1.433, % of Var = 2.6, c% = 54.2)	
Banquet services	**.83540**
Meeting services	**.83519**
Factor 9 (E = 1.349, % of Var = 2.5, c% = 56.7)	
On-premise parking	**.66251**
Vending machines	**.57424**

FIGURE 1   (Continued)

FACTORS	FACTOR LOADING
Convenient to where your business is	.54623
Free local telephone calls	.39212
Factor 10 (E = 1.321, % of Var = 2.4, c% = 59.1)	
Family restaurant	.73879
Snack bar/gift shop	.62943
Factor 11 (E = 1.205, % of Var = 2.2, c% = 61.3)	
Travel agent's recommendation of the hotel	.65947
Medical service	.47546
Factor 12 (E = 1.190, % of Var = 2.2, c% = 63.5)	
Convenient to downtown area	.78154
Bellman service	.46547
Hair dryer	.44353
Factor 13 (E = 1.111, % of Var = 2.0, c% = 65.5)	
Non-smoking rooms	.70758
Wake up calls	–.42156
Factor 14 (E = 1.061, % of Var = 1.9, c% = 67.4)	
Convenient to the airport	.76179
Bar and lounge	.39371

*E = Eigenvalue, % of Var = percent of variance
c% = percent of cumulative variance

Factor 8   Convention services.
Factor 9   Other conveniences.
Factor 10   Eating places.
Factor 11   Travel agent/medical service.
Factor 12   Location/personal assistance.
Factor 13   Nonsmoking rooms.
Factor 14   Airport convenience/lounge.

The first six factors were selected to be utilized in the clustering procedure. Each of these factors explained more than 3 percent of the variance and subsequent factors explained less than 3 percent. For further analysis, these factors were represented by surrogate variables. Hair, Anderson, and Tatham (1987) suggest that the variable with the highest factor loading can be selected as a surrogate to represent for a particular factor dimension. The six surrogate variables for the first six factors explained 48.7 percent of the total variance. Analysis of variance (MANOVA) was run on the six surrogate variables to verify that there were significant differences among them as they related to the clusters. All six of the variables were significant. This was to be expected because they provided the original basis for the clusters.

Cluster Analysis

Cluster analysis is used to identify and classify individuals or variables on the basis of similarities of their characteristics so that a researcher can give a more concise and understandable description of the groups with minimal loss of information (Hair, Anderson, and Tatham, 1987). The six surrogate values obtained from the factor analysis were used to determine the number of homogeneous groups represented by the data. The SPSS (1990) cluster procedure was employed on a random sample of 10 percent of the total respondents. The analysis used the Squared Euclidean Dissimilarity Coefficient Matrix (Euclidean distance) to measure similarity between the pairs of individuals in subgroups. A hierarchical algorithm with the complete linkage procedure was used to place similar responses into groups. By visual inspections of the horizontal icicle dendrogram on the computer printout and the sudden jumps in the agglomeration schedule, a three-cluster solution was identified as appropriate.

The SPSS (1990) quick cluster procedure was then employed on the total sample of 350 respondents. Means tables and cross-tabulations were

FIGURE 2   Interpretation of Cluster

CLUSTERS	MEAN	V. UIMP		UIMP		EITHER		IMP.		V. IMP.	
		N	PERCENT*	N	PERCENT	N	PERCENT	N	PERCENT	N	PERCENT
Cluster 1											
F1 Business/ personal services	1.5766	91	27.0% (66.4)	21	6.2% (15.3)	18	5.3% (13.1)	6	1.8% (4.4)	1	.3% (.7)
F2 Room/hotel basics	4.2847	4	1.2 (2.9)	2	.6 (1.5)	12	3.5 (8.8)	52	15.3 (38.)	67	19.7 (48.9)
F3 Special in-room facilities	1.3188	112	32.8 (81.2)	12	3.5 (8.7)	10	2.9 (7.2)	4	1.2 (2.9)	0	0 (0)
F4 Free extras	3.0515	19	5.7 (14.)	17	5.1 (12.5)	48	14.3 (35.3)	42	12.5 (30.9)	10	3.0 (7.4)
F5 Easy check-in/room service	2.7279	26	7.7 (19.1)	28	8.3 (20.6)	45	13.3 (33.1)	31	9.2 (22.8)	6	1.8 (4.4)
F6 Freq. travel program/advertising	1.8284	66	19.7 (49.3)	33	9.9 (24.6)	28	8.4 (20.9)	6	1.8 (4.5)	1	.3 (.7)
Cluster 2											
F1 Business/ personal services	3.0536	10	3.0% (8.9)	14	4.2% (12.5)	55	16.3% (49.1)	26	7.7% (23.2)	7	2.1% (6.3)
F2 Room/hotel basics	4.5575	1	.3 (.9)	1	.3 (.9)	1	.3 (.9)	41	12.1 (36.3)	69	20.3 (61.1)
F3 Special In-room facilities	2.6579	17	5.0 (14.9)	27	7.9 (23.7)	51	15.0 (44.7)	16	4.7 (14.0)	3	.9 (2.6)
F4 Free extras	4.1081	1	.3 (.9)	2	.6 (1.8)	18	5.4 (16.2)	53	15.8 (47.7)	37	11.0 (33.3)
F5 Easy check-in/room service	3.9558	0	0 (.0)	5	1.5 (4.4)	25	7.4 (22.1)	53	15.7 (46.9)	30	8.9 (26.5)
F6 Freq. travel program/advertising	2.1140	33	9.9 (28.9)	35	10.4 (30.7)	46	13.7 (40.4)	0	0	0	0
Cluster 3											
F1 Business/ personal services	2.9432	13	3.9% (14.8)	15	4.5% (17.0)	31	9.2% (35.2)	22	6.5% (25.0)	7	2.1% (8.0)
F2 Room/ hotel basics	4.5556	0	0 (0)	3	.9 (3.3)	4	1.2 (4.4)	23	6.8 (25.6)	60	17.6 (66.7)
F3 Special In-room facilities	2.3371	27	7.9 (30.3)	18	5.3 (20.2)	35	10.3 (39.3)	5	1.5 (5.6)	4	1.2 (4.5)
F4 Free extras	4.0562	0	0 (0)	3	.9 (3.4)	21	6.3 (23.6)	33	9.8 (37.1)	32	9.5 (36.0)
F5 Easy check-in/room service	3.7416	0	0 (0)	9	2.7 (10.1)	28	8.3 (31.5)	29	8.6 (32.6)	23	6.8 (25.8)
F6 Freq. travel program/advertising	4.2644	0	0 (0)	0	0 (0)	3	.9 (3.4)	58	17.3 (66.7)	26	7.8 (29.8)

*percentage in ( ) is % within the cluster itself;
percentage without ( ) is % of the total sample.

utilized to describe the three groups (clusters) and their relationship with the six surrogate variables. Cluster 1 represented 40.7 percent of the sample, Cluster 2 was 33.2 percent, and Cluster 3 was 26.1 percent of the total sample. To simplify the discussion, the five-point scales used to rate selection attributes were collapsed into three categories of important, unimportant, and neutral. A complete listing of each cluster's response to each factor can be found in Figure 2. The distinguishing features of each group are discussed below.

Cluster 1.   This largest segment in the sample did not consider business and personal services (Factor 1) to be important. Eighty-two percent of the group marked the factor as unimportant. This group placed a great deal of importance on room/hotel basics (Factor 2), but did not view in-room facilities (Factor 3) as important. They were neutral on the importance of free extras (Factor 4), did not find easy check-in/room service to be particularly important as selection criteria and placed little importance on frequent traveler programs.

Cluster 2.   This group considered business and personal services to be more important than did Cluster 1, but still gave them close to a neutral rating as a group. As with the entire sample, and consistent with the results of other studies, this group rated room/hotel basics as being very important. Special in-room facilities were not very important, but having free extras as well as easy check-in/room service were quite important. Frequent guest program availability was only slightly more important for this group than for Cluster 1.

Cluster 3.   Members of this group found the importance of business and personal services to be only slightly less important than did Cluster 2 and were very concerned about room/hotel basics. Special in-room facilities were of little importance. The last three factors were considered important. In particular, Factor 6 (frequent travel program/advertising) was very important, especially when compared with the other two clusters.

Discriminant Analysis

Discriminant analysis was utilized to see how well the six surrogate variables predicted membership in each cluster. The discriminant analysis indicated that five of the six factors significantly predicted cluster membership at a significant level of at least .0001. Room/hotel basics was the only factor that did not discriminate among groups, which can probably be explained by the fact that all groups considered this to be important. The territorial map and scatterplot showed a clear distinction among groups. The classification results for the use of the analysis indicated that the discriminant analysis model could correctly classify 97.66 percent of the individuals into groups in the analysis stage and 90.32 percent of the cases in the validation stage.

Profiling of Clusters

To profile the characteristics of clusters, discriminant analysis is an appropriate statistical method (Hair, Anderson, and Tatham, 1987). The cluster profiles were developed using demographic information and other data which was not previously involved in the cluster procedure. The demographic information includes gender, age, and income; other information includes whether the individual is a frequent or infrequent traveler, overall satisfaction, and the preference for a chain.

The discriminant analysis indicated that age and preference for a hotel chain and were significant discriminators at levels of .0032 and .0110 respectively. The classification matrix showed that this analysis phase could correctly classify 48.85 percent of the cases and the validation phase could correctly classify 40 percent of the cases. (It should be noted, however, that correct classification under the proportional chance criteria would be 34 percent.) Cross-tabulation tables were again utilized to aid in the description of the groups.

When using stepwise discriminant analysis, variables are added in a stepwise procedure with the most significant variable being included first. After a variable is included in the equation the variables are reevaluated for inclusion. Therefore, it is possible for a variable to be significant but not add enough to be included in the final analysis. Because of this possibility, crosstabs were also run on the profiling variables. The chi-square analysis from the cross-tabulations revealed that gender was also a significant demographic variable.

Demographic Profile

Table 1 displays the demographic profile of the three groups in terms of their gender, age, and income. This provides an overview of the demographics of the sample as well as each cluster. Only age and gender will be discussed because they were the only significant discriminating demographic variables.

Cluster 1 had more senior respondents and fewer female respondents than the other two groups. Over 61 percent of the respondents in

TABLE 1   Demographic Profile

GENDER	CLUSTER 1 Percent	(N)	CLUSTER 2 Percent	(N)	CLUSTER 3 Percent	(N)	TOTAL Percent (N)
Male	79.4%	(108)	64.7%	(75)	64.4%	(58)	(241)
Female	19.9	(27)	35.3	(41)	35.6	(32)	(100)
Total	100.0%	(135)	100.0%	(116)	100.0%	(90)	(341)
Age							
Under 25	.7%	(1)					(1)
25–34	2.2	(3)	6.0%	(7)	8.9%	(8)	(18)
35–44	13.9	(19)	24.1	(28)	20.0	(18)	(65)
45–54	21.9	(30)	30.2	(35)	26.7	(24)	(89)
55–64	35.0	(48)	25.9	(30)	31.1	(28)	(106)
Over 64	26.3	(36)	13.8	(16)	13.3	(12)	(64)
Total	100.0%	(137)	100.0%	(116)	100.0%	(90)	(343)
Income							
Less than 25,000	2.4%	(3)	5.4%	(6)	1.2%	(1)	(10)
25,001–50,000	27.6	(35)	28.6	(32)	20.9	(18)	(85)
50,001–75,000	27.6	(35)	28.6	(32)	31.4	(27)	(94)
75,001–100,000	12.6	(16)	10.7	(12)	17.4	(15)	(43)
100,001–150,000	15.0	(19)	14.3	(16)	15.1	(13)	(48)
150,001–200,000	10.2	(13)	3.6	(4)	4.7	(4)	(21)
Over 200,000	4.7	(6)	8.9	(10)	9.3	(8)	(24)
Total	100.0%	(127)	100.0%	(112)	100.0%	(86)	(325)

*Sample sizes vary due to omitted questions.

Cluster 1 were fifty-five years old or older, and only about 20 percent were female. Cluster 2 had 39.7 percent of the respondents fifty-five years old or older, and 35.3 percent were female. Cluster 3 had 44.4 percent of the respondents fifty-five years old or older, and 35.6 percent were female respondents between thirty-five and fifty-four (54.3 percent of the cluster), while the first group had 35.8 percent between thirty-five and fifty-four, and the third group had 46.7 percent in this age group. Cluster 3 had the greatest proportion of young respondents, with nearly 9 percent of the respondents aged thirty-four or younger.

Frequent Business Traveler versus Infrequent Business Traveler

The frequent business traveler in this study was classified as a person who traveled at least ten times within twelve months, and the infrequent traveler was a person who traveled less than ten times in the same time frame. There were more infrequent travelers than frequent travelers in each cluster (see Table 2). Cluster 1 had more infrequent travelers than the other two clusters

(65.2 percent of the respondents in Cluster 1 were infrequent travelers, while Cluster 2 had 62.1 percent and Cluster 3 had 56 percent). The closeness of the percentages gives some insight as to why this variable was not significant in the discriminant analysis.

General Satisfaction

Table 2 shows that, based on the responses to a general satisfaction question, more respondents in all three groups were satisfied rather than dissatisfied with hotel service. This also was not a discriminating variable.

Preference for Hotel Chains

Preference (or no preference) for a particular chain was the second discriminating item. As shown on Table 2, Cluster 1 did not have a strong preference for staying in the same hotel chain when traveling. Forty-two percent of the respondents in Cluster 1 indicated they would not choose a particular chain for their accommodations when they were on the road. Cluster 3 had the highest percentage

TABLE 2   Travel Pattern and Preference

	CLUSTER 1 Percent (N)		CLUSTER 2 Percent (N)		CLUSTER 3 Percent (N)		TOTAL (N)
Frequent vs. Infrequent*							
Frequent	34.8%	(48)	37.9%	(44)	44.0%	(40)	(132)
Infrequent	65.2	(90)	62.1	(72)	56.0	(51)	(213)
Total	100.0%	(138)	100.0%	(116)	100.0%	(91)	(345)
General Satisfaction							
Satisfied	55.1%	(75)	54.8%	(63)	58.0%	(51)	(189)
Dissatisfied	16.9	(23)	14.8	(17)	14.8	(13)	(53)
Neither	27.9	(38)	30.4	(35)	27.3	(24)	(97)
Total	100.0%	(136)	100.0%	(115)	100.0%	(88)	(339)
Preference for a Chain							
Agree	23.5%	(31)	23.5%	(27)	39.8%	(35)	(93)
Disagree	42.4	(56)	40.0	(46)	34.1	(30)	(132)
Neither	34.1	(45)	36.5	(42)	26.1	(23)	(110)
Total	100.0%	(132)	100.0%	(115)	100.0%	(88)	(335)

*10 trips or more within 12 months considered as frequent traveler, less than 10 trips within 12 months as infrequent travelers.
*A traveler had an average of more than 3 nights per trip as long sleeper; 3 nights or less as short sleeper.

of respondents that preferred a particular chain when they traveled (39.8 percent).

Implications for Marketing

The study segmented the business traveler market on the basis of fifty-five hotel selection criteria. Fourteen factors were extracted from fifty-five hotel selection attributes. Six surrogate variables were selected from the fourteen factors to be used to cluster individual respondents into groups. Three clusters were identified based on these six surrogate variables of hotel selection. Discriminant analysis and cross-tabulation were employed to profile the groups.

Cluster 1 was the male-dominated senior business traveler group. Sixty-one percent of the respondents were fifty-five years old or older, and was 79.4 percent male. Fifty-five percent of the respondents had income between $25,001 and $75,000, and two-thirds were infrequent business travelers. They were generally satisfied with hotel services, and most did not have a strong preference for a particular chain. They did not care much about selection criteria except for general service. Most of them were not in hotel frequent traveler programs.

From a consumer behavior standpoint, Cluster 1 seems to represent business travelers who are not particularly loyal to one brand or another. They are probably less demanding as a group, but

also less susceptible to marketing ploys such as frequent guest programs and adding special services. This segment appears to be as concerned about the basics as the other segments, but isn't interested in the fluff. Age was a significant difference, and this segment is older, which may indicate a bit of cynicism toward the hotel industry.

Cluster 2 consisted mainly of the middle-aged business travelers. About two-thirds of the respondents were male, 53.4 percent were between thirty-five and fifty-four years old, and 57.2 percent had an annual income between $25,001 and $75,000. Sixty-two percent of the respondents were infrequent travelers and more than half of them were satisfied with hotel services. Similar to Cluster 1, only 23.5 percent indicated preference for a particular chain. They cared about room/hotel basic services, free extras, and easy check-in/room service. Frequent guest programs were not of major importance.

Cluster 2 would seem to be more susceptible to marketing ploys such as providing free newspapers, free continental breakfast, in-room coffee, and cable TV. Interactions with the front desk and room service staff would be important to this segment.

Cluster 3 was the youngest group among the three groups, with 55.6 percent of them under fifty-five years of age. Similar to Cluster 2, about two-thirds were male and one-third female. Little more than half had an annual income between $25,001 and $75,000. The group had the highest percentage (44 percent) of frequent travelers. This cluster had the highest percentage of satisfaction with hotel service and the highest percentage (39.8 percent) of preference for a particular chain. Like Cluster 2, this segment was concerned about room/hotel basics, easy check-in/room service, and free extras. What set Cluster 3 apart was the importance they placed on a frequent guest program and their preference for a particular chain.

Cluster 3 respondents are likely to be susceptible to good service, "freebies," and easy check-in and check-out. In addition, they are likely to be repeat customers if they can be enrolled in a chain's frequent guest program.

CONCLUSION

The results of this study indicate that there are some distinct subsegments within the business traveler market segment. Hotel marketing managers can use the information in this study to aid in positioning their products and better design their product offerings to more precisely meet the needs of different types of business travelers. For example, all three clusters considered general service important, which indicates hoteliers should maintain the basic services. But younger people seemed most likely to accept FGPs and demonstrate chain loyalty. Therefore, a company can put more efforts in promoting its FGPs to the younger people. Providing "free" extras seems to be effective for keeping both Clusters 2 and 3 happy. On the other hand, stressing the availability of business and personal services, the highest loading factor, does not appear to be an effective way of marketing to Cluster 1, the largest business subsegment.

As has been shown in many studies, the entire business segment expects a high level of performance on the basic services hotels offer. Therefore, expectations regarding basic service is not a strong differentiator among traveler types. Not offering good service is a strong negative, but offering good service is not enough to ensure loyalty and to lure customers away from the competition. By zeroing in on the discriminating factors among market segments, hotel marketers can develop appeals that directly meet the needs of more specific target markets and provide the hotel with a clearer image in consumers' minds.

REFERENCES

Hair, J., Anderson, R. E., and R. L. Tatham, *Multivariate Data Analysis*, 2nd ed. New York: Macmillan, 1987.

Hawes, D. K. "Travel-Related Lifestyle Profiles of Older Women," *Journal of Travel Research*, 27 (1988), 22–23.

Knutson, B. J., "Frequent Travelers: Making Them Happy and Bringing Them Back," *The Cornell H.R.A. Quarterly*, (May 1988), 83–87.

Knutson, B. J., "Profile of the Frequent Traveler: Perceptions of the Economy, Mid-price and Luxury Segments," in *The Stuff of Which Hospitality Marketing is Made*, ed. B. Knutson, K. McCleary, and P. Stevens. East Lansing: Hospitality Resources Inc, 59–72.

Lewis, R. C., "Isolating Differences in Hotel Attributes," *The Cornell H.R.A. Quarterly*, (November 1984), 65–77.

Lewis, R. C., "The Basis of Hotel Selection." *The Cornell H.R.A. Quarterly*, (May 1984), 54–69.

Lewis, R. C., "The Marketing Position: Mapping Guests' Perceptions of Hotel Operations." *The Cornell H.R.A. Quarterly*, (August 1985), 86–99.

Lewis, R. C., "Are Your Listening to Customers—or to Competitors?" *Hotel and Motel Management*, (November 2, 1990), 55.

Lewis, R. C., and M. Nightingale, "Targeting Service to Your Customer," *The Cornell H.R.A. Quarterly*, (August 1991), 18–27.

McCleary, K. W. and P. A. Weaver, "Are Frequent Guest Programs Effective?" *The Cornell H.R.A. Quarterly*, (August 1991), 39–45.

McCleary, K. W. and P. A. Weaver, "Do Business Travelers Who Belong to Frequent Guest Programs Differ from Those Who Don't Belong?" *Hospitality Research Journal* (forthcoming).

Niles, W., "Exposing 10 Myths about Business Travelers." *Proceedings of the Fourteenth Annual Travel Outlook Forum*, Washington, D.C.: U.S. Travel Data Center, 1988, pp. 97–99.

Niles, W., "1988 Outlook for Business Travel." *Proceedings of the Thirteenth Annual Travel Outlook Forum*, Washington, D.C.: U.S. Travel Data Center, 1988, pp. 81–94.

Oppenheim, A. N., *Questionnaire Design and Attitude Measurement*. New York: Basic Books, 1966.

Rivers, M. J., R. S. Toh, and M. Alaoui, "Frequent-Stayer Programs: The Demographic, Behavioral, and Attitudinal Characteristics of Hotel Steady

Sleepers." *Journal of Travel Research,* vol. 30, no. 2 (Fall 1991), 41–45.

Schaffer, J. D., "Competitive Strategies in the Lodging Industry," *International Journal of Hospitality Management,* vol. 6, no. 1 (1987), 33–42.

Shoemaker, S., "Segmentation Of The Senior Pleasure Travel Market," *Journal of Travel Research,* vol. 27, no. 3 (Winter 1989), 14–21.

SPSS, Inc., *SPSSX Reference Guide,* 4th ed. Chicago: SPSS, Inc., 1990.

Taninecz, G., "1990 Business Traveler Survey," *Hotel and Motel Management* (June 1990).

Toh, R. S., M. J. Rivers, and G. Withiam, "Frequent-guest Programs: Do They Fly?" *The Cornell H.R.A. Quarterly,* (August 1991), 46–52.

Weaver, P. A., and K. W. McCleary, "Basics bring 'em back," *Hotel and Motel Management,* June 24, 1991, pp. 29–38.

Weaver, P. A., and H. C. Oh, "Do Frequent and Infrequent Travelers Perceive the Level of Importance of Various Services and Amenities by the Lodging Industry Differently?" *International Journal of Contemporary Hospitality Management* (in press).

CHAPTER 5 The Economic Impact of Tourism

PROJECT _____

Let's turn things around! Tomorrow you will wake up and let's assume that your city/state never had a tourism industry. How would things be different? Try to answer this question by thinking of the number of people that would be unemployed, the loss in income benefits, the loss in tax revenue, the lack of pride people would have in your community, and the lack of cultural assets that now make your town or state the special place that it is.

While tourism affects a place or destination in many ways, its development is invariably based on economic objectives. In this chapter, we will concentrate on the economic benefits (and costs) that result from tourism, looking first at the consequences of tourism as it affects communities in the United States. Then, we will study the economic issues that result from international travel; more specifically, the benefits, costs, and risks to countries that have adopted tourism as a means for economic development and growth.

THE DOMESTIC SCENE _____

Some communities have developed their entire economies around the activities and needs of the traveling public, but even those that have not are affected by tourism. Many individuals in a community profit, either directly or indirectly, from the tourist, through the sale of gasoline, food, lodging, souvenirs, experiences, and many other goods and services. Not all definitions of a tourist are the same. Some define a tourist as anyone who travels to places more than 25 miles from home. Other definitions are based on travel to places 100 miles or more from home. (This definition is criticized as being too restrictive since, throughout the world, most resort areas are located less than 100 miles from major urban population centers.) Regardless of the definition used, several characteristics are common to each: a tourist is defined as someone who has traveled to a destination from some other location and does not plan to stay permanently.

Tourists may be visiting friends or relatives, attending a convention, attending a special event (rodeo, play, musical event), sight-seeing, participating

Missouri Division of Tourism

in a sports event (skiing, canoeing, sailing), passing through en route to another location, or engaging in numerous other activities. Regardless of their reasons for traveling, tourists spend money that helps the economy of the destination.

It is estimated that Americans take nearly 1.3 billion person-trips a year. A *person-trip* is here defined as one person taking a trip to a place 100 or more miles from home.[1] On an average day, approximately 12 million American are traveling away from home. Business person-trips account for approximately one-quarter of all travel in this country, with pleasure travel (visiting friends and relatives, outdoor recreation, vacation, shopping) accounting for the rest. The tourist/travel industry, which expanded dramatically during the past decade, contributes enormously to the United States economy. The travel and tourism industry is the third-largest retail industry, after automotive dealers and food stores. Americans spend more on travel than on clothing, accessories, jewelry, and personal care combined, or on household utilities, including telephone service. In 1990, the United States Travel Data Center estimated that travelers spent $650 billion within the United States alone on trips involving an overnight stay away from home and on day trips to locations 25 or more miles away. This includes money spent by foreign visitors as well as U.S. residents. This activity, in turn, generated 12.9 million jobs and $45 billion in federal, state, and local tax revenue. It is estimated that each $1 billion of spending on tourism directly or indirectly generates 35,000 jobs. Since 1972, payroll jobs in travel-related businesses have more than doubled, while total U.S. payroll employment increased by less than 50 percent. Over the past decade, travel in-

[1]National Travel Survey (Washington, D.C.: U.S. Travel Data Center, 1991).

dustry employment has grown 43 percent, more than twice the growth rate for all U.S. industries. The 2.9 million jobs provided by the industry since 1979 accounted for 15.4 percent of the national increase in employment. Each dollar tourists spend is like a pebble thrown in a pond—it creates ripples which reach every part of the community. Every dollar tourists spend is respent several times. The United States Chamber of Commerce says "cash which a community receives from twenty-four tourists per day is equivalent to a company with an annual payroll of $150,000."[2]

LOCAL BENEFITS FROM TOURISM

Although the economic benefit is often the factor motivating many communities' involvement in tourism, communities identify the following as positive contributions to the community:

- Employment benefits.
- Income benefits.
- Tax revenues.
- Visibility.
- Cultural benefits.

Tourism and Employment

The most impressive contribution of the tourist dollar to the American economy must be measured by jobs. Tourism is a service industry, requiring large numbers of employees in relation to the amount of the investment. That is, tourism relies on relatively large inputs of labor compared to capital, and, thus, generates relatively large numbers of jobs. Tourism stands out among major U.S. industries in creating new jobs, resisting economic downturns, and providing a major source of jobs for minorities, women, and youth. Hawaii, for instance, indicates that 21 percent of its civilian workforce hold jobs created by tourism. While the overall U.S. economy lost millions of jobs during the recession of the early 1980s, the travel industry continued to create new employment (as it has done for twenty-three consecutive years).

Since 1958, the earliest year for which data is available, payroll jobs in the travel industry, including hotels and other lodging places, eating and drinking establishments, air transportation, and intercity bus transportation, increased 200 percent. This is more than twice as fast as the growth in total U.S. payroll employment over this period. The travel industry contributed more than 10 percent of the 39 million new jobs created over these two decades. Direct employment generated by travel in the United States in 1990 exceeded the population of 80 countries of the world. The wage and salary income from tourism was four times that of the United States' steel and auto manufacturing industries combined in 1990.

Of particular importance to local economies, is the fact that small business dominates the tourist/travel industry. Of the 14 million travel-related business firms, 98 percent are classified as small businesses. One of the distinctive characteristics of the American economy, and the one that has contributed the most

---

[2]Tourism Facts: Travel and Tourism (Washington, D.C.: Government Affairs Council, 1991).

to its vitality, is the preponderance of small businesses. More than 500,000 private firms in America provide passenger transportation, lodging, food services, amusement, and recreation.[3]

The employment benefits generated by the tourist industry are many. It creates jobs overall and employs persons of all skill levels. Most jobs are in the support industries, services, and wholesale/retail trade; a good number are in the areas of amusement and recreation. Services include hotels, motels, trailer parks, campgrounds, auto repair, amusement, and recreation. Wholesale/retail includes eating and drinking establishments, gas service stations, and apparel and accessory stores.

Certain groups have traditionally found it more difficult than others to find jobs in our country. The travel industry has proven itself to be a dependable source of job opportunities for these groups. While blacks and other minority groups account for 11 percent of total U.S. employment, they hold 12 percent of the jobs in the travel industry. Women held 45 percent of all U.S. jobs in 1990, but accounted for 58 percent of tourism industry employment. Data on youth employment suggests that the tourism industry provides a disproportionate share of jobs for the young as well. Often the tourism season coincides with school vacations, providing employment opportunities for youth in many communities. A careful analysis of a community's existing employment situation, potential available labor force, and type of tourism operations is critical to any decision with regard to potential employment benefits from tourism.

Tourism and Income

The tourism industry attracts travelers which, in turn, means income and profit for businesses receiving tourist expenditures. New money can be brought into a community through agriculture, mining, manufacturing, and tourism. Many communities are unsuited for the first three, but almost every community has some visitors and therefore has some degree of tourism. In fact, virtually every community in the United States benefits from travel and tourism. Studies by the U.S. Travel Data Center of the economic impact of tourism on over 1,400 counties revealed that only 2 received no benefit from travel and tourism. These economic benefits usually exceed the cost to government in providing highways, parks, and other elements of the tourism infrastructure.

Far from being concentrated in a few well-known resort areas, the economic benefits of tourism in the United States are widespread. Every state in the nation benefits from travel and tourism activity. The tourism industry is among the top three private employers in thirty-six of our fifty states and the District of Colombia. In Hawaii, Nevada, Vermont, and Wyoming, travel activity generates more than 10 percent of total state nonagricultural payroll employment.

Studies have shown that travel expenditures vary almost directly with the number of visits and substantially increase if visitors stay away from home more than one day. However, total expenditures by tourists do not tell the whole story. Two important economic facts must be understood before a reasonable estimate of the impact of tourism on business income can be made. First, some of the goods and materials sold by tourist-related businesses come from outside the community. When these bills are paid, this part of the traveler's dollar does not benefit the community directly. However, the part of the tourist dollar that stays in the area, usually in the form of wages, profits, and

---

[3]See note 2 above.

additional expenditures on locally produced goods and services, does benefit the community. Local income from tourists expenditures is largely respent in the area which leads, in turn, to still more local income, more local expenditures, and so on.

A good example of these direct and indirect benefits is Jackson Hole, Wyoming, a popular outdoor recreation area. Their local study of business generated from tourism showed that 55 percent of total sales in the area resulted from direct tourist expenditures and that an additional 22 percent resulted from the indirect effect of income generated from the initial purchases, for a total of 27 percent of sales related to tourism.

Tax Revenue and Government Benefits

The most important tax from most communities' point of view is the sales tax. When tourist expenditures are high, so are sales tax revenues. Although estimating the impact of these additional tax revenues is difficult, rough estimates indicate a figure of nearly 15 percent of total revenues. Overall, tourism activity generates more than $20 billion a year for federal, state, and local treasuries. Special taxes, aimed specifically at tourists, are often levied by communities. "Occupancy" taxes and entrance fees are based on the premise that tourism imposes certain public costs, such as increased police protection, lifeguards, additional public facilities, and upkeep of monuments and museums. This is particularly true in rural, outdoor recreational areas where tourism and its costs are more clearly identifiable.

In many areas local amenities such as museums, monuments, libraries, historical sites, and entertainment districts, have deteriorated because of inadequate local funding. Other communities are unable to develop parks, recreational areas, and other local attractions because of insufficient funding. These communities sometimes find tourism is a solution that provides the marginal profit and revenue balance needed to maintain or develop these services. These facilities are then available for local use as well.

Tourism and Visibility

Developing a tourist industry has other, less tangible, economic benefits for a community. A very important one is visibility. Visitors are attracted by those little things which are unique to a community: heritage, culture, architecture, scenery. An awareness of the value of these to outsiders can spur renewed interest and pride among residents to conserve and preserve those elements which contribute to the uniqueness. Traditional crafts, ethnic customs and mores, and historic sites and structures are just a few examples of elements which can be enhanced by the realization that they have a value beyond the boundaries of the local community. Citizen and government understanding of the visitor's desire for an aesthetically positive environment as a setting for the tourism experience can be instrumental in forging community goals and actions which result in the conservation of the higher quality aspects of the community and elimination of those which are detractions. Many communities suffer (unreasonably) from bad reputations because of their geographic location, climate, or lack of perceived attributes. The Texas Tourist Development Agency recognized that their communities suffered an image problem when a survey showed that outsiders thought Texas was simply a desert whose only attractions were tumbleweeds and cactus. In Wichita, Kansas, tourist developers thought their business suffered from a misconception that Wichita was nothing but a stopping place for travelers on the way west. North Dakota recently considered changing its name to "Dakota" in an effort to make the state's image sound less remote. The people living in these areas, and those who have explored them, know differently, of course.

An active travel development program can help overcome such misconceptions and be economically beneficial. One benefit stems from community pride. If a community discovers that it has something to offer visitors, something attractive enough to draw people from their home communities to a host community, benefits may naturally be forthcoming. Dodge City, Kansas, is an outstanding example. Pride in its rich "wild West" heritage, helped considerably by the television program "Gunsmoke," spurred local activities in the 1950s. Spearheaded by the Jaycees, their efforts resulted in the rebuilding of historic streets, museums, and cemeteries, and the creation of a number of new attractions. Dodge City, once just another "cowboy town," now attracts nearly 400,000 visitors annually. Community pride enriched the area culturally and economically, and made the community even more attractive. Visitors, when meeting a proud resident, are likely to be shown more hospitality and consequently have a better time. The visitor will stay longer and spend more money. He or she will "spread the word" about "a great place to visit."

Tourism and Cultural Benefits

The potential cultural benefits from tourism, though less obvious than economic benefits, may be equally significant. A well-organized tourist business can benefit the resident through exposure to a variety of ideas, people, languages, and other cultural traits. It can add to the richness of the resident's experience by stimulating an interest in the area's history through restoration and preservation of historical sights. For instance, residents of Savannah, Georgia undertook to restore portions of the old city as a matter of civic pride, but have since discovered that the preservation of their heritage has stimulated tourism. Today, one of the major highlights for the visitor is a tour of the historic district.

Missouri Division of Tourism

Thus, tourism is now an important source of revenue for further historical restoration and preservation. As a Bicentennial project, the city of Mobile, Alabama restored historic Fort Conde Village. The result: a national prize-winning restoration project and an additional incentive for tourists to visit Mobile.

Tourism can also provide an audience and market for the art of local crafts people. Taos, New Mexico, is a case in point. Long a haven for artists and craftspeople, Taos has benefited from tourism and has provided an outlet for local arts and crafts, which, in turn, has served as an incentive for further cultural creativity. Likewise, tourism has encouraged inhabitants of the area around Branson, Missouri, located in the Ozarks, to share their rich heritage of country music with visitors.

Tourism need not result in drastic exploitation of resources or destruction of natural beauty. The famous Azalea Trail in Mobile, Alabama, serves as a city beautification project, a source of community pride, and as a considerable enticement for tourists.

Tourism development can add entertainment facilities which benefit the resident as well as the visitor. Tourism in the tiny community (population 200) of Bishop Hill, Illinois resulted in the construction of restaurants and a bakery which residents, as well as visitors, can enjoy. The Pirate's House, a well-known restaurant, is located in a restored area of Savannah and is a favorite of residents. These examples illustrate how thoughtful development enhances civic satisfaction and pride.

Tourists have more to offer a community than their dollars. They bring a variety of ethnic, geographic, and sociocultural experiences. By establishing contacts between people of different backgrounds, tourism offers opportunities for people to know and understand one another in a direct way.

COSTS AND LIABILITIES OF TOURISM

The jobs created by tourism, the taxes it brings in, and the other benefits are not without cost. Among them are the added demands on public facilities and services, and the operations costs of a tourism industry.

Demands on Public Facilities and Services

In considering the costs of tourism to the community, we must identify all the facilities and services provided by public agencies for the community. How public facilities are affected by tourism is another consideration. Facilities and services are divided into several categories: transportation access to the community; local public works such as roads and streets, parking, information signs, water supply, sewage and trash disposal, and restrooms; public safety, such as police and fire protection; public education; and public health and welfare. Let's discuss each briefly.

Transportation Access.   Historically, tourist attractions have developed only when they became accessible. Today, most centers of tourist travel depend on visitors arriving by private automobile or mass transportation systems —air, rail, bus, and even in some situations, boat. For example, St. George, Utah, was surrounded by dirt roads until a "Five County Association," founded in 1958, pushed for state road funds. This small town with a population of 15,000 is now second in the state in attracting tourists and visitors. Mt. Rushmore did not become a mass tourist attraction until after the completion of an interstate highway across South Dakota in the late 1950s. Now, the Shrine of Democracy is host to over 2 million visitors annually. Disney World is internally self-sufficient, but construction required an early investment by Florida of $5,000,000 for access highways.

Cities that expect to attract tourism business beyond a radius of a few hundred miles should have good, dependable, commercial transportation with reasonably priced, well-scheduled, and well-advertised bus, taxi, or limousine service to the community's tourist attractions and lodging areas.

Local Roads.   One of the most obvious impacts of tourism on the community is the traffic congestion caused by visitors' vehicles on the local roads leading to tourist attractions. City streets may need to be widened, resurfaced, or better maintained to provide adequate passage in the "tourist season." Communities need to institute parking restrictions, one-way streets, traffic lights, and other traffic control features. Lack of adequate parking creates congestion which keeps tourists from returning and creates resentment in the local population.

Signs.   Signs help visitors find their way easily to attractions. Attractive signs, well maintained and replaced as required, can add to the charm of a community at a modest cost. The need for directional signs is also a predominant promotional consideration. Where attractions are close together, a walking tour, outlined in a simple leaflet and marked by attractive signs, can keep the visitor in a community longer.

Water.   While tourists' demand for water for drinking and bathing is small compared with industrial demand, they do want an adequate quantity in a quality that offends neither the eye, nose, or tongue. Most tourist areas can provide this, although some, like Taos, New Mexico, have reason to be concerned about the impact of increasing numbers of visitors on a limited water supply. Other communities must import drinking water and endure some taste or smell in bathing water.

Sewage and Trash Disposal.   Similarly, the demand of tourism on sewage and trash disposal is small compared to heavy industry, yet some communities are not prepared to handle it. The neighboring towns of Ketchum and Sun Valley, Idaho, for example, are under a sewer moratorium limiting construction until the local sewer plant is improved to meet required standards. Trash and litter are inevitable problems when there are crowds. Ample waste receptacles, both public and private, should be provided, and they must be emptied more frequently when tourism is at its peak. Streets and public areas should be kept clean, and this will take added labor and public cost.

Public Safety.   Public safety largely means police and fire protection. As tourism brings more people to the community, additional police will be needed to control crowds, assist visitors, and handle any increase in crime. An influx of people increases the potential for fires, both indoors and out.

Operations Costs.   Measuring the economic contributions of tourism is a complex process. However, as we have learned, it is even more difficult to quantify the economic cost of travel. One area of cost-benefit analysis of vital concern to public officials is the amount government must spend in serving travelers in a state, city, or county compared to how much revenue they earn from visitors. In a major tourism policy study for the State of Delaware, the U.S. Travel Data Center investigated this issue. It compared the traveler cost to the state of constructing and maintaining highways, operating parks, managing fish and wildlife resources, and providing overhead services such as fire prevention. These costs were then compared to the revenue visitors provided in the form of gasoline taxes, park admission fees, hunting and fishing licenses, and other taxes and fees. Although Delaware has no general retail tax, the study found that the state collected a net of $.20 from every visitor to the state. If a state without a general sales tax earns net income from visitors, other governments are likely to profit even more from tourism.

THE INTERNATIONAL SCENE _____

Tourist-Generating Countries

Tourism can affect the balance of payments in two ways: travel payments (expenditures of nationals abroad) and travel receipts (spending by foreign visitors). The governments of major tourist-generating countries are faced with huge travel deficits, since much more money is spent outside the country by its citizens than foreign visitors spend on goods and services in the host country. The Japanese, for example, spent $24 billion in 1990 for foreign travel. They earned $4 billion from foreign visitor spending in Japan that year. A $20 billion deficit! Germans spent $25 billion in foreign countries during 1991 while traveling for pleasure or business. During the same year, total receipts from foreign visitors reached only $9 billion, which resulted in a travel deficit of $16 billion. Dutch citizens spend about twice as much on foreign travel as the Netherlands earns from foreign visitors. It is interesting to note that for the first time in history, the United States registered a travel surplus in 1989. By 1992, 42 million foreign visitors spent $45 billion in the United States, compared with $39 billion spent by 40 million Americans traveling outside the country. The travel item on the balance of payments of most countries includes all expenses incurred by travelers on accommodations, meals, entertainment, transportation, and gifts. However, many other financial transactions also take place between countries because of tourism. This is especially the case between developed and developing countries.[4]

---

[4]Data from World Travel and Tourism Council's 2nd Annual Report (Brussels, Belgium, 1992).

Tourism and Developing Countries

Most developing countries are confronted with a shortage of foreign exchange and have great difficulty financing their economic development. High priority is therefore given to the expansion of export opportunities and to reducing imports. The economic reasons for tourism development are compelling where the available alternatives are few and little or no human or physical resource base exists to develop intensive agriculture or industry.

Tourism activity has a clear advantage as a source of foreign exchange compared with other sectors, particularly in the developing countries. The reasons given in favor of this are the following.

First, tourism depends on international demand, which makes it an exporting activity from the first stages of its development. Development, which is competitive at the international level, cannot be based exclusively on internal demand, which is usually very low in these countries. It can, however, be based on external demand, but at the cost of dependence (capital, technology, skilled labor, and so on) on the developed countries, which calls into question, even in the long term, the possibility of a relatively self-sustaining form of economic development. Most agree that tourism, because of its local or indigenous resource foundation, requires less-sophisticated technology and, possibly, fewer requirements for highly skilled manpower. It can generate a form of development which is, under equal conditions, less dependence-creating than most other industrial alternatives.

Furthermore, industrial development in the developing countries has been hampered by difficulties of access to foreign markets. At the present time in particular, the international marketplace is characterized by a set of tax, tariff, quota obstacles, and the like. On the other hand, tourism demand in developed countries, although it is partly replaced by domestic tourism, is less protected; that is, it is not subject to quotas and does not imply in general any counterpart with respect to the country of origin of the tourists, a situation which is becoming already less frequent in other international economic relations.

The strategic function of tourism as a source of foreign exchange is of special importance in countries which are developing or have limited natural resources and raw materials.

Tourism also contributes to the diversification of existing economic activity. Tourism consumption, through its heterogeneous nature, is directed to many sectors simultaneously, diversifying its direct effects over other various branches or sectors of the economy.

The potential of tourism demand, together with its multiplier effect, makes tourism an activity worth exploring.

Tourism development may bring benefits (or costs) to the people in the host society either as consumers or as producers. As consumers, they may gain access to a wide range of services, such as better roads, improved recreational services, and a greater variety of restaurants; or, they may find their range of choices restricted. In many resorts around the world, it is difficult for the local population to benefit directly from the facilities built for the tourist. Often, the infrastructure may serve the tourist rather than the local people by using resources that might otherwise have improved local living conditions. And, tourist resorts are often designed to discourage interaction between hosts and guests.

As producers, the local population may earn higher returns from its resources, including labor, skills, and land. But for those in competing activities who are not in the tourism industry, these gains to the economy could be individual losses. For example, demand for tourist development land generally increases real estate prices and may make housing very costly for the local population.

RELEVANT ECONOMIC ISSUES

The Employment Factor

Employment generation might not be the major goal of all tourism development, but it is certainly one of its main achievements.

Tourism, as an activity involving services, has a quantitatively significant capacity to generate employment. In recent years, tourism has created a considerable number of jobs in many developing countries and in some it constitutes the most important source of employment.

Three categories of employment result from tourism development: (1) jobs directly related to running the tourism industry; (2) jobs resulting from the development of the industry, such as transportation, agriculture, banking; and (3) jobs indirectly created by tourism, arising from the spending of money by local residents from their tourism incomes. The data from developing countries with established tourism industries indicates considerable differences in employment generation. For example, hotels in the Mediterranean area give rise to about half as much direct employment as hotels in East Africa. On the larger and economically more diversified Caribbean islands, such as Jamaica and Puerto Rico, tourism provides up to 10 percent of total employment. On the smaller islands, the proportion reaches 50 percent; in Bermuda, direct and indirect employment from tourism accounts for three-fourths of the labor force.

Tourism in Mexico creates 2.7 person-years of employment in the construction industry, as well as in the furniture and transportation industries, for each new hotel bed. In large and diversified economies, this is, of course, a positive result. However, in small, underdeveloped economies with little prospect of modern sector development, tourism industry development can create substantial problems. For example, a building boom generated by hotel construction can produce mixed blessings. In the Seychelles, a rapid expansion of the tourism industry, the construction of an international airport, infrastructure work, and new hotels led to an increase in the number of construction workers from roughly 1,300 to over 4,000 or from 10 percent to 25 percent of the labor force. After three years, this dropped to 17.5 percent of the labor force, or 2,750 workers. The unemployed construction workers were not easily absorbed into the hotel industry where their skills were not required, and, in fact, new hotel jobs were more available to women than to men. The construction boom encouraged an exodus from agriculture to higher-paid construction jobs; agricultural labor decreased from 4,500 to around 2,500 during the boom, and picked up only marginally afterward.

Though tourism may be labor intensive, many observers have noted that the quality of jobs created is often relatively low. Case studies have documented the generally low-paying and low-skilled nature of many tourism-related jobs in areas as diverse as the Caribbean, the Mediterranean, the Alps and many parts of the United States. The principal exception to this pattern is a boom period of relatively high paying construction jobs during the rapid growth stage of tourism development. However, this is a temporary phenomenon. Compounding this problem is chronic seasonality which plagues the tourism industry and which often causes many jobs to be of a part-time or temporary nature.

Employment in the agricultural sector of an economy is indirectly affected by tourism. Food production may be stimulated by tourism through increased demand. On the other hand, tourism may draw people from the land and/or lead to a fall in productivity, causing food prices to rise, even for those whose incomes have not improved as a result of tourism development. Particularly in very small economies, agriculture, rather than being stimulated by tourism, may be replaced by it. It may lose out in the competition for labor and land, especially where the agricultural land is in the coastal plains. Experiences around the world vary. In Fuentarrabia, Spain, tourism stimulates agricultural production and the town produces domestic meat, vegetables, and fruit for the tourists. However, the Canary Islands, which should produce much of the necessary foods itself (and actually exports bananas and tomatoes), still imports a large part of the tourist's food needs from Europe. In Tunisia, most agricultural and horticultural products for the tourists are supplied locally, but agricultural productivity seems to be declining. Farmers there are drawn into better paying tourism jobs and lesser-skilled migrant workers from other regions replace them. In Senegal, the profits from village guest houses were invested to improve food production. This gave employment to youths who might otherwise have migrated to towns and, at the same time, local food supplies increased due to the financial benefits of tourism.

The manufacturing of household goods also benefits the host economy though generally only by large-scale tourism development, as in Spain. Furthermore, the transportation facilities, such as airports and other mass transit, and the administrative and banking facilities, which are needed in a tourist destination, provide employment for people of all skill levels.

Tourism and the Balance of Payments

The main objective of developing countries in promoting the tourism industry is the desire to earn foreign exchange. However, a wide range of goods and services, such as aircraft, buses, construction materials, hotel equipment, and food often must be imported to support the tourist industry. For example, many hotels built in developing countries have to import items such as bathroom fixtures and elevators to meet the expectations and needs of the international tourist. Menus in restaurants around the world feature a variety of international dishes, complemented by wines from various regions of the world. These items must be imported, sometimes from far away. Other examples are air fares paid to other countries airlines, the salaries of nationals working in tourist offices abroad, and advertising placed in foreign media.

Increased expenditures by visitors generate a greater demand for services and goods, which provide employment and purchasing power for the local population. Local residents, in turn, often seek to reproduce the consumer pattern of the visitor. This phenomenon, referred to as the *demonstration* or *imitation effect,* in turn adds to the demand for imports, thus causing inflationary effects for local residents.

Efforts to increase receipts from tourism often are offset by an outflow of money used to purchase the imports necessary to develop a successful tourism industry. Among these are:

Imported Goods and Services Consumed by Visitors.   Tourism development generally involves imports of goods and services consumed by tourists as well as raw materials and capital goods directly or indirectly required as a result of the development of the tourism sector. Visitors consume food, drinks, and other imported goods because domestic production is insufficient, either in quantity or in quality. For example, visitors may prefer well-known brands to the local product or, in some cases, there is no domestic output of a particular item.

Other goods the visitors consume, although produced domestically, involve the import of raw materials. Thus, local food may be grown with the aid of imported fertilizer; the bus or rental car used for an excursion was built overseas and uses fuel made from imported crude oil; the electricity used in hotels and other tourist establishments may be generated with imported coal or other fuel, and so on. The import content of international tourism often is greater in the developing countries than in the developed countries; it is very high in some developing countries (often island nations).

Payments Due Abroad.   Payments have to be made by host countries for management fees to foreign organizations. Profits have to be allowed out of the country to foreign investors, including foreign owners of apartments that are rented to visitors. Salaries paid to expatriate staff of hotels and airlines will "leak out" of the domestic economy, as will fees paid to foreign artists and entertainers.

Promotional Expenses.   Governments of destination countries will often spend large amounts promoting the country's image abroad. They use public information media and distribute trade literature and other publicity material to travel agents and other enterprises in the country of potential visitors. Consequently, most of their budget is spent abroad.

Imports of Capital Goods.   These include direct imports of equipment, machinery, vehicles, furniture, and building materials.

Imports Resulting from Increased Consumption by Residents.   As residents receive increased benefits from a growing tourism industry, they, too, may demand imported consumer goods.

Government Subsidies.   More direct costs of tourism development are the subsidies often provided through government programs. Substantial investment is often needed for development of infrastructure, including roads, airports, hotels, and marketing and promotion activities. Financial incentives are often also given to tourism developers, in many cases in the form of easy credit, tax holidays and exemptions, free-enterprise zones, loan guarantees, repatriation of capital and profits, and currency convertibility. These subsidies are particularly vexatious when they pass from relatively low-income residents to relatively high-income tourists without an appropriate return on investment to the local area. Unless tied to local objective, such subsidies can be a highly regressive form of taxation.

Hotels and the Balance of Payments

There is wide variation in the proportion of hotel revenue retained within the host country and that revenue which is lost in the form of payments for imported materials or to expatriate staff. The division depends on the location of ownership and the country's self-sufficiency in providing trained hotel staff, maintenance equipment, and food supplies. In one developing country, a mass tourist destination, approximately four-fifths of the revenue of a hotel owned within the country is retained in the economy. For a hotel in the same country owned by a foreign investor, the proportion retained is only three-fifths. Table 5.1. demonstrates the difference in economic impact related to hotel construction between destinations with will developed local supply industries versus those with less developed supply industries.

Utah Travel Council

TABLE 5–1   Hotel-Related Expenditures

AREAS OF EXPENSE/ WHERE INCURRED	WELL-DEVELOPED LOCAL SUPPLY INDUSTRIES (PERCENTAGES)	LESS-DEVELOPED LOCAL SUPPLY INDUSTRIES (PERCENTAGES)
Construction and capital equipment		
Incurred locally	50%	20%
Incurred abroad (imports)	50	80
Furniture and furnishings		
Incurred locally	90	50
Incurred abroad (imports)	10	50
Hotel operating equipment		
Incurred locally	80	30
Incurred abroad (imports)	20	70

OTHER RELEVANT ECONOMIC ISSUES

An economic by-product of tourism development is the rapid rise in land prices. Not only the price of land is at issue, but also the nationality of those who acquire it. Once tourism develops, the price of commercial land tends to increase to international levels. As a result, local buyers are priced out of the market. These trends have been found to be especially detrimental to traditional economic sectors such as agriculture which cannot persist under the steeply rising real estate tax burden. The transfer of land ownership to nonnationals is a matter of great concern to many countries, because it can severely hinder future development options.

Mexico is a good example of the impact of tourism on the economy. As tourism has developed in Mexico, a concern about foreign ownership of land has led to legislation designed to ensure that development does not lead to foreign control of parts of Mexico. Tourism's contribution to the balance of payments is considerable, since Mexico is a prime tourist destination. The 1960 foreign exchange earnings from tourism represented 11 percent of total goods and services exported by Mexico. By 1973, tourism reached a high of almost 15 percent of total exports. However, since 1973, this contribution has declined as the share of oil revenue increased sharply. In the recent past, tourism revenues have recouped about half of the deficit in Mexico's balance of payments.

Two aspects of foreign scheduled airline operations, servicing and expatriate staff, result in a drain on the economy of the country in which they operate. Few developing countries have facilities to serve foreign airlines, so potential earnings are lost. On average, a staff of five employees is used by scheduled airlines in major overseas stations. The host country receives between 7 and 10 percent of the airline's revenue for a charter flight operated by a charter airline not of the destination country.

Some host countries require that guides be native to the area. Tour operators may prefer local guides, where they have a choice, or they may prefer guides who share a background similar to that of the groups to be served, who have fluency in the language and a knowledge of the customs. The choice of local or foreign guides is another factor that influences the balance of payments. Many countries have introduced training programs to familiarize local guides with the characteristics and requirements of foreign tourists and to teach necessary languages.

Developing countries are concerned about excessive levels of foreign participation in their local tourist industry. They recognize that foreign investment is essential to their tourism development, but feel that the extent of foreign control should be kept within reasonable boundaries.

THE TOURISM MULTIPLIER

The balance of payments for tourism and travel reflects a figure which is simply a total of all tourist expenditures. Money spent by tourists on goods and services will be spent over and over again in the local community, thereby producing employment and income. One of the important effects of tourism is the degree to which money spent by visitors remains in the destination region to be recycled through the local economy. This concept is known as the *multiplier effect*. Tourism provides income for employees of hotels, restaurants, transportation firms, places of entertainment, and, to a lesser degree, most of the nearby commercial businesses. These businesses, in turn, buy products from local suppliers. For example, food bought in a restaurant had to be purchased from a local wholesaler whose need, in turn, was satisfied by the agricultural and transportation sector. Part of the money spent by tourists in hotels, restaurants, and attractions goes to wages for employees, who, in turn, pay rent and buy food. The total of all income is far greater than the sum initially spent by the tourists. This multiplication can be expressed quantitatively and will indicate how much total income will increase as a result of tourist expenditures. The tourism multiplier varies from region to region, and by segment of the industry within a region.

In general, the higher the multiplier, the more money stays and is circulated within the local economy. The economic benefit of tourism is large when the multiplier is high, indicating that much of the original tourist expenditure goes to salaries and wages of local residents and to pay for locally produced goods and services. This is particularly true in countries in which the tourism industry can be supported by locally produced products. Examples include Pakistan, Tibet, and most other countries in the Far East. A low multiplier indicates that less money is spent in the local economy. It often leaks away from local economies.

Leakages in regional economies result from two main problems. First, rural economies are chronically underdeveloped, requiring importation of many goods and services. Payments for these goods and services flow directly out of the local economy. Second businesses are sometimes owned by individuals or companies that are located outside the region and profits from these businesses are not retained in the local economies. Because of chronic leakages in rural, tourism-based economies, the economic benefit of tourism to local residents may sometimes be more apparent than real. That is, relatively large tourist expenditures may have relatively small effects on local residents. A classic example of an area with a relatively low multiplier is the Caribbean. Many goods demanded by the mass tourist need to be imported from the mainland, leaving relatively little benefit to local economies. Exacerbating this situation is the practice of tourists prepaying their entire vacation before they arrive in the host country. The few expenses that remain are often paid for with a credit card, and the transaction is electronically "settled" with little cash ever circulating in the economy of the destination.

As the importance of tourism receipts has increased rapidly in recent years, so have the efforts of many countries to control the outflow of foreign exchange. The local economy will lose money to management fees paid to foreign consultants; income earned by foreign investors, including owners of hotels; salaries to foreign entertainers; commissions to travel agents and tour operators; and expenses related to the promotion of the country's image abroad.

Foreign exchange receipts from tourism are further reduced by the cost of importing goods and services used by visitors. And yet, imports, it seems, are essential to the development of a successful tourism industry. Considerable care needs to be exercised in the use and interpretation of economic multipliers in tourism. The size of the multiplier varies according to the methods used, the scale of the economy, the structure of the economy, seasonality, and the volume of imports used by tourism.

ROLE OF TOUR COMPANIES

The international tourist market is controlled by "intermediary" companies, many of them transnational in character, which have expanded to include interest in all major sectors of the industry. Tour operators consider four major aspects when evaluating a destination: first and foremost, potential demand; second, the availability of suitable accommodations at reasonable rates; third, the presence of good tourist support services; and finally, the attitude of a prospective host government toward mass tourism. Unfortunately, few tour operators conduct research into customer attitudes, behavior, and motivations. They rely largely on in-flight passenger surveys and reports from their guides and local agents. Even more unfortunately, few tour operators consider, in any detail, the social impact of their clients on the country or the people of the country they are visiting. Yet, that impact can be devastating, culturally as well as economically. Tourist development should be a more important aspect of tourism development.

ROLE OF GOVERNMENT

As we have seen, the attitudes toward tourism of developing (receiving) countries differ from those in the developed (generating) countries. To add to the problems these differences create, most receiving countries do not have an established tourism development objective. They are not sure of the type of tourism they wish to attract. This results in a mixture of tourist facilities constructed on an unplanned basis, and frequently recognized only afterward as ill-suited to the country or area. In addition, many countries lack experienced personnel who can assume responsibility for the stimulation and coordination of tourism development.

Despite these shortcomings, governments enter into contracts and agreements with foreign investors and tour operators for the development they urgently require. The results are sometimes damaging to their countries.

It is important for developing countries to establish objectives in relation to the desired level and type of tourism. These objectives should describe the importance of tourism within the national development plan and should specify the government's role in tourism development. A tourism development plan aimed at reducing imports of tourism-related items, to minimize loss of tourism revenue, should be prepared.

It is important that a tourist organization be established, preferably at the national level, and staffed with qualified personnel. This department should be responsible for the full range of government involvement in the nation's

Photo by H. vd Leeden

tourism development, including both economic and social aspects, in much the same way as other departments are responsible for education, trade, or agriculture.

EFFECTS OF SATURATION

The benefits of tourism to a country or state can be relatively easily quantified in terms of tourist expenditures. The regional or local benefits are less easily quantified. Local regions may reach saturation levels, at which time the costs and damages outweigh the benefits of tourism. There is a limit to the number of people that can visit a destination at any time. This limit can be physical, as in a restaurant, or practical, where visitors beyond a certain number simply cannot see or enjoy what is going on.

It may be possible to postpone reaching a saturation point. More hotels can be built, or museums can stay open through the evening. But even then, as long as interest in a destination remains high, a saturation level may eventually be reached. This can create a number of problems.

Land

A first concern arises if the use of land to accommodate tourists denies the use of that land for other, often more important, purposes, such as housing, schools, or open space. This problem varies in intensity from area to area. It is most acute in large cities where hotel construction is seen as economically more advantageous than the construction of new schools, better offices, or more housing units. Conflicts may also exist between the needs of cattle or wildlife, or, as in Africa, the needs of local tribes in less-populated areas.

Employment

A second effect of high saturation levels is on employment. If a town or region becomes too dependent on the tourist industry, its employment structure may be affected adversely. An expansion in hotel construction will increase the number of hotel workers as well as employees in restaurants, nightclubs, and tourist shops. These job requirements are often poorly anticipated by tourism planners. Such jobs require unskilled workers, are seasonal, and pay a minimum wage with few opportunities for advancement.

The resulting side effects may create problems. If the tourism industry is seasonal, labor may be imported from other parts of the country or from overseas. For example, a new 150-room hotel in the Caribbean needed a staff of 225 to operate it. Only 70 were available locally, so nearly three-fourths of the staff had to be imported. They then had to be housed, adding to the demand for housing. Furthermore, staff employed in hotels, restaurants, nightclubs, and other tourist attractions often finish work at a time when public transportation is unavailable. Therefore, many of these employees have to find housing in the center of the city, where there is nearly always a shortage of low-priced housing.

Transportation

A third effect of saturation is the pressure it creates on transportation and the general infrastructure of the area (such as water supply, sewer, taxi services, police service, and air terminals). These problems occur mainly in older tourist cities. Advance planning often keeps these problems from occurring in newer tourist destinations. Traditionally, forecasts were based on the current residential population and its expected increase. The needs of visitors were often ignored. As a result, a survey of the recreational needs of a city often excluded the recreational needs of visitors to that city.

To prevent problems, a generally desirable target is one tourist for every fifty residents for large cities and a maximum of three tourists for fifty residents in smaller towns. Traffic congestion is often the first saturation point to be reached. The police, for example, must devote extra forces to popular sites during the peak season. The problem is aggravated when tourists use facilities more than local residents do. They travel more, shop more, eat out more, produce more waste, and even take more showers.

Negative Effects on Host Population

A fourth effect of saturation is that local residents lose their good will toward tourists. A high-density living situation causes friction. More people means more sharing, and local residents will have to compete with visitors to obtain regular services such as a trip to the theater, a taxi ride, or a place to spread a blanket on the beach.

Beyond this is the negative effect of tourists' often higher standard of living on host populations in developing countries. Seeing such differences may intensify social and political problems in the host country. Tourism often attracts businesses that are perceived as undesirable by local residents, such as casinos, strip shows, and drug traffic. Hotels, especially in Europe, are often located near the entrance to a railroad station, subway station, or bus terminal, not too far from downtown and with a variety of shops and restaurants in the vicinity. Unfortunately, these are the same areas that attract local residents. Another objection to tourist hotels is the fact that they generate a considerable flow of traffic at times of day and night not convenient for those living nearby. It is important that tourists' needs are taken into consideration in general city planning. If this is not done, and a city or region is willing to accept tourists in unlimited numbers, there will be conflict. We must, however, also be fair to the tourist. If it were not for them, residents would be deprived of a wide range of services or would have to pay much more for them. Many cities could not afford their museums or zoos if it were not for the donations made by people from out of town.

IMPORTANCE OF GOVERNMENT PLANNING _____

These four areas, in which high saturation levels may be exceeded, need to be evaluated regularly by local and regional authorities. National or state tourism policies should be such that the flow of tourists to each region is optimal, neither too high nor too low. Beyond a certain level, further increases are counterproductive at the regional level.

A second solution is to establish a maximum number of tourists compatible with an area. That number can then be converted into a corresponding number of accommodation units. This management concept of "carrying capacity" provides a means by which the host society can establish thresholds to limit the numbers of tourists visiting attractions.

A third solution may enable a more efficient use of scarce resources. The notion of multiple use is a strategy that recognizes that a limited supply of recreational resources often can be used for several purposes. It is possible, for example, for some forests to be used for logging as well as for tourism, and for some lakes to be used for commercial fishing as well as for water recreation.

A fourth solution is for local governments to establish taxes on lodging facilities that would increase the price of accommodations and help balance demand with supply. More importantly, these revenues can also be used to improve the services provided by the city to tourists.

It is important that local government officials (both elected and appointed) understand the benefits and costs of tourism. They also need to understand how tourism operates in order to assist properly in the planning and management of its development. Because tourism encompasses many different aspects, local laws may have to be altered or enacted to promote development, while at the same time preserving those things that the community holds dear. A successful tourism economy depends upon a high level of cooperation between the private and public sectors. Local governments are responsible for the basic infrastructure without which tourism cannot operate. It must be concerned with transportation of visitors, public parks, educational programs, litter control, police and fire protection, medical concerns, and a multitude of other support services, all of which will be affected to some degree by increased number of visitors. More than with any other economic development decision, a commitment to tourism development requires a most careful analysis of community goals, priorities, resources, and capabilities by local leaders.

TOURISM ACTIVITY AND ECONOMIC DEVELOPMENT

A final issue regarding the general economic advantages and disadvantages of tourism concerns its relative stability and long-term prospects. There is considerable debate over this issue. Some observers note that tourism is a relatively "fragile" industry and, thus, may be a risky investment. Discretionary travel is, by definition, a luxury item and may be greatly affected by global economic cycles that are well beyond the control of local regions. Local tourism may also be greatly affected by unforeseen national and international events such as political turmoil and currency fluctuations. Outside ownership of tourist development enterprises and services such as hotels, airlines, and travel wholesalers and retailers may also reduce local control. Moreover, tourists' tastes are sometimes seen as "fickle," leaving selected areas and types of developments quickly out of fashion and on the decline.

Tourism, some point out, is too dependent on external demand factors. The chief social, economic, and technological determinants of tourism demand for developing countries are found in the developed countries where most travelers originate. They include factors such as high incomes, increased leisure, good education, new transportation routes, and cheaper forms of transportation. The risk of dependence on external demand is due in the first instance to the fact that international tourism expenditure is generated in a small number of generating or developed countries, thus making tourism development highly dependent on the continued prosperity of these developed countries. Second, in the international tourism market, powerful brokers (airlines, tour operators, and so forth) are active on the demand side, while on the production side (supply) there is dispersion, fragmentation, and a generally lower intensity of organization.

Other observers argue that tourism is a flexible and stable industry with good long-term growth prospects. Tourism is adaptable in that new markets

can be exploited as an alternative to markets lost. In addition, empirical data indicate that tourism growth has been steady over the past three decades, particularly when compared to other industries. Finally, nearly all causative factors including income, leisure time, and mobility are continuing to rise, at least in the major tourist-generating regions of the world, making the long-term prospects of tourism development favorable.

ALTERNATIVE TOURISM DEVELOPMENT

In light of several concerns and problems associated with large-scale tourism development projects, several observers now propose smaller-scale developments.

While large scale tourism can benefit from the higher economic efficiency with regard to marketing, promotion, and a vertical integration of tourist services, it is also important to address the issue of who reaps the economic benefits of tourism and to whom the costs accrue. Smaller-scale tourism development tends to benefit local residents more directly than large-scale tourism development. Analysis of the economic effects of tourism must go beyond total economic impact and address the issue of how economic impact is distributed within and outside the local region. This is particularly true in regard to geographic distribution of benefits, jobs per unit of investment, linkages with other sectors of the local economy, and promotion of local entrepreneurship.

CONCLUSION

For many countries and regions that attract tourists in large numbers, tourism can play an important role in economic growth. Tourism can generate employment and prosperity. Tourism can have important economic benefits for local areas, including income and employment opportunities for residents and tax revenue to local governments. It can be a major source of income for regions that have few natural resources other than a comfortable climate and attractive scenery. It exploits resources that would not be used otherwise (in particular, unskilled labor in developing countries). Tourism is also a major source of income for people who provide transportation, accommodations, entertainment, and other support services and goods. However, employment opportunities created through tourism are often characterized by relatively low pay and a seasonal nature. On the positive side, for the host population, tourism often provides services that the community would not be able to otherwise support.

The primary economic benefits of tourism are generally regarded as: a contribution to foreign exchange earnings and the balance of payments, the generation of employment and of income, the improvement of economic structure, and the encouragement of entrepreneurial activity.

The economic costs of international tourism are considered to include: increased inflation and land values, increased pressure to import, seasonability of production, problems connected with overdependence on one product, unfavorable impact on the balance of payments, heavy infrastructure costs, the effect on growth of having much of the labor force employed in a service industry with poor productivity prospects, and possible impacts on resources and environment.

In summary, tourism results in a complex series of economic, environmental, and social impacts in host societies. Assessing these costs and benefits in many countries is further complicated by difficulties in measurement and lack of local control over the industry. Also, the income multiplier effect of tourism is often relatively low due to leakages in the local and regional economy.

Unless managed professionally, the impact of large numbers of tourists from different cultures and with differing expectations on an established society can cause social and political tensions. Such tensions, in some cases, can negate the economic benefits that tourism can provide.

REVIEW QUESTIONS

1. Identify five positive contributions made by the tourism activity in your community.

2. It is said that the economic benefit of tourism goes well beyond the economic gain of the first recipient. Explain.

3. What is "a travel deficit"?

4. Describe the unique contribution the tourism industry makes as a generator of employment.

5. Tourism is an export industry. What is the item we are exporting?

6. What is the balance of payments?

7. Why should developing countries encourage their hotels to use locally produced building materials, to decorate the hotel with items native to the region, and to serve regional dishes in their restaurants?

8. Identify three job categories that result from tourism development?

9. What are some of the signals that a region is reaching saturation level?

10. List ten positive contributions tourism can make to an area. Contrast this with ten possible negative consequences of tourism development.

Economic Impact Studies: Relating the Positive and Negative Impacts to Tourism Development

William R. Fleming
Economist
U.S. Travel Data
Center

Lorin Toepper
Director
Recreation, Tourism, Travel Institute
Clemson University, South Carolina

In 1988, the U.S. Department of Commerce created a Task Force to examine the issues of accountability and evaluation in travel and tourism research. Since its inception, much of the Task Force's efforts have focused upon the use and abuse of research methods primarily used to evalu-ate the effectiveness of marketing programs conducted by state and local tourism offices as well as private businesses. Often included in such evalu-ation efforts are attempts at estimating the primary economic impact resulting from promotional campaigns. These impacts, estimated in a variety of ways, are then used by the organizations to better allocate scarce promotional dollars among programs which will yield the highest net returns or simply to justify the level of funding received or requested (Burke and Gitelson, 1990).

It should be clear that while recognizing the usefulness of estimating economic impacts through marketing evaluation programs such as conversion studies, the estimates are frequently incomplete. The estimates obtained through conversion studies represent only partial economic impacts generated by inquirers visiting a destination community. Aggregating the estimates from the responses obtained through conversion studies alone may lead to inaccurate total estimates because they are not representative of the entire current or potential visitor population. In addition, some of the studies claim credit for visitor spending which may have occurred without any promotional effort. Lastly, economic impact results obtained through marketing evaluation programs usually only address some of the positive economic impacts to a given destination. Little, if any, effort is made through conversion studies to determine any of the negative economic impacts which often result. Measuring items such as these is usually considered beyond the scope of either conversion or advertising tracking studies. Many residents, faced with increased visitation induced by the successful promotional efforts, are confronted by primarily negative impacts and may have little direct link to the positive impacts touted by tourism development officials. These residents represent a sometimes vocal and often legislatively influential group who seek their versions of "appropriate" tourism development strategies. Therefore, those organizations held accountable for their tourism budgets must often prepare detailed economic impact studies that seek to measure both benefits and costs of tourism efforts, in addition to the more popular marketing evaluation studies.

This article was originally published in the *Journal of Travel Research*, Vol. 29, No. 1 (Summer 1990), 35–41. *The Journal of Travel Research* is published by the Business Research Division at the University of Colorado at Boulder.

This article will provide a brief overview of the growing need for conducting economic impact studies, the general uses of such studies, and some of the basic approaches to measuring positive economic impacts. In addition, this article will present a few illustrations of how negative economic impacts might be measured. It is hoped that this article will serve as a forum for continued in-depth discussion of differing techniques and concerns. Future articles examining each of the major points in much greater detail would certainly seem to be warranted if significant advances in travel and tourism economic impact studies, with respect to accountability and evaluation, are to accrue.

THE NEED FOR ECONOMIC IMPACT STUDIES

While tourism has long been an important part of our lifestyle, only recently has it received increased attention for its role in determining economic importance. Recognition of the potential economic benefits of increased travel (for example, jobs, wages, and tax revenues) has led many nations, states, and local communities to intensify their tourism development efforts. In some cases, this increased tourism development effort has coincided with regional economic slumps brought about by shifts in the underlying economic base. The Midwest, for example, witnessed a decline in its primary industrial base of agriculture and manufacturing during the late 1970s and well into the 1980s. For many of the communities located within the region, tourism was eagerly viewed as an economic savior and still is today. The New England region faces what some economists consider a "mild" recession. This regional recession, along with other sociopolitical factors, has led to relatively large budget deficits in some states. Tourism, as a viable economic alternative to traditional industries (for example, manufacturing, agriculture, and so on) is receiving increased attention as a result.

The positive economic impacts of tourism development have resulted in increased budgets for many of the organizations charged with the task of luring visitors to its state. According to the *Survey of State Travel Offices* (U.S. Travel Data Center, 1989), proposed budgets for fiscal year 1989–90 for the fifty states will total almost $341 million. This figure represents a 6 percent growth from the nearly $321 million budgeted for fiscal year 1988–89 and over a 60 percent increase from fiscal year 1985–86. A very large percentage of these budgets is allocated by the state travel and tourism agencies for primarily promotional purposes.

As these tourism promotional budgets (which are funded predominantly from state and local tax bases) grow, they gain increasing exposure and scrutiny among legislators and their constituencies. With mounting state budget deficits, relatively scarce tax dollars are needed to fund a wide array of government financed programs. Tourism budgets can, therefore, be expected to face greater accountability pressure. In order to justify their existing budgets, not to mention any desired increase, tourism officials are being asked with more frequency to show the benefits and costs of their promotional efforts as well as how these benefits and costs accrue to the state or local community. In addition, tourism promoters are being asked to relate changes in tourism budgets to changes in benefits. According to the U.S. Travel Data Center (1989), twenty-nine states have increased the portion of their total budget which is allocated to advertising in 1990. Subsequently, many of these states will be called upon to justify the new budget levels.

Within the private sector, a softening economy usually leads to reductions in promotional budgets and a decrease in the total demand for advertising space. (Recently, this has been the case in a variety of media situations. The price of advertising space in many mediums has been temporarily reduced). Any reduction in private sector promotional budgets motivates managers to maximize the return for their investment as well as substantiate it. Even in times of positive economic growth, the private sector traditionally holds its managers accountable for how they spend their budgets and for the result it generates.

SOME ISSUES RELATED TO ECONOMIC IMPACT STUDY CREDIBILITY

Recognizing that economic impact studies are becoming very popular venues for illustrating the benefits of travel and tourism naturally leads to concerns with respect to the credibility of such studies. Economic impact studies vary greatly in the methodological approaches utilized as well as in the level of information yielded. Unfortunately, this variability has led to suspicion of the information obtained through economic impact estimation studies and has undermined much of their credibility. This undermining of credibility is due to a number of factors. For example, all too frequently, only the positive economic impacts associated with tourism and its activities are studied and released. The tourism industry has actively publicized the benefits to be gained through tourism development, while residents have grown more concerned and vocal about the negative economic impacts which are brought on, albeit in part, by tourism.

Often, the accuracy of the information obtained through economic impact studies is a function of the budget under which the study is taken. As tax generated funds for tourism marketing and development become even more scarce, many tourism organizations are pressured by industry members to allocate the majority of their limited funds directly upon promotional efforts. Under such a scenario, any amount "leftover" may then be allocated to research efforts such as evaluating the effectiveness of the promotional programs or measuring total economic impacts. While some state agencies and community-level agencies are required to conduct detailed economic impact studies, many are not. Given that detailed economic impact studies cost thousands of dollars, many agencies simply do not conduct them. Or, those that attempt to determine some level of economic impact often settle for a suboptimal level of precision.

Accurately defining what is to be measured within the economic impact study is another factor that influences the results. There is considerable debate over what exactly a "tourist" is. While the issue may seem purely semantical, to the researcher it is not. Definitions of a "tourist" that impose minimal distances traveled or having spent at least one night away from home, and so forth, will lead to entirely different impact estimates than if a "tourist" is loosely defined as "anyone visiting Community A for any reason, for any length of time."

A related issue is whether the economic impact results for one community can be compared with results obtained through economic impact studies from other similar communities. This latter issue is receiving increased attention as many regions desire to monitor their tourism industry's relative performance with that of a similar region. While some economists reject the idea of comparing one region's economic performance to another

region's (that is, "apples and oranges"), others are advocating the formulation of industry-wide standards with respect to definitions and approaches as they relate to measuring and comparing economic impacts across regions.

Lastly, the misuse of information obtained through economic impact studies is of great concern. Applying community-specific multipliers haphazardly from one community to another often yields greatly exaggerated total economic benefits. Incorrect interpretations of the meaning of a multiplier and the underlying assumptions about the time frame within which the multiplying rounds will occur also leads to exaggerated economic impacts. Excessive "rounding" of impact figures has occurred as those held accountable become somewhat overzealous in their attempts to provide statistical evidence of their success. Unfortunately, many tourism officials have been guilty, knowingly or not, of misrepresenting economic impact results through these and other methods.

USES OF ECONOMIC IMPACT STUDIES

Economic impact studies are performed for a variety of reasons and uses. Directors of state travel offices, area and regional travel organizations, and city/county visitor and convention bureaus have traditionally used economic impact studies to assess impact in the form of expenditures, payroll income, jobs, and taxes. These studies have been used to educate legislators, other economic development officials, and the general public about tourism benefits. It should be obvious then that it is very important to have accurate and reliable estimates of economic impacts which have the confidence of its users.

Economic impact studies are also important policy and planning tools which aid both public and private travel promoters in setting goals and objectives for their programs. The effectiveness of promotional programs can be assessed and it can be determined where to focus one's promotional efforts. If standardized, promotional programs can be compared to programs within a state or in other regions. Trends can be tracked and changes in the industries related to travel and tourism can be monitored. Changes in consumer tastes and preference patterns can also be identified by monitoring spending and travel patterns over time.

Information derived from economic impact studies helps travel and tourism developers in determining the feasibility of and site selection for transportation, accommodation, amusement, and recreation facilities. These studies can also be used to measure the costs and benefits of travel and tourism activities. For example, fiscal costs in the form of additional public infrastructure and personnel, and social costs such as congestion and environmental impacts are weighted against the benefits of jobs and tax revenue. These studies may also be used for litigation purposes or where federal and state environmental impact statements are required.

Other uses of economic impact studies have been explored less than the traditional uses of measuring the direct impacts. These studies analyze the total impacts including direct, indirect, and induced impacts of traveler spending on the economy of a state, region, or other economic area. For the most part, these studies have been limited to analyzing the "multiplier" or the "ripple" effect of traveler spending within all economy. For example, for each dollar of tourist expenditures received by one industrial sector, the total requirements (for example, direct, indirect, and induced) from each of the community's industrial sectors can be determined. However, more in-depth analyses can be performed that tell us about the industrial linkages within an economy and how different types of industrial activities effect an economy. An increase or decrease in one industrial sector's activity can then be traced throughout many rounds of spending within a community. In addition to learning about the industrial linkages within an economy, these studies can illustrate how self-sufficient an economy is, where gaps in the structure of an economy exist, and where spending on different activities will have the most or least leakages from one economy to others.

Another growing use of economic impact studies is forecasting and econometric simulation of travel impacts. Forecasting models allow us to predict the direction of travel impacts given past trends and events, together with predictions of social and economic forces which shape trends within travel-related industries. Moreover, some very sophisticated approaches help us understand the determinants of travel behavior patterns and enable us to measure and interpret the causal variables which influence travel behavior. Understanding these social and economic forces is highly useful for program planning, marketing strategies, and policy analysis.

APPROACHES TO MEASURING ECONOMIC IMPACTS

Traditionally, economic impact studies have focused upon establishing categories that assist researchers in the measurement of the total economic impact. These categories typically represent the level at which the impact is believed to occur (for example, direct, indirect, and induced) as well as whether the impacts are perceived to be positive or negative. Direct positive impacts, then, are those that occur as a direct consequence of travel and tourism activity within an area (for example, employment). Indirect positive impacts occur as the recipients of those direct impacts spend part of their receipts upon goods and services required to supply travel-related industries. Induced impacts include the consumption spending of those receiving wages and salaries from tourism-related employment.

Direct and indirect negative economic impacts sometimes can be attributed to tourism development. For years, many within the tourism industry have drawn the public's attention only to the positive economic impacts for which tourism claims responsibility. Recently, increased attention has been focused on acknowledging and addressing the negative economic impacts which often accompany travel and tourism. These include inflation, congestion, environmental degradation, and so on. The growing emphasis upon many of the costs associated with tourism development may lead to citizen-backed imposition of limitations to growth or simply no growth in certain destination areas. The citizens of such destinations may then be deciding which type of tourism retail shops, restaurants, and lodging facilities, they will or will not allow. In response, the travel and tourism industry can no longer provide a one-sided perspective of the positive impacts while paying lip-service (at best) to only a handful of direct negative economic impacts. The industry's myopic outlook might lead to increased regulation and decreased profits. Therefore, detailed positive and negative costs must be studied if the tourism industry is to be perceived in a favorable manner by its various publics and thereby increase its long-term profits.

It should be obvious that while some view the need to build a public medical facility adjacent to a ski resort a negative economic impact, the same facility may be considered a positive economic impact by others. This example highlights the complexity of the issues which need to be addressed within the context of economic impact studies. The next section covers some of the critical aspects of measuring the positive and negative economic impacts.

Measurement of Direct Positive Economic Impacts

Direct positive economic impacts of travel include the economic benefits accrued to an economic area in the form of travel related payroll income, jobs, and taxes that result from traveler spending. The approaches for estimating these economic impacts vary, and generally differ based upon the reliance of primary data collection, the methods used to collect these data, and the manner by which data are aggregated or disaggregated to develop impact estimates.

Survey Methods
The most popular form of primary data collection is to survey travelers returning from trips or in their homes. Although there have been attempts to survey operators of travel-related businesses, this method may be less reliable because operators of many travel-related businesses cannot accurately estimate the percentage of travelers versus local residents that purchase goods and services (California Division of Tourism, 1974). Surveys generally attempt to gain information on the frequency of trips, length of stays, destinations, modes of transportation, types of accommodations, and demographic information about the traveler. Survey questions sometimes will ask travelers about their trip expenditures for different travel-related items. Surveys vary in sample design or selection method of respondents in the medium used to illicit responses.

Some sample designs for selecting respondents include haphazard, representative, quota, and probability samples. Haphazard samples are usually samples of volunteers and are not representative of the population. Results from these samples cannot be generalized beyond the sample. Representative and quota samples rely on the judgment of the researcher that the individuals included in the sample are representative of the population under study. However, experts will often disagree on the best way to select representative individuals. In probability sampling, every individual has a known probability of being selected, and this probability is attained through some operation of randomization. The advantage of probability samples is that they are designed to be statistically evaluated. Statistical inference to the population values can be computed from the sample data, and confidence intervals can be developed which show that sample estimates are within a certain range for a given level of confidence.

The medium by which the survey instrument is administered is also important for reducing nonresponses. Surveys conducted face-to-face generally have the lowest nonresponse rates. However, these intercept surveys are also the most expensive to conduct. Mail surveys tend to be the least expensive medium, but traditionally mail surveys have the highest nonresponse rates. Telephone surveys typically have low nonresponse rates, and are less expensive than face-to-face surveys. The choice of the appropriate medium depends on the population which is being sampled, the sample design, the complexity of the survey instrument, and budget constraints for conducting the survey.

Sample size is concern only to the extent that the size of the sample is adequate. Large sample sizes do not insure accurate samples. In fact, if a sample is biased, increased sample size will only increase the bias. Adequate sample size will depend upon the sampling design, the research question, and the population under study. A comprehensive treatment of survey sampling can be found in Kish (1965).

Modeling Methods
Survey results can describe travel behavior and provide demographic information about travelers, but they cannot measure the traveler generated benefits that accrue to economic areas in the form of payroll, employment, and taxes. Instead, models have been developed to estimate these economic benefits. In general, two kinds of modeling approaches are used for estimating economic benefits. One approach estimates impacts of substate regions (county/city) and aggregates these results upwards to estimate the statewide impact. The other approach estimates the statewide impacts first and then disaggregates the results down to estimate substate regions.

The aggregated method employs survey research to determine expenditure patterns of travelers staying in paid and nonpaid accommodations in the economic area under study (West Virginia University, 1981; California Office of Economic Research, 1988; Georgia Hospitality and Travel Association, 1988). These surveys ask respondents about their expenditures on different travel related items. Some surveys limit expenditure questions to the previous day to reduce the recall bias. These survey data are then used in a model which constructs trip budgets.

A model is used to develop estimates of the aggregate dollars spent by travelers for a given period by combining trip budgets, and data from surveys of accommodations' occupancy and rates, and data from a survey of the incidence of travelers visiting friends and relatives. Some of these models use payroll, employment, and tax data ratios to generate estimates of these impacts from the expenditure estimates. Others use input-output techniques which provide data on employment, personal income, and tax receipts. Analysis of these impacts can be extended to type of accommodations, season, and type of trip.

This disaggregated method is designed to use secondary data on expenditures, payroll, employment, and taxes collected by government and industry sources at the national, state, and local levels together with state specific data on trip patterns from national surveys (Frechtling, 1987). Estimates of traveler-generated expenditures are developed for each travel-related industry category at the national level and for each of the fifty states.

Business receipts of each industry sector are estimated from travel expenditures minus the appropriate sales taxes. Business receipts in an industry category are multiplied by the proportion that payroll earnings comprise of the business receipts to derive payroll income generated in the state in that industry sector. Similarly, employment is derived from the ratio of payroll income to employment for each industry sector. Tax revenue produced by the expenditures, business receipts, and payroll income is estimated directly by applying the relevant tax rates to the appropriate bases. Once state-level estimates have been derived, these are disaggregated among local areas in the state according to the proportion of that industry's activity in the local area as indicated by state and local data from government and industry sources. Analysis of impacts by type of trip, in-state and out-of-state travelers, and type of accommodations can be performed by incorporating trip data from national surveys.

Evaluating Models. Criteria for evaluating direct economic impact models have been addressed in the literature (Frechtling, 1987, p. 328). These criteria include relevance, coverage, accuracy, applicability, and efficiency. Timeliness might be added as a key issue.

Relevance refers to the ability of the approach to measure the impact of economic activities that can be attributed to travelers in the area under study. The approach should be able to distinguish the traveler related impacts on economic activities from the local resident impacts.

Coverage of the approach is judged by the types of expenditures that are measured. While there is disagreement on what expenditures should be included, it seems reasonable that spending for transportation, accommodation, food and beverages, entertainment and recreation, and incidental retail purchases should be captured in the estimates.

Accuracy includes the quality of the input data and the underlying assumptions that express the relationships of travel economic impact in the approach. Data accuracy can be judged by the source and techniques by which it was collected. Judgments about model output accuracy rely upon the acceptance that the model reflects "real world" travel relationships.

Applicability denotes an approach's ability to be consistent and comparable over time and across geographic areas. Estimates of impact for an economic area, such as a state or city, should be comparable to past and future estimates. Additionally, economic impact estimates for a state or city should be comparable to other states' and cities' economic impact estimates.

Efficiency and timeliness are more pragmatic issues than the above criteria for evaluation. Efficiency is simply the ability to produce estimates which meet the above criteria at the lowest possible cost. Timeliness is the amount of time it takes for the data to be available.

Measurement of Indirect and Induced Positive Economic Impacts

Travelers in an economic area produce secondary impacts over that of their original expenditures. Indirect impacts occur when travel related industries, such as hotels, purchase goods and services from suppliers within the economic area. These purchases generate additional output or sales. Those industries supplying the hotel purchase goods and services from their suppliers to meet demand. This chain of purchasing and selling continues in the economic region until the initial traveler purchase completely "leaks out" of the economic area through taxes, purchases or imports from outside the economic region, business savings, and payments to employees.

The other type of secondary impact is the induced effect on sales or output. This results as the employees of industries and their suppliers spend part of their earnings in the economic region. The sum of the indirect and induced effects comprises the total secondary impact of traveler spending in the economic region. The ratio of the sum of primary output generated plus secondary output to initial expenditures alone is commonly known as the multiplier.

Multipliers are often derived from industrial transaction tables such as those found in input-output models. The input-output model is an intraregional flow study that records economic interdependence within a region.

In input-output analysis, the economy is disaggregated into industries and the flow of goods and services among them is examined. It measures the input required by an industry to produce a given output. The more local inputs needed to produce a given output, the greater the economic benefits will be which accrue to the area. Conversely, the more inputs that must be imported from other regions, the more these economic benefits are reduced.

Understanding the linkages within the economic region is important for assessing the feasibility of attracting certain kinds of tourism activities. In addition, it is important to understand the gaps or nonlinkages in an economy which results in leakages. This kind of analysis aids in the planning process for attracting activities that are complimentary to a given economic area. Consider the following simple example:

City A decides to construct a convention center from its tax dollars to attract travelers. However, the labor force, some of the hotels and restaurants, a major amusement complex, and the airport with renal cars are located in nearby County B. Economic benefits will accrue to City A in the form of direct spending for convention related activities, hotels and restaurants, job creation, and taxes. County B will accrue direct benefits from the airport, rental cars, possibly the amusement park, and spillover benefits from the hotels and restaurants depending upon the quality and supply of hotels and restaurants in City A.

City A and County B will both accrue indirect benefits to the extent that suppliers of the activities are located within each economy. Although some of the jobs were created in City A, County B will enjoy the bulk of the benefits of the induced effects because the labor force for the new jobs lives in County B, and these workers will purchase most of their goods and services in County B. They will also pay property taxes in County B. Moreover, City A will accrue more direct and secondary negative effects in the form of commuter congestion, pollution, and added fiscal costs beyond the tax dollars invested in the convention center.

Clearly, it is important to be aware of how certain activities will affect the economy, and the opportunity costs foregone in favor of different options. Input-output models are useful planning tools, as are similar less sophisticated methods such as Burford/Katz, shift-and-share analyses, and location quotions. However, there are some key issues about input-output and multiplier analyses which need to be mentioned briefly.

An important issue with input-output models is how they are constructed. Some input-output models show the transactions of broad industry categories in a 39-by-39 matrix and analyses are based upon broad classifications. Others may contain almost 600 detailed industry classifications, allowing for more precise analysis of industry linkages. Of course, there is a tradeoff. The smaller model with broader classifications is less expensive to build and update, whereas the larger model is much more costly to keep current.

Another key issue is the concept of a tourism multiplier. A tourism multiplier per se does not exist. A multiplier can be derived from the direct expenditures generated by travelers on travel and tourism related industries for a specific economic area. However, a multiplier derived for a specific area cannot be applied to another area because economic areas are different and the same effects are not likely to occur.

Lastly, caution should be used in presenting multiplier estimates. For example, an output multiplier of 1.5 does not mean that for every tourism dollar spent another 50 cents is created. Instead, multiplier of 1.5 implies that in order to meet a dollar of output demand, 50 cents in business activity in the area is stimulated. However, this multiplier effect is a series of events which ripples through an economy in "rounds," and with each successive round the effects diminish due to leakages until the effect of the initial expenditure has completely leaked out. The entire process may take six, seven, or eight rounds or more depending upon the economy, and six to eight rounds may be equal to 15 or 20 years. And, the present value of the total 50 cents is different than the future value of its parts over a 15 to 20 year period.

Measurement of Direct and Indirect Negative Economic Impacts

Direct negative economic impacts associated with travel and tourism include those costs which are directly attributable to tourists being in the destination community. The most obvious direct negative impacts are the fiscal costs to the government (in the form of promotional expenses usually) and occur as a result of successful attempts at luring visitors to their destination communities. These negative economic impacts usually involve the construction and maintenance costs of providing tourism-related facilities and services such as parks, visitor information centers, marketing promotional programs, museums, police and fire protection, and the like. Somewhat less obvious are the opportunity costs of tourism development. For example, money invested by government agencies in tourism-related promotional programs could have been spent on environmental clean-up programs, or, land upon which a resort was built could have been developed for residential housing. Historically, the opportunity costs of tourism have been rarely considered. The opportunity costs should include the monetary costs of development and maintenance of the site or area, along with an accounting of benefits lost by withdrawing the resource from its present or alternative uses.

Additional negative economic impacts include social and environmental costs of tourism. Often referred to as quality-of-life costs, these negative economic impacts include the effects of congestion, destruction of coral reefs and erosion of beaches, crime and prostitution, vandalism, cultural degradation, pollution of lakes, and so on. While some research has focused on each of these issues, translating the social and environmental costs of tourism in monetary terms is difficult and often imprecise. For example, measuring the cost of congestion at crowded beaches is often undertaken by attempting to survey those at the crowded beaches. However, many of those who enjoy beach-related activities may not be at the

beach or may have already left the beach because it is too crowded; consequently, they would not be included within the sample surveyed. The reputation of overcrowding may also influence potential visitors long after situations change. The bias that results must, therefore, be considered.

Indirect negative economic impacts are much less clear and harder to delineate. These are costs which indirectly result from tourism activities. Examples include increased dropout rates as children prefer jobs within the tourism industry to education and the increase in the number of senior citizens retiring within attractive destinations which may place an increased demand on the destination community to provide public transportation and health services. (In general, researchers have shied far away from any notion of an induced negative impact. An example might be an increase in drugs purchased and used by those employed within the tourism industry who now have increased disposable income due to tourism-related employment.)

Many studies do not attempt to measure either the direct or indirect negative impacts such as those listed because of the inherent difficulty. The approaches for estimating the costs vary considerably—especially the quality-of-life costs—and the impacts have often gone uncounted or undercounted as a result. There are five basic methods which can be used to illustrate how negative impacts might be estimated: the survey method, the expert opinion method, the economic or civil engineering method, the referenda method, and the secondary market method. A sixth method might involve some combination of the preceding methods. Each method illustrated in the following section can be used to estimate either direct or indirect negative economic impacts and therefore do not delineate between the two levels. It should be noted at the outset that, in general, each of these methods require simplifying as well as subjective assumptions on the part of the researcher.

Survey Method
The survey method involves surveying either tourists, residents, businesses, or government agencies to determine any costs incurred as a result of tourism activities within the community. Tourists might be surveyed to estimate their demand for government produced goods and services. The information can then be used to determine what portion of a program cost can be

assigned directly to tourists and what portion to residents. For example, tourists could be requested to estimate their existing demand for public transportation within a destination community. The portion of the total program cost which is directly attributable to tourists may then be calculated. Residents might be surveyed to determine their willingness to pay to avoid certain tourism-related negative impacts, such as congestion, in this case. In another instance, businesses could be surveyed to obtain cost estimates for items such as vandalism resulting directly from increased tourism (in those circumstances where it is possible to accurately determine.) Finally, a survey of government agencies could be conducted to determine what programs have been developed directly due to tourism, the costs, and what portion of those program costs can be wholly assigned to tourists. As an example, the police department might be surveyed to determine what percent of their time is spent providing assistance to out-of-state motorists.

Many of the sampling concerns discussed earlier apply equally in this method as well. Care must be taken with respect to sample designs and the criteria for evaluating samples still applies. It should also be noted that such methods certainly face potential recall bias if exit surveys are not utilized. Additional limitations include oversimplification and often highly subjective assumptions which are made within the survey context.

Expert Opinion Method

Sometimes it is necessary to obtain expert opinions about the direct negative economic impacts of tourism when primary data collection is unavailable or cost-prohibitive. Usually, impact estimates are historically based upon a similar destination's experiences and therefore may be biased. However, such experts frequently are very aware of indirect long-run impacts unknown to other types of interviewees. A destination considering entering the bidding process for site selection of an Olympic event might do well to solicit direct and indirect economic cost data from experts for similar cities facing similar constraints and opportunities.

Many simplifying and subjective assumptions are often required in these cases as well to produce useful estimates. If the expert is either pro-tourism development or anti-tourism development as a result of their individual as well as community experience, they may tend to under-

state or overstate the true economic costs incurred because of the approach taken.

Economic or Civil Engineering Method

The economic or civil engineering method is based upon obtaining cost estimates for individual items from building specifications or assumptions about facility demand and aggregating the individual component costs to arrive at reasonable estimate of total cost. For example, to determine the fiscal water and sewage costs to a community for building a hotel, the civil engineer is provided with estimated annual statistics such as occupancy rates, number of occupants per room, days of operation, and so on. Based upon this information, the engineer estimates the additional water and sewage costs of the hotel to the community. This same technique is applied to other relevant individual cost components and then aggregated accordingly.

Once again, this technique parallels the expert opinion and survey methods in that it requires many subjective assumptions and oversimplifications. This method of measuring costs is widely used when conducting cost-benefit analyses of particular projects; its underlying assumptions are often the subject of intense debate at local zoning board hearings.

Referenda Method

Another method used to gain insight into the negative costs of tourism is the referenda method. Perhaps it is only in referendums on specific negative economic cost issues that even a partial reading of the public's opinion for quality of life can be "officially" obtained. This method involves placing an important direct cost issue, such as substantially increasing the state tourism marketing program budget or introducing a bond issue to purchase waterfront property to maintain resident access, before the public in the format of a referendum. If the referendum fails or succeeds, then some insight into the willingness (or the lack thereof) to pay by the residents is reflected in that decision.

Unfortunately, referenda usually present only two dichotomous alternatives and can only be used as a partial gauge by which to measure economic costs. This method is also hampered by the absence of information and the resulting ignorance as well as complacency of the general public.

Secondary Market Method

It is sometimes useful to examine the costs to secondary markets in order to determine the negative economic impacts accompanying tourism development programs. This method works well when market values do not exist as in the case of pollution on a public lake. It is possible to examine the change in sales volume for secondary market goods (for example, bait) for the surrounding areas which might reflect the nature of the economic cost.

A limitation with this method is the difficulty in attributing any loss or gain to specifically one factor. It is also difficult to separate visitor consumption from resident consumption for many businesses which cater to both groups.

FORECASTING AND PLANNING

Forecasts attempt to predict the direction of a trend and measure the magnitude of change in the trend. Forecasting methods range from simple "gut feeling" guess work based upon the past to sophisticated and mathematical models (also based upon past trends). Numerous books have been written about the many different kinds of forecasting techniques (Johnston, 1972; Box and Jenkins, 1970; Theil 1966). A brief overview of the various qualitative and quantitative techniques can be found in Archer (1987). Unfortunately, any detailed coverage of forecasting methods is well beyond the scope of this article. However, the importance of forecasting as a tool for predicting and planning for economic impacts of travel and tourism deserves mention here. Hopefully, more exhaustive treatments of the subject will follow.

Forecasting approaches vary in quality and utility. The more sophisticated approaches are generally expensive, require more data, and are more difficult to use. However, if the approach is too simplistic for the question under study, very inaccurate forecasts will be made. For instance, we would not want to predict travel and tourism impacts solely from trends of hotel stays and personal income indicators. Conclusions drawn from this kind of approach would surely be inaccurate and probably dead wrong. We would instead use a type of time series model (depending upon data availability and precision desired) to predict travel and tourism impacts from past trends of travel and tourism impacts. If we want to learn about the forces (positive and negative) that influence the predicted change in travel and tourism impacts, we would employ a causal technique such as a multiple regression model. To understand how these forces influence travel volume and each

other, and how these forces would react to alternative scenarios, an econometric simulation model could be used. In short, the level of sophistication should be related to the type and complexity of the forecast question.

Forecasting is an essential part of the planning process for managing tourism development. Forecasts of travel volume and expenditures are needed for managing resources and controlling the inventory of tourism products. Managers cannot plan without forecasts. Some type of forecasting must be employed in order to develop goals and the objectives to attain these goals. Moreover, forecasts are needed to predict the future effects of certain policies, and to analyze the effects of alternatives.

Tourism forecasting is relatively new, but its popularity is growing rapidly. For the most part, forecasting in the travel industry has been focused on demand and traffic pattern studies which ultimately can be used to predict expenditures and other positive economic impacts. Studies on the costs of tourism have mainly been limited to the fiscal costs to a particular industry conducting the study. For example, airlines and hotel chains are very active forecasters, but forecasts of the tourism costs are concerned with their capital and labor outlays over time and not the social and fiscal costs of economic areas. Environmental and urban planners have long been engaged in forecasting the fiscal and social costs of development of economic areas. Studies forecasting the social and fiscal costs of airport expansions and resort developments are common examples. We can expect that the growth in tourism as an economic development tool will also be followed with a growth of studies about its forecasted costs.

CONCLUSIONS

Determination of economic benefits is becoming an increasingly common tool used by state and local tourism agencies to justify their existing and proposed promotional budget levels. Likewise, these agencies are being held accountable more often for their estimation of projected returns on investment from their promotional efforts. Greater public scrutiny of these budgets in light of today's scarce tax dollars as well as the mounting public concern of the economic costs of tourism will only lead toward increased use of economic impact studies in the future. The manner in which the results of the economic impact studies are obtained and presented will greatly determine the credibility of the economic impact study and assist the state and local agencies in achieving their goals.

In this article, it has been shown that there exists a variety of methodological approaches for measuring both positive and negative economic impacts of tourism. There are a number of critical issues facing each of the techniques for which a brief overview was provided. Space constraints prohibit the detailed treatment of each approach as well as the inclusion of many more approaches. Similarly, an exhaustive treatment of the issues concerning economic impact studies was not attempted (for example, setting optimal social rates of discount, distributional effects of programs, economic welfare analysis, and so on.) Any attempt at writing a brief definitive guide to economic impact studies would be foolhardy at best.

There is growing sentiment within the economic impact research area for further refinement of existing approaches as well as the development of new approaches to better capture direct and indirect economic impacts such as opportunity costs, environmental costs, and social costs. In addition, there is an attempt being made to determine the desirability of industry-accepted standards concerning the collection and reporting of economic impact estimates. And there is growing need for and use of forecasting tourism demand and its related impacts within the context of tourism planning. Addressing these and other issues presented and implied within this article will improve the usefulness of economic impact studies to the tourism industry.

REFERENCES

Archer, B., "Demand Forecasting and Estimation," in *Travel, Tourism, and Hospitality Research: A Handbook for Managers and Researchers*, ed. J. R. Brent Ritchie and C. R. Goeldner. New York: Wiley, 1987.

Box, G. E. P., and G. M. Jenkins, *Times Series Analysis.* San Francisco: Holden-Day, 1970.

Burke, J. F., and R. Gitelson, "Conversion Studies: Assumptions, Applications, Accuracy, and Abuse," *Journal of Travel Research*, 28 (Winter, 1990), 46–51.

California Division of Tourism, "Tourism Employment Study," Sacramento: California Department of Commerce, 1974.

California Office of Economic Research, "Regional Economic Impacts of California Travel." Sacramento: California Department of Commerce, 1988.

Frechtling, D., "Assessing the Impacts of Travel and Tourism—Introduction to Travel Impact Estimation," in *Travel, Tourism, and Hospitality Research: A Handbook for Managers and Researchers*, ed. J. R. Brent Ritchie and C. R. Goeldner. New York: Wiley, 1987.

Georgia Hospitality and Travel Association, "The Economic Impact of Expenditures by Tourists on Georgia's Nine Tourism Regions 1987," Atlanta, 1988.

Johnston, J., *Economic Methods.* New York: McGraw-Hill, 1972.

Kish, L., *Survey Sampling,* New York: John Wiley & Sons, 1965.

Theil, H., *Applied Economic Forecasting.* Amsterdam: North-Holland, 1966.

U.S. Travel Data Center, "Survey of State Travel Offices," Washington, D.C., 1989.

West Virginia University, "Creating Economic Growth and Jobs through Travel and Tourism." Washington, D.C.: U.S. Government Printing Office, 1981.

CHAPTER 6
The Social Impact of Tourism

PROJECT _____

Initiate correspondence with a contact in a developing country. Invite comments on the impact of tourism development in the country. Formulate specific questions in your letter to make it easier for the recipient to respond. Share the response you received with the class at the end of the course. Be creative when searching for a possible contact or address. Your local minister, rabbi, or priest might be able to pass on an address of a missionary working in that country. Your instructor might have addresses of tourism schools in other countries. Try your local newspaper editor. Your library will have a variety of resources, or write directly to the Government Tourist Office in the host country.

Some of the major issues concerning the social and cultural impact of tourism will be discussed in this chapter. Social and cultural effects of tourism have to do with the way in which tourism affects people and their communities. These effects are often less tangible than economic effects and have been more difficult to quantify. Nevertheless this aspect of tourism has been the subject of much recent research by sociologists, psychologists, and anthropologists. Most earlier studies that evaluated the success of tourism development projects were concerned primarily with their economic benefits. We are now beginning to understand that tourism has often been found to have pervasive effects on residents and host communities of tourist destination areas.

As mentioned earlier, interest in the sociology of tourism is comparatively recent. The first articles appeared in the mid-1960s, but serious recognition of tourism's impact on society and culture only dates from the early 1970s. It is now widely recognized that tourism development, like industrial development, creates social change. Realizing the impact of tourism on people and understanding its social consequences is an important aspect of tourism professionals' career training.

PROS AND CONS OF TOURISM DEVELOPMENT _____

Because tourists today come primarily from the United States, Canada, Western Europe, and, more recently, industrialized countries in Asia, tourism has introduced and spread Western social and cultural values throughout the world. Opponents of tourism argue that its impact is similar to that of mass media. Until the development of sophisticated communications technologies, which enabled the spread of mass media, different people lived in more or less closed societies with their own civilizations and value systems. Increased knowledge of other societies leads to the adoption of different values and to a growing similarity among societies. Tourism, it is argued, works in a similar, though more direct, way because of the actual physical contact. With the development of low-cost, direct air transportation, change is easily introduced into previously isolated societies.

Critics say that the arrival of large numbers of tourists increases the potential for cultural conflict. They point out that some tourists leave their morals and manners at home when on vacation abroad. They seek exotic locales, far removed from the social restrictions of home. And while their behavior may change completely when on vacation, their expectations of material comfort remain the same or increase in their "playground" destination. For example, air conditioning is required and familiar drinks demanded, and, since the tourist has paid for the tour, the host culture must now adapt to fill these needs.

Proponents of tourism disagree. In their view, tourism has a very positive impact. They believe it helps break down superficial social and cultural differences. They believe not only that individual cultures can withstand increased exposure to one another, but that such an interchange is essential for our mutual survival. Tourism can lead to increased intercultural understanding. As people travel to different parts of the world, they learn more about other cultures and may become more tolerant.

In its statement of "fundamental aim," the World Tourism Organization (WTO) views tourism as a means of contributing to "international understanding, peace, prosperity and universal respect for, and observance of, human rights and fundamental freedom for all without distinction as to race, sex, language or religion."

Cord Hansen-Sturm[1] points out that travel may be as important as telecommunications and print media in our modern information society. In his perspective, "good travel experiences become the highlights, the benchmarks of people's lives. They become the information capital of the tourist, his employer, and his country. Nations should be at least as concerned about promoting travel of their citizens abroad, as bringing foreigners to their shores." Mr. Sturm offers strong support of our ever-growing travel and tourism industry. He also issues a resounding warning to the United States, as the only major country in the world without a cabinet-level Minister of Tourism position, indicating that the U.S. has not placed the proper priority on this vital area of influence.

Proponents of tourism also point out the social benefit of tourism as it relates to the psychological rewards that flow to tourists. Tourism can be a constructive and potentially fulfilling use of leisure time. To the extent that tourism can fulfill these needs, it is a useful and productive social phenomenon.

EXPECTATIONS OF HOST AND GUEST

However, tourism has a number of potential social and cultural costs. While tourism can help recognize and promote distinctive cultures, it can also alter

---

[1] Cord Hansen-Sturm. "Info Travel: Travel as an Information Medium." Paper presented at the Fifteenth Annual TTRA Conference, 1984.

Louisiana Office of Tourism

or distort cultural patterns in the process. Most tourists who visit resorts in developing countries are vacationers who have no particular personal or religious ties with these countries. The farther away the destination country, the more important the role of travel brokers—travel agents, transport companies, and tour operators—becomes in organizing and promoting resort tourism. They "package" a series of services and offer access to tourist resources at a price that is otherwise unavailable. For these tourists, contact with the local population is often limited to employees working in the tourism industry. The packaged, standardized culture (shops, dances, sight-seeing) soon leads to a blurring of the distinguishing features of unfamiliar cultures. For many, it does not matter in which country beaches, sunshine, and friendly, tourist-minded people are found; what matters is that they are there and that the price is low. The impersonality of mass tourism is further reinforced by the nature of tourist accommodations—for example, large hotel chains built in Western style, serving primarily Western cuisine along with a few local foods to add a touch of the exotic. In addition, many tourists staying at large resorts are virtually confined to tourist centers. For these reasons, the host often stereotypes the tourist, who seems to come from a place where riches and leisure abound. This reaction is particularly common in poorer countries where the income gap between tourist and resident can be immense. A $4 drink served in a Cancun hotel represents a value equal to a day's salary for the average Mexican worker. Conversely, the tourist views the holiday as an annual occasion that he or she has been looking forward to and intends to get as much out of as possible. However, the host sees a new set of tourists every week or two who act and behave identically, and has no experience with a tourist outside of a vacation setting.

Elements of culture may be changed to appeal more directly to tourists or so they may be more readily consumed by tourists. Sacred dances, once reserved to welcome high priests, are now performed on demand for tourists. Indigenous culture is inaccurately glorified and embellished in order to increase its attractiveness to tourists.

Another cause of cultural distortions are simplified and sometimes inaccurate images created by tourism marketing and promotion. Tourists expect to find the images that attracted them to a given destination, and these destination areas may adopt such cultural elements to satisfy tourist expectations and demand.

We need to be careful not to overdramatize the role of the "mass tourist" and the "island resorts." As we will see, this is but one facet of the industry, and even here good, sensitive planning can reduce or minimize negative impact.

RESULT OF TOURISM DEVELOPMENT

Two important variables determine the likely social and cultural outcomes of tourism development: (1) the size of the country, and (2) the general level of development. Size is essentially a country's physical area, although population is an important component. The level of development is measured by gross national product (GNP) per capita, skill and education levels, degree of urbanization, and the strength or resilience of the native culture.

In small countries, or small islands, where pressure on resources is considerable because of high population density, tourist-host contacts may be widespread and intense. When such countries are also relatively underdeveloped, it is more likely that they will experience negative sociocultural effects from tourism development than larger, more developed countries. Also, negative sociocultural effects will be more intense when tourism facilities are developed rapidly and on a large scale.

The perception of tourism held by residents of host countries changes over time. Historically, tourism usually began without any formal planning and was welcomed by the citizens of the host country because of both the promise of economic benefits and their own human curiosity. In many cases, however, this enthusiasm waned as the number of tourists increased and facilities became overstretched. The local people realized that they were economically dependent on tourism and that they no longer controlled or were even consulted about their environmental destiny.

Thus, the tourist became the focus of resentment against impersonal forces over which the local population had no control. Resentment also occurred when the wide gap between the consumption patterns of the tourist and the standards of living in the host country were readily apparent. This resentment especially occurred where poverty was widespread and a relatively small proportion of the local population benefitted from tourism. Unrealistic expectations often led to frustration and occasionally violence, as was the case in Jamaica in the mid-1970s.

Findings of several studies suggest that tourism development tends to be patterned. Early stages of tourism are characterized by a few adventurous tourists who discover an unspoiled area which has not previously catered to tourists. Visitors are few, as are facilities and services, most of which are owned directly by residents. Contact between host and guest is direct, extensive, and rewarding to both. Tourism, in this stage provides a marginal but welcome source of income to some residents. Early stages of development are followed by a period of growth in both demand and supply. Tourist facilities and services remain largely in the hands of residents, although they begin to adapt to standards of quality more generally demanded by visitors. Host-guest contact remains direct, but becomes more oriented to monetary transactions. Some residents shift out of traditional occupations, earning their livelihood entirely from tourism and thereby increasing their material standard of living. If tourism development continues, it may reach a stage of maturity or institutional mass tourism. In this stage, large numbers of tourists are present, often outnumbering residents. Tourist facilities and services become institutionalized or standardized for the sake of efficiency and to meet the needs of less adventurous visitors. Because of the capital investment and technical expertise needed for this type of development, outside interest in the form of national or international corporations exercise increasing ownership and control within the area (both development and marketing). Contact between hosts and guests is conducted almost entirely on a "service-for-pay" basis. Tourism development may evolve eventually to a stage of decline where both visitors and residents become disenchanted. Crowding and overdevelopment may abase the distinctive features or values of an area that originally attracted tourists. Residents may also resent these impacts, the demands made upon them by visitors, and the feeling of loss of control over their communities. A later development stage of rejuvenation is possible, although it is usually based on contrived or artificial attractions such as gambling.

It is important to note that this pattern of development is not necessarily fixed, and that self-determination can be exercised over this cycle. Nevertheless, there is much evidence to suggest that tourism development often conforms to the classic S-shaped curve characteristic of the traditional product life-cycle.

Initially, the feelings and reactions of the host nation are often positive; tourism appears to present exciting new opportunities. At this stage, tourism exposes the host to new experiences; often increasing independence from religious and/or family environments and awakening confidence in technology. At this stage, too, the host may become aware of the advantages of leading an independent life, the importance of training and vocational skills, the need for active participation in various groups, and the need for more sophisticated information.

These positive expectations and results can be maintained and enhanced through intelligent planning, good management, and a conservative timetable. Effective strategic planning to improve the quality of the environment and to meet the needs of a variety of groups can help to improve chances that tourist destinations will not undergo a major permanent decline in tourist activity as other once-successful tourist areas have. The errors of past exploitation need not be reenacted. There is both the need and the opportunity here for the tourism professional to play a significant role.

CHANGING VALUES AND ATTITUDES _____

A number of attempts have been made to trace the sequence and the timeframe during which values change. For example, Doxey constructed an index of the level of irritation ("irridex"). He believes that irritation resulting from contact between tourist and host cannot be completely avoided and will ultimately destroy tourism unless kept under review and proper control. Doxey's[2] irridex covers four levels of reaction on the part of the host population:

- *Euphoria:* Initial phase; both visitors and investors are welcomed.
- *Apathy:* Transition to this stage varies in length, depending on the speed and amount of development. Tourists are seen as stereotypes and taken for granted.

[2]G. V. Doxey, "Recent Methodological Developments in Travel Research." Paper presented at Sixth Annual TTRA Conference, 1975.

Nebraska Department of Economic Development

- *Annoyance:* Host population begins to express doubts.
- *Antagonism:* Overt expression of irritation; all social and personal problems are attributed to the tourist.

The causes of irritation are numerous and interrelated—social, economic, cultural, and environmental—and point to the need for integrated planning of tourism. Among the causes of this irritation are: fear that hosts are being treated as second-class tourists in their own country; fear that large numbers of tourists may affect the basic rhythm of life; fear that local values and cultural traditions are being threatened; loss of access to facilities (crowded transportation, private beaches); and dislike of tourists' dress and behavior. Resentment may also be based on the extreme, sometimes seemingly bizarre behavior of tourists. Residents can grow to resent the apparently wasteful, frivolous spending patterns of tourists, particularly when there is a large gap in relative wealth between tourists and residents. Even when the gap in relative wealth is not large, tourists spend more freely when on vacation than at other times.

Other forms of tourist behavior can also be interpreted as bizarre and sometimes offensive. After all, tourists are "on vacation" and see themselves largely removed from the constraints of everyday life. The behavior of tourists may become indulgent, often outside the norms of their own society, much less the societal norms of the host community.

Resentment of tourists may also be based on more tangible issues. Tourism development can lead to significantly higher crime rates, and this affects the lives of local residents. Tourist activity can also lead to local crowding and congestion, making it difficult for residents to carry on their daily lives and sometimes restricting access of residents to local recreation resources. Overemphasis in the commercial sector on tourist-related services can reduce shopping options for local residents, leading to more limited shopping opportunities for necessities and artificially higher prices.

Finally, resentment of tourism can be based on a feeling of loss of control over the community. The issue of loss of local control has grown to extreme proportions in some areas, with tourism being termed a form of new colonialism.

Despite these theories (and others), the reasons why the host population may misinterpret and resent the tourist are not fully understood. There are places where such irritation has not occurred. Mexico's Fonatur development sites are prime examples of alternative tourism development. In Indonesia, the Balinese have accommodated tourism into their way of life and culture without the traditional problems associated with the development of tourism. The Balinese distinguish between different types of audiences—religious, local, foreign vacation—and tailor the performance to each. The speed and intensity of the development of irritation on the part of the host community is almost certainly linked to the values and cultural background of the host. The effects of tourism vary with the type of tourism development. In particular, tourism effects are related to stages of tourism development. Where tourism is a supplementary, rather than the only income source, and tourist attractions have an independent, different meaning for the host, this process is slowed. This is true in many parts of Mexico and Latin America.

Although mere numbers of tourists do not, by themselves, constitute the reason for speedy and intense resentment on the part of local residents, most researchers have found that effects of increased interface between tourists and hosts caused by large numbers do result in negative attitudes. There is a point at which irritation grows rapidly. The circumstances that bring about this situation are far from clear. However, they are complex, embracing, and include a contrast of lifestyles as well as such factors as cultural and socioeconomic disparities between tourists and hosts. The land mass of the receiving country, its own historical background, language, structure and economy, level of dependence on tourism, and saturation levels also need to be considered. Again, planning, effective management, and conservative scheduling can preserve a desirable balance, but only with enlightened policies, phasing of supply components, and intensive education and public relations programs.

THE IMITATION EFFECT

Thus far, we have discussed effects of direct contract between tourists and residents of a host country. It is claimed, however, that tourism has an indirect impact on the host, caused by the mere presence of tourists. International tourism acts as a catalyst toward the assimilation of traditional customs by Western cultures in developing societies. Tourists' values may be transferred and adopted by the host population. The local population then seeks to imitate the consumption patterns, for example, of the tourist. The change in the value system and attitudes of the host population may affect dress, accommodation demands, eating habits, and the demand for consumer goods. Ideally, the tourist should be a model worth imitating, but, unfortunately, that is not always the case. Imitation seems to occur most often in the early stages of tourism development. Young people are particularly susceptible and attempt to imitate dress, language, and habits since these seem like exciting alternatives.

Another way of explaining this cause of cultural change related to tourism is by examining the concept of *acculturation*. Acculturation is an anthropological concept describing the melding of two cultures that come in contact with each other. Typically, a process of borrowing takes place between cultures, but with the nondominant culture borrowing more extensively from the dominant culture. Since tourist-generating areas nearly always represent the dominant culture—that is, they are more "highly" developed and advanced—tourist destination areas often undergo substantive social and cultural evolution as a result of contact with tourists.

Positive Effects

It is relevant to pose the question: Are changes in values and the methods of change necessarily harmful to the local population? Many species of wildlife, for example, elephants in East Africa, may have been exterminated without tourism. Tourism has heightened local awareness of natural resources and cultural heritage in other instances as well. In many cases, host countries have overreacted to Western visitors by abandoning traditional dress, cuisine, and customs only to be reminded that it is exactly that which is unique, and that makes their country a desirable tourist destination. Once reminded, their pride is often restored.

Another area in which tourism changes values for the better is in developing countries where the economy is weak, and where, because of outside influences, the people are questioning the validity of their traditional values, rules, and structure. Under these circumstances tourism may suggest some sort of new system: the basic question about such a new system will be whether the country maintains enough of the old system long enough to avoid serious disruptions, and to what extent individuals can adapt to the new system (which may be inconsistent with or inappropriate to their national heritage).

We should remember that tourism is only one factor among many that causes change. Cultural dependence on radio, television, movies, the press, or commercial advertising, also engender imitation.

SOCIOECONOMIC IMPACT

Whether or not tourism serves to change a society's values and whether or not these changes are beneficial to the society, there can be no doubt that the socioeconomic impact of tourism often brings about profound changes in the structure of the host country's society. In developed countries, where the economy is active and well-diversified, tourism has no special socioeconomic effects. However, major changes are inherent when tourism is introduced into developing countries. The most notable change in established value patterns and behavior attributed to tourism occurs when traditional social relations are brought into the economic arena and become part of "making a living." When this happens, it can result in developed and backward regions existing side by side. Modern production techniques, with "normal" behavior in an industrial society coexist with "normal" behavior in a traditional society. This can cause major changes and stress within the socioeconomic fabric. Native cultures and traditional ways of life may be abandoned for the sake of tourism, which frequently results in dramatic generation gaps having a permanent effect on the host society.

Ola Røe, Røe Foto AS

Tourism Employment

Employment in tourism, while not the main goal of all tourism development, is one of its main achievements. We have already established its significance throughout the United States and elsewhere, but we must bear in mind that its importance will vary depending upon the relative importance of tourism to the local economy. In the larger and economically more diversified Caribbean islands, such as Jamaica and Puerto Rico, tourism provides 5 percent of total employment. In the smaller islands, the proportion reaches 50 percent. In Bermuda, direct and indirect employment from tourism accounts for nearly 75 percent of the labor force.

Employment in the tourism sector has a major social impact. In most developing countries, agriculture or fishing are the main means of livelihood. The introduction of tourism allows the local population to become wage earners and gain social status. For example, the attitudes of a farm worker who becomes a hotel worker often change completely. A fisherman can similarly undergo a dramatic change in his way of life and, consequently, his attitude. Tourism can have one of two effects on this fisherman: his material position may be improved because of a new market for his fish or, alternatively, he may use his traditional boat to "entertain" the tourist, for example, using it for fishing expeditions. The latter brings him into direct contact with tourists and often results in a change of status for him—he still fishes but is now part of the show.

In many countries and regions, the resorts become symbols of great activity with high employment, while the fringe areas receive little or no benefit. Therefore, there will be intensive migration to the resort by people looking for jobs that do not exist or for which they are not prepared, with the obvious results.

While a tourism-related job may be preferable to primitive, unpredictable agriculture, the population is most likely to remain employed in low-skill, low-paid jobs such as waiter, busboy, maid, gardener, or dishwasher. Nevertheless, there is evidence that the consistent wage labor generated by tourism is a desirable alternative with brighter future prospects. Even the lowest paid often find the most menial jobs in hotels more attractive than working the land.

Tourism also produces a range of "lower middle class" occupations, such as taxi drivers, cooks, supervisory and office jobs in hotels, entertainers, boat operators, skilled craftsmen, and artists. These, in turn, provide opportunities for the promotion and the growth of small businesses.

The Seasonality of Tourism Affects Employment

The seasonality of tourism can have important social effects. Either employment must be supplemented by other work or the worker is unemployed during the off-season. In some areas, it is possible for hotel employees to return to their traditional employment. In Turkey and Morocco, for example, workers often return to agriculture. Entire communities, including the police force, go down to the coast during the summer months and back to the inland farming areas when the season ends. The effects of this arrangement on the social structure of the communities is unknown. It would seem, however, that a continual transition from a traditional life to a life that caters to tourists must cause major strains. In Turkey, a positive effort has been made by the government to counteract seasonal unemployment and, at the same time, encourage local arts and crafts. Credit facilities are made available to enable otherwise unemployed workers to make handicrafts during the winter months and pay their debts when their goods are sold during the summer tourist season. In addition, all three countries have placed a high priority of tourism development through government-funded hotel facilities and massive advertising campaigns to stimulate "second" season interest and occupancy, which will ultimately make tourism-related employment less seasonal.

Economic Independence of Young People and Women

Most tourism jobs are filled by the younger people of the host nation, which gives them a financial independence they would not otherwise have had. In this way, economic power is transferred from the older to the younger generation, and a social conflict is often created because the young look at the traditional occupations of their parents as inferior.

Tourism can affect the role of women in society. It often gives them a chance to be paid for work that was traditionally considered to have no economic value, such as cleaning and washing. More dramatically, it can bring about economic independence and changes in lifestyle which can have far reaching social effects, as women move into the work force, leave the home and gain self-confidence. Here, too, exposure to their Western counterparts can not only help but provide added motivation. This change can have profound effect on the host society.

SOCIOCULTURAL IMPACT

Many developing countries would have no basis for a tourism industry without their indigenous culture. Many tourists want to experience the cultures of the countries they visit. Tourism has a twofold effect on culture: on the one hand, by creating an economic value, it can help to preserve the culture benefiting both the tourist and host. For example, religious buildings, archaeological sites, and tribal dances are valued by both groups. On the other hand, culture can be destroyed or distorted by tourism when that same cultural charm is replaced by imitations, whether they be copies of artifacts or traditional music. In addition, excessive physical wear and tear may damage buildings and other artifacts.

Regardless of the reason, these distortions of culture present inaccurate images—often only stereotypes—to tourists, thus diminishing the potential for intercultural learning and understanding. They also reduce the significance of these events to residents, thereby threatening their continued existence.

Arts and Handicrafts

There is a consensus that tourism has assisted in the revival of the arts and handicrafts sectors, resulting in both preserving and diversifying the items produced. A related problem is trivialization of native folk art. Certainly tourism can contribute to preservation or revitalization of native arts by creating demand for such products. But alterations in native art forms may also be caused by tourist-generated demand. Unfortunately, the type of art that tourism encourages is often mass-produced art, and it has been said that mass tourism, with its demand for souvenirs, encourages the production of fakes and consequently lowers the quality and standards of art. But the reverse is also true. Tourism has helped preserve and promote art forms that may otherwise have died, thereby helping to preserve the culture. In Morocco, for example, the art of carpet weaving might have disappeared. (An added benefit is that approximately 40,000 to 50,000 artisans are kept employed in Morocco by producing items for the tourist trade). There are also examples where local communities have been able to adapt items of serious social importance to meet tourism needs without making a mockery of them. The kachina, a wooden figure depicting a supernatural spirit mediator between the Pueblo people and their gods, is modified for sale to tourists by removing the significant religious symbols. The cultural significance is retained, but tourists' requirements are also satisfied.

Archaeology and Architecture

Generally, there is evidence that tourism has a beneficial effect on archaeology. Because of their value in attracting tourists, governments are encouraged to protect their country's cultural heritage. In this way, tourism has been responsible for stimulating numerous cultural salvage operations. Another benefit is that local residents are made aware of their cultural originally. UNESCO, the U.N. agency which sponsors many cultural restoration and preservation programs, follows the principle that if a monument has retained its religious, political, and social function, it is necessary to ensure continuity of that function; if not, another use might be found for it. By finding a new purpose for many threatened monuments, tourism has fostered the restoration of the cultural heritage, often financing that restoration. UNESCO has carried out various studies for governments on preservation programs for historic monuments. For instance, it recommended ways of preserving historic monuments in Katmandu Valley to the government of Nepal.

There have been some encouraging signs of attempts to relate hotel architecture to indigenous culture, notably in Africa and the Caribbean. In Tunisia, for example, many new hotels are low and spreading and built around courtyards in the manner of the traditional Arab caravansary, an Eastern inn built around a courtyard where caravans can stop for the night. Another method of developing a hotel style appropriate to the local environment is the conversion of an existing building. In Spain, the government has converted dozens of old homes and castles into deluxe guest houses called "paradores." The holiday village has been talked about for many years by those involved in Caribbean tourism. There are important social and cultural benefits from this

type of development since it emphasizes the use of local designs and indigenous materials. Guest house projects in Senegal successfully integrate contemporary reality into a tourist-host encounter. In addition, the simple comfort of the guest houses reduces the visible economic gap between tourists and local population, and the authentic local involvement of villagers, as members of a cooperative in managing the houses, facilitates genuine contact and exchange between the visitor and the visited.

The Potential for Cultural Conflict

Harry Matthews[3] has analyzed the potential for cultural conflict by identifying clusters of interest in tourism. He points out that tourism interest groups in most communities fall into five major categories: the national government, the tourism industry, local business and professional elites, special interest groups, and citizens.

National Government

In developing regions, if tourism is to serve the national interest in some way, it becomes the responsibility of government to see that optimum benefits are derived. Governmental programs designed to achieve this objective are held up for public criticism by the other three groups. Government's interest in tourism is simple in terms of purpose, but rather complex in terms of method. Its purpose, of course, is to orchestrate tourism policy in order to maximize national benefits from the industry. This includes decisions concerning how much foreign expertise or capital is needed compared to how much and what types of revenue can be derived from tourism without scaring both the tourist and the investor away. The methods of achieving this rather simple purpose, however, are quite complicated. Government, as an interest group, must pur-

[3]Harry Matthews, *International Tourism: A Political and Social Analysis* (Cambridge, MA: Schenkman 1970).

sue this general goal through detailed policies at the national, regional, and international levels. It must negotiate air transport agreements with foreign countries, while, in the meantime, monitor the business practices of local hotels, taxi operators, and storekeepers.

The Tourism Industry

The second important interest group in the host country is the industry itself, especially its managers. As an interest group, tourist managers are a source of helpful information to policy makers in the host countries. They know the industry better than most other people. And, while their political struggles with host governments may often be seen as profit-motivated rather than in the national interest, the two concerns do not always conflict. Managers often suggest certain practices to national officials that would enhance tourism and, at the same time, benefit local residents.

Local Business and Professional Elites

The growth of mass tourism benefits some residents more than others. Business and professional elites tend to welcome a growing tourism industry for obvious reasons. Real estate values and demand for professional services increase as more tourists arrive into the developing region. Lawyers, physicians, and real estate insurance brokers all seem to gain from the presence of a significant tourism industry. Additionally, of course, most retail sales and services are available to tourists and residents alike. Other elite groups tend to challenge tourism more often than do business and professional elites. Among them are other professional people: education elites, church leaders, labor leaders, and, to some extent, communications elites such as newspaper editors. Other critics of tourism include artists, writers, and cultural leaders with varied backgrounds and interest.

There are several reasons why business and professional elites support large-scale tourism in their own country. As mentioned earlier, the obvious reason is the profit to be earned from increased land values and increased demand for retail goods and professional services. A local physician might treat three tourist-patients at a luxury hotel and receive fees equal to those received for a long day's work at his local clinic. Likewise, local lawyers frequently benefit from tourism since hotels, airlines, and banks all need local representation on a day-to-day basis. The retainers received from the expatriate firms are large when compared to fees earned from local clients. Some local elites, not directly tied to the tourism industry, are able to benefit from its growth, yet at the same time be critical of aspects of its development. Perhaps the best example is communications elites, especially newspapers editors. Although the publications receive considerable advertising revenue from the hotels, tourist attractions, airlines, banks, and restaurants, many editors and columnists do speak out on tourism issues.

It is important that commercial businesses, whether local business ventures or developers from elsewhere, understand how tourism operates and what kind of tourism the community wants before making commitments involving planning, design or construction. Too often, public officials and community leaders are eager to accept new investment of almost any kind. As a result, development inappropriate to the long-range good of the community is allowed.

Entrepreneurs who think only of today's profits may create an image of the community as a "tourist trap," an image difficult to eradicate later. Business people and developers insensitive to community aesthetics—especially the visual quality of the entire community—may create a town marred by visual pollution as they change building facades or erect new structures and signs. Such pollution is partly responsible for making people travel, to get away from the eyesores found in most modern cities. A definite part of small-town charm is the lack of plastic and neon culture. If it is allowed to creep in, the charm quickly is lost.

Local bankers and other financiers need to understand tourism in order to make educated decisions in backing tourism development. To many oriented to a "production economy" tourism appears to produce nothing, and therefore they often reject investment opportunities. Tourism development encompasses such a variety of projects with varying returns on investment that financiers have a wide choice; and many of these projects have greater stability and potential for return than any nontourism investment. Without the support of the local financial community, tourism developers will be forced to go elsewhere for financing, taking money out of the community instead of bringing it in.

Special Interest Groups

Some groups and individuals may be primarily concerned about the effects of tourism upon the total population of a society rather than any effect it may have on the individuals or members of a group. This is often referred to as *populism*. Populism can be both a political goal and a political method. When analyzing tourism, special interest groups, or populist groups, we want to know whether the industry benefits the average citizen—that is, the country as a whole. Populist groups monitor the benefits of tourism. If only a few elites benefit, then, in their view, the industry must be changed or abolished. Populist groups promote acceptance. These groups ask critical questions about the effect of mass tourism upon the total society. The numerous special interest groups in this segment include labor unions, churches, university academics, and other cultural or political groups, including political parties.

Citizens

The most important group to be educated in the benefits and costs of tourism, and how it operates, is the citizenry of the community. Without their support, even the best-laid plans cannot succeed. Tourism should and must be a total community effort. Individual citizens can be either the strongest or weakest link in this effort. Their attitude toward the visitor in their community will determine, more than any other factor, whether the tourist will return and also tell others good things about your community. Successful tourism depends upon an intangible host-guest relationship that extends beyond the resort, hotel, restaurant, or recreation establishment. It includes the appearance of private homes, the politeness of people on the street, the knowledge and attitude of the taxi driver, the priced charged in the drugstore. Successful tourism depends, in short, on a healthy, friendly, knowledgeable community, with a commitment to making the visitor's stay as pleasant and enjoyable as an invited guest in the home of one of the residents. The city of Miami requires cab drivers to take a three-hour course to obtain or renew a hack license. The program, funded by American Express and Dade county, encourages them to be courteous to visitors and be knowledgeable about safety and geography. The program, called "Miami Nice," is offered through a local university, St. Thomas, and cabbies who have completed the program report that their tips have gone up an average of 30 percent.

Ola Røe, Røe Foto AS

Commercialization of Culture: An Alternative

Commercialization of culture applies to a phenomenon that takes place when aspects of local culture such as ceremonial dances are staged to serve the tourist. What the local population formerly did as a matter of spontaneous obligation, or ritual, is now performed for reward.

Some results of this are:

- The value of the ceremony to the host population is lessened because the ceremony is moved from the sacred to the secular.
- The choice of local cultural ceremonies to be commercialized is made by the foreign tourist or, more accurately, the tourism organizer, rather than by the host population.
- The artificial ceremonies present a narrow and outdated picture of local culture.

Yet, commercialization of local culture need not necessarily be detrimental to the host community. As noted earlier, the Balinese distinguish between audiences. When the audience is composed mainly of tourists, there is a minimum-attendance stipulation for the performance to take place. For an audience attending for religious purposes, there is no question of cancellation.

Ethnic models or reconstructions of traditional lifestyles may be useful to satisfy tourists' desires to "see how the natives live" without direct invasion of their privacy. Once of the world's most successful experiments in this area is the Polynesian Cultural Center at Laie, Hawaii. The center is an important local economic institution, but also provides additional indirect economic benefits by employing students from distant Polynesian islands. Such employment facilitates students' education at a nearby university campus. The center consists of several reconstructed Polynesian villages, each depicting the aboriginal culture of a different people. Today, the Polynesian Cultural Center attracts more visitors annually than any other tourist attraction in the state of Hawaii.

ENVIRONMENTAL EFFECTS OF TOURISM

The relationship between tourism and the environment is often one of paradox. Tourism has the secondary effect of conserving, as well as conflicting with, aspects of natural and artificial environments. Tourism can focus attention on the importance of natural and cultural resources as tourist attractions and be a powerful force in protecting these resources from other forms of economic development. On the other hand, development associated with tourism itself can impact and alter the very resources upon which tourism depends. The complex relationships between tourism and the environment are explored in this section.

Environmental Benefits and Costs

When a new factory is built in a community, it can entail air, water, and visual pollution, and definitely calls for increased public expenditures for roads, sewer and water lines, new schools, and more services. It also entails the loss of land to new subdivisions and shopping centers. While not totally free from some of these problems, tourism generally is much cleaner in all of the above respects, especially if carefully planned. Tourist facilities such as lodging are more concentrated than housing projects, thereby cutting community costs for provisions of public services. Because tourists only visit, the additional costs for schools, health and other services are minimal compared to other forms of economic development, but there are costs! Without proper planning and controls, a community can suffer from increased auto air pollution, congestion, litter, and higher prices. With careful development, tourism costs communities less than any other form of economic development.

The community qualities that attract tourism—recreation and cultural opportunities, cleanliness, friendliness, and community pride—are the same qualities that will impress other industries in their locational decisions. Although a few communities are suited for tourism as their primary economy, most benefit more with a balanced, mixed economy, with tourism as one segment. A tourist economy is compatible with many other industries, some of which may actually become part of the tourism sector of the community.

The principal environmental benefit of tourism is a rationale for conservation. Tourism often relies on unspoiled natural and cultural environments as basic attractions. Tourism can provide a vital economic justification for maintaining the character and integrity of these environments. In many instances, the highest economic return from these resources is through their conservation as tourist attractions rather than development for commodity production. Classic examples of this relationship are the wildlife refuges of Africa. Without

N.C. Travel and Tourism Division/Photo by Clay Nolen

the economic return provided by tourism, these areas might well be converted to agriculture, forestry, mining or other forms of industrial development, vastly altering their environment.

A second potential benefit of tourism is the environmental improvement which can be associated with tourism development. Tourism, as with other forms of development, can bring with it modern technologies such as sewage-treatment facilities which can protect and even enhance environmental quality.

But tourism development is not without potential environmental costs. The adage of tourism being an "industry without smokestacks" is naive and outdated. Tourism development can and does impact the environment in a variety of specific ways, including damage to soils and vegetation, pollution of water resources, disturbance and loss of wildlife and wildlife habitat, littering and vandalism, and damage to historical or cultural artifacts and buildings.

While these environmental impacts of tourism are important, there can be more insidious and perhaps more detrimental effects of tourism development. Tourism development can introduce incremental changes to the environment and landscape that alter the basic character, integrity, or uniqueness of an area.

The importance of these cumulative environmental effects is rooted in the most fundamental motivation for tourism. In the most rudimentary sense, people engage in tourism to experience different environments. Destinations are attractive to tourists because they possess characteristics that make them distinctive. Contemporary writers often refer to this distinctiveness as "sense of place." Sense of place can be based on features of the natural environment, features of the cultural environment, or some combination of the two. Tourism can diminish an area's sense of place by promoting or allowing inappropriate types or levels of development—development that is not focused upon or consistent with the basic qualities which make an area distinctive.

The type of development can also affect sense of place. The construction of many motels and high-rise hotels in the 1950s and 1960s to accommodate tourism growth has greatly diminished the visual attractiveness of many areas and has altered their sense of place.

The above suggests that tourist environments may be nonrenewable. That is, once an area's sense of place is altered or "consumed" by overdevelopment of improper development, it may be permanently lost. The decline stage of the tourism development cycle implies that once the distinctive characteristics that originally attracted tourists to an area are gone or substantially diminished, tourists move on to new "unspoiled" areas. It is important to recognize, therefore, that tourism development can alter an area's sense of place. It is a paradox, indeed, that the success of tourism can ultimately lead to its own failure.

CONCLUSION

The studies and issues described above illustrate that tourism can have multiple social and cultural effects on people and their communities. Moreover, these effects can be distributed through society in an unequal fashion. The issue of distribution of cost and benefits becomes especially important when economic and social and cultural effects are considered in concert. When economic benefits flow directly to selected individuals either inside or outside the community, but social and cultural costs are borne by the community at large, tourism is inherently inequitable. Recent studies of resident attitudes toward tourism suggest the implications of inequitable distribution of benefits and costs. Residents who were directly tied to the economic benefits of tourism feel generally positive about tourists and their effect on the community, while residents who did not benefit as directly in an economic sense felt more generally negative toward tourism.

Perhaps no other aspect of tourism is more controversial and viewed less objectively than the social and cultural benefits and costs of tourism development. Tourism can distort the cultural patterns of interest to tourists. Cultural distortion may be caused by packaging of cultural elements for tourist consumption, creation of pseudo-events to maintain privacy during the actual events, inaccurate images created by tourism marketing and promotion, and trivialization of native arts. Our aspirations rise on the wings of the greatest hope for world peace and crash in the mediocrity of mass tourism. The previous section on environmental effects of tourism suggested that tourism can help protect and preserve distinctive environments. Often it is an area's cultural history or heritage that makes it distinctive, and tourism can focus sufficient attention on these qualities to protect and even enhance them. There exits a positive relationship between tourism and a reawakening or renewal of cultural heritage.

Environmental conservation in some regions tends to be given a lower order of priority than raising living standards unless it coincides with income-earning possibilities.

Clearly, no single subject offers greater challenge and opportunity for tourism professionals and none may be so critical to the image and continued growth of the industry. The travel and tourism students of today must become the concerned, qualified experts of tomorrow if we are to avoid exploitation through too rapid or excessive development and insensitivity to resident needs. Those experts will take many forms ranging from local, regional, and national tourism marketers to airline executives, hotel developers, tour operators, and travel agents. Each can and must contribute in order to make the benefits far outweigh the negatives of tourism development.

REVIEW QUESTIONS

1. What are some of the arguments used by opponents of tourism development?
2. What are some of the arguments used by proponents of tourism development?
3. Give three examples of how expectations of host and guest may differ.
4. What is "indigenous culture?"
5. Describe the "imitation effect."
6. What is the impact of tourism on locally produced arts and crafts? Give several scenarios.
7. Name the five interest groups that emerge in developing countries as a result of tourism development.
8. What are the pros and cons of ethnic models?
9. Some argue that travel agents should play a more active role in *tourist* development. Discuss.
10. Give examples of how tourism has heightened awareness of cultural heritage in your town or community.

Cultural Tourism: Pitfalls and Possibilities

Anne M. Masterton

On the Indonesian island of Irian Jaya, a Stone Age tribe recently discovered steel axes. This magic tool, introduced to them by Western trekkers, simplified life for these tribal nomads.

Each time they move, tribe members construct new treehouses in a jungle with bird-eating spiders, frogs the size of a man's head, and an incredibly diverse roster of flora and fauna for neighbors. Using stone axes, two months' worth of sunrises passed before the treehouse was completed. With the steel axe, a mere fourteen sunsets guarantees new living quarters.

Off the northern coast of Australia, about 40 miles from Darwin, the Tiwi Aboriginal tribe flourishes on Bathurst and Melville islands, collectively called the Tiwi Islands. The 1,200 strong Nguiu community on Bathurst and the Milikapiti and Pularumpi communities on Melville are self-sufficient, self-governing, self-confident, and savvy about tourism. The Tiwis—who take checks—reap the economic benefits of tourism on their own terms. Visitors are welcome in controlled numbers, but are barred from certain areas and receive comprehensive instructions on cultural etiquette and protocol before landing on the island.

Over in Singapore, where former prime minister Lee Kuan Yew spent his term (1965–1990) modernizing the island by tearing down anything with a history and replacing it with coldly modern structures, tourism officials have recognized that tourists like and look for things traditional and timeless.

Scurrying to capitalize on its culturally diverse population, the island nation is renovating new structures and attractions to look old. Eyeing the success of cultural programs and historic attractions in neighboring destinations, Singapore recently launched a heritage preservation program, staging festivals, producing cultural shows in hotel dining rooms, and developing attractions underscoring Singapore's short history.

These are all examples of the burgeoning product category called cultural tourism. Warning that this type of travel is "potentially exploitative," anthropologist Barbara R. Johnston broadly defined cultural tourism as "ventures that are consciously designed to enhance the socio-economic milieu of the host while educating and entertaining the guest."

Cultural tourism covers a broad range of activities, from observing performances of traditional music and dance in a city center to visiting with isolated, rural villagers in their own homes. The common component is that the product is people.

The problem inherent in this form of tourism is that culture is not a commodity: it's a way of living developed by a specific group of people so they can survive and thrive in a particular environment. And while some aspects of a culture can remain relatively intact after being isolated, removed from their original context, and presented for viewing by outsiders, others cannot. In particular, cultural tourism that involves direct interaction between Westernized tourists and indigenous people in developing rural areas is ripe with the potential to go wrong.

This article was originally published in *Island Destinations*, a supplement to *Tour & Travel News*, November 30, 1992, pp. 58–63.

Anne M. Masterton, a former senior editor at Tour & Travel News, *has covered tourism development in Asia and the Pacific for six years, two of them as editor of Singapore-based* ASIA Travel Trade. *In 1990, she was named journalist of the year by the Pacific Asia Travel Association for her exhaustive coverage of issues affecting tourism in the Pacific Rim. While in Asia, she specialized in environmental issues.*

Exposure alone has consequences. Tourists, decked out in modern garb and armed with video cameras, nifty luggage, instant snacks, Walkman stereos and glittering gold and silver jewelry, etch an impression on the locals, an impression that can spark changes, often profound ones, in traditional methods of living, loving, and worshipping. It's not just impressions that Western tourists leave behind: sometimes artifacts from a different culture, like the ax in Indonesia, remain, and these can have a profound impact on people's lives.

At its worst, cultural tourism can be an exploitative, debasing, and corrosive phenomenon for everybody involved. But at its best, conducted with sensitivity and respect, cultural tourism can be the conduit for a mutually beneficial exchange, in both human and financial terms.

It can give visitors a precious opportunity to make contact with people who live differently and hold different values than themselves, opening the path to real understanding. And it can give indigenous cultures a tool to use their own heritage to move into a self-determined future.

BOTTOM-LINE CONCERNS

Cultural tourism and eco-tourism are sister products; they share many characteristics, but they are not the same thing. The mushrooming consumer demand for environmentally responsible travel, now commonly acknowledged and fully documented, is just beginning to extend to travel products involving cultural tourism. Almost everyone agrees in theory that cultural preservation and mutual respect are desirable goals.

However, the bottom line is the bottom line, and everybody involved is struggling to find a way to balance the commercial imperatives of tourism with the cultural integrity of a host community. The truth is that cultural tourism is not very profitable for tour operators. Suppliers, for example, almost never offer volume-based pricing or other types of concessions to companies specializing in cultural tourism.

"It's the 'more is better' mentality that pervades not only the industry, but our society as well," said Chuck Gee, dean of the School of Travel Industry Management at the University of Hawaii.

"Talk about mixed signals," said a retail agent whose sister company operates tours in Asia. "Mass-market companies get all the breaks."

"And people don't understand why cultural tourism products are more expensive than other types of products," she added. "Travelers accustomed to paying top dollar for luxurious five-star hotels, sleek limos, and first-class air transportation cannot reconcile that trekking to rural villages or scaling a remote mountain to reach a crumbling, ancient temple revered by tribes dwelling in the valley beneath cost several thousand dollars."

Tour operators who adhere to the values, implicit in cultural tourism walk a fine line. Pricing and packaging difficulties aside, they cannot appear patronizing by suggesting that developing countries need their assistance or protection, a move that would put the indigenous community in a dependency relationship. Nor can operators presume that all indigenous people are either simple or naive, incapable of conducting their own business affairs and making sound business decisions.

They also face problems in the distribution channel.

"As the industry changes its view of cultural tourism, retailers need to adjust their self-perception—that of a work machine—which in turn will affect the way suppliers and consumers view them," said Jeannie Graves, operations manager for Forum International, a California-based not-for-profit corporation selling highly specialized tours and a pioneer in culturally and environmentally responsible travel products.

"Retailers tend to think, partly because this is the industry attitude, that `I can do mechanical functions, I can work the computer and deliver tickets. Many retailers don't have much interest in specialized fields, and cultural tourism is a specialized field at the moment. But as clients generate more interest, I'd like to see retailers become more knowledgeable. To do that, we all [wholesalers and suppliers] need to educate and encourage them. It's in our best interests. This is one of the fastest-growing segments of the travel industry."

The broad category of adventure travel, which includes cultural tourism, is booming. Last year alone, Americans spent $7.5 billion on gear for outdoor activities, according to the Adventure Travel Society in Englewood, Colo. That figure is expected to climb this year, as are the numbers of folks out to satisfy their curiosity about the ways other people in other countries live.

What's more, there are more than 10 million "dues-paying" environmental/cultural conservationists in the United States, and, according to the U.S. Travel Data Center, they're willing to pay up to 8.5 percent more than the going market rate for culturally responsible tourism products. There is significant growth potential, but cultural tourism remains problematic to all involved.

CHALLENGES FOR ALL INVOLVED

Operators have problems with pricing, packaging, and access, and they must devise responsible ways to provide an appropriate lifestyle experience to clients, at a profit, without compromising the culture of indigenous communities. Retailers must educate themselves and their clients. Consumers must understand the concept of value and be willing to pay, in money, attitude, and expectations, for the privilege of looking in on another's lifestyle.

But the most prodigious challenge falls to indigenous communities themselves.

According to George Wallace, an associate professor in the Department of Recreation Resources and Landscape Architecture at Colorado State University, and an expert in this field of travel, "Indigenous or traditional peoples cannot be asked to live their lives in a bell jar, to maintain the old way for tourists. It's true that there are many local traditions that demonstrate a wisdom about nature including sustainable agricultural practices, important native crop varieties, and cultural practices that we outsiders admire.

"There is a better chance that these will be maintained, however, if we allow local people to wrestle with the issue of how much contact with outsiders and new technology is appropriate, when and where it should occur, and what traditions, if any, they should change. For this to happen, they cannot be isolated from changes or overwhelmed by them."

Although misconceptions about pricing is one of cultural tourism's prickliest thorns (it should cost less to sleep in a local guest house than an international standard hotel), tour operators emphasize that cultural tourism is a supply-driven market, and the best way to protect that supply is to charge high prices for it. Tour operators also point out that because cultural tourism is driven by supply, it continually challenges the operator's values.

CHARGING THROUGH

"I always feel as if I'm intruding," said one guide who asked not to be identified but whose company sells and operates cultural tours in Asia. "No matter how respectful my group is, and no matter how welcoming the locals are, I still feel as if I'm charging through someone's living room."

A fisherman on Bali named Marudin offered his point of view: "When the tourists are around, I feel not whole. I can't fish my way [by hand with a net], because there's too much moving in the water from people. I can't do my type of art; people up at the hotel tell me I'm too native. Before all the people come to Nusa Dua, we don't have lots of ringetts [Indonesian currency], but we smile a lot. Now, some of us have lots of ringetts, but we have to smile for the cameras of the white people, too."

Bali's Nusa Dua is an exquisite example of cultural debasement spawned by the rapid and unregulated boom in tourism development. Temples were disrupted by camera-toting, often offensively dressed tourists. The woodcarvers and painters of Mas and Ubud started producing cheap reproductions of "authentic" Balinese art as souvenirs. And the batik makers produced fewer traditional patterns as they came to understand Western preferences in color and style.

Ironically, Bali's cultural decline and disappointment as a tourist destination underscores the basic tenets of cultural tourism, many of which are also fundamental to sustainable tourism: control visitor numbers; keep decision making within the local community to ensure the involvement and cooperation of local people; and channel tourism earnings back into the community, either directly or through contributions to non-profit agencies specializing in the host area.

PEACE AND PROFITS

Despite some disturbing examples to the contrary, tour operations and indigenous cultures do peacefully, respectfully, and profitably coexist on island destinations throughout Asia and the Pacific.

The Ambua Lodge in Papua New Guinea unequivocally illustrates that an indigenous people can retain cultural traditions, selectively integrate outside influences, and support itself in the bargain.

Located in the Tari Valley, and owned by inbound operator Trans Niugini Tours, the Ambua Lodge is smack in the middle of the 75,000-strong Huli Tribe. With the exception of an expatriate manager, Ambua is staffed by Huli villagers. The food used at the lodge is not imported; it comes from the gardens and stock of villages in the Tari Basin. Most of the materials used to build the lodge came from Papua New Guinea. Local villagers helped design the hut-like accommodations and the compound has its own gravitational water supply, also designed by local tribespeople.

In conjunction with the birth of the lodge, completed in 1990, the Huli chose to share their ceremonies and lifestyle for monetary gain, in order to build schools, obtain medical supplies, and generally improve their economic circumstances. Some villagers built visitor accommodation huts on their property, which are used by Trans Niugini Tours in its trekking programs, and allowed visitors limited participation in their lives. Other villages, for a fee, allow visitors to simply stroll around and observe the male-dominated activities of Huli life. Most of the money generated by tourism stays in the Huli community, and Trans Niugini Tours plans nothing without consulting the Huli elders.

INNOVATION IN FIJI

But the most ambitious and culturally pure undertaking in the region is the Vatukarasa Culture Hotel in Fiji, an evolving project facilitated by Australian Mark Aussie-Stone.

Aussie-Stone has devoted most of his adult life to finding out why indigenous communities and habitats, which can easily welcome visitors, cannot own and operate their own hotels. He is founder and president of Bluepeace Pacific, World Habitat and Culture Conservation Society, and is managing director of Vatukarasa Village Ecotourism Culture Hotel Project, which he has privately funded over the past ten years.

Aussie-Stone's model calls for a 100-percent locally owned and operated cultural hotel, which will enable the village to be self-sustaining without being self-effacing. By constructing a duplicate sister village to allow visitors to experience traditional village life and customs, without ever visiting and perhaps corrupting the actual habitat, the privacy of the real village remains intact. Community members interested in exchanges with visitors can participate in the second village; those who prefer their privacy need not leave the security of the real village.

All monies paid by visitors go to the village elders, who supervise traditional distribution methods. At least 70 percent of the hotel's profits will be passed on to assist other Fijian villages building their own sister projects. Moreover, guests will be charged at the same rate they would pay for a similar facility in their own country. The stronger their own currency against the host currency, the more they will pay. Such a policy permits all people to be able to afford to visit and share hospitality with other indigenous peoples. For example, a Nepalese may pay only $20 a night; while a Japanese visitor may pay $600 a night.

It doesn't sound like a particularly radical idea. But developers and even culturally sensitive tour operators have somehow always managed to wrest control, to some degree or other, from the indigenous community. The first step toward a happy partnership is an acknowledgment from the travel industry that indigenous communities are not there to serve the tourist trade.

CHAPTER 7 Community Tourism Planning

Mass tourism is a relatively recent phenomenon. It was not until the late 1950s that changing lifestyles and advances in transportation technology revolutionized the way people vacationed. Much of the early development in the tourism industry was demand driven; destinations provided attractions and services to the large number of new travelers. Hotels, restaurants, and attractions were built as demand exceeded supply. Often, development took place without much consideration for maintaining the overall attractiveness of an area, environmental consequences, or long-term challenges. Tourism development was often the result of entrepreneurial initiative without the benefit of coordinated planning. Often as a result of haphazard developments, destinations lost popularity with tourists.

    To be a truly successful part of a community's economy, tourism must be sustainable, even if only on a seasonal basis. To be sustainable, it must be prop-

Parts of this chapter are based on material originally contained in *Tourism USA; Guidelines for Tourism Development,* published by U.S. Department of Commerce, Washington, D.C., 1991.

erly planned and managed to ensure a continuing high-quality experience for the visitor.

It is through planning that the tourism industry can satisfy the public's consumer needs, coordinate programs, and guide developments to meet tourism's economic benefits while minimizing social and environmental problems. This chapter points to the need for planning and appropriate, controlled development.

WHAT IS TOURISM PLANNING?

Tourism planning is a decision-making process aimed to guide future tourism development actions and solve future problems. Tourism planning is also the process of selecting objectives and deciding what should be done to attain them. It involves the initiation and implementation of ideas and action. The process is a dynamic means of determining goals, systematically considering alternative actions to achieve those goals, implementing the chosen alternative, and evaluating that choice to determine success. The use of planning to guide development of a tourism initiative will allow a community to adapt to the unexpected, create the desirable, and avoid the undesirable. Tourism planning is the activity aimed at developing and enhancing the positive aspects of tourism development, while avoiding or controlling tourism's negative aspects.

Planning is a prerequisite for success; it forces the consideration of assumptions about the future, it allows for the consideration of alternatives, it increases options, it avoids misunderstandings, it helps avoid decline, it establishes responsibility, and it causes planners to use time as a resource. Planning for tourism development also promotes the opportunity for improving the total community rather than improving one part of the community at the expense of other parts. Planning requires the involvement of the citizens of a community and considers their environment. That environment includes political, physical, social, economic, and environmental elements which must be viewed as interrelated and interdependent components of the community development system. Community use of the integrated planning process provides

Wyoming Division of Tourism

for an assessment of the impact of selected tourism activities and programs on those elements within the total environment. Planning also provides for consideration of the effects that each element has on the other as a comprehensive tourism program is developed.

THE PLANNING PROCESS

Tourism is a large and complex system of industries and activities. It has far-reaching, deep, positive, and negative effects on people, economies, and the environment. To appreciate the role of planning in tourism it is important to understand the nature of the tourism system and its social, economic, and environmental effects. The tourism system can best be understood as consisting of a demand (market) and supply (attractions and services) component, linked together by the elements of transportation and promotion.

Planning is a decision-making process aimed to guide future action and solve future problems. Planning is a continuous process because it allows for future goals and objectives as well as change.

The planning procedure or process can be most easily understood and used as a sequence of steps.

Step   1. The planner becomes educated and informed on the issue(s).
Step   2. The planner specifies the problem or area of need.
Step   3. The planner analyzes current resources (supply) and assesses the market (demand).
Step   4. The planner identifies the program objective.
Step   5. The planner generates alternative plans of action to reach the goals and objectives.
Step   6. The planner selects an optimum alternative for implementation.
Step   7. The planner selects a program design.
Step   8. The planner develops an implementation strategy.
Step   9. The planner implements the plan.
Step 10. The planner evaluates the plan.

While it is easy to learn and to think about the planning process as a sequence of steps it is important to remember that the planning process is dynamic. Plans must be continuously reviewed and revised because mistakes in choosing between alternatives can be made, circumstances might change, and unseen obstacles (or opportunities) may present themselves at any time during the planning process.

CONVENTIONAL VERSUS STRATEGIC PLANNING

Traditional views of planning suggest that the planner's task consists primarily of defining goals and then manipulating them in order to achieve these goals. However, in today's turbulent and rapidly changing world, the planner is often forced to reevaluate both means and goals throughout all planning and development phases of a tourism project. Plans for the establishment of a theme park might need to be changed due to consumer research findings, the rerouting of a nearby highway, or the actions of a competitor.

Strategic tourism planning, therefore, suggests that planners and developers constantly scan their environments for factors that might affect the achievement of objectives. These opportunities and threats often require a change in goals and strategies. Strategic planning, unlike conventional planning, is action-oriented, flexible, ongoing, and subject to constant evaluation of goals and strategies.

WHY CONSIDER TOURISM DEVELOPMENT?

Some local business people who do not deal directly with tourists sometimes find it difficult to support activities that attract and/or service the visitor population. However, the spending of a tourist dollar is like tossing a rock into a pond; the initial impact makes the largest splash, but the effects—like the ripples created on the pond's surface—continue into all parts of the business community.

The general citizenry benefits directly from tourism in two ways. First, tourists pay sales tax and, sometimes, special taxes such as those on hotel rooms. These help provide public services for citizens without taking additional tax payments from citizens' pockets. Second, tourism generates and supports ventures such as restaurants, museums, specialty shops and recreational facilities which can be enjoyed by residents as well as visitors, thus enhancing the quality of local life.

Employment Opportunities

Tourism is a labor-intensive service industry, requiring large numbers of employees in relation to the amount of the investment. These jobs generally require moderate education and skills with short-term and inexpensive training. However, many tourism jobs are seasonal in nature, and careful thought must be given to what happens to these people during the off-season. Often the tourism season coincides with school vacations, providing employment opportunities for youth in the community. Unlike most industries, tourism is also an employer of older citizens. Careful analysis of the community's existing employment situation, potential available labor force, and type of tourism operations is critical to any decision to develop tourism.

Economic Benefits

New money can be brought into a community through agriculture, extractive industries (such as mining), manufacturing, and tourism. Many communities are unsuited for the first three, but almost every community has some visitors and therefore has some degree of tourism. The question is, does a community have the potential to expand this visitor rate, and does it really want to?

Heritage Tourism

Visitors are attracted by those little things that are unique to the community— heritage, culture, architecture, scenery. An awareness of the value of these to outsiders can spur renewed interest and pride among residents to conserve and preserve those elements that contribute to this uniqueness. Traditional crafts, ethnic customs and mores, and historic sites and structures are just a few examples of elements that can be enhanced by the realization that they have a value beyond the boundaries of the local community. Citizen and government understanding of the visitor's desire for an aesthetically positive environment

as a setting for the tourism experience can be instrumental in forging community goals and actions that result in the conservation of the higher-quality aspects of the community and elimination of those that are detractions.

Need for Community Support

All sectors of the community need to be aware of what tourism development can do for them, because successful development can only take place in a town, county, or country where the government, commercial business and developers, financiers and the general citizenry have a positive and assertive attitude toward establishing a tourism economy. This is an educational process that needs to be ongoing.

Local government officials need to understand the benefits and costs of tourism in order to make the decision to promote its development. They also need to understand how it operates in order to properly plan and manage its development. Because tourism encompasses many different aspects, local laws may have to be altered or enacted to promote development, while at the same time preserving those things which the community holds dear. A successful tourism economy depends upon a high level of cooperation between the private and public sectors. Local governments are responsible for the basic infrastructure, without which tourism cannot operate. It must be concerned with transportation, medical concerns, and a multitude of other support services, all of which will be affected to some degree by increased numbers of visitors. More than with any other economic development decision, a commitment to tourism development requires a most careful analysis of community goals, priorities, resources and capabilities of local leaders.

Commercial Developers

Commercial businesses, whether local business people or developers from elsewhere, need to understand how tourism operates and what kind of tourism the community wants before making commitments involving planning, design or construction. Too often, public officials and community leaders are eager to accept new investments of almost any kind. As a result, development inappropriate to the long-range good of the community is allowed.

Business people who think only of today's profits may create an image of the community as a "tourist trap," an image difficult to eradicate later. Business people and developers insensitive to community aesthetics—especially the visual quality of the entire community—may create a town marred by visual pollution as they change building facades, or erect new structures and signs. Such pollution is partly responsible for making people travel, to get away from the eyesores found in most modern cities. A definite part of small-town charm is the lack of plastic and neon clutter. If it is allowed to creep in, the charm is quickly lost.

Financial Support

Local bankers and other financiers need to understand tourism in order to make educated decisions in backing tourism development. To many oriented toward a "production economy," tourism appears to produce nothing and, therefore, they often reject investment opportunities out-of-hand. Tourism development encompasses such a variety of projects—with varying returns on investment—that financiers have a wide choice; and many of these projects will have greater stability and potential for return than any nontourism investment.

Without the support of the local financial community, tourism developers will be forced to go elsewhere for financing, taking money out of the community instead of bringing it in.

The Community

The most important group to be educated in the benefits and costs of tourism, and how it operates, is the citizenry of a community. Without their support, even the best laid plans cannot succeed. Tourism should and must be a total community effort. Individual citizens can be either the strongest or weakest link in this effort. Their attitude toward the visitor in their community will determine, more than any other factor, whether the tourist will return and also tell others good things about their community. Successful tourism depends upon a hotel, restaurant, or recreational establishment. It includes the appearance of private homes, the politeness of people on the street, the knowledge and attitude of the taxi driver, the prices charged in the drugstore. Successful tourism depends, in short, on a healthy, friendly, knowledgeable community, with a commitment to making the visitor's stay as pleasant and enjoyable as an invited guest in the home of one of the residents.

UNDERSTANDING TOURISTS

The tourism industry is a very competitive one. In order for a community to reach its fullest potential in the competitive arena, its leaders must understand what motivates people to travel, how they travel, and the patterns they follow. Knowing these will help in planning and development. Knowing what causes these patterns to sometimes change, allows contingency plans to be established which can be implemented when conditions call for such change. Planners also need to understand the complementary role of attractions and infrastructure and the linkages which must be provided for a total and positive tourism experience. Finally, because the world is shrinking into a global community of business and pleasure travelers, local tourism developers and promoters must be appreciative of the special needs of foreign international visitors.

Attracting Visitors

Visitors may come to your community for many reasons. The official definition of a tourist is one who travels at least 100 miles away from home primarily for pleasure, but actually any visitor to your locality requires similar services. Most vacationers stay with friends or relatives during their trips and patronize the local drugstore as well as the local tourist boutique. When business people attend a convention, they travel for professional purposes, but the convention site is chosen for its recreational and entertainment offerings as well as its convention facilities. The local restaurant may, on the same evening, cater to business people, conventioneers, tourists, and local residents.

All visitors look for a few basics: cleanliness, friendliness, politeness, safety, and service—at a price the visitor considers reasonable for the satisfaction derived. Almost every community has some potential for successful tourism development as long as these basic needs are met. The degree of success will depend upon the community's ability to accomplish the three basic steps in visitor promotion:

1. Attract the visitor to your community.
2. Persuade the visitor to stay as long as possible.
3. Persuade the visitor to make return visits, and to tell friends about the pleasures of your community.

Colloquially, this can be boiled down to a simple liturgy: "Get 'em, Keep 'em, and Bring 'em back!"

Understanding Travel Patterns

The family automobile or recreational vehicle is still the primary mode of transportation for vacationing North Americans. Often a stop to visit friends or relatives is included in travel plans. If the trip to the destination takes more than one day, most make advance lodging reservations, a distinct change from earlier days when the majority took their chances of finding overnight accommodations whenever they felt like stopping. There is a general tendency for more trip planning than ever before.

Some areas of transportation have seen significant change over the past decade and are worth noting. The growth of package tours has been

phenomenal. A package is created when two or more of the basic essentials of a tour—transportation, lodging, food services, attractions—are joined by a single price. An "all-inclusive" tour contains all four; some even include tips and baggage handling fees.

For years, package tours were synonymous with motorcoaches. Today more than 60 percent of all packages include air transportation, often in a fly-drive (rental car), fly-ride (motorcoach) or fly-cruise (cruise ship) combination. Packaging appeals to many because the total tour cost is known ahead of time, and generally the package costs less than if all elements were purchased separately.

Growth in the cruise ship industry may be of interest only to coastal or island communities. Because ships provide lodging and dining as well as transportation, those communities need not worry about development of hotels and restaurants as inland communities must. Income generation must be concentrated on the sale of local products and foods, admission to entertainment events or historical sites, and fees for local scenic tours, diving and fishing, or other recreational and cultural activities.

More people than ever now travel with credit cards and traveler's checks rather than cash. Hotels, restaurants, shops and banks need to be prepared to accept these. Travel vouchers, usually associated with packaged tours, are also on the increase. Some vouchers are written on major banking companies, while others are to the account of the tour packaging company.

People are traveling lighter, with more casual apparel, as formal dress codes have all but vanished. This trend creates opportunities for adjunct services such as self-service laundromats.

How people arrive at, and get around in, a destination, has implications for the community's promotional literature, information and directional system, internal transportation system, and other ancillary services.

Travelers today want more and better information than has been available in the past. Tourists need to have accurate, current information available to them. Two types of information available to tourists are directed and nondirected. "Directed" information consists of messages that have been intentionally prepared for the visitor. This type of information includes magazine articles, guidebooks, advertising, tourist maps, and the like. "Nondirected" information that reaches tourists through the mass media or general literature without the initiative of the host community. This type of information is difficult to control and often very powerful.

Unpredictability of Travel Patterns

Travel and tourism has sometimes been labeled a recession-proof industry. This is not entirely true. Business travel is usually one of the first items curtailed during economic downturns. Conferences and conventions, mostly supported by white-collar professionals, usually experience less of an impact. The impact may be much more visible if the conference site is in a more expensive or remote location than usual, relative to the membership's expectations.

For individual or family vacations, the very affluent and the very poor are little-affected by recession. It is the middle class whose travel patterns are most altered when pocketbooks become tight. Interestingly, studies show that North Americans, at least, take as many pleasure trips during recessions as in good economic times. However, they do not travel as far, they choose less-expensive destinations, and they tend to opt more for friend and relatives as a place of lodging. As a result, both en-route and destination expenditures tend to be less.

Usually severe weather (hurricanes, drought), natural disasters (floods, earthquake), and political upheavals (riots, civil wars) all produce a temporary curtailment of travel to specific destinations. Another travel destination may be substituted. In 1986, for example, the threat of terrorism directed at United States' citizens caused a dramatic drop in the demand for European and Mediterranean destinations. Severe hurricanes in South Florida and Hawaii caused serious interruptions in tourist flows to these destinations in 1992. How long such situations last is unknown. Successful tourism calls for the development of alternative packaging and promotional strategies to deal with such contingencies. Fluctuations in the value of local currency vis-à-vis that of visitor-origin countries and the price of aviation fuel can create fluctuations in business for those communities dependent on foreign visitors.

Attractions and Infrastructure

There are two basic categories necessary to any tourism development: attractions and support facilities or services (normally referred to as infrastructure). These two categories are not always distinct. For example, some support facilities may themselves be attractions, such as the carriage rides in historic Charleston, South Carolina. As with cruise ships, this transportation mode becomes part of the recreation experience.

Attractions cover a vast variety and scope—both existing and potential. They may have wide appeal, such as a panoramic natural vista in the mountains, the ocean and its beaches, and almost any major festival. On the other hand, they may appeal only to specific markets, such as a tobacco auction, an archaeological dig, or a cemetery for a particular ethnic group. Types of attractions can be categorized as (1) natural, scenic or environmental; (2) man-made, historical, cultural and ethnic; (3) recreational attractions; and (4) special events.

It is necessary to inventory potential attractions in a community as a preliminary step to further planning. It is of critical importance after inventorying all existing or potential attractions in an area to assess their market potential and market match. Are the attractions appealing to a general or specific public? Are they unique or can they be found elsewhere? Will they draw visitors from overseas, across the nation, from the remainder of the state, or strictly from the local area? Properly marketed, even attractions with only local appeal can be profitable to the community. But one shouldn't spend a fortune on wasted national advertising or development in such cases.

Support facilities and services (infrastructure) should be inventoried and analyzed as carefully as attractions. These generally fall under the major categories of transportation (internal and external), information-signing, lodging, food-service, and retail commercial. Major deficiencies in either quality or quantity of such things as water, sewer or power can ruin proper tourism development for even the finest of attractions. Although attractions draw visitors to your area, it is from the employment, income, and taxes generated by support facilities and services that most communities profit. Tourism development organizers must always keep in mind that effective tourism is the selling of a total experience to the visitor.

Improperly developed or maintained facilities and services are usually the prime cause for tourism not reaching its fullest potential or in some cases causing total failure.

The distinction between *attractions* and *services* is important. Attractions are aided by services, attractions are promotional, attractions are prime motivators for travel, attractions are often the focus of the planning activity, attractions are site-specific, attractions are often publicly owned and managed, and attractions are more permanent.

Services, on the other hand, require attractions, services are expected by the tourist, services are satisfiers, services are often beyond the planner's control, services are more likely to be privately owned, services are more changeable, and many services are needed to support one attraction.

Interestingly, while attractions "attract" the visitor, it is services that are most likely to generate the economic benefit expected from tourism development. Both attractions and services must be flexible and changeable; in order to sustain themselves, they must change to keep up with new trends and new markets.

Linkages

How tourists get to their destination is an important part of tourism planning. Transportation is the vital link between a destination and the tourists; therefore, it must be inexpensive, frequent, comfortable, fast, and safe.

Travel linkages are essentially part of the infrastructure system, but because they are often ignored, they are given special mention here. Linkages are associated with transportation, but there are also visual and temporal linkages.

For the common traveler, consideration must be given to linking airports, train stations, and bus terminals with other transportation modes, infrastructure, or attractions. These intermodal linkages must not only exist, but they must also be designed for the visitor's convenience. Parking is a prime consideration for auto travelers. Because tourists generally are carrying more valuables in their cars than they would in their day-to-day business at home, the security of their vehicles is paramount in their minds. Even though a community may have adequate transportation facilities, it should be recognized that visitors need information about the system that local citizens might not. Often, signs

on the outside of public transit buses state "have exact fare ready!" Regular commuters know the fare; visitors do not. The warning only served to create apprehension, and thus detract from the visitor experience. Travel information stations, roadside signing, transit system maps showing attractions and support facilities, are all important linkages in keeping the visitor from becoming lost, disoriented, or confused—any of which will detract from the positive tourism experience and can well lead to unfavorable images passed on to other potential visitors. Other linkages can be enhanced by color-coding pedestrian paths or signing for walking tours, and by insuring attractive entrances to attractions. Use of the standardized international scheme for traffic signs will go far toward assisting foreign visitors, as well as those from closer to home, in easily finding their way about.

Few private attractions operate around the clock. There is always some "down-time," especially in smaller communities. Yet the tourist is motivated by his vacation time limits to "do as much as possible" in the allotted time. Therefore there must be linkages, in the form of "filler" opportunities for visitors to enjoy in between major attractions or events. Attractive public parks and recreational facilities offer just one way of filling this time constructively and enjoyably, even if it is only a fifteen-minute respite from extended auto travel. Because these facilities are generally free or at a nominal cost, they also offer the visitor a "breather" from the higher cost of private recreation attractions. The same rule applies to public facilities as to private ones: the more diverse the opportunities, the more potential exists for satisfying the visitor's demand for a fully enriching experience, and the more likely he or she is to stay longer, make return visits, and tell friends.

A note of caution in the provision of public facilities: they should always complement rather than compete with private attractions. Before deciding to develop or improve a public attraction, consideration should be given to whether it might be developed privately, thereby providing income to the community, rather than acting as a financial drain.

International Visitors

The United States has only recently become practical as a major destination for visitors from other countries. 1979 was the first year in modern travel history that foreign arrivals to the U.S. outnumbered U.S. citizens' departures for other countries. By 1980, foreigners actually spent more in this country than Americans spent overseas, thus helping our international balance of payments. In spite of their relatively smaller numbers, foreign visitors generally spend more per trip than visitors from other states.

In 1992, 42 million international visitors spent $45 billion in the United States, directly supporting 900,000 jobs and making travel the largest export industry for this country. More sensitivity to the servicing of international visitors by the United States tourism community can only add to the attractiveness of the United States as an international destination.[1]

Fortunately, most services required by foreign visitors are not unique—they need the same basics that domestic travelers need. However, there are items of language, currency exchange, information, and social, cultural, and religious customs that must be given special consideration by the community that desires to tap this lucrative market. Some of these considerations are best addressed by the public sector; examples of these would be signs and multilingual information stations. As for private industry, banks should be prepared to assist local businesses in currency exchange, and local hoteliers, restaurateurs, and attraction operators should be prepared to invest in multilingual menus, employees, and, in some cases, special foods. Just as North Americans expect their VISA credit cards and American Express travelers' checks to be honored in Europe, so must local business be prepared to accept Lloyds of London travelers' checks or Eurocards.

"Language banks" are another relatively simple method of assisting foreign visitors whose English may be lacking to some degree. One really needs only to survey the community to find out who speaks which foreign language and is willing to be called upon to act as an interpreter should that be necessary. A list of volunteers can be kept at the local police station, hospitals, hotels, restaurants, and service stations. Language banks of various types exist across North America and in many foreign countries.

DO WE REALLY WANT TOURISM?

The first question to be asked before leaping into any extensive development scheme is, "Do we really want more tourism in our community?" Tourism development isn't free, and it requires both resources and commitment which might better be directed elsewhere. A quick look at some of the pros and cons of tourism development may be helpful in making this decision.

Preliminary Considerations

Pros

1. Tourism can be a major income generator, providing jobs, profits, and a tax base like other industries.

---

[1]Data from *Tourism Facts: Travel and Tourism.* (Washington, D.C.: Government Affairs Council, 1991).

2. Nearly all community segments profit financially from tourism.

3. Tourism often makes services available to residents that the community could not otherwise support, such as theaters, parks, sport facilities, and food services.

4. Travel is vital to most all modern industries. Travel and living amenities associated with successful community tourism development may encourage expansion of industries other than those that are directly tourism-related.

5. Tourism-related enterprises provide entry-level jobs for youth and those with minimum skills, and often part-time or seasonal jobs adapt well to the needs of secondary family wage earners.

6. Travel is personally rewarding to most who undertake it. Playing host to those travelers can provide a community with increased pride and sense of direction.

7. The tourism dollar is relatively "clean:" it does not require commitment to new schools, sewers, and roads, which other industries generally necessitate.

Cons

1. Tourism brings strangers into your community whose activities may conflict with those of residents. In communities, this has developed into a "tourism industry" versus a "rest of the community" feeling.

2. The tourism industry is often highly seasonal, and many tourism-related jobs are low-paying.

3. People-pressure on local resources and services may cause environmental deterioration and pollution.

4. Travel requires a high level of energy use in an energy-scarce world.

5. Tourism development often creates inflated prices in a community, which are most detrimental to persons on fixed incomes.

Careful analysis, organization, and planning can help enhance the positive aspects of tourism development and alleviate the negative. Because each community is unique, each must make its decisions based on local circumstances. What has worked in one community may not apply in another.

THE DEVELOPMENT OF TOURISM

If a community decides to move ahead with tourism development, the first step is to perform a preliminary feasibility study to determine, in an objective manner, the assets and liabilities of the community as a tourist destination. This study includes an inventory, analysis of results, and recommendations on directions developments should take. Following or concurrent with the study is the development of a community tourism organization responsible for further membership development, planning, promotion and management control.

Preliminary Feasibility Study

As mentioned earlier, a preliminary feasibility study should enable community leaders to determine if increased tourism development would be beneficial to them and the citizenry. Such a study can be conducted by an individual or group

Norwegian National Tourist Office

in the community. However, sometimes it is best to have a nonbiased outside analysis. If a professional consultant is too expensive, local or nearby colleges and universities often provide help through a contractual arrangement or student projects.

A study of this type is called "preliminary" because it is broad in scope and generally contains no economic cost-benefit figures—merely recommendations for general directions tourism development might take. Should these recommendations call for development of major facilities then a detailed financial feasibility study should follow. The kinds of items to be included in a preliminary feasibility study are:

Location.

Accessibility.

History.

Climate.

Population/demographics.

Labor force.

Industrial base/major employers.

Educational/training opportunities.

Attractions—existing and potential.

Infrastructure.

Legal climate/local-state law.

Community attitudes.

Analysis.

Recommendations.

Some detail on each of the above items follows:

Location.   Where is the community situated vis-à-vis major visitor-generating markets? Is it near other tourist destinations? Is it on a major transportation corridor? What competition might it face?

Accessibility.   How can visitors reach the community? Are air, rail, or water terminals nearby? Is it near an interstate or other major highway system? In what condition are transportation facilities? Is local transport (taxi, bus, limousine service) available within the community? Most small towns are visited by tourists in autos, campers, and motorcoaches. Highway access and good directional signage are therefore of paramount importance.

History.   Every town has a history. Is it significant (or unique) enough to draw visitors from outside the local region? Are there structures or sites which are listed on either the National or State Register of Historic Places? Historical personages or sites of merely local significance may not be capable of drawing visitors from any distance, but can be used to "flesh out" a visitor's stay in the community, just as minor attractions can be used to complement major ones.

Climate.   Tourists are generally drawn to areas of mild climate. Perennial rain, fog, thunderstorms, or blizzards will deter even the most avid outdoor enthusiast. Seasonal climatic conditions will also dictate outdoor event planning. Seasonal pests, such as mosquitoes and black flies, will also deter outdoor activities.

Population/Demographics.   What is the composition of the local populace? Is it primarily elderly or youthful? Are local citizens well educated? What is their income level, ethnic background, sex, family size, and type of housing? All of this information is available through the national census. Tourism tends to provide more jobs for teenagers and the elderly than other industries, although most are not highly paid positions.

Labor Force.   Where are local people employed? How many of working age are unemployed? If the unemployment rate is extremely low, additional tourism development may require importing labor.

Industrial Base/Major Employers.   What are the major industries and employers in the area? Are they growing, declining, or stable? Is there a good mix of industry, or is it a "one-factory" town? Sometimes by default, tourism becomes the major industry in a community. In most areas, however, it is best developed as part of a varied industrial base, lending greater economic stability to the community.

Educational/Training Opportunities.   What kinds of schools are there in the area? Are there opportunities for vocational training or retraining nearby? Are there colleges and universities available to offer assistance in research and development of tourism opportunities, perhaps through extension services? In areas in which residents are being laid off from factory jobs, retraining for the tourism industry can be accomplished with minimal expense if educational facilities in the local area can do the job.

Attractions—Existing and Potential. Attractions are the core of all tourism. They can be natural, scenic, architectural, historic, adventuresome, educational, culinary, festive, or cultural. Often an attraction is a combination of several of the above. What attractions already exist in the community? Who visits them? How are they promoted? Are there other potential attractions which so far have no visitors because of lack of accessibility, visitor amenities or promotion? If attractions are few or nonexistent, can the community create one? This is not meant to imply that a community should create a Disney World, but remember, most special events and festivals are examples of created attractions.

Infrastructure. Infrastructure is a term to describe all the facilities and services that support tourist attractions. Water, sewerage, electrical power, lodging, restaurants, roads, parking, directional signage, bridges, ferries, police, fire and medical services are all necessary to make a place comfortable for visitors. Increased tourism development cannot occur in a vacuum; support facilities and services must be in place. The extent of infrastructure needed will depend upon the type of development contemplated. An annual festival can operate with field parking and portable toilets. If the local water and sewer facilities are operating at maximum capacity, no new motel can be constructed unless those facilities are expanded.

Legal Climate/Local-State Laws. Many states have "blue laws" that prohibit the sale of certain items on Sunday. Some localities prohibit outdoor food service, a deterrent to festival development and sidewalk cafes. On the other hand, most rural communities lack zoning regulations, architectural and signage ordinances, or other legal means to control the type and quality of tourism development. Visual pollution is often the result. Most legislation is restrictive in nature. From the above examples, it is obvious that some restrictions are good for tourism, some detrimental. What form of government exists locally and how easy is it to change state or local legislation to favor tourism development? The legal climate of a community is often a reflection of community attitudes.

Community Attitudes. Tourism cannot flourish, especially in a small town, without support from both the business community and the general citizenry. Apathy or opposition to tourism generally stems from lack of knowledge of

Italian Government Travel Office

tourism benefits. An educational program can often offset these attitudes. In some cases, however, a strong aversion to strangers for whatever reason may nip plans in the bud for increased tourism development.

Analysis. Each of the above categories should be examined, both on its own and in relation to others, to determine what advantages and disadvantages exist toward increasing tourism. If the latter outweigh the former, and cannot easily be alleviated, then community leaders should consider some alternative means for economic development. How can advantages be exploited to their fullest; how can disadvantages be overcome, neutralized or erased? Do you really want to proceed with tourism development?

Recommendations. If the analysis is generally positive toward tourism development, what directions should this development take? The most common route taken by small towns as the first step in tourism development is via a special event, such as a festival.

ORGANIZATION

If the decision is made in favor of tourism development, then organization becomes the key to successful implementation. Traditional community structure will determine the form this organizing effort takes. In some communities, it may be a special tourism committee appointed by the mayor, administrator, council or supervisor. In others, it may be the Chamber of Commerce that is the driving force. Four basic responsibilities will fall to this organizing group: membership development, planning, promotion, and management control.

Involvement by the entire community is an ideal situation in tourism development, but one which seldom happens. It is crucial that as many sectors of the community as possible be represented in the planning and management processes. Leaders of these sectors need to be educated about their role in tourism development and must be committed to performing that role. Critical to success are recruits from the business, banking, arts, historic preservation, recreation, and government sectors. These should be people who have the ability to get things done, and who can be called on for their expertise, labor, or financial assistance. Politicians should leave the planning to professionals.

THE MASTER PLAN

The initial assessment of development potential must now be detailed, based on established goals for the scope and direction of tourism development in the community. If the community has a master plan for development, tourism should be incorporated as an integral part. A review of all local ordinances which might affect tourism development and operations, such as those related to traffic, alcoholic beverages, food services, zoning and signage, should be accomplished, making modifications where necessary. A review of any state and federal legislation that might impact potential tourism development is also advisable. This is of particular importance in coastal areas, where numerous restrictions on certain kinds of development exists. Necessary facilities and services to support a tourism economy should be specified and cost estimated, whether these are public or private. If outside help is needed at this stage, it must be obtained.

The master plan is a procedure for surveying the structure of the destination, its resources, and its attractions. It calls for an evaluation of these resources against existing and potential tourist markets in order to determine travel flows and the main priorities and preferred locations for the further physical development of attractions and services.

The following parts are part of a community tourism development master plan.

I. Surveys and analysis, required in three main areas:
Analysis of the destination area (supply).
Market assessment (demand).
Regional and national policies (to define political, administrative and financial framework which will be involved in the implementation of tourism initiatives and development).

  A. Resource analysis.

    1. Physical surveys of existing and potential resources.
Positive and negative factors.
The alternative use of resources.
The carrying capacity of particular resources.
The difficulty and cost of accessibility.
Natural resources.
  The climate.
  The geomorphology.
  The vegetation cover.
  The hydrology.
  The wildlife.
  The land ownership.
Cultural resources.
  The archaeology.
  Urban developments.
  Achievements.
  Traditions.
  Events.
Negative features.
  Natural drawbacks.
  Dangers to health.

    2. Both existing and planned facilities must be examined.
Details must include:
Tourist facilities, such as hotels, motels, restaurants.
  Their actual facilities.
  Their clientele.
  Their operation.
  Their local and regional impact.
Present tourism product.
  Characteristics
  Organization and management.
Transportation.
  Means of access.
  Transport infrastructure.
Technical infrastructure.
  Water supply.
  Electricity.

Telecommunications.
Sewage and garbage disposal.
Service infrastructure.
Social and demographic structure.
Labor force.
Training facilities.

B. Market assessment (parallel with resource analysis).

1. Identification of the main tourist flows.
    Establish means of classification for identifying groups and flows of origin, by main motivation, by level of spending, by type of travel, by season, by destination or facilities used.
    Outgoing local tourism has to be considered as implying a loss of exchange.

2. Analysis of main tourist flows.
    Their volume, seasonal variations, trends.
    Their socio-economic characteristics.
    Their main motivations and the extent to which these are met in the destination areas.
    Their consumption characteristics.
    The competitive destinations offered.

3. Main potential tourist flows.
    Assessment of future markets is based both on projections of present demands and on an analysis of capacities and quality of resources. At least three main categories of tourism should be distinguished: domestic, international, business. Forecasts are qualitative (type of product, facilities needed, motivation) and quantitative (number of visitors, duration of stay, expenditures, mainly based on:
    Description of present market.
    Trends and influences.
    Analysis of resources.
    Attractions.
    Image comparisons with competitive areas.

4. Markets for future activities.
    Identification of the main type of activities.
    Analysis of present clientele.
    Assessment of trends and future demands.

C. Assessment of the region's structures and policies.
    Tourism development must consider the means of implementation.
    The planning proposals must be within the mainstream of existing political agendas and policies.
    Economic surveys.
    Survey of existing development plans.
    Survey of regional, statewide objectives in tourism development.

II. Determination of priority tourist flows.

A. Goals and priorities for tourism development.

B. Tourist flows and corresponding facilities.

C. Analysis of tourist facilities.
    Elements to be considered:
    Implementability.

Accountability.
Competitiveness.
Compatibility.
Timing.
Impact.

III. The Physical Master Plan.

A. Main elements.

B. Program of additional facilities needed.

C. Main potential users of the facilities.

D. Market performance.

IV. Strategy for implementation.

A. Necessity for coordinated strategy.
   Avoiding deficiencies.
   Achieving coordination of public/private sector, etc.

B. Main aspects of implementation.
   Adapting financing techniques.
   Implementing and controlling facilities.
   Training tourism human resources.
   Transporting tourists.
   Organizing the tourism product.
   Advertising/promotion.
   Land ownership/control.

PROMOTION

The best-laid plan for tourism development and financing are of little value if potential visitors don't know about them. The type of promotion and publicity in which a community invests will be determined by the size and scope of planned tourism operations, the targeted visitor market area, financing available, and availability of supportive promotion from outside the community, such as regional and state travel organizations.

The most common and least-expensive method of advertising is the brochure; the most expensive is the electronic media—radio and television. Coordination and pooling of promotional funds and efforts within the community and with agencies outside the community generally offer more "bang for the buck" and provide for greater exposure than if each attraction attempts to advertise individually.

Management Control

Management control basically covers two areas: coordination of activities and ethics. Tourism activities, particularly festivals and other special events, need to be organized and scheduled to maximize their attraction potential. Sales by retailers can be coordinated with special community events to attract a wider range of visitor types. Operating hours may be staggered from one attraction to another in order to provide activities to appeal to visitors throughout the day, evening, and the entire week.

Poor service, poor product quality, and price-gouging will generally put the perpetrator out of business, but in the meantime these practices—even by only one operator in the community—can reflect badly on the entire community.

Because travelers return to their own locality after a trip, they don't have the opportunity to return faulty merchandise and can't readily complain about sloppy or overpriced service. They do have one devastating recourse—they won't come back, and they may tell others not to visit. Therefore, the community tourism organization must act as a "watchdog" over the ethics of tourism operations. A total community understanding of the importance of ethical practices to the success of tourism can prevent such actions from ever taking place. The International Institute for Quality and Ethics in Services and Tourism suggests the following questions to test for ethics: (1) Is it legal? (2) Does it hurt anyone? (3) Is it fair? (4) Am I being honest? (5) Can I live with myself? (6) Would I publicize my decision? and, (7) What if everyone did it?

Pitfalls to Avoid

Don't overrate a community's attractions. Good schools, churches and libraries may be important to residents, but have little value in attracting visitors. Similarly, a local waterfall may be very attractive, but is it unique enough to draw travelers from the highway?

Don't go "second rate" on promotion. Even if the only advertising is a brochure, it has to be accurate, attractive, and the best the community can afford. Modern travelers are sophisticated, and demand a high-quality experience. In anticipation of this experience, they will be attracted by high-quality advertising.

Planning for tourism development should not be done in secret. The community needs to know what is being done. Conflicts and problems can be settled earlier, and the more everyone feels part of the enterprise, the more support will be generated.

Successful tourism development can be measured by several yardsticks: local business profits, taxes generated to the government, increased employment, favorable community publicity, heightened community spirit, and pride. Seldom do these benefits accrue in equal measure to everyone in the community, and all come at some cost, which is unlikely to be shared any more equally than the benefits. For the general community's sake, the most successful development is when the maximum number of people share the benefits at the minimum cost to each and to the community as a whole.

THE HOSTING FUNCTION

As the tourism industry has expanded, there has been a growing awareness of the importance of tourism to the national economy. Tourism is now a top generator of income and employment in the United States. As the industrial and manufacturing base of this country's economy has continued to decline, the number of service industries has continued to increase. Areas which perhaps never before envisioned themselves as attractive to tourists are suddenly interacting with them on a daily basis. With the influx of tourists comes a need to provide the very best in visitor services.

On the more obvious level, visitor services consist of those elements which sustain the visitor once he or she has come into the area. They differ from attractions in that they do not provide the primary motivation for visiting the area; rather, they enhance the overall visitor experience and provide a wealth of memories and tales. The memories of the services are often that which a visitor will relate to family and friends at home. Stories of a vacation consist of personal encounters more frequently than they consist of descriptions of the scenery or the hotel room. Impressions are apt to be positive or negative, and almost invariably the negative ones remain foremost in the mind, especially if they are not countered with more positive experiences. Because of this tendency of human nature, it is the responsibility of those involved in visitor services to do their utmost to provide only the best to the visitor.

It sounds like a nearly impossible task, and in some instances it can be. However, the majority of visitors will relax and respond cheerfully when treated with the respect they feel they deserve. This is not to suggest, however, that the host need be subservient. In contrast, the host should treat visitors as intelligent equals. The whole idea behind visitors' services is to look beyond the tourist with lodging, food, and parking and concentrate on offering a total experience.

The first step in the process is an understanding of the concept of hosting. Just like guests in a private home, visitors to a community have certain expectations. Hosting is a function of hospitality, knowledge, and caring; it is an attitude that permits a visitor to feel warmly welcomed the instant he or she enters a community. Many visitors to an unfamiliar area will remain uncomfortable until given the signal to relax and enjoy the assistance that is close at hand.

Providing visitor services begins with an analysis of needs. This includes not only capacity requirements, but also the need for additional public services, such as police, sanitation workers and facilities, tourist information personnel, and adequate signage. Needs must be anticipated and planned for accordingly if visitor satisfaction is to result. Ideally, visitor services planning should be included or at least incorporated into the tourism master plan.

The provision of visitor services can be quite costly, and many members of the community will question the legitimacy of such spending and ask: "What's in it for me?" Granted, some of the funding will come from the community, but much of it will come from the visitor in the form of user fees. Parking and admission charges, and lodging and entertainment taxes will come out of the pocket of the visitor, not the resident. As this is not exactly obvious to the average citizen (or lawmaker), education of the local community is the key to successful tourism planning.

Perhaps the way in which residents will most readily relate to the importance of tourism to the community is to educate them on the economic impact. Unfortunately, the means to this end are not always readily available. Ideally, young adults should learn the economics of tourism in the local school system so that they can develop a greater tolerance of tourists. But because children are raised to share the attitudes of their parents, the adults in the community must likewise receive an education. Rather than just being told, "Oh, there is a convention in town, please be extra courteous to the attendees," people must understand why it is so essential that a tourist leave an area as a happy, satisfied customer.

From waiters and waitresses to cab and bus drivers to clerks in fast food restaurants and in the local drug store, the more knowledgeable the local residents are, the better equipped they are to answer questions. The better answer a tourist receives the more satisfied is he or she, and the more likely he or she is to return to a destination and/or to encourage others to visit it. Local enthusiasm is contagious, and transfers itself readily to the visitor. If the visitor perceives a positive community self-image, his or her impression will likewise be positive and the overall experience favorable.

Utah Travel Council

Of course, education and awareness do not just happen. Training programs must be implemented for all persons who meet and serve tourists. Training should have as its focus hosting, the ability to meet and greet tourists, recognizing both their needs and motivations and their importance to the community. Training programs should encompass those who render personal services, those who perform specialized services, the general community, and those staffing tourist information centers.

Personal-services personnel have the most frequent contact with tourists (although perhaps police officers and gas station attendants come close) and should therefore have the most extensive training. Such workers should be made aware of the economic impact of tourism and the importance of the tourists to their own positions in addition to learning how to interact with the wide variety of people they will encounter. Even more importantly, employees should be familiar with the local area so as to be better prepared to deal with inquiries. Some type of familiarization tour may be appropriate for those who interact continuously with the visitors.

Specialized service personnel and the local community must also be prepared to handle tourists. A vital aspect of this education is a community awareness program that enlightens the citizens to the benefits that accrue to them from the tourist dollar.

The aim of a community awareness program is to build a welcoming attitude towards the tourist. In order to achieve this goal, such a program must both convince the members of the community of the value of tourism and help to build an understanding of the tourist. Because of the diversity within the community, efforts at raising awareness must be targeted towards various sectors. The public awareness program must strive to help each sector to understand, in varying degrees, the direct and indirect benefits of tourism; therefore, each group will require emphasis to be placed on the benefit that is most meaningful to the member of the particular group.

The second aim of the community awareness program is to build an understanding of the tourist. Certainly tourists are often regarded as nuisances as they drive slowly, snap photos, and ask for directions. However, any person who has ever vacationed in an unfamiliar area has done the same type of things. It is important that the members of the community realize that the tourist is no different than the locals, just a little bit out of his or her element and feeling a bit confused and defensive. It is difficult to be patient with tourists, particularly in an area inundated with them, but if the hosting function is to be a success, it is essential.

It is easy to say that visitors' services and community awareness programs must be established, but it is far more difficult to implement them. To compound the problem, turnover in service industries is often so high that training sessions would need to be continual in order to be successful. Local cable stations often air segments on tourism and community events, but people rarely tune in to such stations for any length of time unless they perceive some tangible benefits to doing so. Destinations wishing to raise community awareness need to engage in a variety of activities. From seminars to public service announcements, communication is the key.

If it is possible, the most effective means of raising awareness is direct experience. Oftentimes the visitor is more knowledgeable about the area from an attraction angle than the resident because he or she has been given the opportunity to participate in whatever it is that the community has to offer. Special community days, discounted admissions, and off-season rates and season passes are excellent ways in which to generate community enthusiasm. Again, this enthusiasm is easily transferred to the interested visitor.

Basically, the conclusion here is that community relations is a very important aspect of the successful marketing efforts of a destination. Much of the above mentioned activities have fallen into the hands of the convention and visitors' bureau (CVB). The CVB of an area does not exist solely to market the destination to outsiders, but also to market it to "insiders." Indeed, the success of external marketing is interwoven with the effectiveness of internal marketing. The CVB can serve as the avenue by which community awareness is raised. It can sponsor seminars, television programs, and community calendars. The bureau can do much to solidify the relationship between a community and its visitors. Efforts such as these do much to advance the selling of the area to victors. CVBs can sponsor teacher-education programs and take presentations into the schools. On a national scale, the Tourism Awareness Council has designated "Tourism Awareness Days" and has adopted as its mascot "Buck the Tourism Dollar." The Council travels to various trade shows, provides press releases, and sells "Buck" memorabilia to serve as reminders of the importance of tourism to the community.

CONCLUSION

The degree to which the members of a community are educated in regard to both the assets of the area and tourism in general has a significant impact upon the success of tourism. An educated community is better equipped to make decisions about its own future as a tourist destination. Heightened awareness can lead to a greater sense of control, and then to a greater interest in projecting a positive image to outsiders. In short, the success of a destination ultimately rests upon the ability of the community to welcome outsiders and conduct itself as a gracious host.

REVIEW QUESTIONS

1. Why plan for tourism development?
2. Identify and briefly describe the major steps of the planning process.
3. Differentiate between conventional and strategic planning.
4. What is "heritage" tourism?
5. Differentiate between attractions and services. Why are these differences important for tourism planners?
6. Name special provisions that might need to be planned in consideration of international visitors to a community.
7. Define the "hosting function."
8. Why are marketing and promotion considerations important to successful tourism planning?
9. Economic development cannot be tourism planning's exclusive goal. What are other goals of tourism planning?
10. It has been said that "taking the trouble out of travel is the biggest challenge that faces tourism planners." Do you agree?

The Social Impacts of Tourism and Their Effects on Attitudes toward a Major Cultural Attraction

Laurel Reid

Brock University

Allison Boyd

Shaw Festival
Niagara-on-the-Lake, Ontario

INTRODUCTION

The importance of a region's cultural resources in attracting visitors is undeniable. Cultural attractions afford the opportunity to enhance tourism's economic contribution to a region. Venues such as festivals, performing arts (activities) and hallmark events often present opportunities to stimulate tourism through cultural means. Such pursuits help maintain tourist interest in a particular destination and often have the added advantage of extending the tourism season (Tighe, 1986).

While local residents may enjoy initial outside interest in their community, the notoriety and economic gain that accompany such attractions are not without trappings. Tourism visits to a community/region are attended by numerous social impacts. When the influx of tourists is perceived to disrupt existing resident lifestyles, social impacts are predominantly negative. At times, this disruption intensifies so that residents begin to devalue tourism. Intrusions into resident activities may foster unfavorable attitudes toward tourists and these attitudes may, in turn, spread to the entire industry. Since cultural attractions often serve as a catalyst for drawing substantial numbers of tourists, local residents may hold the attraction responsible for some of the effects of the tourist influx. If so, irritation and resentment toward the cultural attraction may surface.

This article was originally published in the *Proceedings of the Twenty-Second Annual Conference of the Travel and Tourism Research Association*, Salt Lake City, Utah, 1991.

When this scenario is present, community leaders may feel pressure from residents to: (1) block legislation that might otherwise be beneficial to the attraction, (2) create zoning regulations that inhibit expansion, (3) restrict development that enhances the attraction, and/or (4) encourage reduced patronage of the attraction by locals. Cultural attractions, by their very nature, often depend on community support for continued existence. Consequently, such venues cannot afford to alienate residents.

The question then arises: do the social impacts of tourism result in negative attitudes toward cultural attractions? If so, which impacts are most pronounced in affecting such attitudes? The answers to these questions would permit cultural attractions to take action in mitigating negative resident perceptions regarding their role in fostering negative social impacts. This paper examines resident perceptions of the social impacts of tourism and their effects on resident attitudes towards the Shaw Festival Theatre, a major cultural attraction located in Canada.

BACKGROUND

Niagara-on-the-Lake, Ontario, Canada has been a popular tourist destination for many years. This destination was chosen for the study since the town depends on tourism for its economic survival and is the home of the internationally acclaimed Shaw Festival Theatre. No other economic force is as strong as tourism for this community. With a population of 4,000, the town employs approximately 40 percent in the tourism industry. (Not all employees live in the town.) More than 2 million visitors flock to the town annually. The most recent estimate valued tourist expenditures at (Cdn.) $35.7 million (Dyck, 1985). For every dollar spent on theatre tickets by tourists, a multiplier effect occurs. Mitchell and Wall (1985) estimated that in 1985, an additional $2.37 was spent on other goods/services in the community for every dollar spent on Shaw tickets.

Founded in 1962, the Shaw Festival is located in the town's center and serves as the catalyst for the multimillion dollar tourism business. In 1990, 265,000 of the total visitors purchased at least one ticket to a Shaw Festival performance (Shaw Festival, 1991). With a total operating budget of (Cnd.) $9.3 million, the Shaw is one of the largest theaters in Canada. There is no denying the Festival's economic value to the town. In 1985, it was estimated that $11.2 million was injected directly into the local economy as a result of the Shaw and the activity of its patrons (Mitchell and Wall, 1985).

The Shaw has long been a controversial topic among residents; it fosters economic prosperity for some and bitterness for others (Lacey, 1988; Cobb, 1986). The Theatre's growth has been accompanied by an increase in the number of tourists to the area. During recent years, locals have not been entirely supportive. Both the popular press and researchers have documented Niagara-on-the-Lake residents as having negative attitudes toward tourism (Anonymous, 1988; Lacey, 1988; Doxey, 1976). Doxey (1976) suggested that the increasing number of visitors posed a threat to resident lifestyles. This author also claimed that locals perceived that "commercialism and greed" had overtaken the town.

A parallel situation existed at the Stratford Shakespearean Theatre, another large Canadian theatre located in the small community of Stratford, Ontario. This Theatre experienced a rapprochement between locals and theatre people when it was established (Lacey, 1988; MacFarlane, 1979). MacFarlane (1979) documents that residents appeared to be primarily concerned about two issues: (1) the "types" of employees that would be hired by a theatre, and (2) the adverse affects the influx of tourists would have on the community.

Such attitudes led Niagara-on-the-Lake residents to vocalize their resentment toward both tourists and those who supported, facilitated, or offered activities associated with tourism (Anonymous, 1988; Doxey, 1976). Some of this irritation was manifested toward the Shaw. In several instances, locals threw stones at tour buses headed for the Theatre. Indeed, Mitchell and Wall (1985) note that even some business proprietors felt the Shaw was "too big" or "beyond the reach of local residents."

Clearly, this community is affected by tourism. Although the economic benefits of tourism to Niagara-on-the-Lake are well documented, little research exists on the social impacts of tourism in the community. Moreover, there is no information on how such impacts can affect resident attitudes towards a major cultural tourist attraction.

TOURISM'S SOCIAL IMPACTS

Although many tourism attractions provide much of the energizing power in a community's tourism system, they are often underappreciated and viewed as "commercial" (Gunn, 1988) Consequently, conflicting goals and interests of the community and its attractions (for example, quality-of-life issues versus profit-motive concerns) can arise and cause rifts. One unfortunate consequence of such upsets is visitor-host hostility and social dissension, leading to lack of support for the cultural attraction that draws visitors.

Sociocultural impacts that arise from tourism have been addressed by a number of scholars (Dogan, 1989; Crandall, 1987; Mathieson and Wall, 1982; Thomason, Crompton and Kamp, 1979; Belisle and Hoy, 1980; Pizam, 1978; Dann, 1977). The negative social effects of tourism can manifest themselves in numerous ways, such as a decline of traditions, materialism, an increase in crime rates, social conflict, and crowding (Dogan, 1989; Belisle and Hoy, 1980; Thomason and others, 1979). The literature frequently cites the following social impacts of tourism as negatively affecting a region: (1) conflicting activities of residents and tourists, (2) growth in undesirable activities, (3) seasonal employment, (4) social dualism, (5) the demonstration effect, (6) congestion, and (7) culture viewed as a commodity. The potential effect of perceptions about these impacts on resident attitudes toward a major cultural attraction are depicted in the model shown in Figure 1 and elaborated on below.

Apart from resident perceptions of social impacts, the model also poses two additional

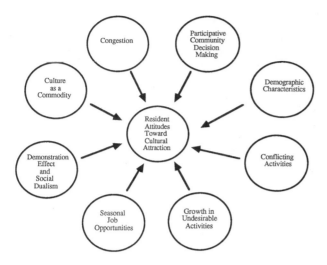

FIGURE 1. Resident Perceptions of Tourism's Social Impacts Effects on Attitudes Toward a Major Cultural

dimensions as having an impact on resident attitudes toward cultural attractions. Both resident demographic characteristics and their participation in community decision making are included as important components of the model. Although not an impact of tourism, per se, the need for participative decision making (consideration and consultation with residents opinions about tourism decisions) has been identified by several authors (Frisby and Getz, 1989; Getz and Frisby, 1988; Gunn, 1988; Cooke, 1982). Allen, Long, Perdue and Kieselbach (1988) suggest that negative resident attitudes towards tourism are partially a result of the lack of resident involvement in tourism-related decisions. The inclusion of residents in decision-making is critical since tourism involves so many facets of the community (Gunn, 1988). Locals should be both solicited for opinions and informed about decisions. Resident input can often provide valuable innovative solutions for decision makers, who sometimes lack the objectivity to clearly see the situation. Whether residents have control over tourism development in their community appears to affect the way they perceive tourists, tourism, and tourist attractions. Resident input also appears to confer more benefits since residents have a vested interest in positive outcomes (Allen and others, 1988).

Conflicting activities of residents and tourists involve tourist activities that interrupt daily resident lifestyles (Dogan, 1989). For example, tourists may use facilities normally frequented by residents, such as restaurants and retail outlets, which places a strain on community services (Thomason and others, 1979). Encounters between the host community and tourists that affect daily resident habits and routines are often a source of psychological tension (Dogan, 1989; Doxey, 1976). Residents may find it harder to purchase tickets for local attractions (Lui, Sheldon, and Var, 1987), and simple chores like going to the grocery store, post office, and/or bank become tedious and frustrating due to the "competition" with tourists for parking spaces and in line-ups. As a result, residents have to alter their behaviors by adapting and adjusting to the tourist influx (Allen and others, 1988; Dogan, 1988; Dann, 1977). Indeed, Mathieson and Wall (1982) suggest that the physical presence of tourists (sharing facilities) is a major source of tourist resentment by residents. If a major cultural attraction is believed to be responsible for much of the tourist flow, such conflicting activities should be correlated with negative attitudes toward attraction.

The influx of tourists into a community can also increase the amount of *undesirable activities* in a town. Activities such as crime, loitering, gambling, prostitution, and alcoholism (Mathieson and Wall, 1982) among others, are ones which no community desires. If these phenomena surface concurrently with the increase in visitors, attitudes toward the attraction are likely to be negative.

In addition to undesirable activities, the customs and traditions that tourists may bring to a destination can also affect residents. This occurrence is termed *social dualism*. If residents view tourists as different from themselves, they may: (1) adopt some tourists' customs as their own, and/or (2) have a tendency to cling to their own customs and traditions (Crandall, 1987). Dogan (1989) suggests that in developing regions, a loss of authenticity/identity of a traditional culture results from the host community's tendency to imitate tourists. Although this impact would appear to be most pronounced in the case of developing countries, social dualism is included in the model since, if residents perceive themselves as different from tourists, they many manifest resentment toward visitors to the Shaw.

When there is a disparity between the income of tourists and residents, the *demonstration effect* may be in evidence, where locals want the same luxuries as those of tourists (Crandall, 1987). The demonstration effect can have an impact when residents perceive that tourists have substantially higher incomes than themselves. Several researchers (Crandall, 1987; de Kadt, 1979; Cleverdon, 1979) have been primarily concerned with this effect as it applies to developing countries. However, such an effect could also occur in developed countries, either in poorer regions or in areas where the reverse is true (that is, residents perceive they have substantially higher incomes than tourists). While the former perceptions might lead to resentment (Mathieson and Wall, 1982), the latter may lead to feelings of superiority on the part of residents.

Seasonal employment is a socioeconomic impact that often occurs in a town dependent on tourism for prosperity. Tourism's seasonal nature has an effect on the job market (Crandall, 1987). One might hypothesize that favorable attitudes should exist toward a cultural attraction in such a town since it creates additional seasonal jobs. However, Mathieson and Wall (1982) suggest that the resident resentment exists when seasonal employment due to tourism dominates a community. Even though employment increases during peak periods, many available jobs have traditionally been low-paying since they are perceived as requiring few skills. Moreover, the creation of such jobs may mean workers are unemployed for the remainder of the year and/or must find alternative employment. Consequently, it is important to know whether residents view seasonal employment opportunities in a positive light and how these views translate to attitudes toward the Shaw.

An additional social impact of tourism can be referred to as *culture as a commodity*. Crandall (1987) suggests that this occurs when the culture and traditions of the town become marketable commodities. On the one hand, traditions may lose their meaning in residents' eyes since ceremonies/rituals are performed to attract tourists who may have little understanding of the underlying importance of such activities (Cleverdon, 1979; de Kadt, 1979). On the other hand, tourism may preserve or revive the heritage of a community in the form of architecture, monuments, arts and crafts (Crandall, 1987). When the former situation prevails, attitudes toward a cultural attraction are likely to be negative. However, in the latter case, the attraction is likely to be viewed in a more positive light since it represents an agent of cultural preservation and heritage.

Congestion is a final social impact of tourism. This phenomenon occurs when the daily lifestyles of residents are affected by increased vehicle and pedestrian traffic due to the influx of tourists. Tourist town populations are in a state of continual expansion and contraction; a year for such towns can be divided into peak and lull periods (Rothman, 1978). Consequently, overcrowding and congestion, in the instances of both vehicle and pedestrian traffic, often occur during peak periods. Ritchie and Aitken (1984) found that prior to hosting a hallmark event, Calgary, Alberta residents were extremely concerned about congestion and traffic. If such congestion is primarily attributed to the attraction, negative attitudes toward the attraction are likely to surface.

In summary, the social impacts of tourism prove to be negative if the influx of tourists disrupts resident lifestyles. When the effects of tourism are perceived negatively by members of the host community, resident reactions often take the form of resistance (Dogan, 1989). This resistance may manifest itself in negative attitudes toward tourism and the cultural attraction which precipitates tourists visits.

The above discussion points to a need for addressing the factors that have an impact on attitudes toward cultural attractions. The study poses a conceptual model for examining the social impacts of tourism as related to attitudes toward a cultural attraction. It is anticipated that negatively perceived social impacts will result in negative attitudes toward the cultural attraction, while positively perceived impacts will result in positive attitudes. The research investigation outlined below examines: (a) perceptions of tourism's social impacts, and (b) the variables that have the most effect on attitudes toward a cultural attraction.

METHODS

The study employed a survey research design. With a total of 4,000 residents, the "old town" of Niagara-on-the-Lake represented the population under investigation. This district is the location of the Shaw Festival and the area most directly affected by tourism. The tourist season was defined as the months of April through September, inclusive.

A systematic random sample (n=110) was drawn from a list of names in the telephone directory. Potential respondents were restricted to those eighteen years of age or older who were not employed by or serving on the Board of Directors for the Shaw Festival Theatre. A telephone questionnaire was developed, pretested, then administered by five trained interviewers over three week nights during April 1990. In the event of a "no answer" or selection of an inappropriate respondent, the next number on the list was selected.

The questionnaire consisted of structured, closed-ended questions and was divided into two major sections: (a) resident degree of agreement with statements describing tourism's social impacts and attitudes toward the Shaw Festival, and (b) demographic characteristics. Questions addressing respondent attitudes and perceptions were measured using a five-point Likert scale,

ranging from strongly disagree to strongly agree or extremely unfavorable to extremely favorable. Respondent scores were averaged creating an attitude index measuring the degree to which residents agreed/disagreed with statements about tourism's social impacts in different categories. Data were also analyzed using stepwise multiple regression. The results of these analyses are presented below.

RESULTS AND DISCUSSION

Respondents paint a picture of living in a stable, upscale retirement community. Half (49.3 percent) are over fifty years of age. Locals are also relatively well educated; 50 percent have a college

TABLE 1   Resident Perceptions of Tourism's Social Impacts

(n = 98)	MEAN[a]	STANDARD DEVIATION
DEPENDENT VARIABLE		
• Attitudes Toward the Shaw Festival[b]	3.948	1.228
INDEPENDENT VARIABLES		
• Participative Decision Making		
-Town organizations involved in tourism planning should consider resident opinions	4.086	.996
-Resident opinions have been considered in tourism planning	2.333	1.155
• Conflicting Activities		
-Parking spaces more difficult to find during tourist season	4.693	.524
-Bank lines are longer during tourist season	3.650	.925
-Grocery store lines are longer during tourist season	3.307	1.007
-Post office lines are longer during tourist season	3.119	.962
-Commuting to work takes longer during tourist season	2.378	1.284
• Undesirable Activities		
-Loitering increases during tourist season	3.099	1.171
-Crime has increased in the past five years	2.798	.990
-Increased crime is the result of the volume of tourists	2.280	.792
• Social Dualism & Demonstration Effect		
-Perceived income of tourists[c]	3.345	1.256
-Tourists are different than myself	2.653	.984
• Seasonal Employment		
-Job opportunities for residents increase during tourist season	4.297	.701
• Culture as a Commodity		
-Plays at the Shaw are targeted primarily at tourists	3.475	1.064
-Historical buildings restored primarily to make town appealing to tourists	3.069	1.079
• Congestion		
-Vehicle traffic volume increases during tourist season	4.723	.634
-Pedestrian traffic increases during tourist season	4.644	.540
-Increased vehicle traffic volume interrupts daily patterns of residents	3.929	1.096
-Increased pedestrian traffic interrupts daily patterns of residents	3.677	1.141

[a]Mean measured on a five-point Likert scale ranging from 1 (strongly disagree) to 5 (strongly agree).
[b]Five-point Likert scale ranging from 1 (extremely unfavorable) to 5 (extremely favorable).
[c]Perceived tourist income measured on six-point scale (1=less than $20,999; 2=$21,000-30,999, 2=$31,000-40,999 . . . 6=$61,000 plus).

education or more and incomes of at least $30,000. Sixty-seven percent have lived in the town for more than ten years and only about one-fourth (21 percent) are employed in tourism.

Resident attitudes toward the Shaw Festival and tourism's perceived social impacts are presented in Table 1. With regard to attitudes toward the Shaw Festival, the dependent variable, respondents are generally favorable (x = 3.948). The support for the Shaw Festival is likely due to resident knowledge/awareness that the town is economically dependent on tourism for its survival and the active role the Shaw Festival plays in attracting visitors. Since relatively few respondents are directly employed in tourism (only 21 percent were employed in tourism), these favorable attitudes are not attributed to individual economic reliance on the tourism industry. These results are parallel to those found for residents of Stratford, Ontario who held favorable attitudes toward the Stratford Shakespearean Festival, in spite of the changes that the attraction brought to their town (MacFarlane, 1979). Similarly, Niagara-on-the-Lake residents experience some social impacts of tourism but still maintain favorable attitudes towards the Shaw Festival.

With respect to the independent variables, Table 1 shows that residents strongly agree that organizations involved in tourism planning should *consider resident opinions* (x = 4.086), but most residents feel that their opinions have not been considered in the past (x = 2.333). Although not a direct social impact of tourism, resident participation in tourism development and planning often affects their perceptions of tourism (Allen and others, 1988). Perhaps resident involvement in planning and development efforts by the Shaw Festival would mitigate some of the social impacts of tourism, as suggested by Cooke (1982).

The most negatively perceived social impacts of tourism are in the areas of: (1) conflicting activities (parking spaces are more difficult to find during the tourist season (x = 4.693), (2) job opportunities for residents during the tourist season (x = 4.297), and (3) congestion in the forms of: (a) increased vehicle traffic (x = 4.723), and (b) increased pedestrian traffic (x - 4.644).

In terms of *conflicting activities*, most respondents indicate that with two possible exceptions, most of their daily activities do not conflict with tourists. The difficulty of find a parking space downtown during the tourist season is perceived as the major conflicting activity (x = 4.693),

while bank lines are thought to be somewhat longer during the tourist season (x = 3.65). The relative neutrality of respondent attitudes about other potentially conflicting activities may be due to the fact that residents have adjusted for the tourist influx during the summer by carrying out their daily activities in facilities outside of Niagara-on-the-Lake and/or during off-peak hours during the day. These findings may indicate that residents are adopting a strategy of *"retreatism"* (Dogan, 1989), perhaps more aptly termed *"avoidance,"* where residents attempt to avoid contact with visitors.

Undesirable activities are not perceived as major social impacts in Niagara-on-the-Lake. Gambling and prostitution are not addressed since neither of these activities is in evidence in the town. Neither crime (x = 2.798) nor loitering (x = 3.099) are perceived to increase during the tourist season. Respondents are neutral in these categories. The perception that crime has not increased may be due to the town's: (a) relatively small population (4,000), (b) demographic make-up (over one-third of respondents were over sixty years of age), and/or (c) historical/cultural character, which is not conducive to such activities.

Social dualism and the demonstration effect are not viewed as tourist impacts, as reflected in the findings. With regard to *social dualism*, respondents do not perceive tourists to be substantially different than themselves (x = 2.653). Niagara-on-the-Lake tourists are primarily drawn from Canada and the United States, thus residents and tourists share many of the same customs and traditions. Consequently, tourism does not appear to be linked with disrupting culture and/or ways of life. Social dualism is an impact that seems to be more often evident in countries that obtain a high percentage of foreign visitors where customs and traditions differ noticeably from those of residents.

The *demonstration effect* involves differing income levels and/or consumption patterns by residents and tourists. This construct is measured by resident perceptions about the income of tourists. The mean reported income of respondents and mean of perceived tourist incomes were approximately the same (both between $31,000–$40,000 yearly). This finding suggests that residents perceive that there is little difference between their incomes and those of tourists. Consequently, there is little evidence of the demonstration effect in Niagara-on-the-Lake.

As anticipated, residents perceive that *job opportunities* increase during the tourist season (x = 4.297). Tourism thus creates the opportunity for residents to be employed in seasonal jobs and may offer residents income opportunities that would otherwise be unavailable. Such jobs may free up resident time during the winter months, an important consideration if one is retired, as is the case with over 30 percent of the town's resident population. In addition, the average length of residency indicates the presence of well-established families. Consequently, even though residents may not pursue seasonal job opportunities, it is likely that their children and/or grandchildren do.

Respondents are relatively neutral (x = 3.069) regarding the perceptions of the town as *cultural commodity*. Doxey's (1976) assertion that "commercialism and greed" have permeated the town seems overstated. Even though residents perceive that building restorations and many town improvements are for tourist purposes, many respondents acknowledged that such activities were necessary for a town that is economically dependent on tourism. In addition, the town's heritage has been preserved in many ways in the form of parks, historic attractions and architectural restoration. Residents thus enjoy an aesthetically pleasing environment.

The most emphasized impact of tourism in Niagara-on-the-Lake appears to be *congestion*. Since congestion is highly visible and can have an immediate and direct impact on anyone walking or driving, residents appear to have developed strong attitudes about this issue. While other impacts may be given cursory attention by residents, it is difficult to ignore an excess number of vehicles and pedestrians on streets and sidewalks during the tourist season. Perceived increases in both vehicle (x = 4.723) and pedestrian (x = 4.644) traffic may have simply led many residents to avoid the downtown area completely during peak periods. In fact, unsolicited comments from respondents regarding their adoption of these avoidance strategies illustrate how many residents seem to adjust their schedules due to tourist congestion.

PREDICTING ATTITUDES TOWARD THE CULTURAL ATTRACTION

In order to assess which social impacts had the most effect on attitudes toward the Shaw Festival, stepwise multiple regression was performed. De-mographic variables entered into the equation included age, education, and income level, and number of years of residence. Additional independent variables were selected for inclusion in the regression equation on the basis of: (a) the statistical significance of their associations with the dependent variable, and (b) representation of each major category identified in Table 1 (and the model in Figure 1). The model was refined based on theoretical considerations, relative beta weight contributions, examination of partial correlation coefficients, and the statistical significance of each variable in the model. The final regression equation is presented in Table 2.

As Table 2 shows, only three variables were found to be significant in explaining attitudes toward the Shaw Festival. The results show that resident education levels and the perceptions of (a) loitering and (b) job opportunities for residents during the tourist season, collectively explain 14.8 percent of the variation in resident attitudes toward the Shaw Festival. Education levels of the resident sample explains 7 percent of the variation in attitudes toward the Shaw Festival. The inclusion of loitering increases the model's explanatory power by an additional 5 percent, while perceived job opportunities adds to the model's prediction capability by only 2.5 percent. Although the model explains a relatively small amount of variance in attitudes toward the Shaw Festival (R^2 = .1476), the equation is highly significant (p ≤ .005). By examining the standardized beta weights, one can conclude that resident education levels, perception of loitering, and perceived seasonal job opportunities represent the "best" predictors of attitudes toward the Shaw Festival, in descending order of importance.

Figure 2 visually depicts the results of the regression. As one might expect, the higher the education of residents, the more favorable are attitudes toward the Shaw Festival. Respondents are relatively well educated. Half (49.3 percent) have obtained formal education beyond high school in the form of a college diploma, university degree, or graduate degree; an additional 42.3 percent have at least a high school education. It is likely that residents with these education levels are aware of the Shaw Festival's importance to the town in attracting tourists and keep abreast of community developments of which the Shaw is part.

The findings suggest that educational efforts to inform residents about the benefits of the Shaw and its activities are likely to be well re-

TABLE 2   Regression Model for Predicting Attitudes Toward the Shaw Festival*

VARIABLE	ADJUST. R SQR.	STD. ERROR	BETA COEF.	SIGNIF. (t)
Demographics (Education of Residents)	.0708	.085	.312	.0023
Undesirable Activities (Loitering)	.1230	.103	−.250	.0125
Perceived Job Opportunities for Residents	.1476	.171	.155	.0504

*Adjusted R squared = .1476; Multiple R = .377
  F = 7.437
  Model Significance = p < .0044; n = 91
  Durbin Watson d = 1.927

ceived by the community. These results also have implications for the types of promotional approaches that can be used by the Shaw Festival to inform residents about tourist related activities with which they are involved. These efforts can help maintain community support.

The model also shows that the greater the perception of increased loitering (an undesirable activity), the less-favorable resident attitudes are likely to be toward the Shaw. Since loitering is not perceived as a major impact of tourism, it is difficult to assess the meaning of these results. One must examine the incidence of loitering as well as the identity of the loiterers. Since most of the loitering occurs in downtown Niagara-on-the-Lake during the evening, it may be directly linked by residents to Shaw performances. Residents have recently expressed some concerns over loitering by teen-aged residents since "there is nothing to do," especially in the evening (*Niagara Advance*, 1990, p. 4). In recent months, there has been a strongly supported proposal for a youth center to alleviate this problem.

In addition to the above variables, the greater the perceived job opportunities for residents during the tourist season, the more likely residents are to have favorable attitudes toward the Shaw Festival. Since the Shaw Festival is viewed as a catalyst for tourism to the town, it appears to be linked to creation of job opportunities for residents. Most retail and service establishments either commence operation or hire additional employees when the Shaw season begins. Many employees are hired from the surrounding area. Numerous families are long established in the area, so it is likely that if one is not employed in tourism, a relative who lives nearby is. As long as seasonal demand for the destination continues the Shaw will probably be linked to job creation since such employment opportunities may not otherwise exist.

Interestingly, congestion, a major perceived impact, does not appear to have any effect on attitudes toward the Shaw. Perhaps congestion is not linked to the Shaw due to the fact that visitors also travel to other attractions in the region. Winery tours and fruit markets as well as the scenic Niagara Parkway have all spawned additional traffic to the Peninsula. Since driving is the major mode of transportation into the town (the only other way is by boat), it is understandable that this may have an impact on residents during peak times. However, traffic irritation may also be a phenomenon that is instantaneous—a response of the moment—that does not carry over to the Shaw, but rather is directed at the individual driver.

LIMITATIONS

Three limitations affect the scope of this research. First, the sample is limited to Niagara-on-the-Lake

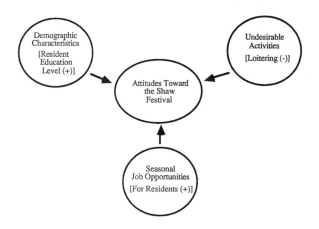

* A minus sign (-) indicates that an *increase* in this category (variable) statistically results in *less* favorable attitudes toward the Shaw Festival. A plus sign (+) indicates that an *increase* in this category (variable) statistically results in *more* favorable attitudes toward the Shaw Festival.

FIGURE 2.   Empirically Tested Model of Perceived Social Impacts and Their Effects on Attitudes Toward the Shaw Festival*

residents who are eighteen years of age or older, have telephones, and could be reached at home during the specified calling times. Second, the specificity of the site limits the generalizability of the study to other tourist communities. Finally, in some instances, only one variable was used to measure the construct under investigation. Alternate measures should be included to enhance the validity of the operationalized variables.

CONCLUSIONS

In conclusion, Niagara-on-the-Lake residents perceive four social impacts as having the greatest effect: (1) vehicle congestion, (2) the difficulty of finding parking spaces (conflicting activity), (3) pedestrian congestion, and (4) increased job opportunities for residents. In addition, residents generally have positive attitudes toward the Shaw Festival.

Although residents experience these tourism impacts, the results of this study indicate that heavy tourism to an area and its associated social impacts do not lead to negative perceptions of a cultural attraction. The study isolates only three factors that affect attitudes toward the Shaw Festival: (1) resident education levels, (2) perceptions of loitering, and (3) perceived job opportunities for residents. The major negative social impact of tourism (that is, congestion) is not linked to attitudes toward the Shaw.

These findings point to the need for the Shaw to continue its efforts to inform the community about its activities, including in the area of employment of area residents. In addition, it is recommended that the Shaw be represented on the Board of Directors of the proposed youth center. The Theatre might also consider offering "acting" or "props" workshops to youths.

This paper offers several insights into the perceived social impacts of tourism in a small community. The paper also points to three factors that have an effect on resident attitudes toward a major cultural attraction.

REFERENCES

Allen, L. R., P. T. Long, R. R. Perdue, and S. Kieselbach, "The Impact of Tourism Development on Residents' Perceptions of Community Life," *Journal of Travel Research*, 10 (1) (1988), 16–21.

Anonymous, *Hamilton Spectator*, June 22, 1988, p. A-1.

Belisle, F. J. and D. R. Hoy, "The Perceived Impact of Tourism by Residents: A Case Study in Santa Marta, Columbia," *Annals of Tourism Research*, 7 (1) (1980), 83–101.

Cleverdon, R., *The Economic and Social Impact of International Tourism on Developing Countries*, E.I.U. Special Report No. 60, London: Economist Intelligence Unit, 1979.

Cobb, D., "Voices Offstage," *Toronto Life*, June 1986, 44–45, 76–88.

Cooke, C., "Guidelines for Socially Appropriate Tourism Development in British Columbia," *Journal of Travel Research*, 21(1) (1982), 22–28.

Crandall, D., "The Social Impact of Tourism on Developing Regions and its Measurement," ed. *Travel, Tourism, and Hospitality Research: A Handbook for Managers and Researchers*, J. R. Ritchie and C. R. Goeldner. New York: Wiley, pp. 373–383.

Dann, G., "Anomie, Ego-enhancement and Tourism," *Annals of Tourism Research*, 4 (1977), 184–194.

de Kadt, E., "Social Planning for Tourism in the Developing Countries," *Annals of Tourism Research*, 6(2) (1979), 36–48.

Dogan, H. Z., "Forms of Adjustment: Sociocultural Impacts of Tourism," *Annals of Tourism Research*, 16 (2) (1989), 216–234.

Doxey, G. V., "When Enough's Enough: the Natives are Restless in Old Niagara," *Heritage Canada*, 2 (2) (1976), 26–27.

Dyck, Judith, *Economic Impact of Tourism in the Community of Niagara-on-the-Lake*, Niagara-on-the-Lake, Ontario: Chamber of Commerce, 1985.

Frisby, W., and D. Getz, "Festival Management: A Case Study Perspective," *Journal of Travel Research*, 28 (1) (1989), 7–11.

Getz, D., and W. Frisby, "Evaluating Management Effectiveness in Community-Run Festivals," *Journal of Travel Research*, 27 (1) (1988), 22–27.

Gunn, Clare, *Tourism Planning*. New York: Taylor and Francis, 1988.

Lacey, L. "A Tale of Two Cities," *The Globe and Mail*, July 1988, C1, C7.

Lui J., P. Sheldon, and T. Var, "Resident Perceptions of the Environmental Impacts of Tourism," *Annals of Tourism Research*, 14 (1) (1987), 17–37.

MacFarlane, R. N., *Social Impact of Tourism: Resident Attitudes in Stratford*, (Unpublished Masters Thesis, London, Ontario: University of Western Ontario, 1979).

Mathieson, A., and G. Wall, *Tourism: Economic, Physical, and Social Impacts.* New York: Longman, 1982.

Mitchell, C., and G. Wall, *The Impact of the Shaw Festival* (Research Report). Waterloo, Ontario: Department of Geography, University of Waterloo, Ontario Ministry of Citizenship and Culture and the Shaw Festival Theatre Foundation, December, 1985.

Niagara Advance, June 18, 1990, 1,4.

Pizam, A., "Tourism's Impacts: The Social Costs to the Destination Community as Perceived by its Residents," *Journal of Travel Research*, 16 (2) (1978), 8–12.

Ritchie, J. R. B., "Assessing the Impact of Hallmark Events: Conceptual and Research Issues," *Journal of Travel Research*, 23 (1) (1984), 2–11.

Ritchie, J. R. B., and C. E. Aitken, "Olympulse II: Evolving Resident Attitudes Toward the 1988 Olympic Winter Games," *Journal of Travel Research*, 23 (3) (1984), 28–33.

Rothman, R. A., "Residents and Transients: Community Reaction to Seasonal Visitors," *Journal of Travel Research*, 16 (3) (1978), 8–13.

Shaw Festival, *Facts about the Shaw*, Niagara-on-the-Lake: Shaw Festival Theatre Foundation, 1991.

Thomason, P., J. L. Crompton, and B. D. Kamp, "A Study of the Attitudes of Impacted Groups Within a Host Community Toward Prolonged Stay Tourist Visitors," *Journal of Travel Research*, 17 (1) (1979), 2–6.

Tighe, A. J. "The Arts/Tourism Partnership," *Journal of Travel Research*, 24 (3) (1986), 2–6.

The Heritage Resource
as Seen by the Tourist:
The Heritage Connection

Karen Ida Peterson

President, Principal
Davidson-Peterson Associates, Inc.
18 Brickyard Court
York, Maine 03909

Over the past several years, we have noted the increasing importance of heritage tourism to the growth and development of tourism destinations with whom we have worked. One reason may well be that our heritage resource and the history of a town, city, or region is totally unique. Tourism attractions such as amusement parks, water slides, zoos, or other modern-day activities for tourists can easily be duplicated in many areas; historic resources cannot. They provide a sense of place, a sense of difference, a uniqueness for any community or area. As such, they offer a reason to visit a destination area or an attractive place to visit for tourists who come to the area for other reasons.

WHAT IS HERITAGE TOURISM?

Perhaps it would be helpful to review what tourists see as the heritage resource. In general, tourists do not subscribe to the definition that age makes a resource historic. Indeed, some of the most popular historic sites for tourists are, from the historian's perspective, quite modern—the Kennedy Space Center, for example. Indeed, in a recent Florida tourism survey, the Kennedy Space Center emerged as one of the state's top attrac-

tions thought of as historic sites. The other was Disneyworld's Epcot Center.

Although tourists include a wide variety of different types of resources in their heritage tourism category, I'd like to focus today on what we may think of as more traditional heritage tourism—*visiting historic sites. Historic* can be defined very broadly—from he colonial period of the 1600s through the second World War to NASA space centers; from the colonization of the U.S. to our civil rights struggles in the 1960s. We think of heritage tourism as visitation to sites or areas which make the visitor think of an earlier time.

CATEGORIES OF VISITORS TO HERITAGE SITES

Our work has suggested four different types of heritage tourism visitors. At one end of the scale are the true *aficionados*—preservationists, perhaps nearly professional in studying history. They are interested in the historic resource in great depth; they are often focused on a particular period in history, a particular type of artifact, or a particular architectural style. They visit a historic site to learn and enjoy—but to do so on a very detailed, involved level. They may be heritage professionals—or well-qualified amateurs. But they represent only a very small portion of the visitors to any historic site. And, I will not be presenting their views of heritage tourism today.

This article was originally presented at the twenty-first annual conference of the Travel and Tourism Research Association, 1990.

At the other end of the scale are those individuals whom we have labeled *casual visitors*. These visitors use historic sites almost as parks, as safe, green spaces to which they go to enjoy an afternoon of rest and relaxation. We saw these visitors at historic sites in the Hudson River valley, and north of Boston—only a short distance from the cities where they live in massive apartment buildings. For them, the historic site has become a safe haven, a place to enjoy the outdoors, essentially an urban backyard. For them, the site is important for its grounds, not for its history. We'll not be discussing these casual visitors today either.

A third group of site visitors we have called *event visitors*. Many historic sites hold events on the property to heighten both interest in and visitation to the site. Both local residents and tourists are drawn to attending an event at a historic site—if they are interested in the event itself. These events include *major military reenactments*, such as the one held several years ago in San Antonio, in which key events in the battle and siege of the Alamo were staged by costumed characters to the delight of the assembled crowds of residents and tourists. Such an event is one of major proportions—key to tourism to the Alamo, San Antonio, and the state.

But all reenactments or military events aren't so dramatic. Sometimes Civil War soldiers simply camp at a relevant historic site, cooking meals as soldiers would have and sleeping in their typical overnight accommodations. These soldiers are then available to talk with visitors and explain and teach about military life. Even the colonial militia do reenactments and encampments, drawing tourists and residents alike.

Other events at historic sites might include arts festivals, concerts, ethnic festivals, and so on. These large festivals draw crowds, who may not use the historic resource especially deeply. The site becomes a stage—and one sometimes lost sight of. Perhaps historic crafts and tasks festivals provide a stronger heritage focus for the events.

These smaller events are specifically developed and designed by historic attractions to provide local residents with a reason to visit the historic resource—to create a sense of liveliness, action and a reason for visiting *today*. These events are important considerations for a historic site, but event visitors are most often locals—not tourists.

Finally, our fourth and most important category of heritage visitors—the *tourists*. Our heritage tourism connection focuses primarily on this group of visitors, those who are out of their normal routine, away from home and visiting historic sites.

TYPES OF SITES

Some historic sites are destinations. Tourists plan a vacation or weekend getaway to visit the historic site. Examples might be areas such as Colonial Williamsburg, Greenfield Village, or Living History Farms in Iowa. These historic sites have sufficient mass, sufficient advertising and marketing, and sufficient appeal to hold a tourist's interest for a day or longer. They offer a lot to see and do, special programs, and tours of interest to different tourists. They are historic *attractors*.

Most historic sites, however, are *attractions*. They provide something to see or do in a destination area when the tourist has arrived there for other reasons. Some may be well enough known to be on the visitor's list of places to go in the area before he or she arrives, but most will be learned of when the tourist arrives in the area.

But some historic resources are also used today as a stage for other activities. Adaptive reuse permits the renovation of historic warehouses, factories, or other buildings as sites for shopping, dining, and other tourist activities. Ghiradelli Square in San Francisco, Quincy Market in Boston, and Larimer Square in Denver would be examples. Why, then, do these heritage tourists choose to make a trip to enjoy historic sites or visit those sites when they are traveling?

PROS AND CONS OF VISITING HISTORIC SITES

Using the traditional focused group discussion method, we have talked with many tourists who visit historic sites about their reasons for so doing. The group method has allowed us to delve into motivations and reasons for visiting as well as into attitudes toward the historic site components of a fun and interesting vacation.

From those conversations, we can parse out three major reasons for visiting historic sites. For many, the joy of a historic site visit is in *experiencing a different time or place*. With the frenetic hectic pace of today, it is important to experience what has gone before, to feel how life was different at different times. This historic experience is often sensory, providing the participant with a feeling which cannot be obtained elsewhere. This joy in visiting historic sites does not depend on a particular famous person or event. Rather, it depends on the ability to sense and feel a different place and time.

Visitors also go to historic sites to *learn*—to enjoy a cerebral experience. They wish to learn more about what has gone before. Some are especially intrigued with learning about specific individuals—a visit to Monticello cannot fail to impress one with the specialness of Thomas Jefferson as a man and as a creative genius. Some are intrigued by what events have taken place. The resurgence of interest in Civil War battlefields, in retracing the steps of early pioneers, in seeing the sites of the gold rush are testimony to this interest in being where something important (or even not so important) actually happened.

Finally, some tourists want to share with others or teach their children what they know about the history of our country. Parents are even more anxious today than they have been in the past to show their children their heritage, their roots, the history which is relevant to them. As we will see, this reason for visiting may be the greatest challenge to historic site managers and guides. Children need to participate, to be involved, to learn from doing as well as seeing. A historic site which offers only passive, observational experiences may do more to *reduce* children's interest than to heighten it!

And, why do some travelers and tourists avoid historic sites when they are visiting an area? "History is boring!"

Although the group interested in heritage tourism is growing, there remain many in our population who remember dreadfully dull history lessons or terribly boring visits to historic sites who have no interest in being bored further during their vacation trips. Heritage tourism development and marketing will need to address these resistances as we strive to persuade even more travelers to visit our historic sites.

For those who enjoy historic sites, what constitutes a good visit? What makes a visitor go home and tell his or her friends that a particular site is worth visiting?

First, the site needs to provide a strong sense that the visitor has *"stepped back in time."* They want to feel they have truly experienced another place in time, to learn or understand how life was then. The phrase—stepping back in time—is per-

haps the quintessential description of a good historic visit experience.

Many enjoy making *"connections"* between our time and an earlier time. They leave a site happily when they have developed a sense of appreciation for how different, and often how difficult life was "then" as well as a sense of appreciation for how lucky we are "now."

Most importantly, however, a visit will be successful if the guest has developed a good understanding of the *people* who lived, worked, or played in the historic resource in other times. Most historic site visitors are interested primarily in the people—not just the artifacts or the structure. They want to know how people lived, how they worked, how they played, how their lives were different from our lives today. And, they love historic gossip—the fun stories which bring those people to life. They want the stories to be true. But they want them to be fun, too.

What makes a historic site visit a less-than-positive experience? It is the physical barriers that create psychological barriers between the visitor and the experience of history. If what the visitor wants most is to step back in time and to feel the historic space, what turns him or her off most is being prevented from doing so. When visitors are prevented from being in the space, from experiencing and feeling what life was like in that space, they do not enjoy the visit.

Most heinous is the plexiglass shield that lets one see into a room from outside—but not to enter. Ropes that allow visitors only to see in or to stand in a 3-foot square area in the room also reduce the intensity of the experience to almost nil. "Please do not touch" signs also create barriers—ones especially difficult for children to deal with.

MAXIMIZING VISITORS' POSITIVE EXPERIENCES

The key goal needs to be to *involve the visitors* in the historic period that is being interpreted, to make them feel that they are experiencing the resource the way the original residents or workers did.

One way to do this is to involve visitors through dramatizations. The Astor Mansion in Newport, Rhode Island, does a wonderful job of involving its visitors. As you approach the front door of the mansion, you are greeted by the butler for Mrs. Astor who welcomes you as guests for the party that evening. He and a cast of other "mansion residents and servants" take you through the house, all the while pretending that you are guests and explaining the house and its contents through the people who lived and worked there.

The play makes a wonderful vehicle for involving the visitors with the mansion and its owners and guests. One leaves with the feeling that he or she really knows what it was like to live and work in this home. It might be worth noting that this mansion is run by a private, for-profit corporation. The other mansions in Newport are owned and managed by the historic society, and permit visitors to identify with wonder and awe at the homes almost in spite of their interpretation, which focuses dryly on the provenance of the artifacts or the details of the architecture. Only in the Astor Mansion does one have a sense of people living there.

Living history demonstrations are also excellent ways for visitors to become involved in the historic resource. Colonial Williamsburg is a prime example of how these methods can be used to enrich the visitor's experience. Men and women dressed in colonial dress undertake the crafts and tasks which their counterparts would have done in earlier times. They actually make products—guns, newspapers, wrought iron, glass, and pottery—as they would have been made in colonial days. Visitors can talk with them about what they're doing, understanding the jobs and tasks which had to be done then. The key is *interaction*—learning and understanding by talking with interpreters and craftspeople as they do their work.

Living History Farms in Iowa offer visitors the opportunity to understand how farming was done at several different periods in our history. The work of the farm is done in each case using methods, tools, and practices which would have been used at that time. Visitors can talk with the farmers and learn what they are doing and why, permitting them to grow in understanding of the lives and work of the earlier farmers. Sturbridge Village and Plimoth Plantation in Massachusetts offer similar types of experiences.

Visitors told us, however, that the experiences are quite different, depending on whether the interpreter working on the site is willing to *talk* with visitors and explain what he or she is doing. In some instances, the interpreters are so busy with their own work that they do not talk with visitors or portray an unwillingness to share. Nat-

urally, that reduces the intensity of the experience for the visitor.

In some places, of course, it isn't possible to have interpreters actually doing work or crafts from a previous period. However, if interpreters are costumed and can present interesting stories about the people who lived, worked or played at the site in previous times, the effect will be positive for the visitor.

Let me stress again the *importance of people* to the historic site visitor. Most visitors are far more interested in the *who* and *why* than in the what and when. They want to understand people and life in a previous time—not to learn about specific objects or architectural details.

The architectural gestalt and the artifacts are, of course, important. They set the stage for understanding how the people lived and worked at the site. But they are far less important in and of themselves than the *people* stories which can be told about those who used the artifacts and lived or worked in the building.

When the people with whom a site is associated are famous, the artifacts take on more significance from the person than from the artifact itself. The bed George Washington slept in is important for that fact—not for its furniture style, cabinetmaker, or provenance.

So, wherever possible to do so, a historic site, area or city will enhance the visitors' experience by focusing on the people whose lives are entwined with the area rather than on the artifacts or architecture in the interpretation.

The focus on people can also be accomplished by the tour companies who show the historic resource. There is a tour offering in San Francisco whose operator is interpreting the 1930s and 1940s for his clients. The tour visits famous Art Deco buildings, but perhaps the most important aspect of the tour is the characters who board the coach to personalize the period. "Rosie the Riveter" comes on board and sings a medley of songs from the period. Also included are "sailors shipping out to war" and "longshoremen working on the docks." In the Great Frisco Crime Tour, the same operator transports his clients back to a time when the city was known for its rascals and rogues. Costumed performers join the tour to play specific historical or literary characters—Black Bart, Dashiel Hammett, the brothel madam, Sally Stanford, and the variety performer, Lotta Crabtree.

In Macon, Georgia, the city tour is guided by Macon's most famous historic resident, the poet,

Sydney Lanier, dressed in top hat and period costume. He speaks as Sydney, telling stories of life during his time in Macon. His clients have an excellent opportunity to understand and appreciate the ante-bellum period through the eyes of someone who lived at that time.

The historic site visit can be further enhanced in many instances by *engaging all the visitors' senses.* To intensify the historic experience, to enable the visitor to imagine life in a particular time and place, we can add the sounds and smells of that time. Playing period music in a ballroom enhances visitors' understanding of entertainment and fun during that period. Cooking and baking in the old style in historic homes offer the visitor an additional sensory experience to help him or her step back in time. There's a wonderful Victorian home in Saint Paul, Minnesota—The Ramsey House—where interpreters bake cookies in the old-fashioned kitchen and offer them to visitors. What a wonderful way to experience the past!

Candlelight tours of period homes during the Christmas season gives visitors a marvelous opportunity to live in earlier times. They see how dim the lighting was, how the homes were decorated for Christmas at different periods, and smell the pine boughs used for decoration. When interpreters are also cooking the Christmas goose or making syllabub and telling visitors what they're doing, the experience is further enhanced.

Strawberry Banke in Portsmouth, New Hampshire opens five of its historic homes for the Christmas Candlelight Stroll which show the progression of Christmas decorations from the colonial period, when no celebration was permitted, through the excesses of the Victorian Christmas to the bubble lights of the 1950s.

Historic site visits are even more involving when the visitor is permitted to handle the artifacts, or perhaps reproductions of the artifacts. In the Indian Mound Museum Visitor Center in Natchez, Mississippi, there is a wonderful children's exhibit with a most unusual sign for a historic site: "Please Touch." A play area on the floor contains pottery pieces and other native American artifacts and encourages the children to handle them. Even if these pieces are reproductions—and I suspect they are—how much better for the child's experience to handle the artifacts and *sense* and *feel* the way the ancient native Americans must have than to press one's nose against the glass and only *see* these artifacts.

In the Washington, D.C. area, there is a colonial site that encourages visitors to participate by actually *doing* the crafts and tasks of an earlier period. They are invited to spin wool into yarn, to make candles by dipping, to make soap, and so on. Most of the tools they use are reproductions, but they are still able to experience the earlier period by working themselves in the way that their forbears did. That is a very compelling experience for the visitor who is interested in learning how life was different then.

If the best, most positive visit to a historic site, involves the visitor in the experience, personalizes the lives and stories of those who lived there, and expands horizons by allowing the visitor to use all of his or her senses to understand the period, what is a bad, boring, dull historic visit?

Probably the worst experience for the visitor is the preferred one for the preservationist. The worst experience is one in which the visitors are *prevented* by physical and psychological barriers from experiencing the historic period. They are kept away from the artifacts and the historic spaces by plexiglass shields, ropes and "do not touch" signs—or by interpreters constantly saying "stay on the runner," "don't touch the furniture," "don't handle anything," and "keep your hands behind your back."

The preservationists prevent visitors from entering the historic spaces to preserve those places and their artifacts for the enjoyment of this and future generations. Saving the historic spaces and the artifacts is, of course, *critical* to perpetuating the resource and providing historic experiences for the future.

Here is where preservationists and heritage tourism developers are on a collision course. Preservationists want to remove the damaging effects of visitors, and visitors won't visit unless they can enjoy the experience. We must begin to work on a compromise, to find ways to allow the visitors to enjoy the experience without seriously damaging the historic resource.

AVOIDING A COLLISION BETWEEN PRESERVATIONISTS AND TOURISM DEVELOPERS

One compromise has been suggested already— protect the real artifacts from visitors but allow them to use, touch, and handle reproductions to understand more fully the lives of the former residents. If cooking or baking in the historic home will damage the resource—and of course it will, at least to some extent—then create a place for such cooking with reproduction equipment to allow the visitors to sense, smell, and learn how it was done and make the important connections to their own lives.

In York, Maine, the Old York Historic Society has created such an experience in a building which is colonial, but was modified improperly by earlier preservations. Today Jefferd's Tavern is used to demonstrate colonial methods of preserving and cooking food. You can see fish and beans drying, spices hanging on the walls, and stews cooking on the open hearth. Samples of peas-porridge and ginger cookies make learning even more fun for both adults and children.

If the sap from pine boughs will damage the finishes on furniture and mantelpieces, don't eliminate the real pine decorations and their delicious smell—protect the furniture. To be sure, other compromises need to be developed to assure the conservation and preservation of our historic resources while making them historic experiences for our guests.

Beyond these interpretive methods, there is one more key to whether visitors enjoy a positive experience in a historic site—the guides. Guides are the historic site's front-line service people. They make or break the experience for the visitors.

THE ROLE OF HERITAGE TOUR GUIDES

Good guides *involve* their tour participants, personalize and enliven the stories of the people, communicate excitement and enthusiasm for the historic resource, and enhance the visitor's experience. Bad ones easily destroy a visit in many ways—boring recitation of irrelevant, uninteresting facts, overemphasis on the provenance of artifacts or architectural details, rudeness to a tour participant, overzealous protecting of the resource, and so on. You've all had a bad guide; unfortunately, they abound.

The historic-site management challenge here is to keep guides excited and enthusiastic about the resource when they are essentially performing what could be a routine and boring job—not notably paying a high salary. If the boredom is communicated to the visitor, disaster occurs. Further, as with all tourism service jobs, guides have to deal with a fickle, demanding, and sometimes difficult public—all the while smiling and welcoming people. That task, as we all know, is fraught with problems.

During our research for historic sites, we developed what we call a monitored site-visit technique. Essentially, a member of our professional staff tours with a group of visitors, observing the way they interact with each other and the guide, when they are bored and turn away, when they are interested and excited. After the tour, our staff person interviews participants to have them talk about their feelings during the tour and their reactions to specific components. Perhaps similar techniques or approaches need to be developed by historic site managers to measure directly the ways the guide staff is dealing with the public and the experiences they create for visitors. If growth in tourism visits is desired, the guide staff will need to enhance and enliven the visit, not make it a difficult and boring time.

PACKAGING HERITAGE TOURISM

One way to address the staffing, training and motivating issues is to eliminate guides and employ an audiotape tour—not a dull tape, but a special approach to personalize the experience. For example, several years ago, we were in Nashville and visited The Hermatige, Andrew Jackson's home there. The historic resource was wonderful, but the visit a disaster. We are herded from roped-off room to roped-off room to listen to boring guides provide uninteresting details about the rugs, chandeliers, and furniture. Jackson and his family were nowhere to be found.

But this year, a friend had an exciting, involving historic experience at The Hermitage. Today, the tour is on tape. It guides you through the house and grounds—and it does so with Jackson, his family, and slaves as your guides. With actors reading Jackson's words, guiding you in the first person, you can really identify with the people who lived and worked at The Hermitage, stepping back in time and making the all important connections. That is a truly exciting experience. And, it requires *no* guides!

To review, tourists find historic site experience fun and interesting when

- They can step back in time—can see, feel, hear, touch, and smell—what it was like to live, work or play in an earlier time.
- When they can learn about the *people* who lived then, and;
- When they can relate to the guide who shows them the site and introduces them to the people.

And, if they have a good experience, they'll spread the word, telling friends and relatives about the fun time they had at your site.

But, importantly, tourists who visit your site are not in your area *just* to visit your site. They come to have a good time, to rest and relax, to enjoy themselves on a vacation or short pleasure trip. Their main reason for being in your area may be to visit friends and relatives or to enjoy today's modern amusements, to attend a major sporting event or play a little themselves. They may be in town to view a special museum exhibit. All of these are members of the tourism community. All can offer you opportunities for marketing communications, cross-selling, and working together to expand the number of visitors to your heritage site. We need to begin the dialogue with the tourism managers for these attractions and with your CVBs and chambers of commerce to build tourism to your area *together* as a team. Our attitude needs to be cooperation, not confrontation. Tourism enterprises should be viewed as our partners, not our foes.

Let's go back to our tourist again. We've talked about some of the activities they may do in your area. But on those same trips, tourists need some basic essentials. They need a place to stay: high-rise hotels, charming properties in historic areas, or even historic properties such as this one. Hotels, of course, are also a part of the tourism industry, and we have good opportunities for developing business by working with property managers to develop packages and promotions for hotel guests. Have them include a visit to your site in their weekend promotions.

And, finally—there are two more critical components for every tourist. The first is **food.** It seems to me that tourists have much in common with Napoleon's army—they travel on their stomachs! They need a variety of foods, from fast food to snack food to special foods to fun foods to fine dining. Helping tourists find a place to eat—or, indeed, offering them snacks, teas, or suitable dining experiences—can contribute importantly to your guests enjoyment of the experience you offer.

And, the only activity more important to tourists than anything we've talked about is **shopping.** Apparently, a vacation just isn't a vacation unless one shops—in museum shops, in historic shops, in crafts shops, in outlet malls, and in discount stores.

Clearly, then, the tourists who will visit your area have other needs when they are *in* your area—they need overnight accommodations, fun things to do and see, food and shopping opportunities. Your growth will be enhanced if you team with other members to provide a "package" for your area and make it accessible to tourists.

What today's traveling public lacks is time— time to plan, time to figure out a day's itinerary in your area, time to do all the research that's necessary to put a trip together. If the historic site managers can team with others in the community to facilitate the planning process for the ultimate tourist, then visitation will grow much more dramatically.

CONCLUSION

Let me share with you a brochure which recently crossed my desk. In reviewing some materials sent to me by the Scottish Tourist Board, I found one small brochure which made me feel that the author had read my mind—or at least these comments. Let me share the few words from this brochure for Cawdor Castle with you:

Cawdor Castle: Step Right Into Scottish History

Cawdor. A magical name, romantically linked by Shakespeare with Macbeth. A superb fairy-tale Castle, and just what every visitor is looking for . . . "living" Scottish history that you can touch and see and sense for yourself. Cawdor Castle is not another cold monument, but a splendid house and Lord and Lady Cawdor's home.

So, come in over the drawbridge and gaze into Scotland's medieval past. Look up and around and feel the unyielding solidity of the ancient stonework. Enter the low doorways; climb the winding stairs; look out from the windows set deep in the massive walls and you will understand the necessity of the warmth of the beautiful woven tapestries. See the snug sitting-room in the core of the Tower, and the forbidding dungeon; the freshwater well; imagine the cooks preparing a feast in the original kitchens and you will be swept back centuries in time.

Yet a day out at Cawdor is not merely the romance of ancient walls and the delight of fine furnishings.

Stroll through beautiful gardens and across the lawns; snooze in the sun; walk one of our four popular nature trails meandering through majestic trees besides tinkling streams; feed the ducks. Picnic in the park; have an ice-cream from the snackbar or a square meal and drink in our licensed restaurant. And to "top-off" your day, buy that special souvenir of Cawdor and Scotland or that forgotten present from the gift shop.

It makes a super day out for the whole family; rain or shine; connoisseurs or kids.

Are you ready to go? I am! And the tourists I've interviewed about historic sites would already be there if they could. Communicating with prospective tourists about the experience they can anticipate at our historic resources needs to promise the exciting historic experience—and describe the *whole* tourism experience in your area.

In our judgment, if the experiences are good, tourists are ready and willing to visit historic sites, to get in touch with the past, to make connections to the present, to enjoy and to learn, to share and to teach. Historic site marketers need to assess the experiences they offer, improve them if necessary, and communicate them to prospective visitors. If that is done, the opportunities for further, dramatic growth in historic tourism are exciting.

CHAPTER
8   The Years Ahead

PROJECT _____

Write an essay on possible future trends of the tourism industry in your state. What might tourism be like at the beginning of the twenty-first century? Include modes of transportation, origin of tourists, and outlook for business travel. Ask the assistance of the tourist office as well as the convention and visitors' bureaus in major cities. Use your imagination for this project.

History has taught us that forecasting trends and developments in tourism is difficult. At one time, the DC-3 was considered the ultimate in air transportation, especially after a steward was put on board to look after the passengers. Then the DC-4s came, able to fly the Atlantic with two stops and cross the United States with only one stop. Today, commercial airlines fly one-fourth of the way around the globe without refueling.

By the early 1970s, the world was awaiting the introduction of the first supersonic passenger aircraft. It was expected that the new plane would change the nature of international travel forever. Two years after its introduction in 1975, however, the aircraft was taken out of production after only twelve had been built. The Concorde, with its capacity of only 100 seats, was uneconomical to operate because of its limited range and fuel inefficiency.

There is no question about whether or not people will continue to travel. It is almost impossible to predict the who, what, where, when, why, and how of the future travel. Throughout history, the demand for travel has grown as time and money for leisure travel became available. Over the next decade there is every indication that these prerequisites for tourism growth will be increasingly available, and for a larger segment of the world population.

TRENDS INFLUENCING FUTURE TOURISM DEMAND _____

The basic motivation for travel and modes of travel satisfying needs have remained fairly static over time, but attractions sought, activities engaged in, and forms they have taken have changed dramatically over time. Planning for future tourism requires the crystal ball that does not exist. The best that can be done is to observe patterns of change and note their impact and

Swedish Tourist Board

potential on tourism. The following trends are (re)shaping the tourism industry of tomorrow.

Pace of Life

A quickening pace of life is one of the major changes dividing the past from the present from the future. This change in pace has and will continue to influence travel. It has already resulted in an increase in minivacations and pleasure travel attached to business trips. It is also evidenced in the focus of tourist experience on specific places, events and experiences that are at the end point of a journey, rather than on the journey itself. Interstate highways long ago displaced travel on regional highways where visitors saw small towns, factories, farms and homes along their travel routes and were aware of the changing landscape and culture. Tourists instead became dependent on contrived interpretations of regions and places visited. Air travel and short holidays have increased geographical alienation and dependence on touristic interpretations. Air travel also makes exotic places accessible for short vacations for those who can afford it.

A fast-paced life with multiple short vacations will increase regional travel and recreation expenditures within regions, but growing air travel will mean that distant places will be competitive for those with money. For example, skiing within the New England region will increase because of short holidays, but there will also be more short ski holidays in Colorado by those with high discretionary income.

While many will thrive on the new rapid pace, others will want to "get off the merry-go-round." Opportunities will also abound for specialized services to those who react strongly against any further acceleration of change. On the one hand, there is a need for the vivid, compressed experience that technology makes possible; on the other, there is the need for a quieter trip where authenticity and continuity support the traveler.

Transience

Transience is not unexpected in a world with a fast pace of life. With a more rapid pace and accelerated change, places, people, and ideas get used up more quickly. Such change makes life difficult in the tourist business. Destinations that are "in" one day are "out" the next. Theme parks that provide the ultimate in experience one year are technologically bypassed in a short time. The South Pacific is now accessible, so the new tourist frontier is Antarctica.

Changing Demographics

Important age-related trends are rapidly reshaping the make up of America's population. A brief overview of current demographic trends that affect the tourism industry includes the following highlights: One-third of the current population of the United States was born in the eighteen years between 1946 and 1964. Because of their numbers, the needs and tastes of this baby-boom generation have shaped the American lifestyle at every stage of their growth. By the end of this decade, the majority of baby boomers will have reached the age of forty. They represent a highly educated market; one out of every five Americans is college-educated; one out of every three baby boomers has earned a college degree.

One-fourth of the United States' population is now over the age of fifty. Many are in good health and enjoy large amounts of discretionary incomes. In fact, older Americans have double the income of the average American citizen.

Other interesting facts which indicate changing trends for the 1990s include:

- Nearly 40 percent of all business travelers are women.
- Today's travelers are more experienced and sophisticated than ever before.
- Since 1985, there has been a 30 percent increase in weekend vacations due to difficulty in scheduling the free time of two partners.
- Only one out of five of all households in the United States are nuclear (mom, dad, kids.).
- Minorities will make up one-fifth of the population in the year 2000. In 1980 the figure was one-twelfth.
- Persons entering the job market today should expect seven careers in his or her lifetime and a job change every three to five years.

Technology

Technology has changed the world of amusement/education/interpretative attractions. Multimedia experiences, increased projection speed on film, wrap-around screens, lasers, and "virtual reality" can produce effects never before achieved. Interactive participation will soon dominate the entertainment experience.

New Experiences in Tourism

A common theme in all discussions of new directions in tourism is the importance of the designed experience. These experiences may be individualized or designed for a mass market. Involvement varies from the tourist being the central participant to his being a distant spectator.

LONG-TERM PREDICTIONS

Long-term forecasts for tourism growth have been made by planners, financial institutions, aircraft manufacturers, and individual countries. Estimates are that tourism will continue to grow at an annual rate of between 7 and 14 percent over the next twenty years.[1]

Outbound travel will probably grow faster in certain regions of the world than it will in others. Substantial increases in outbound travel are anticipated from countries in North and South America and in the Middle East. Japan and Italy will also generate substantial future growth. Germany and the United States will remain the leaders in international travel expenditures. In 1992, Germany, with a population of 130 million people, spent nearly $31 billion on foreign travel. The United States, with a population of 245 million people, spent $39 billion on overseas travel expenditures.[2]

Group and charter travel will probably continue to grow. Experts predict that the demand for charter flights should grow at a rate that is much greater than the demand for scheduled air service. These growth rates are largely based on predictable changes in future demographics. One of the most important factors affecting future tourism is the decrease in numbers of the youthful population within Western societies. By 1995, the group of Americans between the ages of fourteen and twenty-four will drop by 6.4 million. In 1985, for the first time, people over sixty-five outnumbered teenagers in the United States, and, by the year 2025, the margin will increase to more than two to one. The elderly population has grown from 4 percent of the total in 1900 to more than 15 percent in 1990. The number of those over sixty-five is projected to grow from today's 26 million to an estimated 40 million by 2010, when they will constitute almost 20 percent of the nation's population.[3]

Business Travel versus Pleasure Travel

Business travel, historically the backbone of the air carrier business, will continue to decline as a percentage of total travel volume. Vacation travel, however, has a very favorable long-term outlook. Increased discretionary income, increased leisure time, and higher educational levels are primarily responsible

---

[1]Data from World Travel and Tourism Council's 2nd Annual Report (Brussels, Belgium, 1992).
[2]See note 1 above.
[3]Data from Current Population Reports (Washington, D.C.: U.S. Bureau of the Census, May 1992).

for this. In addition, it is expected that the technology associated with serving future tourist needs will improve greatly.

Consumer lifestyles and aspirations are changing from a "goods" orientation to interest in "nonmaterial" experiences. Also, the cost of travel has either stayed constant or dropped relative to inflation. Travel promotions have increased over the last several years, creating more interest in travel across all income levels. All of these factors suggest that the need for travel services will continue.

The North American Market

After some twenty-five years of consistent growth of travel to and from North America, an unstable economy since the mid-1970s has created uncertainty regarding the future of this travel market. Major destinations of travelers from North America have been Western Europe, Mexico, and the Caribbean. Most travel to these regions have been vacation- and pleasure-oriented, while travel to other parts of the world included a much higher percentage of business-related travel. North American travel has been important on all continents except Africa.

Highly competitive air fares including student, family, and excursion rates, charter flights, the recent strength of the dollar, and promotional devices by carriers have encouraged the rapid growth of pleasure travel from North America to these regions. Major promotion efforts by governments of overseas countries, the development of better accommodations, and the establishment

Wyoming Division of Tourism

of a travel environment oriented to the demand of North American travelers have also stimulated these growth patterns. The United States has for many years been an important generator of visitors to the United Kingdom, Italy, Germany, Greece, Japan, Venezuela, and all islands of the Caribbean (except Cuba).

In recent years, the share of travel to the Pacific and Latin America from North America has increased steadily, although it is still relatively low. Until now, travel by North Americans to Africa, the Middle East (except Israel), and Asia (except Japan and South Korea) has been limited by relatively long distances, high cost, lack of close business ties, political disturbances, and lack of suitable accommodations and related services.

Indications for the next five years suggest that growth in outbound travel from North American will be moderate, largely because of a weak American dollar. While factors that disrupted travel patterns between 1950 and 1975 were primarily politically oriented and relatively short-term, economic considerations will predominate and will have long-term effects in the future. Real disposable income is somewhat lower in North America than it has been in the past, and the weak dollar continues to make overseas travel unattractive. However, spreading urbanization in industrialized societies will result in an increasing psychological need for holidays away from home. People in North America and Western Europe appeared unwilling to give up vacation travel even during the recessionary period of the mid-1970s, the era of high-interest rates in the 1980s, and the recent recession. New concepts and approaches are being developed within the travel industry, such as time-sharing, one-stop charters, and fly-drive packages, which will stimulate the continued growth of tourism.

Fluctuating currency exchange rates will continue to cause unexpected travel bargains. This helped set records in the number of Americans visiting Europe in 1985 and encouraged travel to North America in the early 1990s.

Historically, the desire of North American travelers to tour internationally has been strong and is expected to remain so. If not restricted by economic realities and the absence of highly publicized terrorist activity, people from the United States will give priority to that long-awaited international trip. On the other hand, Europeans are eager to visit the "New World" and will find the means to make that dream come true. As industrialization increases in the developing countries during the coming decades, more of the populations of these countries will participate in international travel, including travel to North America. Mexico will continue to provide the majority of visitors to North America, but Japan is surpassing Western Europe as the primary overseas place of origin. Tourist industries in Guam and Hawaii will continue to benefit from this development. Australia, the Middle East, Eastern Europe, and the Commonwealth of Independent States will also gain some importance as travel-generating areas. Sub-Sahara Africa will continue to be the least important generator and recipient of travel to and from North America.

Group Travel

Group rather than individual travel will characterize the pleasure travel market by the end of the century. Most countries and regions that have expressed or implied disinterest in, or displeasure with, low-cost group travel will alter their policies and regulations so that they can participate in the economic benefits of this type of travel. Many will increase their tourism promotion budgets to stimulate the interest of this group of travelers. Moreover, increased leisure time and the growing ability of younger persons to travel will result in a steady lowering of the average age of nonstudent travelers to and from North America (particularly of Americans, Canadians, Germans, and Japanese). These younger travelers will generally be well suited, philosophically and socially, to group travel.

Business Travel

The relationship between business and pleasure travel on a region-to-region basis is and will continue to be closely related to volume. As the volume of travelers to North America increases from regions where they are currently low, and as North American travel increases to regions now visited infrequently, pleasure travel will expand relatively more rapidly than business travel.

Business traveling will continue to be an important segment of the traveling public. With increased domestic and international trade, the growth of business travel will continue, and airlines and hotels will cater to the specific needs of this lucrative market.

Government Involvement

Governments of many countries are attentive to the economic effects of tourism as a major foreign exchange earner for their economies. The United States government, which operates under a laissez-faire attitude toward the tourism industry, should give greater attention to the industry as a whole and overseas promotion in particular. The current budget targeted for overseas promotions of the United States' tourism product is equal to that of the country of Togo or to that of the city of Amsterdam. It is unfortunate that the United States does not recognize the important role its government would play in promoting international travel to this country. It is the responsibility of everyone involved in tourism to help bring about a change in this situation.

Table 8–1 demonstrates the U.S. government's lack of resolve with regard to funding tourism promotional efforts.

Global Patterns

Global patterns indicate that during the next five years, Germany and the United States will remain by far the largest tourist-originating countries, with a 20 and 18 percent share, respectively, expected in the year 2000. Japan will move into third place with a 15 percent share.

Travel from France, the United Kingdom, the Netherlands, and Italy will all be of fairly similar magnitudes by 2000, each having 4 to 6 percent of the market, a considerable increase in the case of Italy, and a decline for France and (less markedly) for the United Kingdom.

Canada, Mexico, and Belgium form the next group of countries, with around 3 percent of the market each. They are followed by Austria and Sweden with about 2 percent each, and by Switzerland, Denmark, Australia, and Norway, with about 1 percent each.

These sixteen countries accounted for about 82 percent of the world traveler total in 1992, a figure similar to that of 1975, and somewhat higher than the 80 percent they accounted for in 1966. Of the remaining originating countries, the Middle East is likely to increase its share of the total, while the Asian (except for Taiwan, Singapore, and South Korea) and African shares seem likely to fall significantly. Other areas should more or less retain their positions, but

TABLE 8–1   Budgets of National Tourism Administrations

COUNTRY	TOTAL NTO BUDGET (1988) (IN MILLIONS, U.S. 1988 DOLLARS)	FOREIGN PROMOTIONAL BUDGET (1988) (IN MILLIONS, U.S. 1988 DOLLARS)
Australia	$27.8	$27.8
Austria	60.8	19.7
Canada	44.9	N.A.
Cyprus	9.4	3.3
Greece	115.7	6.6
Ireland	45.9	23.0
Italy	976.8	N.A.
Japan	19.4	11.5
Malaysia	45.0	32.9
Morocco	18.0	7.8
Netherlands	30.9	12.3
Panama	5.4	0.3
Peru	9.4	4.8
Philippines	6.6	1.0
Portugal	14.7	N.A.
Singapore	29.3	14.4
Spain	81.0	32.2
Switzerland	23.9	14.9
Tunisia	36.7	9.1
United Kingdom	42.4	17.9
United States	**$11.7**	**$ 8.3**

Source: United States Travel and Tourism Administration.

more liberal attitudes might result in increases in the share of East European countries and the Commonwealth of Independent States, where there is a big untapped potential.

Systems for receiving and dispatching travelers across international borders will be streamlined, but security concerns might cause delays at airport terminals. More international gateway airports will become available around the world. Reception and dispersal systems in North America and other major destinations will be better organized and more diversified. Except in specialized operations oriented to high-income markets, the availability of luxury services will diminish greatly, and standard facilities and services will dominate most tourist operations.

There appears to be a large potential for growth in international travel since it is now largely limited to a small number of countries in the industrialized nations of Western Europe, North America, and Japan. Further, it is restricted to a small proportion of the population of these areas. One would expect that in the future (as in the recent past), international tourism will expand as greater numbers of the world's population increase their educational level and gain more disposable income and longer paid vacations. However, because of differences in lifestyles and cultures, the people of some nations are likely to develop a greater propensity to travel to foreign countries than others.

Japan National Tourist Organization

In summary, looking at the next ten years, the bulk of international travel is likely to continue to be within and between the developed countries, but there should also be increases in the flow of visitors to the developing countries. Sizable growth is also likely in travel from Japan to nearby destinations and from Australia and New Zealand to destinations in the South Pacific. Other areas of expansion will be in travel between the countries of South America.

Other major changes are likely to be in the types of tourist services needed. Today's traveler, even at the low-cost end of the market, is a person with diverse expectations, and the tourism industry will have to be innovative in order to satisfy changing demands.

Destinations

With regard to the travel destinations of North Americans, Europe, Mexico, Canada and the Caribbean will be the principal foreign destinations. Control of travel costs in Latin American countries, the stabilization of the Commonwealth of Independent States and selected other areas, as well as improved travel infrastructures and services worldwide, will also stimulate larger numbers of North Americans to visit a greater variety of destination areas than in past years. In general, U.S. domestic travel will continue the popularity it earned during the recent recession, and North America will continue to be a significant source of visitors to other Western Hemisphere countries, although it will no longer be the dominant force in travel to other regions. As travel patterns change, the historic gap between numbers of travelers from and visitors to North America has already reversed itself.

CHANGES IN TRANSPORTATION

Automobiles

During the early 1990s, the automobile industry experienced significant changes that are likely to continue through the remainder of the decade. Ongoing concerns with high fuel prices have been responsible for an increase in the number of smaller, more fuel efficient automobiles. In the 1960s, cars were designed to be comfortable; in the 1970s, cars were built to be fuel-efficient. Today, cars are engineered to be economical, comfortable, and practical. Greater use of electronics and onboard computers will improve the competitive position of car manufacturers. The 55-mile-per-hour speed limit has been eliminated in some states but will be supported in many parts of this country, since its safety record and its role in energy conservation have been widely recognized.

Airlines

The airline industry is going through a period of uncertainty as a result of a decline in demand. The proportion of those traveling for pleasure will increase more rapidly than the proportion of those traveling for business. The expansion of the actual and potential market for pleasure trips is significant to the airline industry. Pleasure travelers are very cost sensitive; they enter the market when fares are low and withdraw when they are high. In contrast, business travelers' plans are dictated by business needs and not by fares. The growing share of leisure travelers will make the demand for travel more elastic, which means, in general, that the lower the fare, the higher the demand. The challenge is to translate these higher load factors into positive yield figures.

Airline management in the future will attempt to fill more seats in each plane to compensate for high cost of operating the aircraft. With high fuel and labor costs, the airlines will be forced to stabilize their fares, pushing the industry back into the inelastic demand segment of the market.

Airlines will continue to further develop the hub-and-spoke systems developed in the deregulated environment that enable them to control their own traffic. New marketing techniques will be implemented in an effort to fill every seat in order to get the most profit out of every departure. There will be various classes of full service, and there will be an astonishing variety of discount and promotional fares. There will also be an increase in the various classes of passage, widening the level of services between those who pay full fare and those who do not. Fares will differ according to season, according to size of group, according to the number of children and their ages, and other marketable factors not yet identified.

The airlines' motive is simple: considering the low profit margin available, there should be no seat left empty. Marketing departments of airlines will be busy during the coming decade inventing easy-to-remember names for hard-to-determine fares. Fortunately, the wide-ranging diversity in the needs of passengers will be matched by an increasing variety in aircraft types that will become available in the 1980s. Large numbers of early-generation jets, voracious consumers of high-cost fuel, will be taken out of service. The operating efficiency and comfort of large planes such as the Boeing 747 and the McDonnell Douglas DC-10, will continue to improve. A wider variety of intermediate aircraft for short- and medium-haul routes will be available (such as the MD-11), offering wide-body comfort for a smaller number of seats, as provided by the Boeings 757 and 767 and the European Airbus AB-300.

All air travelers wonder, at one time or another, about the future of air transportation. An industry that has developed from the first powered flight to a moon landing in less than seventy-five years can obviously work wonders. No one in 1903 could predict 500-passenger 747s or the worldwide aviation network of today. Even now, although skills are more highly developed, technology is changing so fast that it would be futile to describe airplanes seventy-five or even fifty years in the future. Even looking thirty years ahead is difficult. The passenger might speculate on this subject in terms of future travel time, convenience, comfort, and, of course, safety. The managers of an airline, on the other hand, in addition to the all-important issue of safety, must consider investment requirements, operating economics, fuel consumption, maintenance needs, route/schedule impact, and airport congestion. Aircraft manufacturers search for combinations of existing and developing technologies that eventually can be integrated into safe, efficient, comfortable, and economical transports for the future. Commercial air transportation will continue to be strongly influenced by market, environmental, energy, legal, financial, and technological factors.

Tremendous progress has been made in the past seventy-five years in commercial aviation. There is no reason to believe that this won't continue. One particular problem confronting the growth of the airline industry, however, is the congestion of airports and traffic-control facilities. Even the sky could become a limit to the growth of aviation.

Railroads

America's passenger trains have been remodeled and refurbished, and high-speed trains have been introduced, improving passenger comfort. Amtrak has further improved its automated reservation system and has committed itself to working closely with the network of travel agencies around the country. Yet the railroad passenger business continues to decline, and Amtrak has been forced to discontinue service on many interregional routes. Rail travel will play a significant role in future transportation in Europe and Japan. In the United States, however, passenger rail travel will probably only be available in a few highly urbanized regions; for example, between Boston, New York, and Washington, D.C.

Accommodations

The future of the hospitality industry looks bright. Improvements in computerized reservation systems will continue, as will the growth in the meeting and convention business. Hotel facilities will become more complete, with facilities for recreation, shopping, and meetings and conventions. Technological developments in hotel construction will continue to be spectacular, with multipurpose lobby spaces, glass elevators, and year-round temperature-controlled environments.

Japan National Tourist Organization

In addition to development in the conventional aspects of accommodations, economic pressures will bring about an increase in the development of timeshare facilities. Shared ownership of apartments or cabins in beach areas or ski resorts, for example, will tend to replace the individually owned vacation home. Some of these timesharing arrangements will allow owners to trade their weeks or months of time in one location for equivalent time in another—a beachfront condominium in Florida for a chalet in Colorado—or perhaps even for accommodations overseas.

Another trend that started in the mid-1980s is expected to continue: hotel chains will expand their product offerings, including the all-suite hotels, the luxury hotel, and the economy hotel. Recently, several chains have introduced new all-suite hotels, such as Radisson and Quality Inn. The luxury hotel market has grown with such additions as Holiday Inn's Crowne Plaza, Howard Johnson's Plaza Hotels, and Ramada's Renaissance properties. However, economy lodging is the fastest-growing sector of the U.S. hotel industry today. In 1970, there were fewer than ten budget chains, with 20,000 rooms; today there are more than sixty chains, with 250,000 rooms.

Other future developments affecting the hospitality component of the industry will include the rapid growth and improvement of world communication. It is not unlikely that home television screens will be used to display computerized information on hotel availability and prices, as well as full-color pictures of the hotel, the view from the hotel window, and even some of the local sight-seeing attractions.

In the hotel industry, we will also see more foreign investments in U.S. hotels in the wake of recent foreign ownership and foreign investments in such companies as Westin, Inter-Continental, Hilton International, and Omni.

Travel Agents

The role of the travel agent will shift even further from that of a ticket agent to that of a professional travel advisor. Indeed, increased automation could mean that the travel agent's function as ticket agent will become obsolete as travelers can secure seat reservations directly via computer. The successful travel agent of the future will be a professional who will guide clients through the enormous variety of available itineraries. Clients will be charged a fee for the professional help they receive.

These travel professionals of the future will have to be ready to face even more changes than have already occurred, especially in the field of automation. The changes brought about in tourism by automation thus far are impressive: close to 85 percent of all travel agencies in the United States today are automated. Today's travel agent is operating in an ever-changing environment. Computer technology has contributed to the complexity of this industry component. Furthermore, deregulation has removed the antitrust immunity the airlines had in dealing with agency accreditation. The result will be a further deregulation of the retail travel industry itself. Some industry experts predict a growth in the number of chain-operated giant agencies, which would reduce the number of small and midsize agencies. Others see an opportunity for non-travel-related businesses, such as department stores or banks, to start selling airline tickets and provide other travel services.

The growth in the number of corporate travel departments is a trend that is irreversible. Potentially, this may prompt airlines to deal directly with corporations on a large scale, cutting out travel agencies as middlemen. Nevertheless, the industry's requirement for trained professionals remains urgent. The current changes will provide a myriad of new and challenging job opportunities and will make careers in the travel industry more diverse and rewarding.

CONCLUSION

Robert Hazard, President and CEO of Quality International, recently identified the following five trends which he believes will shape the travel industry over the next decade.[4]

Accelerated industry consolidation.   There will be an increase in new mergers, joint ventures, and acquisitions in every sector of the travel industry. A handful of industry mega-giants will emerge to dominate the travel landscape. Today, the top twenty-five hotel companies control more than half of all rooms. Already, six airlines control 90 percent of domestic air traffic. By the year 2000, some experts predict that as few as twenty giant global airlines will dominate the international market. Right now there are twenty to thirty major travel agency companies and consortia. Over the next two decades, two or three major international players will emerge from the pack. In the future we will see more strategic alliances linking hotels, rental cars, airlines, and travel agencies.

Greater globalization.   Spurred by relatively healthy oversees economies, the once stagnant U.S. travel industry could become one of the hottest growth in-

---

[4]Data from "The Industry of the Future" (Secaucus, N.J.: Reed Travel Group).

dustries of the 1990s. In 1988, international airline arrivals to the United States rose a dramatic 20 percent. The following years would see a decrease in the number because of worldwide political uncertainty, but with 400 million travelers in the international marketplace, the potential for increased inbound business is enormous.

More segmentation and niche marketing. Travel companies will seek a competitive advantage by developing unique and targeted travel products. Within the hotel industry today, Marriott, Holiday Inn, and Quality International alone market a total of twenty brands of hotels. Segmentation and niche marketing will accelerate in the years ahead. Witness the emergence of the individual incentive package, the nonsmoking hotel room, luxury air carriers, and budget airlines.

Technological change. Travel marketing automation is still in its infancy. Soon we will see laser disk imaging, better guest recognition systems, and a new generation of global reservation systems. New industry partnerships will improve the quality and flow of information to the traveling public. New accounting and yield management systems will drive rates and fares on a minute-by-minute, space-available basis. From video displays to automated satellite ticketing outlets, the consumer will become more directly involved in the process of buying travel products.

The quest for service. The travel industry's future lies not with bonus-type frequent-travel programs or rate discounting, but in superior service to the customer. Worldwide, travelers are growing increasingly frustrated with rude, inept, uninformed, insensitive, or unpleasant service. Companies that unlock their employees' potential, not through slogans or smile buttons, but through professional recruitment, massive retraining, and innovative incentive motivation programs, will emerge as the market leaders. Mr. Hazard goes on to say that with the "baby bust" years upon us, the competitive battle for good people will become an all-out war. Winning travel companies will find, train, motivate, and promote the best people to provide the best service to tomorrow's traveler.

Thus tourism professionals will always be part of an industry and a world that is constantly changing, as long as they are prepared to adapt to those changes.

Another very hopeful prediction may be made about the effect of tourism on the world we live in. As advancements in transportation, communication, and destination development continue, tourism will grow. As the industry grows, it will become even more intertwined with the economic health of the nations it affects, and the number of nations it affects will increase. This should substantially reduce the risk of international conflict, because nations will know that open conflict endangers profitable economic relationships. Tourism and international travel, therefore, will play an important part in establishing political stability in most of the heavily traveled regions of the world.

REVIEW QUESTIONS

1. Which countries are likely to generate more international travel in the future?
2. How will the decrease in size of the youthful population in Western societies effect the tourism industry?

3. Name three overseas destinations that are travel bargains due to current currency exchange rates.

4. Explain the reason behind the positive outlook for group travel in the future.

5. Present the arguments in favor of and against the use of government funding for international travel promotions.

6. What are the factors that influence the operation of international air transportation?

7. Discuss solutions to current airport congestion problems.

8. How will the role of the travel agent change in the future?

9. Describe "segmentation" as a recent trend in the lodging industry.

10. Explain how the tourism industry can help reduce the risk of future international conflicts.

Tourism Impacts
Related to EC 92:
A Look Ahead

Brian J. Mihalik

Associate Professor
Cecil B. Day School
of Hospitality Administration
Georgia State University

In 1993 an historic event occurred within twelve countries in Europe. EC 92 will signify a United States of Europe representing 322 million people and $4.5 trillion per year in goods and services. The removal of internal trade, customs, and people barriers, and the development of European industrial, agricultural, service, monetary, and social standards should have a major impact on the world. It will affect world trade, economies, and tourism in EC and non-EC countries (Wolf, 1989).

Because tourism plays such an important role in the European economy, the events of 1992 could have a major impact on tourism both within Europe and internationally. Tourism has expanded tremendously in the European Community over the last twenty years and plays a significant role in the economies of the twelve member countries. For example, tourism represents 5.5 percent of the European Community's gross domestic product (Akerhielm and others, 1990). In 1987, travel and tourism was the largest employer in France and the United Kingdom, and the European Community tourism sector directly employed 7.5 million people. In 1987, Europe accounted for $161 billion, or 58 percent of travel and tourism capital investment. Europe's

This article was originally published in the *Journal of Travel Research*, Vol. 31, No. 2 (Fall 1992), 27–33.

tourist trade is the largest in the world, accounting for approximately 62 percent of all international travelers and 50 percent of the world's tourism receipts (Savignac, 1990).

Yet in spite of the economic significance of tourism to the European Commission countries of Belgium, Denmark, France, Great Britain, Greece, Ireland, Italy, Luxembourg, Netherlands, Portugal, Spain, and West Germany, the European delegation in Brussels is relegating tourism to a lesser role. For example, agriculture and manufacturing have been receiving more attention in the planning process for the upcoming 1992 initiatives. This lack of tourism understanding is historical, with its roots deeply ingrained in the past.

HISTORICAL PERSPECTIVE

The European Community laid its foundation under the leadership of Robert Schuman, who proposed the pooling of the European coal and steel industries in 1951. He developed the European Coal and Steel Community Treaty, which led to a 129 percent increase in steel and coal trade between the countries of Belgium, Germany, Italy, Netherlands, Luxembourg, and France. This success led to the Treaty of Rome in 1957, which dismantled customs unions and quotas and established common policies in primarily agricultural and manufacturing areas (Perry, 1987).

Then, in 1985, a White Paper was completed on a unified Europe which led to the 1986 European Council approval of the Single European Act. This act had as its goal the removal of obstacles to the free movement of goods, people, services, and capital within the twelve member countries. With its roots deeply buried in manufacturing and agriculture, these areas dominated its expansion with about 65 percent of the total EC budget in the 1980s. Thus it came as no surprise that tourism has not been a major topic of discussion in the planning process of the European Community 1992 efforts (Perry, 1987).

Further, a recent content analysis of an official European Commission publication entitled *The European Community* (1987) cited seventeen different industries within its cover, including energy, public health, agriculture, textiles, manufacturing, fishing, pharmaceuticals, telecommunications, and information technology equipment. Numerous charts accompanied much of the text regarding the above mentioned industries, but not once did the word "tourism" appear anywhere in the publication.

The agriculture sector, which received about 66 percent of the 1987 EC 92 budget, was perceived as "a cornerstone of economic integration and one of the binding forces of the Community" (Perry, 1987). The closest the document got to the tourism issue was a brief mention of culture and sports and a discussion of air transportation. Yet, European households devoted between 14 and 16 percent of their 1986 consumer budgets to travel; West Germany and U.K. households spent more than twice as much on travel as on health care. Finally, the French spent more on travel than on all consumer durables (WEFA, 1988).

Another content analysis of a more recent publication, *Europe 1992: The Facts*, published by the Department of Trade and Industry and the Central Office of Information in the United Kingdom, again gives examples of the lack of focus of individual countries on the topic of tourism. If tourism was as important as agriculture, environment, science, telecommunications, and employment, the delegation in Brussels would have designated tourism as a Directorate-General (DGs) with a commissioner responsible for its work. In this text, the authors state, "Many of the DGs are of relevance to business. Some of the key ones are . . . " without any mention of tourism. Yet, clearly, tourism is relevant to Europe's business.

Finally, a literature review of the 1991 version of the computer data base titled Infotrac, a review of 1990 and 1991 U.S. Government Accounting Office (GAO) Reports, and a 1990 visit to the EC 1992 library in Washington, D.C., revealed nineteen additional articles or publications on EC 1992. These publications included *Inc., Business Week, Vital Speeches of the Day* and *Europe* magazines, internal government documents of respective EC countries, *New York Times* articles, GAO publications, and European Commission press releases and internal documents. In this collection of EC 92 references, not a single mention of tourism appeared.

It is clear that the EC views tourism not as a single, important entity such as agriculture or telecommunications, but attempts to address it in bits and pieces under a variety of Directorates such as Transport, Environment, Consumer Protection and Nuclear Safety, Financial Institutions and Company Law and Employment, Social Affairs, and Education. Again, after examining *Europe 1992: The Facts*, one finds brief mention of tourism components under the Physical Barriers and Transport, Environment Policy, Freedom to Work in the Single Market, Social Dimension, and Anti-Trust sections. If previous EC 92 budgetary priorities and official publications are any indication of the relative importance of tourism to the planners in Brussels, tourism is of secondary importance to the European delegation.

POTENTIAL TOURISM ISSUES

It is anticipated that EC 92 will create 5 million new jobs after the initial shakeout of lost government and private jobs currently needed because of the existing, burdensome bureaucracy. EC 92 is expected to boost the gross domestic product of member countries from 4.2 to 6.6 percent with an accompanying drop in the inflation rate of 1.5 percent. Further price savings because of streamlined bureaucracy and the development of Europe-wide standards in areas such as manufacturing and agriculture are expected to drop prices 6 percent for European citizens. All these factors indicate increased affluence for a population already the largest sector of international travelers in the world (Spielman, 1989).

Recent actions by the EC 92 Commission have attempted to correct some of the problems of the lack of importance of tourism. Of the 286 measures contained in the 1985 White Paper, 76 may affect tourism directly or indirectly (Akerhielm, Dev, and Noden, 1990). Some of the major issues that affect tourism which will be addressed in this article are taxation, deregulation of the airlines, and impacts on the hotel industry.

TAXATION

Value-Added Tax

One of the most significant fiscal issues affecting EC countries is the variety of value-added tax rates imposed on travelers. These value-added taxes can represent a large source of income for EC countries. Harmonization of the value-added tax has far reaching consequences. A partial harmonization of tax rates will result in a substantial drop in revenue for France and Denmark; while Italy, Luxembourg, and the United Kingdom would be winners.

Value-added tax rates range from 6 percent in Luxembourg, Netherlands, and Greek restaurants and hotels to 22 percent in Danish restaurants and hotels. The variation on food purchases is even wider. In the United Kingdom take-away food is taxed at a zero rate while restaurant meals are charged 15 percent. Fish in Italy is taxed at 2 percent while in Belgium shellfish are taxed at 28 percent. French and United Kingdom bed-and-breakfast establishments do not pay the tax, but hoteliers in France pay 18 percent and in the United Kingdom they pay 15 percent. Clearly, the increasingly popular bed-and-breakfast establishments have a significant price advantage over their hotel counterparts because of the absence of taxes (Lichorish, 1989).

VAT is levied on other tourism services besides restaurants and accommodations. It is passed on to tourism services including travel agents, tour packages, entertainment, recreational services, cultural attractions, and the arts. Passenger transportation rates can range from zero to 18 percent for rental cars in the United Kingdom (Lichorish, 1989). VAT on intraEuropean flights, once VAT-free, will be instituted.

Excise Tax

Excise taxes are another problem. Four of the five principle sources of excise tax revenue are cigarettes, beer, wine, alcohol, and petrol. Of these five tax sources, four have potential tourism impacts. For example, the tax on a single beer ranges from a low of .03 ECUs in Spain and France to a high of 1.13 ECUs in Ireland. One bottle of wine is taxed from a low of zero ECUs in Germany, Greece, Portugal, and Spain to rates of 1.54 ECUs in the United Kingdom, 1.57 ECUs in Denmark, and a high of 2.79 ECUs in Ireland. One bottle of alcohol (40 percent volume) is taxed from a low of .14 ECUs per bottle in Greece to a high of 10.50 ECUs in Denmark. One liter of petrol is taxed from a rate of .20 ECUs in Luxembourg to .55 ECUs in Italy.

Table 1 clearly indicates the potential impacts tax reform could have on different countries.

Tax Harmonization

Implications of the tax rate changes will not be confined to national budgets, but will have implications on the cost of tourism services offered. In an attempt to harmonize the tax issue, a two-tiered value-added tax system with a reduced tax rate for basic needs and a normal rate for all other products will be instituted. Member countries will be allowed to choose rates that require the minimum of change. The European Commission is proposing that normal, value-added rates range from 14 to 20 percent in individual countries,

TABLE 1   Revenue from the Indirect Taxation As a Percent of GNP (1982)

COUNTRIES[a]	VALUE-ADDED TAX	EXCISE DUTY[b]	VAT AND EXCISE DUTY
Belgium	7.67%	2.29%	10.06%
Denmark	9.84	3.27	15.71
France	9.19	2.12	11.41
Germany	6.34	2.58	9.04
Ireland	8.22	7.63	17.13
Italy	5.48	2.72	8.32
Luxembourg	6.04	3.75	10.28
Netherlands	6.83	1.92	9.19
United Kingdom	5.22	4.35	9.79
Weighted EC average:			
EC average	7.05	3.37	10.68

Source: Lichorish (1989).

[a]Excluding Greece, Portugal, and Spain.

[b]Tobacco, beer, wine, alcohol, and petrol.

which should affect tourism services such as international transport, travel agencies bookings, hotel and restaurant bills, entertainment and recreational services, cultural attractions, and the arts. The reduced rate will range from 4 to 9 percent for tourism items such as food, beverages, energy for heating and lighting, water and human transport. However, the National Hotel and Restaurant Association in the European Community (Hotrec) is actively lobbying for the European Commission to apply the reduced VAT to the hotel and tourism industry. This association believes that for Europe to remain competitive in an international tourism marketplace, it needs a lower tax rate (*Hotels,* 1990).

With regard to a harmonization of the excise tax, the European Commission is recommending a single ECU charge of 3.81 ECUs per item on alcohol, .17 on one beer, and .34 ECUs on one liter of motor fuel (Lichorish, 1989). Because tourism services in individual countries will not all be taxed at the same rate, tourists will be well advised to ask questions about the tax rates of major tourist expenditures when planning foreign visits. Because the final price of a tourist expenditure will vary based on the price plus tax rates, not all tourist expenditures will be equal in all EC countries.

AIRLINE DEREGULATION

With the deregulation of the United States airline industry in 1978, the European Commission can look to its American counterparts for a well documented history of what could happen in a completely deregulated, free market environment. These changes can affect both the charter and scheduled carrier components of the European airline industry. Between 1977 and 1989, business receipts based on 1982 U.S. dollars for the U.S. air transportation industry increased. Additionally, the lodging and entertainment industry receipts showed similar gains, which could partially be explained by the increased air travel of the American tourist (U.S. Travel Data Center, 1989). With the exception of the oil crisis and inflation problems of 1980–82, the trend in U.S. travel related business receipts is clearly increasing. The deregulation of the U.S. airline industry stimulated a growth in U.S. air transportation receipts between 1977 and 1988. Lodging receipts showed a similar trend with increased receipts over the same period. Based upon the United States experience, deregulation of the European airline industry could have a positive influence on other tourism-related industries.

Scheduled Carriers

Currently, the European countries run state-supported airlines which have tried to avoid the free-market requirements of the EC 92 single market. However, the 1986 EC Court of Justice ruled that government-run airlines were not exempt from free trade policies and must begin the deregulation process. New EC air transport policy is expected to push the air transport industry towards total deregulation by the year 2000. It is expected that a deregulated European airline industry will be responsible for a 15 to 20 percent decrease in scheduled carrier airfares especially in the early stages of competition. Currently, the cost of a scheduled carrier airline ticket for comparable routes in a regulated Europe is 35 to 40 percent higher than in a deregulated America (Speilman, 1989).

Additionally, increased competition in the European airline industry may mirror the United States industry with a reduction and consolidation of the scheduled carrier airlines and a possible reduction in charter airlines. The EC 92 legislation could cause unhealthy, scheduled carrier airlines managed by bureaucrats who are not familiar with free market businesses to make poor management decisions. These could include inappropriate mergers or acquisitions or pricing themselves to the verge of bankruptcy or out of business by advertising cheap airfares similar to the United States counterparts like Eastern, Braniff, Pan Am, Continental, and TWA airlines (Huff, 1991).

To counteract the potential for cutthroat competition that has seen the United States airline industry reduced to just eight carriers carrying 95 percent of the market as of 1988 (U.S. Travel Data Center, 1989), the EC developed price fixing, pooling, and route-access regulations. With regard to price fixing, airlines are allowed to set their fares if their governments approve. Other governments can only disapprove if the new fares are proved to be predatory. Pooling requires airlines to move from the historic 50 percent share for each carrier to a 40 to 60 percent range in 1990. Route-access regulations have been developed to allow new airlines easier market entry (*Aviation Week and Space Technology,* 1989).

Consolidation and Mergers

Consolidation, friendly partnerships, and mergers may produce as few as five European super carriers. The anticipated survivors could be British Airways, KLM, Air France, SAS, and Lufthansa (Berger, 1990). Already, Sabena has begun negotiations with KLM and British Airways in which British Airways and KLM will each receive a 20 percent stake in Sabena's airline. Sabena's chairman, Carlos Van Rafelghem, stated, "Under deregulation a l'European, the bigger ones (airlines) will dominate and others may disappear. We have to grow rapidly" (Sturken, 1989).

However, the EC will have veto authority to bar mergers or require that specific conditions be observed before allowing a merger to be finalized. If the European Commission views the European merger to be a violation of its antitrust powers, it can veto the merger. With regard to antitrust violations, the EC further can fine an airline 10 percent of its annual sales volume without the EC court approval (*Aviation Week and Space Technology*, 1989). Finally, deregulation is expected to increase the importance of major international gateway cities such as London, Paris, and Frankfurt as business hubs because of increased air passenger traffic. Brussels also is poised to increase in importance because it is the home of the European Economic Community and NATO and is one of the few European airports that is still uncrowded and can accommodate a significant increase in business.

Foreign ownership of European and U.S. carriers is another aspect of mergers and consolidation that will probably grow but will be monitored closely by both the European Commission and the U.S. Department of Transportation. Currently, majority foreign ownership of both European and U.S. airlines is prohibited. Countries from which new owners may come probably will be allowed ownership of European carriers so long as European business can own an equal share of airlines in the other country. Swiss Air owns 5 percent of Delta and KLM owns 49 percent of Northwest Airlines but only has 25 percent of the stockholder voting rights. Delta has purchased an equal share of Swiss Air, which opens possible marketing opportunities for both carriers. KLM is expected to begin new U.S. service in 1991 and will utilize Northwest's hub operations for feed traffic (Poling, 1991).

Charter Service

While deregulation will certainly affect the scheduled airline industry, its implications for the approximately 50 percent of the population that travels internationally by charter flights is less clear. One representative of Lufthansa stated in a presentation that he expects a trimming of charter carriers because of greater fare flexibility and competition in the commercial airline sector. He stated that "EC 92 is expected to begin the demise of charter flights for tourist travel" (Huff, 1991).

This position also is supported by a representative in the U.S. Department of Transportation: "After deregulation, there was a real hit to the (U.S.) charter industry because of prize competition and elimination of route regulations" (Szrom, 1991). Price differentials between scheduled carriers and charter airlines evaporated because of scheduled carrier competition with more discounted fares such as super-saver rates. Route regulations were eliminated which removed geographic authorizations. The presence of larger U.S. charter carriers is a thing of the past in the U.S. market since deregulation in 1978 (Szrom, 1991). Although the European Commission is moving slower with its deregulation and is creating more liberal, artificial market shares, there is no reason to believe that Europe's charter business will not be affected by deregulation of its major competitor, the scheduled airline.

For example, the need for Lufthansa Airline charter subsidiaries such as Viva and Condor may become a needless expense of the past. Lufthansa invested in these airlines to simply allow it access to previously restricted routes in such countries as Spain and the United States. As the airlines are allowed access to previously restricted routes and their market shares can vary based on market competition, they will have to rethink their investments in charter carriers because of the financial resources needed to compete in a global marketplace.

Potential Deregulation Problems

The United States airline industry and airports experienced problems of delays and congestion, and EC 92 countries are bracing for similar problems. Increased competition is expected to increase domestic and international travel leading to European airport congestion and delays. This problem is one of the major factors in the increased construction of additional high-speed rail networks in EC countries.

High-speed rail systems can compete successfully with the European carriers because of the relative short distances of intraEuropean travel. The efficiency of a potential European hub-and-spoke-system of air travel management so popular in the United States may prove less profitable in Europe because the travel distances are shorter. This inefficiency, combined with air-traffic congestion and lack of new airport construction, can move passenger traffic from European airlines to high-speed trains. This event, in turn, could force European carriers to concentrate on the overseas, long haul traffic. However, they then will have to compete with the more experienced market-driven U.S. mega-carriers of Delta, United, and American airlines.

The lack of civilian north/south air corridors previously set aside only for military traffic will be reexamined because of the rapidly changing political face of Eastern Europe. Since some European north/south air-traffic corridors were restricted for only military flights, the European carriers were hampered further with unnecessary flight delays. More civilian air corridors can help reduce air traffic congestion. Slot allocation at existing airports will be examined in light of the increased competition. Serious air traffic control problems are anticipated because of the twenty-three different air traffic control systems currently in operation in EC countries. Yet the potential safety problems and delays associated with twenty-three separate European air traffic control systems necessitate action by government and European Commission planners.

The issue of expanded evening operating hours for existing airports is under discussion. The expansion of flights into the previously restricted evening hours will be a major issue for citizens living adjacent to existing airports but unaccustomed to evening flights like their American counterparts. Still, by increasing north/south flight corridors, standardization of air traffic control systems and expanding existing airport hours of operation should help in addressing air traffic congestion due to increased leisure and business tourism traffic.

Cabotage

With the creation of a more competitive airline market, select air carrier agreements of the past will get new scrutiny. The issue of cabotage—that is, one nation's carrier moving passengers within another nation—will be negotiated in Europe with a possible spillover to renegotiations within the United States. Currently, European airlines have limited landing rights within another foreign country. However, EC 92 could allow, for example, the German airline, Lufthansa, to fly internal domestic routes in France at the same time Air France can service German cities.

Foreign countries like the United States and Japan could see their bilateral, individual country agreements renegotiated. EC officials will try to coordinate a European policy for all member countries to follow while at the same time will not try to cancel individual country agreements (*Aviation Week and Space Technology*, 1989). Thus, European airlines have the potential to gain landing rights in U.S. cities because of potential new negotiations. Currently, U.S. airlines have access to fifty EC cities while EC airlines have access to only twenty U.S. cities (Akerhielm and others, 1990). Increased European airline presence in a free market environment can stimulate international competition between U.S. and European airlines. This increased competition could result in a lowering of international airfares and an increase in international tourism flows both to Europe and North America.

The presence of more European airlines at U.S. gateway cities could increase pressure on both European and U.S. government officials to increase or allow foreign airlines operational rights within the borders of another country. The potential presence of five European supercarriers competing with the current oligopolistic U.S. airline industry could rekindle the internal U.S. competitive environment of the late 1970s and early 1980s. This position is further supported by Martin Shugrue, former Trustee of Eastern Airlines, who stated "We now face the daunting possibility that our industry could be so monopolized by so few carriers that the government would be hard-pressed not to allow foreign competition with domestic markets" (Fredericks, 1991).

Finally, the emergence of five potential European super-carriers in a part of the world already responsible for 62 percent of all international travelers can lead to the creation of a new international standard for a central, computerized reservation system. Just as U.S. carriers have complained about the potential disadvantages and biases of U.S. carrier reservation systems, U.S. and non-European airlines fear international reservation discrimination because of potential computer code differences (DePace, 1991). This is further incentive for both European Commission and foreign government representatives to increase the importance of tourism planning in EC 1992 negotiations.

HOTEL INDUSTRY

Increased business activity associated with an economically recharged Europe and potential airline competition brought about by EC decree should lead to increased hotel occupancy because of increased passenger traffic. Increased hotel occupancy should lead to potential new capital investment through new hotel construction. Further helping to fuel a potential new hotel construction period are new EC regulations to streamline the banking, insurance, and construction industries which should lower new construction costs.

Banking and insurance costs are projected to be lower because of Europe-wide standardization of the currency, banking, and insurance regulations. It has been stated that "the liberalization of financial services will reduce the price of financial products by up to 25 percent in countries such as Spain and Italy" (*Real Estate Journal*, 1991). Thus the cost of borrowing new capital investment money is expected to be lower. Construction codes and building materials will become uniform, which is expected to lower construction costs through standardization of building materials and construction practices.

Increased hotel occupancy and construction should increase hotel employment. Further, the removal of restrictions to the free movement of people via the European Community passport and the elimination of police checks for EC residents at the border crossings will allow people in high unemployment countries to move and work in those EC countries experiencing a tourism expansion. Regional employment shifts are expected, with subsequent negative pressure on those regions losing employees. Currently, the

employment situation favors Northern Europe. Expanded hotel occupancy should create the need for more multilingual staff as increased business travel puts more demands on the hotel meeting planning staff.

Mergers and Acquisitions

Just as the airline industry is expected to see an increase in mergers, friendly acquisitions, and consolidation, the hotel industry is well positioned for increased merger and acquisition activity. Since the European hospitality industry is a fragmented industry with low overall entry barriers, erratic sales fluctuations, diverse market needs and a high degree of product differentiation, the potential for consolidation is great (Crawford-Welch and Tse, 1990).

For a nine-month period in 1987, general business acquisitions numbered 1,634, with 93.3 percent of the acquisitions by EC companies. In the same period of 1988 general business acquisitions were 1,899, with only 6.5 percent coming from non-EC companies; 28 percent of the non-EC company acquisitions in 1988 came from U.S. companies. An additional 19.5 percent came from Swiss companies.

Specifically, in the hospitality industry, a total of 325 merger and acquisition transactions were identified for the 1981–1988 period with a total value of U.S. $19,877 million; 75 percent took place in the eating and drinking sector and 25 percent occurred in the lodging sector. While the total number of lodging acquisitions was small, the dollar amount was $360 million higher than the $9,758 value of the eating and drinking establishment mergers (Crawford-Welch and Tse, 1990). Clearly, the trend is for increased acquisition and mergers within the hospitality industry.

Other Hotel Impacts

Because EC 92 is expected to lower overall European prices between 4 to 6 percent, hotel operating costs can be expected to be lower. Decreased costs can translate into lower room rates, increased profits, or increased expansion. It is projected that insurance, banking, interest, and energy costs will be lower. Since these costs can represent up to 19 percent of the cost of a European's hotel's operation, savings in these four areas could have a positive impact on hotel operations (Pannell Kerr Foster, 1988).

The presence of EC wide standards in a variety of hotel operational components should help to lower hotel operating costs. Information technology, telecommunications, fire safety, and even appliance outlet standardization are a few items that can help to lower hotel operational costs. The emergence of information technology standards could help increase computerization of the hotel industry and lower operational costs associated with computer standardization. Telecommunication standardization should further reduce hotel costs through simplification of telephone and reservation operations. EC-wide fire safety standards should allow hotels to purchase the needed equipment at reduced costs.

Increased hotel traffic should influence the competitive nature of hotel operations. Increased competition should put pressure on prices and increase the need for service distinctiveness. Franchising could increase as new hotels are built. A variety of hotel industry experts predict that the growth market for Europe after 1992 will be in the low- and medium-priced hotels, not in the inner-city tourism core areas. The need for more market research should grow because a more competitive environment will require a greater understanding of market segmentation and appropriate advertising strategies. Increased competition and increased hotel traffic should have a subsequent positive effect on the tourism economic multiplier associated with the hotel industry.

OTHER TOURISM IMPACTS

EC 1992 and the potentially positive impact of EC 92 will extend to such sectors as foodservice, car rental sales, increased travel agent and tour operator business, and increased retail purchases associated with travel. Additional potential positive impacts include increased business tourism via trade shows and attraction attendance.

EC 92 will continue to allow more companies to think globally in the twenty-first century. It is projected that EC 92 will stimulate more trade between North American and European companies. Participating in international trade shows provides a cost-effective forum for alleviating the lack of information about doing business between two countries in a global market. EC 92 may give Germany a major trade show advantage because of its huge trade fair facilities, experience with large trade shows, transportation infrastruc-

ture, and existing hospitality services (*Tradeshow Week*, 1991).

Increased attraction attendance coupled with the anticipated lowering of banking and insurance costs could spur new attraction capital investment which, in turn, should increase employment within the construction and attraction industries. Already, EuroDisney opened in April 1992. Six Flags, U.S.A. also is holding discussions regarding an amusement park in Spain (Richardson, 1991). Again, a positive economic effect should occur locally because the economic multiplier associated with these tourism expenditures should increase. It should increase because of less economic leakage associated with the local nature of the purchases of goods and services needed to operate these amusement parks.

ECU Currency

Potential currency standardization with the EC currency will further help lower travel costs when visiting multiple European countries. There is already a thrust to encourage the European Commission to use the ECU for travelers checks (*Hotels*, 1990). Once the United Kingdom removes its objections to the ECU currency, travelers will experience a further price bonanza: "if you start with $1,000 U.S. in London and simply changed it again and again at every border crossing in the community, you would end up with only about $500 in your pocket" (Burnstein, 1990). This will occur because of the service charges and bank policies associated with converting one foreign currency to another. For example, banks will not convert foreign coins or small denomination currency from one country to another. The standardization of the ECU currency should have a positive impact on the tourism sector especially for multiple country travelers.

External Departures from European Countries

Because of the anticipated 4 to 6 percent decrease in EC prices and a 1 to 2 percent decrease in inflation, discretionary income should increase for the individual. Since Europeans already spend 14 to 16 percent of their consumer budgets on travel, it would seem that some of this increase in disposal income would be channeled to travel. Already the West Germans and United Kingdom households spend more than twice as much on travel as on health care. The French spend more on travel than on all consumer durables (WEFA, 1988). There is no reason to expect these trends to be reversed because of an increase in discretionary income. Rather, travel should increase especially for government-targeted travel groups such as youths. For example, the European Community designated 1990 as the European Year of Tourism and engaged in special promotional programs designed specifically for people under the age of twenty six. It was the objective of these programs to promote travel within Europe "with a view to creating a greater awareness of the different cultures on the Continent" (Akerhielm, Dev, and Noden, 1990).

European visitation to the United States and other foreign countries should increase. Europeans are expected to spend $22 billion a year in the United States on travel (Axtell, 1990). This should have a positive impact on those countries and individual states within the United States that have established or will increase destination awareness within EC countries.

ISSUES FOR FUTURE STUDY

Many issues regarding the impact of tourism relating to EC 1992 deserve continual review and evaluation. Since many of the governments of Europe have not ratified all of the European Community's directives and initiatives, it will be interesting to examine the actual outcomes of EC 92 and tourism in the future. What is called EC 92 may actually be EC 2002, especially when it comes to the complete deregulation of such tourism related components as the European airline industry.

The airline issue is one important area that will continue to evolve and have impact not only on intraEuropean flights, but the international and U.S. domestic airline industry. For example, will foreign airlines be allowed to own 49 percent of the voting rights of other country airlines or even a majority ownership? Will a truly "free skies" policy be adopted by all countries as recently proposed by (former) U.S. Department of Transportation Secretary Andrew Card? Card stated that the U.S. is prepared to begin talks with all European countries that are "willing to permit U.S. carriers essentially free access to their markets" (Poling, 1992). Will the big three airlines of the U.S. dominate the global skies by the year 2002 as feared by the European carriers? All these issues are important and deserve continual examination throughout the 1990s.

With respect to the hotel, foodservice, and attraction industries, a future examination of the proposed hospitality mergers and acquisitions should prove useful to ascertain whether the projections regarding growth are accurate. Will the hotel growth in Europe be concentrated in new medium and economy properties away from the central core cities? Will U.S. based fast-food operations expand their holdings in Europe in anticipation of tourism growth or simply as a result of oversaturation in the U.S. market? An examination of the impact new attractions such as EuroDisney will have on the local French economy will give tourism planners valuable data regarding new tourism product development.

CONCLUSION

Although the European Commission has not given as much policy and subsequent budgetary support to the tourism issue as to agriculture and manufacturing, the events of EC 92 will greatly affect Europe's tourism industry. The impact of airline deregulation could be the engine that will drive the tourism growth in years following the complete deregulation of the European airline industry. Just as the United States airlines experienced a 108 percent increase in passenger revenue from 1977 to 1989 based on 1982 dollars, Europe should experience similar results so long as European government pricing and free market factors will be allowed to emerge in the European airline market (U.S. Travel Data Center, 1989).

Even though the EC court rules that the airline industry was not exempt from free market economies, the government-owned airlines have used some loopholes in the 1987 EC court ruling to avoid a truly free-market, competitive situation. More work on the part of the European Commission is needed to develop a truly free-market airline industry. An examination of the impact on a deregulated airline industry in the United States clearly shows the positive impact it will have on other tourism components such as hotel and entertainment revenue.

However, often when government policy analysts and planners ignore crucial tourism planning issues, negative impacts of unanticipated tourism growth can occur. For example, the free movement of employees will be a boom to those expanding tourism areas but a major problem to those regions experiencing a loss of the labor force. It will be more difficult for the European Commission to target certain regional areas for increased economic development using tourism as an economic development tool if the European Commission does not address all the potential ramifications of European Community policies within all EC countries.

As Europe moves closer to 1992, the Commission is beginning to address more tourism issues (Kosters, 1991). However, the absence of planning at the earliest stages of the Commission's efforts has sent a signal that tourism is not as important as agriculture or manufacturing. Clearly, if EC countries are to remain competitive in a global tourist market, they must plan accordingly and devote EC economic and human resources to the issue of European tourism after 1992.

REFERENCES

Akerhielm, P., C. Dev, and M. Noden, "1990 Europe 1992: Neglecting the Tourism Opportunity," *The Cornell Hotel and Restaurant Administration Quarterly, 31* (1), 104–11 (1990).

Aviation Week and Space Technology, (1990) "Common Market Begins to Wrestle with Rules to Govern Competition," *Aviation Week and Space Technology,* June 12, 1989, 89–95.

Axtell, R., Keynote Presentation at the Meeting Planners International Symposium in Munich, West Germany, 1990.

Berger, L., *Corporate Travel,* (June 1, 1990).

Burstein, D., "Here's to 1992," *Travel Holiday,* June 1990, 30–33.

Crawford-Welch, S., and E. Tse, "Mergers, Acquisitions and Alliances in the European Hospitality Industry,"*International Business Communication, 2* (3) (1990), 42–48.

DePace, S., Presentation to Georgia State University Hospitality Administration Senior Seminar Students, Atlanta, GA, 1990.

Europe 1992: The Facts, London: Department of Trade, and Industry and the Central Office of Information, 1990.

Fredericks, A., "Industry Outlook," *Travel Weekly: The 1991 Economic Survey of the Travel Industry, 50* (1991), 1, 7.

Hotels, "Is Your Hotel Group Ready for 1992?" *Hotels,* (April 1990), 48–51.

Huff, H., Presentation to Georgia State University Hospitality Administration Senior Seminar Students, Atlanta, GA, February 20, 1991.

Kosters, M., Personal letter, 1991.

Lichorish, L., "European Tourism 1992—The Internal Market," *Tourism Management, 10* (2) (1989), 100–10.

Pannell Kerr Foster, *Trends in the Hotel Industry.* Houston: PKF, 1988.

Perry, Suzanne (ed.), *The European Community.* Brussels: The Commission of the European Communities, 1987.

Poling, B., "Skinner Unveils Eased Policy on Foreign Stakes in U.S. Airlines," *Travel Weekly, 50* (9) (1991), 1 +.

———"DOT Secretary Offers 'Open Skies' Agreements to 'Willing' European Countries," *Travel Weekly, 51* (28) (1992),5.

Real Estate Journal, "Tumbling Walls: Emerging Opportunities in Europe, (Spring 1991), 14–19.

Richardson, S., Presentation to Georgia State University Hospitality Administration Senior Seminar Students, Atlanta, GA, May 13, 1991.

Savignac, Antonio Enrique, Presentation at the ITIX Trade Show in Chicago, IL, 1990.

Spielman, M., "Europe 92. The European Internal Market: 'The Great Occasion.'" Hamburg: Gruner and Jahr AG, 1989.

Sturken, B. "Sabena Chief: Belgian Line is Poised for Major Growth," *Travel Weekly, 48,* (70) (1989), 1 +.

Szrom, P., Telephone interview, April 18, 1991. U.S. Department of Transportation, Washington, D.C.

Tradeshow Week, "Global Competition for Meetings and Tradeshows Expected to Heat Up: Factors That Will Influence Who Comes Out Ahead," *Tradeshow Week,* April 8, 1991, pp. 1 +.

U.S. Travel Data Center, *The 1989-90 Economic Review of Travel in America.* Washington, D.C.: USTDC, 1989.

WEFA Group, Wharton Econometric Forecasting Associates, *The Contribution of the World Travel and Tourism Industry to the Global Economy.* Prepared for the American Express Travel Related Services Company. New York: American Express, 1988.

Wolf, M., "New Ventures on a Well Traveled Road," *L&H Perspective, 15* (1) (1989), 3-7+.

Environmental Ethics

Anne M. Masterton

Before an InnerAsia Expeditions tour group gets under way, passengers are briefed on the proper environmental and cultural etiquette to be observed in the host country. During the trip, guides haul kerosene for fuel rather than destroy trees by burning firewood.Tour members carry out all nonbiodegradable waste when they depart and return all plastics to the United States for recycling. Trip leaders are expected to be conversant on everything from regional geology to local customs to the current political situation. Group sizes are controlled to minimize damage to fragile ecosystems.

InnerAsia uses only local ground operators and suppliers and pledges a certain percentage of its profit from the tour to a non-profit group that shares InnerAsia's principles. The company encourages its clients to do the same.

A lot of rules? Maybe. But InnerAsia vice presi-dent Jim Sano has no doubts about the responsibilities the travel industry should shoulder for environmental conservation. "It's simple: it's our job to protect what we use. If we don't, then we're out of business," said Sano, whose twenty years in the travel industry have been devoted to conservation and advancing environmentally responsible tourism. "I've come to the conclusion that solutions for developing an environmentally sustainable travel industry ultimately require an integrated approach, blending scientific, economic, political and sociological disciplines," Sano said.

"We clearly have to police ourselves," added Karen Johnson, president of Preferred Adventure Ltd., a St. Paul–based retail agency specializing in ecotourism. "Conservation isn't aesthetics; its survival. Our priority has to be the survival of the earth. And the agent has a crucial role in ecotourism. It's the agent who has the first opportunity in a sale to sell nature without selling it out." Preferred has an official policy governing conduct toward the destinations it sells.

Not everyone thinks this way. The complexity of the issue and the enormous impact environmental ethics can have on business patterns and profit levels have nurtured extensive buck-passing concerning the travel industry's obligations to safeguard destinations it sells.

Retailers say tour operators should bear the burden of protecting the destinations in which they operate. Large-volume, mainstream tour operators straddle the fence by blaming both retailers ("we sell what they ask for") and the host governments ("we give them the revenue they're looking for"). Government policymakers claim developers have pillaged the land: they also blame the dollar-wielding consumers themselves, for fostering degradation with their self-centered demands.

The result—with the exception of most authentic adventure tour operators and a handful of mainstream operators—is gridlock.

Almost all tour operators and retail agents interviewed for this piece agreed that abusing the earth is a bad thing, at least in theory. In practice, the story is a little different.

Most leading tour operators to Hawaii, the Caribbean, and the Greek islands contacted for this article did not want to discuss their responsibility to ensure environmentally responsible tourism, including how that role shapes tour package design. At least part of the reason appears to be rooted in the off-the-record comment made by one spokesperson for a major tour operator, who noted that her company has no environmental policy and has never considered creating any such policy. "It just never came up," she said.

At GWV International, which does a brisk Caribbean business, marketing chief Nick Coda said his company would be willing to consider es-

This article was originally published in *Island Destinations, a supplement to Tour & Travel News,* November 30, 1992, pp. 16–18.

Anne M. Masterton, a former senior editor at Tour & Travel News *has covered tourism development in Asia and the Pacific for six years, two of them as editor of Singapore-based* ASIA Travel Trade. *In 1990, she was named journalist of the year by the Pacific Asia Travel Association for her exhaustive coverage of issues affecting tourism in the Pacific Rim. While in Asia, she specialized in environmental issues.*

tablishing environmenal guidelines in operations and tour development, but has none now.

"Nobody's ever asked us about this before," he said. "Ultimately, though, I think the responsibility for environmental preservation belongs to the island policymakers. And although we sit on a number of advisory councils, as a rule the policymakers don't pay much attention to our recommendations. We'd like to see the islands preserved. Obviously, if a destination crumbles, so does our business. But it's just not within our power to do it. Wholesalers almost never find themselves in a position of empowerment."

Or leadership. Classic Hawaiian president Ron Letterman said although he would support controlled growth of Hawaii's tourism industry, protecting the environment is a Pandora's box better left to folks other than tour operators. "Who defines what protection is?" Letterman asked. "We can't build our own bias into something like that. There is no single source [in Hawaii] that has consistently voiced concerns over the lack of a clear environment charter, or has charted a clear understanding of what the tourist industry's role should be. If there was a catalyst, a vehicle for change, we'd become a part of that group. But we would not take a leadership role."

According to a Travel Industry Association of America report on how the industry can cope with the challenges presented by the growing environmental movement, fully 80 percent of travel industry operations are either directly dependent or based on natural resources. Yet, many travel retailers and wholesalers still function in a conservation vacuum and resist what they see as the politicization of tourism.

"I see very little demand from consumers for retail agents to make product choices based on environmental dictates," said Richard Copeland, chief executive of Hillside Travel in Queens, N.Y. "And while agents certainly give direction to clients in many areas during the travel decision process, it's not our function to steer them toward, or away from, a particular area because somebody considers that area to be environmentally unsound. We're not qualified to determine the environmental status of a destination."

That may be true. But Prof. George Wallace of the Department of Recreation Resources and Landscape Architecture at Colorado State University, a leading proponent of ecotourism, thinks that the industry may be shirking the issue, either out of fear or ignorance. "Ethically responsible ecotourism should be recognized for what it is and no more—a moderately useful tool for locally directed participatory rural development and wildlife protection," he says. "And anyone involved in it has a responsibility toward the resources that are being consumed."

Resources? Development? Protection? What happened to the business of making dreams and fantasies come true, particularly in selling island destinations?

It went south. Tourism is big business, in fact the primary source of foreign exchange earnings worldwide. Tourism receipts for 1991 totalled $212 billion, according to the World Tourism Organization. By 1995, the WTO expects that figure to jump to $343 billion, and to hit $527 billion by the year 2000. That's a 61.6 percent increase, and most of it will be fueled by the catch-all category of ecotourism.

In fact, the proliferation of environmentally correct products has overwhelmed the industry, especially retailers, who don't always have the time to investigate claims made by unscrupulous operators. Companies large and small have discovered that anything "green" has tremendous marketing potential. Recent studies by a host of organizations, including the Ecotourism Society, show that green consumerism is the biggest marketing challenge facing companies across the board in the 1990s. In unprecedented numbers, consumers weigh environmental factors before purchasing everything from toilet paper to travel to tuna.

Although there are many things agents can do to start themselves on the road to environmentally responsible operations, they are not without cost. For example, it takes time, energy, and money to develop an environmental policy that governs business operations, or help fund a nature preserve from company profits, or screen out environmentally unfriendly tour operators, destinations and clients. The latter practice could also result in a temporary loss of business, a hard concession to make in an industry notorious for its shoestring profit margins. In addition to financial losses, agents fear rocking the boat, opting to leave the innovative approaches and first moves to someone else.

"On a theoretical level, yes, I'm sorry to see overbuilt nightmares like Bali, Cancun, or some of the Mediterranean islands," said one retail agent who requested anonymity. "But realistically, what can I do? Who has time to read up on the pollution in the South China Sea, for example, when my computer keeps going down? Or when the airlines keep me on the phone for half the day with annoying—and unending—fare changes? I have to make a living, and if people want to go to polluted, or overcrowded, or disgustingly commercial tourist traps, then they're going to go. So why shouldn't I get the commission for their trip?"

It is on this point that tour operators and industry associations disagree most with the retail community.

Smaller group sizes, one of the tenets of environmentally ethical tourism, produce total package prices that exceed mass-market group tours. Thus, commissions are higher, which should be an inducement for retailers to promote ecotourism and help nurture the destinations they sell. But agents tend to look at the short-term gain rather than the long-term benefits, said most of the tour companies specializing in ecotourism.

Most ecotourism operators have developed and adopted environmentally responsible company codes of conduct. They, along with organizations like the American Society of Travel Agents, the Ecotourism Society, the Pacific Asia Travel Association, the Adventure Club, and the World Tourism Organization have also introduced guidelines governing the behavior of travelers when abroad. Lists of questions for both retailers and consumers to ask their travel company concerning its use of natural resources are also in circulation.

Indeed, InnerAsia's Sano insists that in order to promote resource conservation on a tour, the company selling the tour must practice a business ethic that sets a high environmental standard at home. InnerAsia, for example, operates under the Valdez principles, a set of environmentally sound and culturally responsible business practices, including a clause ensuring that companies "take responsibility for harm we cause to the environment by making every effort to fully restore the environment and to compensate persons adversely affected."

InnerAsia has introduced recycling and water conservation programs in its San Francisco office, encourages its employees to use public transportation (60 percent of them do) and fosters employee involvement in non-profit organizations by allowing employees to do volunteer work on company time.

Is InnerAsia a typical company? Not yet. Will it be in ten years? Maybe. But as more and more companies follow InnerAsia's example, fueled by consumer demand, the industry's consciousness is shifting. And eventually, so will the attitude of government policymakers toward tourism development. It's hard for the travel community to seriously consider problems that are routinely ignored by government policymakers more concerned with quick bucks than environmental integrity. It took a fecal contamination level of 87 percent (the measurement of untreated waste) in the water off Pattaya in Thailand to squeeze some regulatory action out of the Thai government, but it did happen.

For the first time, market forces have replaced legislation in orchestrating changes in attitude and conduct with respect to the environment.

In the case of Pattaya, retail travel agents were largely responsible for flogging the Thai government into action. They simply refused to feed customers into Pattaya until changes were made. Whether retailers are ready for the responsibility or not, they are the fulcrum joining the travel industry with environmentalists in a collaborative fashion.

"Travel agents have an enormous responsibility," said Sir Edmund Hillary, an avid traveler, conservationist, and the first human to scale Mount Everest. "They have the power to direct the vast flow of tourism into almost any direction they wish, to mold the attitudes of their customers into constructive channels, to spread the flow . . . of tourists widely. The future of tourism and our beautiful earth may well rest in their hands."

APPENDIX A

Employment Opportunities
in Tourism

AIRLINES

More than 300,000 people work in America's aviation industry (excluding military aviation). Salary levels are relatively high in the airlines. Short-term economic stresses may cause some problems, but long-term prospects for airline careers are bright. In particular, the smaller, commuter airlines have excellent potential for growth, and thus will offer good employment opportunities during the next decade. Airline employment is exciting and attractive to the adventurous, whether in the air or on the ground servicing the carriers between flights.

Flight Attendant

The position of flight attendant has evolved from the career that once was called "stewardess," "hostess," or "steward." In the past, employees who filled this position were young, female, unmarried, attractive, short, (because of aircraft space limitations) and (at one time) were also required to be nurses. After a lawsuit filed by a young man claiming he was denied a stewardess position on the basis of his sex, the airlines had to consider both men and women for the position. Thus, the evolution of the flight attendant.

The flight attendant's primary responsibility is to see to the comfort of the passengers. These in-flight public relations representatives are the most visible employees of the airlines, and travelers often form their impressions of the airline—whether positive or negative—on their experiences with the person who fills this position.

The flight attendant makes in-flight announcements, demonstrates the use of oxygen masks and life jacket equipment, serves cocktails and meals, and acts as host or hostess for the passengers. It is demanding and tiring work. Some international flights last more than twelve hours. The ability to remain calm and pleasant, coupled with the physical stamina necessary to remain on duty for hours at a time, are primary requirements for flight attendants.

Flight attendants are no longer required to be unmarried. They are, however, required to live in the city designated by the airline. The attendant is no longer required to be short, but should be average to tall in height, be able to reach the pillows, blankets, and small luggage that are now stored overhead. The attendant's weight must be in proportion to height.

A high school education or better is the usual educational requirement. Post-high-school training is preferred. Excellent English language skills are required, and, if one hopes to work on an airline with international routes, a second language is an asset. General health should be excellent since the flight attendant must be physically ready to cope with all emergencies. All airlines stress the importance of good appearance. The various airlines provide individual programs of training for flight attendants.

Advancement from the flight attendant position comes with seniority and merit. The job of flight service director, who is in charge of the cabin crew, is a position one can attain starting as a flight attendant. Nonflying positions into which flight attendants may be promoted include instructor, customer service director, and recruiting representative. Flight attendants may also become members of an airline's advertising and public relations staff.

A key benefit of flight attendant work is the availability of free or reduced rate travel. Many airlines offer this benefit not only to their own employees but also to employees of competitive airlines. Thus the flight attendants' choices of trips are not limited to their own employer's routes, but include the routes offered by other carriers that may have exchange agreements with their employer.

Ticket Agents, Reservation Agents, Clerks

Reservation agents and clerks who work for the major carriers work in large central offices where they become the link between telephone inquiries and the computer terminal. The agents answer questions on flight schedules, and seat availability, and make reservations. Their work brings them in telephone contact with the general public, travel agents, and their own company's ticket agents.

Ticket agents work at airport ticket counters and in central-city ticket offices. Their tasks include answering questions about fares and schedules, handing out timetables and literature, checking with the reservation agent on seat availability, and selling tickets. In addition, they check baggage, add excess-weight charges if necessary, and issue boarding passes. Ticket agents are in direct contact with the public. For that reason they must be pleasant and present a professional appearance. They wear uniforms that represent their carrier employer. The usual educational requirement for this position is two or more years of college. Possibilities of advancement to other positions are improved if one has college level courses in traffic management and other phases of transportation.

Airline Food Service

Airlines have finally recognized the need for quality meals to attract potential passengers. Travelers have now come to expect a meal on board, or at least a snack if the flight is short. Many airlines may even plan international meals characteristic of the destination or of the airline itself. An airline may have its own food service division or arrange for a private catering service to prepare inflight meals.

This is a behind-the-scenes position but an essential one in the workings of the airline. Educational training in food service or practical experience in the hotel or restaurant field is a prerequisite for a position in airline food service.

Flight Dispatcher

The flight dispatcher gives permission for aircraft of specific airlines to take off. That is, Pan Am's flight dispatcher (for example) oversees all Pan Am carriers at a given airport. The dispatcher evaluates all factors of the flight including the airplane's status, the crew, weather information, and other details. Constant communication between the dispatcher and crew keeps the latter informed of any delays at the airport caused by weather or crowded airspace conditions.

Operations/Stations/Ramp Agents

The supervision and loading and baggage and cargo are the responsibilities of person in these positions. Cargo weight must be evenly distributed by these agents, with corresponding lists of numbers and passengers recorded. They coordinate the transfer of baggage for connecting flights while taking on new luggage at stop-over airports. These agents may also be responsible for announcing arrivals and departures.

Sales Managers/District Sales Managers

These airline employees are responsible for all sales efforts. They oversee ticket and reservations offices, supervise sales representatives, and promote traffic on their airlines. Sales managers and district sales managers maintain contact with local travel agents and tour operators to keep them informed on the latest airline promotions. This relationship often means a discount to the travel agent or operators for their clients; however, the sales manager will maintain a profit for the airline on the basis of volume in these cases.

Of course, these descriptions cover only a few of the more familiar airlines careers. Below is a listing of job descriptions for airline-related jobs, taken from the *Dictionary of Occupational Titles* published by the United States Department of Labor.

Airline Lounge Receptionist

Admits members and guests to airline lounge, serves beverages and snacks and provides other personal services as requested. Opens door to lounge in response to sound of buzzer, verifies membership cards and admits and seats members and guests. Serves refreshments such as cocktails, coffee and snacks. Answers questions regarding scheduled flights and terminal facilities. Verifies passengers' reservations.

Directs or accompanies passengers to departure gates, restrooms and other terminal facilities. Relays requests for paging service, using telephone. Opens cans, bottles and packages; brews coffee; and arranges pastry, nuts and appetizers on serving trays. Removes used ash trays, glasses and dishes from tables and picks up trash.

Airplane Flight Attendant

Performs variety of personal services conducive to safety and comfort of airline passengers during flight. Greets passengers, verifies tickets, records destinations and assigns seats. Explains use of safety equipment, such as seat belts, oxygen masks and life jackets. Serves previously prepared meals and beverages.

Observes passengers to detect signs of discomfort, and issues palliatives to relieve them of ailments, such as air sickness and insomnia. Answers questions regarding performance of aircraft, stopovers and flight schedules. Performs other personal services, such as distributing reading material and pointing out places of interest.

Prepares reports showing place of departure and destination, passenger ticket numbers, meal and beverage inventories, palliatives issued, and lost and found articles. May collect money for meals and beverages.

Airplane-Flight Attendant Supervisor

Supervises and coordinates activities of flight attendants. Assigns duties and areas of work to **Airplane-Flight Attendant** (air trans.) to provide services for airline passengers. Observes activities of employees to evaluate work performance and maintains personnel records. Explains and demonstrates methods and procedures for performing tasks.

Prepares evaluation reports on performance of employees. Analyzes, records and prepares reports of personnel activities. Interprets company policies and practices for workers. May update local procedures manuals and guides according to directives and oral instructions.

Ramp Flight Attendant

Checks Airplane-Flight Attendant's conformance to personal appearance standard and performance of preflight duties during boarding stage of scheduled airline flights, and complies report of findings. Inspects appearance and grooming of personnel for comformance to company standards.

Observes performance of on-board airplane preflight duties and inspections by personnel for conformance, adequacy and completeness. Records errors, inadequacies and reasons for deviation on daily checksheet and forwards to supervisor. Extracts information from check-sheets and writes performance reports for inclusion in personnel folders.

Consolidates trip report and daily checklist information regarding work performed, emergency equipment, safety procedures, and appearance standards for use by supervisor. Prepares flight register and schedules to indicate assignments. Notifies personnel of changes in schedules.

Administrative Clerk

Compiles and maintains records of business transactions and office activities of establishment, performing variety of following or similar clerical duties and utilizing knowledge of systems or procedures. Copies data and compiles records and reports. Tabulates and posts data in record books. Computes wages, taxes, premiums, commissions and payments. Records orders for merchandise or service.

Gives information to and interviews customers, claimants, employees and sales personnel. Receives, counts and pays out cash. Prepares, issues and sends out receipts, bills, policies, invoices, statements and checks. Prepares stock inventory.

Adjusts complaints. Operates office machines, such as typewriter, adding, calculating and duplicating machines. Opens and routes incoming mail, answers correspondence and prepares outgoing mail.

May take dictation. May prepare payroll. May keep books. May purchase supplies.

Crew Scheduler

Compiles duty rosters of flight crews and maintains records of crew members' flying time for scheduled airline flights. Prepares flight register which crew members sign to indicate their preference and availability for flights and time they wish to be called prior to each flight. Types names of crew members onto flight schedule in order of seniority to indicate flights to which crew members are assigned. Posts names of extra crew members in order of seniority on reserve list. Selects replacements from reserve list and notifies replacement when needed.

Computes and logs cumulative flight time for crew members and removes crew member's name from flight schedule when flying time limit, as prescribed by Federal Aviation Administration, has been reached. Schedules vacations as requested by crew members. May notify crew members of assignments, using telephone.

Flight-Crew-Time Clerk

Compiles flight time record of flight officers for payroll and crew scheduling departments to ensure accuracy of payroll and legality of flights. Posts data, such as time in flight, type of aircraft, mileage flown, and weight of aircraft, onto flight time records, using posting machine.

Reviews union agreements to ascertain payroll factors, such as meal expense allowance, billeting allotment and rates of pay. Computes pay (**Payroll Clerk**). Compares figures with flight officer's log to detect and reconcile discrepancies. Notifies **Crew Schedulers** of total accumulated flight time of each officer and submits pay records to payroll section.

Flight Reservations Manager

Directs and coordinates, through subordinate supervisory personnel, flight reservation activities for certificated commercial or transport company. Reviews flight reservation reports, statistical data on passenger miles flown, and conducts comparison studies on other airline reservations to develop methods and procedures designed to improve operating efficiency and increase reservations for company flights.

Interprets and implements, through supervisory personnel, company policies and procedures regarding customer relations and contact with public. Analyzes economic statistics as applies to air transportation and other factors, such as weather conditions, special flight rates, and package deals, to estimate future volume of flight reservations.

Prepares estimates of work force required to process workload and equipment requirements in order to formulate budget estimate. Reviews performance evaluations on reservations personnel and initiates personnel actions as required. Schedules notation of worker assignments to improve capabilities of personnel and develop worker overall knowledge of department activities.

Directs investigation of customer complaints regarding reservation service and prepares correspondence designed to improve customer relations. Endeavors to resolve personnel grievances and submits unresolved grievance to higher authority.

Gate Agent

Assists passengers and checks flight tickets at entrance gate or station when boarding or disembarking airplane of commercial airline. Examines passenger tickets to ensure that passengers have correct flight or seat, or directs passengers to correct boarding area, using passenger manifest, seating chart and flight schedules.

Verifies names on passenger manifest or separates portions of passenger's ticket and stamps or marks tickets or issues boarding pass to authorize passengers to board airplane. Assists elderly, disabled or young passengers to board or depart from airplane such as moving passengers in wheelchairs.

May announce flight information, using public-address system. May post flight information on flight board.

Gate Services Supervisor

Supervises and coordinates activities of workers engaged in admitting departing passengers to airplanes and assisting passengers disembark at terminal exit of commercial airline. Reviews flight schedules, passenger manifests and information obtained from staff to ascertain staffing requirements that will ensure efficient passenger embarking and disembarking; and assigns staff accordingly.

Observes workers to ensure that services to passengers are performed courteously and correctly. Directs, explains and demonstrates improved work practices and procedures to attain efficient utilization of manpower. Evaluates work performance of personnel and prepares recommendations for retention, dismissal, transfer or promotion. Prepares daily personnel and activity reports. May perform tasks of **Gate Agent.**

Ground Host/Hostess

Renders personal services to passengers in airline terminal to facilitate movement of passengers through terminal and create goodwill. Greets and welcomes passengers to terminal. Answers questions and advises passengers concerning flight schedules and accommodations, such as arrival or departure time, location of concourses and gates and selection of seat on aircraft. Performs such tasks as assembling and forwarding luggage to departing flight, or guiding and escorting passengers to designated gate for boarding of aircraft, to expedite transfer of passengers between airline flights. Informs passengers, upon request, concerning fares, airline schedules and travel itineraries and distributes brochures to promote interest and sale of air travel. Informs passengers of terminal facilities, such as restrooms and snackbar to promote comfort and well being of passengers.

Passenger Service Representative

Renders variety of personal services to airline passengers requiring other than normal service, such as company officials, distinguished persons, foreign speaking passengers, invalids and unaccompanied children. Greets and escorts distinguished persons to lounge or waiting area. Transports special passengers between lobby and boarding area, using electric cart. Gives aid to ill or injured passengers and obtains medical assistance. Informs relative of passenger's whereabouts and condition.

Assists elderly persons and unaccompanied children in claiming personal belongings and baggage. Prepares baby food for mothers with infants. Accompanies foreign speaking passengers, or aliens traveling without visas, abroad airplane and introduces them to **Airplane-Flight Attendant.** Arranges for air commuter and ground transportation. Teletypes or telephones downline stations regarding special services for arriving passengers.

Reservations Agent

Makes and confirms reservations for passengers on scheduled airline flights. Arranges reservations and routing for passengers at request of **Ticket Agent** or customer, using timetables, airline manuals, reference guides and tariff book.

Types requested flight number on keyboard of on-line computer reservation system and scans screen to determine space availability. Telephones customer or **Ticket Agent** to advise of changes in flight plan or to cancel or confirm reservation.

May maintain advance or current inventory of available passenger space on flights. May advise load control personnel and other stations of changes in passenger itinerary to control space and ensure utilization of seating capacity on flights.

Senior Reservations Agent

Supervises and coordinates activities of workers engaged in reserving seat space for passengers on scheduled airline flights. Assigns workers to tasks in accordance with abilities and personnel requirements. Observes work procedures, monitors telephone calls, and reviews completed work to ensure adherence to quality and efficiency standards and to rules and regulations. Directs, explains and demonstrates improved work practices and procedures to attain efficient utilization of personnel.

Writes revisions to procedure guides and memoranda describing changes in reservations methods, flight schedules and rates. Records teletypewriter messages and telephones passenger service personnel to obtain information regarding flight cancellations and schedule changes and to determine disposition of passengers holding reservations on cancelled or rescheduled flights.

Posts flight schedule changes and passenger disposition information on bulletin board, and directs staff to telephone passengers to notify of schedule and reservation changes.

Ticketing Clerk

Compiles and records information to assemble airline tickets for transmittal or mailing to passengers. Reads coded data on booking card to ascertain destination, carrier, flight number, type of accommodation and stopovers enroute.

Selects ticket blank, invoice and customer account card if applicable, and compiles, computes and records identification and fare data, using tariff manuals, rate tables, flight schedules, and pen or ticket imprinter. Separates and files copies of completed tickets.

Clips completed tickets and invoices to booking cards and routes to other workers for teletype transmittal or mails tickets to customers. Computes total daily fares, using adding machine, to compile daily revenue report.

Aircraft-Log Clerk

Keeps records of usage and time intervals between inspection and maintenance of designated airplane parts. Compiles data from flight schedules and computes and posts amount of time airplanes and individual parts are in use daily, using calculating machine. Maintains card file for individual parts with notations of time used and facts taken from inspection records.

Notifies inspection department when parts and airplanes approach date for inspection, including accumulated time and routing schedule. Records work notations onto inspection report forms, using typewriter. Prepares reports on schedule delays caused by mechanical difficulties to be filed with Federal Aviation Administration. May keep reports on amounts of gasoline used daily. May keep employees' time records.

Airport Attendant

Performs any combination of following duties in maintenance of small airports and in servicing aircraft: periodically inspects buildings and hangars to detect fire hazards and violations of airport regulations. Examines firefighting equipment to detect malfunctions and fills depleted fire extinguishers. Performs necessary minor repairs to fire trucks and tractors. Fills light bombs with kerosene and positions bombs on landing field to illuminate danger areas. Cleans, fills, and lights smokepots used to indicate wind direction, and repairs or replaces windsock and other wind indicating devices. Replaces defective bulbs or burnt-out fuses in lighting equipment, such as landing lights and boundary lights. Fills holes and levels low places and bumps in runways and taxiing areas. Cuts grass on airport grounds (**Laborer, Airport Maintenance**). Patrols airfield to ensure security of aircraft and facilities. Verifies and reports specified amount of gasoline and oil supplies. Blocks and stakes down airplanes. Records airport data, such as number of planes stored in hangars, plane landings and departures, and number of passengers carried on planes. May wash and clean cabins and exterior surfaces of air-

planes. May fill airplane tanks with gasoline and oil (**Line-service Attendant**). May be required to possess Red Cross first-aid certificate to render emergency treatment to victims.

Flight Information Expediter

Determines flight times of airplanes and transmits information to flight operations and Air Traffic Command centers. Evaluates data, such as weather conditions, flight plans, ramp delays and enroute stopovers, to determine arrival and departure times for each flight, using aids, such as weather charts, slide rule and computer.

Transmits identity and type of airplane, flight locations, time of arrival and departure, and names of crew members to Air Traffic Command to obtain clearance for flight over restricted areas. Notifies departments of airline of pending arrival of inbound flight to ensure that personnel are available to load or unload fuel, baggage and cargo.

Airport Manager

Plans, directs, and coordinates, through subordinate personnel, activities concerned with construction and maintenance of airport facilities and operation of airport in accordance with governmental agency or commission policies and regulations.

Consults with commission members, governmental officials, or representatives of airlines to discuss and plan such matters as design and development of airport facilities, formulation of operating rules, regulations, and procedures, and aircraft landing, taxiing, and take-off patterns for various types of aircraft.

Negotiates with representatives of airlines, utility companies, or individuals for acquisition of property for development of airport, lease of airport buildings and facilities, or use of rights-of-way over private property. Formulates procedures for use in event of aircraft accidents, fires, or other emergencies. Inspects airport facilities, such as runways, buildings, beacons and lighting, and automotive or construction equipment, or reviews inspection reports, to determine repairs, replacement, or improvements required.

Coordinates activities of personnel involved in repair and maintenance of airport facilities, buildings, and equipment to minimize interruption of airport operations and improve efficiency. Directs personnel in investigating violations of aerial or ground traffic regulations, reviews investigation reports, and initiates actions to be taken against violators. Directs studies on noise abatement resulting from complaints of excessive noise from low flying aircraft or other operations.

Reviews reports of expenditures for previous fiscal year, proposed improvements to facilities, and estimated increase in volume of traffic, in order to prepare budget estimates for upcoming fiscal year. Represents airport before civic or other organizational groups, courts, boards, and commissions.

Station Manager

Directs and coordinates airline station activities at transport station or terminal point located at airport to provide services for scheduled flight operations. Reviews station activity reports to ascertain data required for planning station operations.

Directs preparation of work schedules to obtain optimum utilization of manpower and facilities. Coordinates activities of passenger reservations and ticketing, passenger services, ramp and cargo services, and dispatching of aircraft to ensure operations to meet company and government policies and regulations.

Directs preparation of passenger lists, cargo manifests, and plans for stowage of cargo and baggage aboard aircraft. Evaluates training and performance records of employees to determine and formulate training designed to increase employee efficiency.

May direct activities of **Transportation Agents** in expediting movement of freight, mail, baggage and passengers through station or from other company's terminal to station.

Chief Airport Guide

Supervises and coordinates activities of workers engaged in conducting guided tours at airport. Arranges tours according to interests of groups, such as school children, foreign visitors and civic or private organizations. Schedules tours to avoid interruption of airport operations and minimize congestion.

Assigns workers to guide tours. Provides information to workers about interest of specific groups. Coaches workers on organization, history and function of airport and use of airport facilities. Observes workers' dress and performance on guided tours to assure conformance to department standards. Confers with public relations personnel to plan special event programs. Prepares reports showing number of people taking tours, type of tours and public reaction.

Traffic Agent

Solicits freight business from industrial and commercial firms and passenger-travel business from travel agencies, schools, clubs and other organizations. Calls on prospective shippers to explain advantages of using company facilities. Quotes tariffs, rates and train schedules.

Explains available routes, load limits and special equipment available, and offers suggestions in method of loading, crating and handling freight. Calls on travel agents, schools, clubs and other organizations to explain available accommodations offered by company. Quotes fares, schedules, and available itineraries offered to groups by company. Speaks to members of groups and organizations and exhibits travel movies showing points of interest along routes to stimulate interest in travel.

Distributes descriptive pamphlets. Acts as liaison between shipper and carrier to obtain information for settling complaints. May specialize in soliciting freight or passenger contracts or may travel from community to community to solicit freight and passenger patronage.

TRAVEL AGENCIES

The career we know today as **retail travel agent** was created by one man, Thomas Cook of London, in 1841. Although he probably did not realize it, his arrangement of a fee for a rail tour on behalf of a group of travelers marked the beginning of the travel agent's service to travelers. As time went on, Cook realized people were attracted by the idea of travel at low prices. The operation of tours for entertainment, education, and business grew into a profitable business. Cook even issued circular notes, which evolved into the modern day traveler's check.

Travel agents must provide all types of travel information for the clients they service. While it is impossible to know every fact about hundreds of destinations, travel agents will have access to much information and with experience will become knowledgeable about sources and contacts in the industry. Travel agents must know how to locate any information that is not immediately available.

This position is basically a sales position. After all, no money is made unless a prospective client actually books travel services. Travel agents have a tremendous responsibility to their clients, to relay accurate and complete information about destinations. Satisfied customers will be likely to return when it comes time to book their next vacation. It is this repeat business that is a travel agent's livelihood. It takes a great amount of training and experience to be able to quickly locate information on schedules, fares, special excursion rates, car rentals, guided and group tour packages. However, travel agents must be able to do this. As well, they must keep alert to changes in all of these areas, in order to give their clients the most current information.

Travel agents are representatives of all the businesses whose services are being sold at the agency. Many people look to travel agents as consultants for planning information. For this reason, travel agents must be patient and willing to spend a great deal of time with clients. People tend to want all the possibilities they see, and may change their plans many times before the trip is finalized.

While the retail travel agent is the occupation most familiar to most people, similar careers exist in other areas. Large corporations may include in-house travel agencies that service only their needs. Government agencies may also employ travel agents for their own purposes. All government- or community-sponsored tourism development programs, such as travel information centers, may have openings for personnel knowledgeable in planning trips and events in specific areas.

As time goes on, travel agents are usually offered "fam" or familiarization trips by carriers and destinations. These free trips to potential destinations for clients are one of the benefits and attractions of the career.

Tour Operators

The tour operator is the wholesale agent of the travel industry. The design of tours and travel packages on a large scale is the primary function of the wholesaler, who markets these packages to the retail travel agent and the major airline carriers. Organizing a tour is time consuming. It involves many details. The tour operator is in a position to buy travel services at rates unavailable to the agent on the retail level, and thus makes a profit on volume.

The tour operator must plan entire itineraries, taking into account the most scenic routes from place to place, the availability of rest stops for refreshments, when tourist attractions are open, whether the tour size can be accommodated on a particular day, and whether adequate overnight accommodations can be arranged. Local transportation must be arranged months in advance of the scheduled tour. Tour guides for escorted tours must be recruited and trained in the itinerary of the planned destinations.

Tour operators range from the very large, such as American Express, to small independent operators specializing in specific geographic regions. Many tour operators become specialists in one or two specific areas and will tend to organize tours for these given areas only. The travel benefits available to the tour operator are similar to those of the travel agent mentioned earlier. Free or reduced air travel and trips to potential promotable destinations are frequently available.

Positions available within a tour operator company include reservationist, operations clerk, sales representative and tour guide. If the firm is a large one, supervisors may be necessary for an efficiently run organization.

Following are descriptions of the travel agency related jobs based on material included in the *Dictionary of Occupations Titles* published by the United States Department of Labor.

Travel Agent

Plans intineraries, and arranges accommodations and other travel services for customers of travel agency. Converses with customer to determine destination, mode of transportation, travel dates, financial considerations and accommodations required. Plans or describes and sells itinerary package tour.

Gives customer brochures and publications concerning travel and containing information regarding local customs, points of interest, and special events occurring in various locations; or foreign country regulations, such as consular requirements, rates of monetary exchange and currency limitations. Computes cost of travel and accommodations, using calculating machine, carrier tariff books and hotel rate books, or quotes costs of package tours. Books customer on transportation carrier and makes hotel reservations, using telephone or teletypewriter. Writes or obtains travel tickets for transportation or tour and collects payment.

May specialize in foreign or domestic service, individual or group travel, specific geographical area, airplane charters or package tours by bus. May act as wholesaler and assemble tour packages.

Travel-Information Center Supervisor (Government Service)

Supervises and coordinates activities of workers engaged in greeting and welcoming motorists at state highway information centers. Provides information, such as directions, road conditions and vehicular travel regulations. Provides maps, brochures and pamphlets to assist motorists in locating points of interest or in reaching destination. Performs duties as described under **Supervisor.**

May direct tourists to rest areas, camps, resorts, historical points or other tourist attractions.

Travel Clerk

Plans itinerary and schedules travel accommodations for military and civilian personnel and dependents according to travel orders, using knowledge of routes, types of carriers, and travel regulations. Verifies travel orders to ensure authorization. Studies routes and regulations and considers cost, availability and convenience of different types of carriers to select most advantageous route and carrier.

Notifies personnel of travel dates, baggage limits, and medical and visa requirements, and determines that all clearances have been obtained. Assists personnel in completing travel forms and other business transactions pertaining to travel. May deliver personnel files and travel orders to persons prior to departure. May meet and inform arriving personnel of available facilities and housing, and furnish other information. May arrange for motor transportation for arriving or departing personnel.

Automobile Club Travel Counselor

Plans trips for members of automobile club. Confers with member in person or by telephone to answer questions and explain services. Marks suitable roads and possible detours on road map, showing route from point of origin to destination and return. Indicates points of interest, restaurants, hotels or other housing accommodations and emergency repair services available along route.

Reserves hotel, motel or resort accommodations by telephone, telegraph or letter. Calculates mileage of marked route and estimates travel expenses. Informs patron of bus, ship, train and plane connections.

Consults hotel directories, road maps, circulars, timetables and other sources to obtain current information. Provides members with guides, directories, brochures and maps.

May plan trips for members in response to mail requests. May plan foreign trips and perform duties, such as arranging for automobile rental, purchase and shipment, and be designated as **World Travel Counselor.** May review itineraries prepared by other travel counselors for factors such as accuracy, pricing and date and timetable sequencing, and be designated **Travel-Ticketing Reviewer.**

Tourist Information Assistant

Provides travel information and other services to tourists at state information center. Greets tourists, in person or by telephone, and answers questions and gives information on resorts, historical sights, scenic areas and other tourist attractions. Assists tourists in planning itineraries and advises them of traffic regulations. Sells hunting and fishing licenses and provides information on fishing, hunting and camping regulations. Composes letters in response to inquires. Maintains personnel, license sales, and other records. Contacts motel, hotel and resort operators by mail or telephone to obtain advertising literature.

Reservation Clerk

Obtains travel and hotel accommodations for guests and employees of industrial concern, issues tickets, types itineraries and compiles reports of transactions. Obtains confirmation of travel and lodging space and rate information. Issues and validates airline tickets from stock or teleticketer and obtains rail and bus tickets from carriers. Prepares passenger travel booklet containing tickets, copy of itinerary, written lodging confirmations, pertinent credit cards and travel suggestions.

Keeps current directory of hotels, motels and timetables, and answers inquiries concerning routes, fares and accommodations. Reviews routine invoices of transportation charges, and types and submits reports to company and to transportation agencies. Prepares and types claim forms for refunds and adjustments and reports of transactions processed.

Travel Guide

Arranges transportation and other accommodations for groups of tourists, following planned itinerary, and escorts groups during entire trip, within single area or at specified stopping points of tour. Makes reservations on ships, trains and other modes of transportation, and arranges for other accommodations, such as baggage handling, dining and lodging facilities, and recreational activities, using communication media, such as cable, telegraph or telephone.

Accompanies tour group and describes points of interest. May assist tourists to plan itinerary, obtain travel certificates, such as visas, passports and health certificates, and convert currency into travelers' checks or foreign monies.

Sightseeing Guide

Drives motor vehicle to transport sightseers and lectures group concerning points of interest during sightseeing tour. Drives limousine or sightseeing bus, stopping vehicle at establishments or locations, such as art gallery, museum, battlefield and cave, to permit group to be escorted through buildings by **Establishment Guide.**

Describes points of interest along route of tour, using public address system or megaphone. May collect fees or tickets and plan refreshment and rest stops. May escort group through establishment and describe points of interest.

Guide

Escorts visitors around city or town. Advises visitors, such as convention delegates, foreign government personnel, or salesmen, as to location of buildings, points of interest and other sites, or escorts visitors to designated locations, using private or public transportation. May carry equipment, luggage or sample cases for visitors. May be required to speak foreign language when communicating with foreign visitors.

HOTELS AND MOTELS

Approximately one million persons are employed in the United States lodging industry today.

While a hotel or motel can be run by one or two persons or by as many as 1,000 or more employees, most establishments fall somewhere between these extremes.

Larger establishments have a clearly defined organizational structure. Management usually includes representatives from all phases of the establishment's operations. The front desk staff includes the manager and various clerical staff to check guests in and out, take phone reservations and follow through on mail inquiries and written reservation requests. In larger hotels, a separate accounting department has the responsibility of collecting daily receipts and balancing the financial records.

Other hotel and motel positions include the housekeeping and maintenance staff and the food service staff. In very modern establishments additional staff members are responsible for running bars, nightclubs, lounges, pool and/or athletic facilities, meeting rooms for business travelers and various convenience shops: beauty salons, boutiques, gift shops, and car rental services.

An educational background in hotel and motel management is a good start toward a management trainee position. There is room for advancement in the larger hotel chains. Another benefit of working for a chain is the opportunity to stay at the various properties free or at a reduced rate. However, a potential disadvantage of employment with any hotel or motel may be the necessity of working nights, weekends and holidays.

Hotel/motel employees must adjust their lifestyles, including personal vacations, in order to be available for the busy season in this industry. The key to a well-run property is the concern of all employees for the guests' comfort and needs. A satisfied guest will not only return, but will recommend the establishment to friends and associates.

Following are the descriptions of hotel/motel related jobs based on material in the *Dictionary of Occupational Titles* published by the United States Department of Labor.

Manager, Hotel or Motel

Manages hotel or motel to ensure efficient and profitable operation. Establishes standards for personnel administration and performance, service to patrons, room rates, advertising publicity, credit, food selection and service, and type of patronage to be solicited. Plans dining room, bar and banquet operations. Allocates funds, authorizes expenditures and assists in planning budgets for departments. Hires personnel. Delegates authority and assigns responsibilities to department heads. In small hotels or motels, processes reservations and adjusts guests' complaints.

Night Auditor

Verifies and balances entries and records of financial transactions reported by various hotel departments during the day, using adding, bookkeeping and calculating machines. May perform duties of **Hotel Clerk** in smaller establishment.

Cashier's Supervisor

Supervises and coordinates activities of workers engaged in receiving cash or credit-card payment for merchandise or services and keeping records of funds received in retail establishments or places of public accommodation. Performs cashiering and other clerical duties to relieve subordinates during peak work periods. Searches records to assist subordinates in locating and reconciling posting errors on customers' invoices, such as hotel bills or sales tickets, or compares cash register totals with receipts in register to verify accuracy of transactions.

Withdraws monies from bank and keeps custody of operating funds, or retains next day's operating funds from daily receipts. Allocates operating funds to cashiering stations. Totals and summarizes funds received, endorses checks and prepares bank deposit slip.

Hotel Clerk

Performs combination of duties for guests of hotel, motel, motor lodge or condominium-hotel, registers and assigns rooms to guests. Issues room key and escort instruction to **Bellhop.** Date-stamps, sorts and racks incoming mail and messages. Transmits and receives messages, using equipment, such as telegraph, telephone, teletype and switchboard. Answers inquiries pertaining to hotel services, registration of guests, and shopping, dining, entertainment and travel directions.

Keeps records of room availability and guests' accounts. Computes bill, collects payment and makes change for guests. Makes and confirms reservations. May sell tobacco, candy and news-

papers. May post charges, such as room, food, liquor or telephone to cashbooks by hand or by machine. May make restaurant, transportation, or entertainment reservations, and arrange for tours.

May deposit guests' valuables in hotel safe or safe-deposit box. May order complimentary flowers or champagne for honeymoon couples or special guests. May rent dock space at marina-hotel.

Travel Clerk

Provides travel information and arranges accommodations for tourists: answers inquiries, offers suggestions and provides descriptive literature pertaining to trips, excursions, sports events, concerts and plays. Discusses routes, time schedules, rates and type of accommodations with patrons to determine preferences and make reservations.

Verifies arrival and departure times, traces routes on maps and arranges for baggage handling and other services requested by guests. May deliver tickets. May arrange for visas and other documents required by foreign travelers. May contact individuals and groups to inform them of package tours.

Sales Representative

Contacts representatives of government, business and social groups to solicit business for hotel, motel or resort. Selects prospective customers by reviewing information concerning functions such as sales meetings, conventions, training classes and routine travel by organization members. Calls on prospects, analyzes requirements of occasion, outlines types of service offered and quotes prices. Verifies reservations by letter or draws up contract and obtains signatures.

Confers with customer and hotel department heads to plan function details, such as space requirements, publicity, time schedule, food service and decorations. May serve as convention advisor or hotel agent during function to minimize confusion and resolve problems, such as space adjustment and need for additional equipment. May select and release hotel's publicity.

Lodging Facilities Manager

Manages and maintains temporary or permanent lodging facilities, such as small apartment houses, motels, small hotels, trailer parks and boat marinas. Shows and rents or assigns accommodations. Registers guests, collects rents and records data pertaining to rent funds and expenditures. Resolves occupants' complaints.

Purchases supplies and arranges for outside services, such as fuel delivery, laundry, maintenance and repair, and trash collection. Provides telephone answering service for tenants, delivers mail and packages, and answers inquiries concerning travel routes, recreational facilities, scenic attractions and eating establishments. Cleans public areas, such as entrances, halls and laundry rooms, and fire boilers.

Makes minor electrical, plumbing and structural repairs. Mows and waters lawns and cultivates flower beds and shrubbery. Cleans accommodations after guests' departure. Provides daily maid service in overnight accommodations. May rent equipment, such as rowboats, water skis and fishing tackle. May coordinate intramural activities of patrons of park. May arrange for medical air for park patrons. May sell light lunches, candy, tobacco and other sundry items.

Parlor Chaperone

Chaperones young people attending social functions held in hotels or restaurants. Greets guests and answers questions regarding program. Arranges for entertainment, such as games, concerts and motion pictures. Asks guests to observe rules of establishment or reports offenders to **House Officer.** May collect tickets for admission to events.

CRUISE LINES

Some of the most exciting careers in the tourism field are provided by cruise lines. It is not unusual for a ship that will accommodate up to 1,000 passengers to have a crew of at least 250. About one-third of these jobs require extensive marine or maritime training. They include engineer, radio officers, electrical officers, navigation personnel and experienced seamen.

Jobs most readily available to people with a background in tourism and hospitality include those that are directly related to passenger service and well-being. Since a cruise ship can be compared to a floating hotel, it is not surprising that many job descriptions closely resemble those previously discussed under "Hotels and Motels." The hotel aspects include the usual activities and responsibilities of a resort or shore-

side hotel. A background in hotel training or experience is helpful.

Training in the hospitality management and a background in food and beverage preparation are essential for personnel in charge of all dining room facilities aboard ship.

The cruise director is responsible for all daily activity planning, entertainment, and port of call information for passengers. This requires a strong background in the entertainment field, an exceptional ability to work well with people, and the ability to handle administrative details. A cruise director's staff, usually four to six people, handles various activities under the director's supervision; and the position also requires a background in the entertainment field and the ability to work well with people. Since many ships call in foreign ports and carry passengers from many different nations, the ability to speak a foreign language will increase the chances for employment by a cruise line.

While employee turnover in the cruise lines is one of the lowest in the industry, a number of cruise line companies recently announced the construction of new ships. It can be anticipated that this will greatly increase employment opportunities for people with training in tourism and hospitality management.

Following are descriptions of cruise line related jobs based on material in the *Dictionary of Occupational Titles*, published by the United States Department of Labor.

Documentation Supervisor

Supervises and coordinates activities of workers engaged in preparing shipping documents and related reports and in classifying and rating cargo according to established tariff rates. Reviews ships' schedules and booking records to plan and schedule work activities.

Assigns rating activities to workers and reviews ratings to ensure that cargo has been classified in accordance with established tariff rates. Verifies codes assigned shippers against bills of lading and manifests, and compiles tonnage, demurrage and storage reports.

Examines reports and documents for completeness and accuracy and gives instructions to workers regarding corrections. Issues bills of lading to shippers' representatives to clarify problems and resolve complaints. May supervise and coordinate activities or workers engaged in passenger baggage handling.

Cargo Checker

Compiles records of amount, kind and condition of cargo loaded on or unloaded from ship. Verifies amount of cargo against lists compiled from bills of lading or shipping manifests. Measures dimensions of cargo and computes cubic feet required for stowage aboard ship. Records condition of damaged cargo containers unloaded from ship. May prepare cargo or stowage plan showing location of cargo stowed aboard ship.

Booking Supervisor

Supervises and coordinates activities of workers engaged in booking shipments of cargo on ships and keeping booking control records to ensure maximum utilization of cargo spaces. Reviews records of bookings, studies plans of cargo spaces to determine type of tonnage that can be booked on each ship in order to obtain maximum revenue and utilize available cargo space. Assigns booking duties to workers and gives work directions regarding tonnage or cubic feet of storage space that can be booked for refrigerated cargo or container cargo.

Coordinates booking and space control activities to insure that each ship is booked to capacity. Trains workers in booking procedures and demonstrates methods of converting cubic feet of storage space into tonnage. Submits booking sheets to documentation department for preparation of shipping documents.

Chief Steward/Stewardess

Supervises and coordinates activities of personnel in steward's department aboard passenger vessel. Supervises workers engaged in housekeeping and meal serving. Arranges space for shipboard recreation activities. Inspects passenger areas for cleanliness. Observes services rendered by steward personnel for conformance to company standards. Collaborates with **Chef** to plan menus. Requisitions stores, such as food, sundries and furniture. Obtains replacements for personnel leaving ship.

Social Director

Plans and organizes recreational activities and creates friendly atmosphere for guests in hotels or resorts or for passengers on board ship. Greets new arrivals, introduces them to other guests, acquaints them with recreation facilities, and encourages them to participate in group activities.

Ascertains interests of group and evaluates available equipment and facilities to plan activities such as card parties, games, tournaments, dances, musicals and field trips.

Arranges for activity requirements such as setting up equipment, transportation, decorations, refreshments and entertainment. Associates with lonely guests and visits those who are ill. May greet and seat guests in dining room. May assist management in resolving guests' complaints.

RAILROADS

Americans are beginning to take a fresh look at rail transportation as a convenient, efficient transportation mode. Crowds at Amtrak stations and on many trains are becoming the rule as ridership continues to grow.

Despite recent route reductions, substantial increases in passenger miles have been achieved. This is important to the economic viability of the American railroad industry. In addition, equipment improvements and the introduction of new equipment such as the Superliner between Chicago and Seattle have increased the level of passenger satisfaction.

The future of a healthy national railroad passenger system is uncertain at the moment, but a recent increase in popularity of rail transportation by the American traveler could indicate the beginning of a new and exciting era in railroad transportation. The train deserves to hold a prominent place in a well-balanced American transportation system.

Here are some descriptions of rail travel related jobs based on material in the *Dictionary of Occupational Titles* published by the United States Department of Labor.

Documentation Billing Clerk

Compiles and types transportation billing documents listing details of freight shipped by carrier. Types information on manifest, such as name of shipper, weight, destination and charges from bills of lading and shipper's declaration. Computes totals of document items, using adding machine. Compares figures and totals on documents with statement of accounts submitted by accounting department to verify accuracy of documents.

Notifies **Cargo Checker** to examine shipment when discrepancies are found. Resolves discrepancies on accounting records or manifest. May prepare manifest, using billing machine. May notify shipper's agent of consular visa and official stamps required and attaches to documents when presented by agent.

Interline Clerk

Compiles and computes freight and passenger charges payable to participating carriers on interline business. Examines way bills and ticket sales records to compute number of miles each carrier transported freight or passengers. Computes freight or passenger charges payable to each carrier, using basic rates from rate table and calculating machine. Records results of calculations on special forms. Reviews statement submitted by other companies to determine if portion of charges received is correct.

May compile records of daily freight car rental fees due to other carriers and be designated **Per-diem Clerk.**

Passenger Rate Clerk

Using rate tables, provides fare information to passengers traveling on nonscheduled or chartered motor trips. Interviews customer or reviews written requests to obtain data on proposed trips. Studies maps to select or lay out and measure travel route.

Refers to rate tables to gather rate data considering such items as type of vehicle, distance, destination, estimated travel and waiting times, cost of tolls and passenger or freight service. Computes rates, using calculator. Prepares written report on rates or informs customer orally. May arrange travel accommodations for tourists.

Dispatcher Clerk

Schedules work for train crew or individual workers and keeps time records. Enters names of workers on assignment sheet for each trip on basis of seniority. Notifies workers of assignment, establishes availability of departure and return of crew or worker for each trip, recording total time worked and number of miles traveled, using a calculator.

Voucher Clerk

Compiles data to prorate cost of lost or damaged goods among interline railroad carriers. Receives claim for lost or damaged goods filed by shipper or consignee. Verifies records to substantiate claim

of shipment and requests **Customer Complaint Clerk** to investigate claim and to submit estimate of value of lost or damaged goods.

Receives estimate, verifies records to ascertain names of carriers involved in transporting goods. Computes number of miles each carrier transported goods. Prorates and computes cost to be charged to interline carriers according to comparative mileage in transit over each railroad, using calculating machine. Records name of each interline carrier involved and amount prorated to each.

Train Clerk

Records time each train arrives and departs from station or terminal. Records number of train, engine and exact time train departs or arrives. Compares time of arrival or departure with train schedules to ascertain number of minutes train was off schedule. Ascertains from train crew or **Yard Manager** reasons or causes for delays.

Transmits train-movement data to electronic data-processing system, using on-line console or telegraphic typewriter. May type operating information, such as switching lists and personnel assignments, according to instructions from **Yard Manager.**

Railroad Maintenance Clerk

Compiles and records information pertaining to track and right-of-way repair and maintenance by railroad section crews, such as materials used, types and locations or repairs made, and hours expended. Types or writes requisitions for materials needed.

May keep daily time records and compile maintenance reports for specific section crew and be designated **Road Clerk.** May compile daily, weekly and monthly composite reports from data submitted by **Road Clerks** and be designated **Section Crews Activities Clerk.**

Reservation Clerk

Receives requests for and assigns space on trains to passengers. Accepts requests for space assignments and examines diagram charts of each car on train to verify available space on specified train. Informs **Station Agents I** or **Information Clerks** of available space. Marks blocks on diagram to indicate that space is reserved.

Prepares teletype requests to other interline carriers to complete passage. Informs **Station Agents I** and **Information Clerks** upon completion of booking arrangement. Informs **Reservations Clerks** at other cities and towns of space reserved or space remaining available.

Railroad Dining Car Steward/Stewardess

Supervises and coordinates activities of workers engaged in preparing, cooking and serving food to passengers in railroad dining car. Requisitions food supplies necessary to fill menu and prepares requisitions for linen, crockery and silverware from commissary. Examines supplies for quality and completeness of orders. Supervises workers engaged in storing food in car. Receives bills and money from **Dining Car Waiter/Waitress** and makes change. Maintains record of all cash received during each day. Informs the **Cook** of approximate number of persons expected to board train. Assigns work stations to **Dining Car Waiters/Waitresses.** May coordinate sale and serving of beverages in lounge car and be designated **Club Car Steward/Stewardess.**

Passenger Service Representative

Renders personal services to railroad passengers to make their trip pleasant and comfortable. Straightens seat cushions and window shades to prepare cars for passengers. Greets passengers boarding trains and introduces passengers to each other. Answers questions about train schedules, travel routes and railway service. Assists in feeding and caring for children during transit. Assists ill passengers.

The Passenger Service Representative may also stand at the gate in a railroad or rapid-transit station to admit passengers holding tickets or tokens, or at an exit to prevent unauthorized entrance of passengers. Tears or punches tickets to prevent their reuse. Many count tickets to tally number of passengers boarding train. May give passengers and guests boarding passes.

Baggage and Mail Agent

Supervises and coordinates activities of workers engaged in loading and unloading mail and baggage. Coordinates work schedules in accordance with train schedules to ensure that transfer of mail and luggage is completed in allotted time. Assigns duties to workers. Observes workers serving passengers to ensure workers are courteous and helpful.

Supervises workers sorting, loading and unloading sacks of mail. Notifies **Station Agent I** when transfer of mail and baggage has been completed following prescribed rules and regulations. Recommends new methods of transferring mail and luggage onto and from trains. Reviews workflow and production charts to determine need for additional workers.

Freight Loading Supervisor

Supervises and coordinates activities of workers engaged in loading and unloading incoming and outgoing freight at railroad stations. Determines number of workers and equipment required to load or unload freight, using information obtained from waybills, other shipping records and personal experience. Examines each item of freight for size and weight to determine sequence of loading so that maximum amount of freight can be loaded into each car.

Gives instructions to **Material Handler** to load freight into cars. Records description of each item of freight and number of car in which it is loaded. Compares items of freight loaded or unloaded with listing on waybill or other shipping records to ensure that all freight is routed to specified destination. Informs adjustment department of damaged freight. May notify railway clerical employee to affix door seal when freight car has been loaded. Performs other duties as described under **Supervisor.**

Station Agent

Supervises and coordinates activities of workers engaged in selling tickets and checking baggage at railroad station not served by **Station Manager.** Assigns shift schedules to workers to ensure adequate service to patrons. Keeps daily records of attendance. Sells tickets to patrons. Answers inquiries from patrons concerning schedules and departures and arrivals of trains. Requisitions supplies. Relays train orders and messages.

Inspects buildings to detect maintenance needs. Verifies records of daily ticket sales and cash receipts. May train new employees. May supervise and coordinate activities of workers engaged in maintaining buildings and grounds of railroad station. May perform duties of **Express Clerk.**

Passenger Representative

Accompanies conductor through train, verifies tickets and seat reservations and records information such as number of passengers scheduled to leave train at each stop. Answers passengers' questions and suggests activities and accommodations available at the passenger's destination. May assist or relieve **Passenger Car Conductor** by taking tickets in designated coaches or entire train. May inspect kitchen and dining area to insure sanitation requirements are maintained. May investigate passenger complaints.

CAR RENTAL COMPANIES

The practice of renting a car while on vacation or on a business trip has become second nature to the United States traveler. Opportunities in leased- or rental-car businesses are excellent for the qualified individual.

Sales Rental Agent

The sales rental agent greets customers and helps them find suitable cars for their needs. Since this position requires public contact, persons must possess pleasant and outgoing personalities and have an overall good appearance. Agents are trained in computerized reservations and billing procedures as well as communications skills, such as proper telephone manners and customer relations. Preferred applicants will have a travel-related educational background and knowledge of computerized reservations.

Reservation Agent

Reservation agents work directly over the phone with requests from airline reservationists, travel agents, and the general public. They check the availability of cars in the city requested and take all pertinent information, including a credit card number to secure the reservation. Applicants with some background in computerized reservations are preferred for this position.

Car Rental Sales Representative

The car rental sales representative's responsibilities are similar to those of this same position in the airlines. Many representatives are assigned to call on business accounts to promote car rental service to the business traveler segment. Others deal with travel agents and airlines with the goal of increasing sales through the establishment of corporate package deals on a large volume basis.

This description of a car-rental related job is based on material in the *Dictionary of Occupational Titles* published by the United States Department of Labor.

Automobile Rental Clerk

Rents automobiles to customers at airports, hotels, marinas and other locations. Talks to customer to determine type of automobile desired and accessories, such as power-steering or air-conditioning, location where car is to be picked up and returned, and number of days required. Examines customer's driver's license and determines amount of deposit required.

Quotes cost of rental, based on per-day and per-mile rates. Completes rental contract and obtains customer's signature and deposit, or checks charge-plate number against list of disapproved charge-plates. Telephones storage and requests delivery of automobile, and to check automobile upon return for damage and to record mileage reading. Computes rental charges based on rental time, miles traveled, type of car rented, taxes and other incidental charges incurred.

May reconcile cash and rental agreements and charge slips and send them to management. May deliver automobile to customer. May keep log of location of rented automobiles.

MOTORCOACHES

While the bus industry in North America is dominated by the two giants, Greyhound and Trailways, smaller companies are sharing in the economic growth that this industry is experiencing at the moment.

With higher fuel prices, the bus has once again earned its reputation as the most energy efficient means of transportation. Today more passengers are transported by bus to more communities than by any other mode of transportation. While buses have long been widely used as a means of public transportation, the tourism industry also discovered early that buses provide an excellent means of transportation for transfers, local sightseeing, excursion trips and group tours.

The modern tour bus is a truly deluxe transportation vehicle, often equipped with restroom facilities, panoramic view windows and sometimes even a lounge area. Motorcoach tours are currently extremely popular with the elderly segment of the population and it can be expected that the popularity of vacations by bus will increase during the decades ahead.

Frequently, a public bus company will expand its operations into the tour operating business. Many tour operators have purchased and operate their private fleets of buses. The Gray Line company is a leader in this field.

Following are descriptions of motorcoach related jobs based on material in the *Dictionary of Occupational Titles* published by the U.S. Department of Labor.

Bus Attendant

Renders a variety of personal services to bus passengers to make their trip pleasant. Welcomes passengers boarding bus. Adjusts seating arrangement to accommodate passengers when requested. Answers question about bus schedules, travel routes and bus services. Points out places of interest. Distributes magazines, newspapers, pillows and blankets. Mails passengers' letters and arranges for dispatch of telegrams. Tends tape recorder to provide music. Serves refreshments. Lists names of passengers on manifest. Maintains inventory to account for food served during the trip and food on hand. May warm bottles for babies.

Interstate Bus Dispatcher

Dispatches interstate or long-distance buses according to schedule and oversees **Bus Drivers** and **Bus Attendants** while they are at terminal. Issues orders for station departure of buses at specified hours or according to schedule.

Arranges for extra buses and drivers in case of accidents or heavy traffic. Announces incoming and outgoing buses over public address system in bus terminal. May supervise loading, unloading and checking of baggage or express shipped by bus. May inspect driver's appearance and physical condition prior to dispatch.

Dispatcher Clerk

Schedules work for bus crew or individual workers and keeps time records. Enters names of workers on assignment sheet for each trip on basis of seniority. Notifies workers of assignment, establishes availability and assigns replacement crew when needed. Keeps record of departure and return of crew or worker for each trip, recording total time worked, and number of miles covered, using calculator.

A FINAL WORD

The travel industry, like many other businesses, offers employment opportunities for candidates with backgrounds and skills that are not necessarily travel oriented. Experience in any of these areas, combined with an interest in or commitment to the tourism and travel industry can often open doors to the exciting world of travel. Students who, in addition to their travel classes, have taken courses in accounting, secretarial science, computer programming and/or business management are well advised to include these skills on their resumes or job applications. Such skills may well lead to a first job in the chosen field.

It would be difficult to list and describe all of the many employment opportunities which are available in the travel and tourism industries. In addition to the career areas and jobs presented above, the travel and tourism professional will be prepared to work for local, state, regional and national tourist agencies. Every convention and visitors' bureau needs people with training and people with experience in travel and tourism. Local chambers of commerce are usually tied very directly to the tourism businesses of their communities and thus need professional skills in travel and tourism.

Destination sites such as Disney World, Mt. Rushmore, Yellowstone, Grand Canyon, Wall Drug, Cypress Gardens, The Alamo and Knott's Berry Farm are busy tourist centers, as are national parks, ski resorts and camper vacation resorts. The specific types of positions available at destination sites range from managerial to travel planning, from marketing to accounting, and from marina fishing guide to supervisor of activities at a dude ranch.

Where you begin will depend on your interests and training. Your advancement in the industry will depend on interest, performance and continued learning, both through experience and formal study. The more skills you bring to a job, the higher your starting salary is likely to be and the more opportunities you will have to advance.

Following are descriptions of business related jobs which are available in all facets of the travel industry. This material is based on information in the *Dictionary of Occupational Titles* published by the United States Department of Labor.

Accountant

Directs and coordinates activities of workers engaged in general accounting, or applies principles of accounting to devise and implement system for general accounting. Directs and coordinates activities of workers engaged in keeping accounts and records, or performing such payments.

Prepares individual, division or consolidated balance sheets to reflect company's assets, liabilities and capital. Prepares profit and loss statements for specified accounting period. Audits contracts, orders and vouchers and prepares reports to substantiate individual transactions prior to settlement.

May represent company before government agencies upon certification by agency involved.

Accounting Clerk

Performs any combination of routine calculating, posting and verifying duties to obtain primary financial data for use in maintaining accounting records. Posts details of business transactions, such as allotments, disbursements, deductions from payrolls, pay and expense vouchers, remittances paid and due, checks and claims.

Totals accounts, using adding machine. Computes and records interest charges, refunds, cost of lost or damages goods, freight or express charges, rentals and similar items.

May type vouchers, invoices, account statements, payrolls, periodic reports and other records. May reconcile bank statements. May be designated according to type of accounting performed as **Accounts-Payable Clerk; Accounts Receivable Clerk; Advance-Payment Clerk; Bill-Recapitulation Clerk; Cash-Posting Clerk; Rent and Miscellaneous Remittance Clerk; Tax-Record Clerk.**

Bookkeeper

Keeps complete records of financial transactions of establishment. Verifies and enters details of transactions as they occur in account and cash journals from items such as sales slips, invoices, check stubs, inventory records and requisitions. Summarizes details on separate ledgers, using adding or calculating machine, and transfers data to general ledger.

Balances books and compiles reports to show statistics, such as cash receipts and expenditures, accounts payable and receivable, profit and loss and other items pertinent to operation of the business. Calculates employee wages from plant records or timecards and prepares checks or withdraws cash from bank for payment of wages.

May prepare withholding, Social Security and other tax reports. May compute, type and mail monthly statements to customers. May complete books to or through trial balance. May operate bookkeeping machines or computer terminal.

Business Programmer

Converts symbolic statements of administrative data or business problems to detailed logical flow charts for coding into computer language. Analyzes all or part of workflow chart or diagram representing business problems by applying knowledge of computer capabilities, subject matter, algebra and symbolic logic to develop sequence of program steps. Confers with supervisor and representatives of departments concerned with program to resolve questions of program intent, output requirements, input data acquisition, extent of automatic programming and coding use and modifications and inclusion of internal checks and controls.

Writes detailed logical flow chart in symbolic form to represent work order of data to be processed by computer system, and to describe input, output, and arithmetic and logical operations involved. Converts detailed logical flow chart to language processable by computer **Detail Programmer.**

Devises sample input data to provide test of program adequacy. Prepares block diagrams to specify equipment configuration. Observes or operates computer to test coded program, using actual or sample input data. Corrects program errors by such methods as altering program steps and sequence. Prepares written instructions (run book) to guide operating personnel during production runs.

Analyzes, reviews and rewrites programs to increase operating efficiency or adapt to new requirements. Compiles documentation of program development subsequent revisions. May specialize in writing programs for one make and type of computer.

Computer Operations Supervisor

Supervises and coordinates activities of workers engaged in operating electronic data-processing machines and operates computer system to test new or revised programs. Assigns personnel and schedules work-flow to facilitate production. Directs training or trains personnel in operation of computers and peripheral and off-line auxiliary equipment. Confers with programming personnel and operates computer systems to test new and revised programs.

Develops operating methods to process data, such as devising wiring programs for peripheral equipment control panels, and making minor changes in canned (standardized) programs or routines to modify output content or format. Directs insertion of program instructions and input data into computer, and observes operations. Operates computers to assist operators in locating and overcoming error conditions.

Makes minor program and input data revisions through computer console to maintain operations. Notifies programming and maintenance personnel if unable to locate and correct cause of error or failure. Revises operating schedule to adjust for delays. Prepares or reviews records and reports of production, operating, and down time. Recommends changes in programs, routines and quality control standards.

Consults with **Manager** about problems, such as including new program test and operating runs in schedule and arranging for preventive maintenance time. Coordinates flow of work between shifts to ensure continuity. May supervise personnel engaged in key punching, data typing and tabulating.

Office Manager

Coordinates activities of clerical personnel in establishment or organization. Analyzes and organizes office operations and procedures, such as typing, bookkeeping, preparation of payrolls, flow of correspondence, filing, requisition of supplies and other clerical services. Evaluates office production, revises procedures or devises new forms to improve efficiency of work flow. Establishes uniform correspondence procedures and style practices. Formulates procedures for systematic retention, protection, retrieval and transfer and disposal of records. Plans office layouts and initiates cost reduction programs. Reviews clerical and personnel records to ensure completeness, accuracy and timeliness. Prepares activities reports for guidance of management. Prepares employee rating and conducts employee benefit and insurance programs. Coordinates activities of various clerical departments or workers within department.

Receptionist

Receives callers at establishment, determines nature of business and directs callers to destination. Obtains caller's name and arranges for appointment with person called upon. Directs caller to destination and records name, time of call, nature of business and person called upon.

May issue visitor's pass when required. May make future appointments and answer inquiries. May perform variety of clerical duties. May collect and distribute mail and messages.

Secretary

Schedules appointments, gives information to callers, takes dictation and otherwise relieves officials of clerical work and minor administrative and business details. Reads and routes incoming mail. Locates and attaches appropriate file to correspondence to be answered by employer. Takes dictation in shorthand or by machine and transcribes notes on typewriter or transcribes from voice recordings.

Composes and types routine correspondence. Files correspondence and other records. Answers telephone and gives information to callers or routes call to appropriate official and places outgoing calls. Schedules appointments for employer. Greets visitors, ascertains nature of business and conducts visitors to employer or to appropriate person.

May not take dictation. May arrange travel schedule and reservations. May compile and type statistical reports. May oversee clerical workers. May keep personnel records. May record minutes of staff meetings. May make copies of correspondence or other printed matter, using copying or duplicating machine. May prepare outgoing mail, using postage-metering machine.

Terminal Operator

Operates on-line computer typewriter terminal to transmit data to or to receive data from computer at remote location. Types alphabetic or numeric input data or request for data output on keyboard of computer terminal from source documents, using knowledge of coding system. Inserts specified paper into typewriter carriage and presses key to obtain printout or activates machine to display facsimile on viewing screen of information input or stored.

Compares data on printout or screen with source documents to detect errors. Backspaces and strikes over original matter, using terminal keyboard to correct errors. Presses code key to transmit corrected data via telephone lines to computer.

May operate terminal to record data on perforated tape. May place tape in transmitter to transmit data to remote computer. May maintain incoming and outgoing message logs.

Traffic Rate Clerk

Compiles and computes freight rates, passenger fares and other charges for transportation services, according to rate tables and tariff regulations. Examines shipping bills to obtain description of freight and classifies freight according to rate-book description.

Consults rate schedule to obtain specific rate for each item classified depending on distance shipped. Computes total freight charge, using calculator, and records charges on shipping order. Calculates and records storage, redelivery and reconsignment charges when applicable. Answers mail or telephone inquiries from shippers regarding rates, routing, packing procedures and interline transportation procedures.

May examine bills of lading and file claims with transportation companies for overcharges. May keep records of freight movements.

CONCLUSION

A challenging and exciting future may be yours in one of the positions described previously, or in a position which is not yet designed. The fields of travel, tourism and hospitality are constantly growing and changing. The individual who has the necessary motivation, education and experience will have the opportunity to enjoy a highly satisfactory career or several careers if he or she is willing to continue to learn and to explore new challenges.

In today's world of work there are few career fields which provide such a variety of opportunities for excitement and personal choice in both professional and personal life. An individual who wants security and stability will find many opportunities in a variety of desirable locations to earn an adequate income while providing a necessary and important professional service to friends, neighbors and other members of the community.

Individuals who want mobility literally have the world from which to choose. Not only is there great mobility within a given field, such as a travel agency, but also among the many career fields. A well-trained professional can provide the same kinds of competencies for airlines, cruise lines, bus companies, state or local tourist agencies and a variety of hospitality-related fields as well.

What other career field permits you to work where you want to live; earn a competitive salary; have extensive travel opportunities; have security or be an entrepreneur; be able to advance rapidly in your profession; and which constantly brings you into contact with some of the most interesting and exciting people in the world . . . those who travel?

PROJECT

1. Select three jobs, either from those described in this chapter or elsewhere, in which you think you might like to be employed after you complete this program.

2. For each job you select, prepare a complete job description, using this text as well as other references which you have available.

3. Analyze your current program of study to determine whether or not you will need additional study beyond that provided by the program in order to qualify you for any of the three positions you selected. (Remember that although your current program of study does train you for many positions, it is possible that further specific skills will be needed. Many companies have in-house training programs for this purpose once they have selected an employee with a good basic education.)

4. Start a job file by collecting job advertisements from newspapers, journals and special announcements.

5. Identify at least five companies that employ people in the three jobs you selected. Gather information about those companies relative to the history of the company, locations, number of employees, salaries and so forth.

   This project should run throughout your program of study. Items 1, 2 and 3 should be completed as soon as possible, however. Your instructors will tell you about other due dates.

APPENDIX B
Directory of Useful Addresses

AIRLINES

Aer Lingus
122 E. 42nd Street
New York, NY 10168
(212) 557-1090

Aerolineas Argentinas
9 Rockefeller Plaza
New York, NY 10020
(212) 698-2050

Aeromexico
13405 N.W. Freeway, Ste 140
Houston, TX 77040
(719) 939-1862

Air Canada
Place Air Canada
500 Dorchester West
Montreal, Quebec
Canada H2Z 1X5
(514) 879-7000

Air Europe
136 East 57th Street
Suite 1602
New York, NY 10022
(212) 888-7010

Air France
888 Seventh Avenue
New York, NY 10106
(212) 830-4442

Air-India
345 Park Avenue
New York, NY 10154
(212) 407-1300

Air Jamaica
95–25 Queens Blvd., 9th floor
Rego Park, NY 11374
(718) 830-0622

Air Mauritius
560 Sylvan Avenue
Englewood Cliffs, NJ 07632
(201) 871-8381

Air New Zealand
1960 East Grand Avenue
Suite 900
El Segunda, CA 90245
(213) 648-7100

Air Pacific Ltd
6151 West Century Blvd
Suite 524
Los Angeles, CA 90045
(213) 417-2236

Alaska Airlines
P.O. Box 68900
Seattle, WA 98168
(206) 433-3200

ALIA
535 Fifth Avenue
New York, NY 10017
(212) 949-0050

Alitalia
666 Fifth Avenue
New York, NY 10103
(212) 903-3441

All Nippon Airways
630 Fifth Avenue
Suite 537
New York, NY 10111
(212) 956-8200

ALM Antillean Airlines
1150 Northwest 72nd Ave.
Miami, FL 33126
(800) 327-7197

Aloha Airlines
P.O. Box 30028
Honolulu, HI 96820
(808) 836-1111

America West Airlines
4000 E. Sky Harbour Blvd.
Phoenix, AZ 85034
(602) 350-3256

American Airlines
P.O. Box 61916 MD 5366
DFW Airport, TX 75261
(817) 355-2670

Ansett Airlines
9841 Airport Blvd
Suite 418
Los Angeles, CA 90045
(213) 642-7487

Aspen Airways
Hangar Five
Stapleton Int'l Airport
Denver, CO 80207
(303) 320-4747

Australian Airlines
510 West Sixth Street
Suite 312
Los Angeles, CA 90014
(213) 626-2352

Austrian Airlines
17–20 Whitestone Expwy
Whitestone, NY 11357
(718) 670-8600

Avianca Airlines
6 West 49th Street
New York, NY 10017
(212) 399-0800

British Airways
245 Park Avenue
New York, NY 10017
(212) 878-0740

Cathay Pacific
300 N. Continental Blvd.
El Segundo, CA 90245
(213) 615-1113

China Airlines
6053 West Century Blvd
Suite 800
Los Angeles, CA 90045
(213) 641-8888

Continental Air Lines
P.O. Box 60455
Houston, TX 77205
(800) 525-1700

Delta Air Lines
Hartsfield International Airport
Atlanta, GA 30320
(404) 765-2600

El Al Israel Airlines
120 W. 45th Street
New York, NY 10022
(212) 852-0603

Ethiopian Airlines
123 E. 42nd Street
New York, NY 10017
(212) 867-3830

Finnair
10 East 40th Street
New York, NY 10016
(212) 689-9300

Garuda Indonesian Airways
9841 Airport Road
Los Angeles, CA 90045
(213) 986-4500

Hawaiian Airlines
Box 30008
Honolulu, HI 96820
(808) 525-5511

Iberia Airlines
6500 Wilshire Blvd
Suite 1900
Los Angeles, CA 90048
(213) 658-7100

Icelandair
360 West 31st Street
New York, NY 10001
(212) 330-1400

Japan Air Lines
655 Fifth Avenue
New York, NY 10022
(212) 310-1200

JAT
630 Fifth Avenue
New York, NY 10020
(212) 759-2400

KLM Royal Dutch Airlines
437 Madison Avenue
New York, NY 10022
(212) 223-2860

Korean Airlines
6101 West Imperial Highway
Los Angeles, CA 90045
(213) 417-5200

Kuwait Airways
405 Park Avenue
New York, NY 10022
(212) 319-1222

Lan-Chile Airlines
9700 S. Dixie Hwy.
11th floor
Miami, FL 33156
(305) 670-1961

LOT Polish Airlines
500 Fifth Avenue, Suite 325
New York, NY 10110
(212) 944-8116

Lufthansa German Airlines
750 Lexington Ave.
New York, NY 10022
(212) 745-0700

Malaysian Airline System
5933 West Century Blvd
Suite 506
Los Angeles, CA 90045
(213) 642-0849

Martinair Holland
1165 Northern Blvd
Manhasset, NY 11030
(516) 365-6146

Mexicana Airlines
9841 Airport Boulevard
Los Angeles, CA 90045
(213) 646-9975

Middle East Airlines
680 Fifth Avenue
New York, NY 10019
(212) 489-5400

New York Air
Hangar 5
La Guardia Airport
Flushing, NY 11371
(718) 507-5136

Northwest Airlines
Minneapolis-St. Paul International
   Airport
5101 Northwest Drive
ST. Paul, MN 55111
(612) 726-2351

Olympic Airways
647 Fifth Avenue
New York, NY 10022
(212) 735-0200

Pakistan International Airlines
545 Fifth Avenue

New York, NY 10017
(212) 370-9150

Philippine Airlines
447 Sutter St.
San Francisco, CA 94108
(415) 391-0270

Qantas Airways
6151 West Century Blvd., Suite 500
Los Angeles, CA 90045
(213) 215-4407

Royal Air Maroc
55 East 59th Street
New York, NY 10022
(212) 750-5115

Royal Jordanian Airlines
535 Fifth Avenue
New York, NY 10017

Sabena Belgian World Airlines
1155 Northern Blvd
Manhasset, NY 11030
(516) 562-9200

Scandinavian Airlines System
138–02 Queens Blvd.
Jamaica, NY 11435
(212) 657-2575

Singapore Airlines
5670 Wilshire Blvd.
Los Angeles, CA 90036
(213) 934-8833

South African Airways
900 Third Avenue
New York, NY 10017
(212) 826-0995

Southwest Airlines Co.
Box 36611
Love Field
Dallas, TX 75235
(214) 353-6100

Swissair
608 Fifth Avenue
New York, NY 10020
(212) 969-5734

TAP-Air Portugal
399 Market Street
Newark, NJ 07105
(201) 344-4490

Texas International Airlines
P.O. Box 12788
Houston, TX 77017
(713) 640-5000

Thai Airways International
720 Olive Way, Suite 1400
Seattle, WA 98101
(206) 467-9898

Trans World Airlines
110 S. Bedford Road
Mt. Kisco, NY 10549
(914) 242-3000

Turkish Airlines
821 United Nations Plaza, 14th floor
New York, NY 10017
(212) 867-8922

United Airlines
P.O. Box 66100
Chicago, IL 69666
(312) 952-4000

USAir
Washington National Airport
Washington, DC 20001
(703) 892-7000

Varig-Brasilian Airlines
622 Third Avenue
New York, NY 10017

VIASA Airlines
1101 Brickel Ave., Suite 600
Miami, FL 33131
(305) 358-3900

RAILROADS

Amtrak
60 Massachusetts Ave.
Washington, DC 20002
(202) 906-3964

VIA Rail Canada Inc.
P.O. Box 8116
Montreal, P.Q. H3C 3N3
(514) 871-9888

BUS LINES

Greyhound Lines, Inc.
1810 Greyhound Tower
Phoenix, AZ 85077
(602) 248-5276 or
(602) 248-4000

CAR RENTALS

Agency Rent A Car
3000 Aurora Rd
Solon, OH 44139
(800) 232-9555

Alamo Rent A Car
110 Tower
110 Southwest Sixth Street
Ft. Lauderdale, FL 33301
(305) 527-4758

Avis Rent A Car System
900 Old Country Road
Garden City, NY 11530
(516) 222-3175

Budget Rent A Car Corporation
4225 Naperville Road
Lisle, IL 60532
(708) 855-7799

The Hertz Corporation
225 Brae Blvd
Park Ridge, NJ 07656
(201) 307-2000

National Car Rental Systems, Inc.
7700 France Avenue South
Minneapolis, MN 55435
(612) 830-2537

Thrifty Rent A Car System, Inc.
4907 Walden Circle
Orlando, FL 32811

Value Rent-A-Car
2510 Jetport Drive
Orlando, FL 32809
(407) 438-7106

CRUISE LINES

Admiral Cruises
Box 010882
Miami, FL 33101
(305) 374-1611

American Canadian Line
Box 368
Warren, RI 02885
(401) 247-0955

American Hawaii Cruises
550 Kearny Street
San Francisco, CA 94108
(415) 392-9400

Bermuda Star Line
1086 Teaneck Road
Teaneck, NJ 07666
(201) 837-0400

Carnival Cruise Lines
5225 NW 87th Avenue
Miami, FL 33166
(305) 599-2600

Chandris Fantasy Cruises
900 Third Avenue
New York, NY 10022
(212) 586-8370

Clipper Cruise Line
7711 Bonhomme Avenue
St. Louis, MO 63105
(314) 727-2929

Commodore Cruise Line
1007 N. America Way
Miami, FL 33132
(800) 327-5617

Costa Crusie
One Biscayne Tower
Suite 3190
Miami, FL 33131
(305) 358-7300 or
800-462-6782

Crown Cruise Line
Box 3000
Boca Raton, FL 33431
(305) 394-7450

Cunard Line
555 Fifth Avenue
New York, NY 10017
(212) 880-7500

Delta Queen Steamboat Co.
30 Robin Street Wharf
New Orleans, LA 70130
(504) 586-0631

Dolphin Cruises
1007 N. America Way
Miami, FL 33132
(305) 358-2111

Epirotiki Lines
551 Fifth Avenue
New York, NY 10176
(212) 599-1750

Exploration Cruises
1500 Metropolitan Park Bldg
Seattle, WA 98101
(206) 624-8551

Hellenic Mediterranean Lines
One Hillside Plaza
San Francisco, CA 94102
(415) 989-7434

Holland America Cruises-Westours
300 Elliot Avenue West
Seattle, WA 98119
(206) 281-3535

Home Line Cruises Inc.
One World Trade Center
Suite 3969
New York, NY 10048
(212) 432-1414

Italian Line Cruises International
One Whitehall
New York, NY 10014
(212) 344-5657

"K" Lines-Hellenic Cruises
645 Fifth Avenue
New York, NY 10022
(212) 751-2435

KD German Rhine Line
Rhine Cruise Agency
170 Hamilton Avenue
White Plains, NY 10601
(914) 948-3600

Lindblad Travel
8 Wright Street
Westport, CT 06880
(203) 226-8531

Med Sun Lines
849 Lexington Avenue
New York, NY 10021
(212) 249-3053

Norwegian Caribbean Lines
One Biscayne Tower
Miami, FL 33131
(305) 358-6670 or
(800) 327-9020

Ocean Cruise Lines
1510 SE 17th Street
Ft. Lauderdale, FL 33316
(305) 764-5566

Polish Ocean Lines
McLean Kennedy, Inc.
410 Saint Nicholas St.
Room 119
Montreal, PQ H2Y 2P5
(514) 849-6111

Premier Cruise Lines
Box 573
Cape Canaveral, FL 32920
(305) 783-5061

Princess Cruises
2029 Century Park East
Los Angeles, CA 90067
(213) 553-1770

Regency Cruises
260 Madison Avenue
New York, NY 10016
(212) 972-4774

Royal Caribbean Cruise Line
903 South America Way
Miami, FL 33132
(305) 379-2601

Royal Cruise Line
One Maritime Plaza
Suite 660
San Francisco, CA 94111
(415) 956-7200

Royal Viking Line
One Embarcadero Center
San Francisco, CA 94111
(415) 398-8000

SeaEscape
1080 Port Blvd
Miami, FL 33132
(305) 377-9000

Sitmar Cruises
10100 Santa Monica Blvd.
Los Angeles, CA 90067
(213) 553-1666

Society Expeditions
3131 Elliott Avenue
Seattle, WA 98121
(206) 285-9400

Sun Line Cruises
One Rockefeller Plaza
Suite 315
New York, NY 10020
(212) 397-6400

Windjammer Barefoot Cruises
824 S. Miami Avenue
P.O. Box 120
Miami Beach, FL 33139
(305) 373-2466

HOTELS

Best Western, Inc.
Best Western Way
6201 N. 24 Parkway
Box 10203
Phoenix, AZ 85064
(602) 957-4200

CP Hotels
900 Rene Levesque Blvd. W.
Montreal, Que. H3B 4A5

Canada
(514) 861-3511

Choice Hotels
10750 Columbia Pike
Silver Springs, MD 20901
(301) 593-5600

Club Med, Inc.
40 W. 57th Street
New York, NY 10019
(212) 977-2100

Days Inns of America, Inc.
2751 Buford Highway North East
Atlanta, GA 30324
(404) 325-2525

Fairmont Hotel Co.
950 Mason Street
San Francisco, CA 94106
(415) 772-5000

Four Seasons Hotels
1165 Leslie Street
Don Mills, Ontario M3C 2K8
(416) 449-1750

Glacier Park Inc.
Glacier Park Lodge
East Glacier Park, MT 69434
(406) 226-9311

Golden Tulip International Hotels
437 Madison Avenue
New York, NY 10022
(212) 838-6554

Hilton Hotels Corporation
Corporate Office
9336 Civic Center Drive
Beverly Hills, CA 90209
(213) 278-4321

Hilton International Co.
301 Park Avenue
New York, NY 10022
(212) 688-2240

Holiday Inns, Inc.
3796 Lamar Avenue
Memphis, TN 38195
(901) 362-4001

Howard Johnson's Company
One Monarch Drive
N. Quincy, MA 02269
(617) 847-2288

Hyatt Hotels Corporation
200 West Madison
Chicago, IL 60606
(312) 750-1234

Inter-Continental Hotels
200 Park Avenue
New York, NY 10017
(212) 880-1558

La Quinta Motor Inns, Inc.
P.O. Box 32064
Century Building
84 North East Loop 410
San Antonio, TX 78216
(512) 349-1221

Loews Hotels
One Park Avenue
New York, NY 10016
(212) 545-2000

Marriott Hotels, Inc.
One Marriott Drive
Washington, DC 20058
(301) 897-9000

Meridian Hotels
888 Seventh Avenue
New York, NY 10106
(212) 956-3501

Omni Hotels
500 Lafayette Road
Hampton, NH 03842
(603) 926-8911

Radisson Hotel Corporation
12805 State Highway 55
Minneapolis, MN 55441
(612) 540-5526

Ramada Inns, Inc.
3838 E. Van Buren
P.O. Box 590
Phoenix, AZ 85001
(602) 273-4000

Sheraton Hotels and Motor Inns
Sixty State Street
Boston, MA 02109
(617) 367-3600

Sonesta Hotels
6 East 43rd Street
New York, NY 10017
(212) 661-1220

Steigenberger Hotels Corporation
Bethmanstr. 33
P.O. Box 16440
D-600 Frankfurt 16, Germany
28,1926

Stouffer Hotels
29800 Bainbridge Road

Solon, OH 44139
(216) 248-3600

Trust Houses Forte Ltd.
71–75 Uxbridge Road
London W5 5SL, England
1-839-1158

United Inns, Inc.
5100 Poplar Avenue
Suite 3200
Memphis, TN 38137
(901) 767-2800

Westin Hotels
2001 6th Avenue
Seattle, WA 98121
(206) 443-5000

GOVERNMENT TOURIST OFFICES (IN THE U.S.)

Antigua Tourist Board
610 Fifth Avenue
Suite 311
New York, NY 10020
(212) 541-4117

Argentina Tourist Information
330 West 56th Street
New York, NY 10019
(212) 765-8834

Aruba Tourist Bureau
521 Fifth Avenue, 12th floor
New York, NY 10175
(201) 330-0800

Australian Tourist Commission
2121 Avenue of the Stars
Los Angeles, CA 90067
(213) 552-1988

Austrian National Tourist Office
500 Fifth Avenue
New York, NY 10110
(212) 944-6880

Bahamas Tourist Office
150 East 52nd Street
New York, NY 10022
(212) 758-2777

Barbados Board of Tourism
800 Second Avenue
New York, NY 10017
(212) 986-6516

Belgian National Tourist Office
745 Fifth Avenue
New York, NY 10151
(212) 758-8130

Bermuda Department of Tourism
310 Madison Avenue
New York, NY 10017
(212) 818-9800

Bonaire Tourist Information Office
275 Seventh Avenue
New York, NY 10001
(212) 832-0779

Brazilian Tourism Authority
3006 Massachusetts Avenue NW
Washington, DC 20008
(202) 745-2712

British Tourist Authority
40 West 57th Street
New York, NY 10019
(212) 581-4700

612 South Flower Street
Suite 401
Los Angeles, CA 90017
(213) 623-8196

British Virgin Islands Tourist Board
370 Lexington Avenue
New York, NY 10017
(212) 696-0400

Bulgarian Tourist Office
161 East 84th Street
New York, NY 10028
(212) 722-1110

Canadian Consulate General
  Tourism Section
1251 Avenue of the Americas
Room 1030
New York, NY 10020
(212) 622-1029 or

One Maritime Plaza, 11th Floor
San Francisco, CA 94111
(415) 981-8541

Caribbean Tourism Association
20 East 46th Street
New York, NY 10017
(212) 682-0435

Cayman Islands Department of
  Tourism
250 Catalonia Avenue
Suite 604
Coral Gables, FL 33134
(305) 444-6551

Ceylon/Sri Lanka Tourist Board
609 Fifth AVenue
Suite 714
New York, NY 10017
(212) 935-0369

Chile, Tourist Office of
630 Fifth Avenue
Suite 809
New York, NY 10111
(212) 582-3250 or

510 West Sixth Street
Suite 408
Los Angeles, CA 90014
(213) 627-4293

China, National Tourist Office
60 East 42nd Street
Suite 465
New York, NY 10165
(212) 867-0271 or

166 Geary Street
Suite 1605
San Francisco, CA 94108
(415) 989-8677

Colombian Government Tourist
Office
140 East 57th Street
New York, NY 10022
(212) 688-0151

Commonwealth of Independent
States Intourist
630 Fifth Avenue
New York, NY 10111
(212) 757-3884

Curacao Tourist Board
400 Madison Avenue
Suite 311
New York, NY 10017
(212) 751-8266 or

330 Biscayne Blvd.
Suite 806
Miami, FL 33132
(305) 374-5812

Cyprus Tourist Office
13 East 40th Street
New York, NY 10016
(212) 689-9720

Danish Tourist Board
655 Third Avenue
New York, NY 10017
(212) 949-2333 or

P.O. Box 3240
Los Angeles, CA 90028
(213) 906-0646

Dominican Tourist Information
Center
485 Madison Avenue
New York, NY 10022
(212) 768-2480

Eastern Caribbean Tourist
Association
220 East 42nd Street
Ney York, NY 10017
(212) 986-9370

Egyption Government Tourist Office
630 Fifth Avenue
New York, NY 10020
(212) 246-6960

323 Geary Street
San Francisco, CA 94102
(415) 533-7562

El Salvidor Tourist Information
Office
Radio City Station
46 Park Avenue
New York, NY 10016
(212) 889-3608

Finnish Tourist Board
655 Third Avenue
New York, NY 10017
(212) 370-5540

French Government Tourist Office
610 Fifth Avenue
Suite 222
New York, NY 10020
(212) 757-1125

9401 Wilshire Blvd.
Suite 840
Beverly Hills, CA 90212
(213)272-2661

French West Indies Tourist Board
Fifth Avenue
Suite 222
New York, NY 10020
(212) 755-1125

9401 Wilshire Blvd.
Beverly Hills, CA 90212
(213) 272-2661

German National Tourist Office
747 Third Avenue
New York, NY 10017
(212) 308-3300

444 South Flower Street
Suite 2207
Los Angeles, CA 90071
(213) 688-7332

Greek National Tourist Organization
Olympic Tower
645 Fifth Avenue, Fifth Floor
New York, NY 10022
(212) 421-5777

611 West Sixth Street
Suite 1998
Los Angeles, CA 90017
(213) 626-6696

Grenada Department of Tourism
141 East 44th Street
Suite 803
New York, NY 10017
(212) 687-9554

Haiti Government Tourist Bureau
630 Fifth Avenue
New York, NY 10020
(212) 757-3517

Honduras Tourist Bureau
1140 Freemont Avenue
S. Pasadeno, CA 91030
(213) 682-3377

Hong Kong Tourist Association
590 Fifth Avenue
New York, NY 10036
(212) 869-5008

421 Powell Street
Suite 200
San Francisco, CA 94102
(415) 481-4582

Hungarian Travel Bureau-IBUSZ
630 Fifth Avenue
New York, NY 10111
(212) 582-7412

Icelandic National Tourist Board
655 Third Avenue
New York, NY 10017
(212) 949-2333

India Tourist Office
30 Rockefeller Plaza
14-N Mezzanine
New York, NY 10020
(212) 586-4901

3550 Wilshire Blvd.
Suite 204
Los Angeles, CA 90010
(213) 380-8855

Indonesia Tourist Promotion Office
3457 Wilshire Blvd
Los Angeles, CA 90010
(213) 387-2078

Irish Tourist Board
757 Third Avenue
New York, NY 10017
(212) 418-0800

    681 Market Street
    San Francisco, CA 94104
    (415) 781-5688

Israel Ministry of Tourism
350 Fifth Avenue
New York, NY 10118
(212) 560-0620

    6380 Wilshire Blvd.
    Suite 1700
    Los Angeles, CA 90048
    (213) 658-7462

Italian Government Travel Office
630 Fifth Avenue
New York, NY 10111
(212) 245-4961

    360 Post Street
    Suite 801
    San Francisco, CA 94108
    (415) 392-6206

Jamaica Tourist Board
866 Second Avenue
New York, NY 10017
(212) 688-7650

    3440 Wilshire Blvd.
    Suite 1207
    Los Angeles, CA 90010
    (212) 384-1123

Japan National Tourist Organization
630 Fifth Avenue
New York, NY 10111
(212) 757-5640

    624 South Grand Avenue
    Suite 2640
    Los Angeles, CA 90017
    (213) 623-1952

Jordan Information Bureau
2319 Wyoming Avenue NW
Washington, DC 20006
(202) 265-1606

Kenya Tourist Office
424 Madison Avenue
New York, NY 10017
(212) 486-1300

9100 Wilshire Blvd.
Suite 111
Beverly Hills, CA 90212
(213) 274-6635

Korea National Tourism Corporation
460 Park Avenue
Suite 400
New York, NY 10022
(212) 752-1700 or

    510 West Sixth Avenue
    Suite 323
    Los Angeles, CA 90014
    (213) 623-1226

Luxembourg National Tourist Office
801 Second Avenue
New York, NY 10017
(212) 370-9850

Macau Tourist Information Bureau
3133 Lake Hollywood Drive
Los Angeles, CA 90068
(213) 851-3400

Malta, Consulate of the Republic of
249 East 35th Street
New York, NY 10016
(212) 725-2345

Malaysian Tourist Information
  Centre
818 West Seventh Street
Los Angeles, CA 90017
(213) 689-9702

Mexican Government Tourist
  Council
405 Park Avenue
Suite 1002
New York, NY 10022
(212) 755-7261

    10100 Santa Monica Blvd.
    Los Angeles, CA 90067
    (213) 203-8151

Monaco Government Tourist Office
845 Third Avenue
New York, NY 10022
(212) 759-5227

Moroccan National Tourist Office
20 East 46th Street
Suite 503
New York, NY 10017
(212) 557-2520

Netherlands Board of Tourism
355 Lexington Avenue

New York, NY 10017
(212) 370-7367

    681 Market Street
    Suite 941
    San Francisco, CA 94105
    (415) 781-3387

New Zealand Government Tourist
  Office
630 Fifth Avenue
Suite 530
New York, NY 10111
(212) 586-0060

    Alcoa Building
    Suite 970
    One Maritime Plaza
    San Francisco, CA 94111
    (415) 788-7404

Nigerian Information Services
575 Lexington Avenue
New York, NY 10022

    369 Hayes Street
    San Francisco, CA 94102
    (415) 552-0334

Northern Ireland Tourist Board
680 Fifth Avenue, 2nd Floor
New York, NY 10019
(212) 765-5144

Norwegian Tourist Board
655 Third Avenue
New York, NY 10017
(212) 949-2333

Pacific Area Travel Association
228 Grant Avenue
San Francisco, CA 94108
(415) 986-4545

Panama Tourist Bureau
2355 Salzedo Street
Suite 201
Coral Gables, FL 33134
(315) 442-1892

Peru National Tourist Office
999 S. Bayshore Drive
Miami, Fl 33131
(305) 374-0023

Philippines Ministry of Tourism
556 Fifth Avenue
New York, NY 10036
(212) 575-7915

3325 Wilshire Blvd.
Suite 606
Los Angeles, CA 90010
(213) 487-4525

Polish National Tourist Office
333 N. Michigan Avenue
Chicago, IL 60601
(312) 326-9013

Portuguese National Tourist Office
590 Fifth Avenue
New York, NY 10036
(212) 354-4403

Puerto Rico Tourism Company
575 Fifth Avenue
New York, NY 10017
(212) 599-6262

Romanian Natinal Tourist Office
573 Third Avenue
New York, NY 10016
(212) 697-6971

Saint Lucia Tourist Board
820 Second Avenue
New York, NY 10017
(212) 867-2950

Saint Maarten/Saba/Saint Eustatius
Tourist Office
275 Seventh Avenue
New York, NY 10001
(212) 989-0000

Saint Vincent and the Grenadines
801 Second Avenue
New York, NY 10017
(212) 687-4981

Scandinavian National Tourist
Offices
75 Rockefeller Plaza
New York, NY 10019
(212) 582-2802

Senegal Government Tourist Bureau
Pan Am Building East Lobby
200 Park Avenue
New York, NY 10017
(212) 682-4695

Singapore Tourist Promotion Board
251 Post Street
Suite 308
San Francisco, CA 94108
(415) 391-8476 or

590 Fifth Avenue
New York, NY 10036
(212) 302-4861

South African Tourist Corporation
747 Third Avenue
New York, NY 10017
(212) 838-8841

9465 Wilshire Blvd.
Suite 721
Beverly Hills, CA 90212
(213) 275-4111

Spanish National Tourist Office
665 Fifth Avenue
New York, NY 10022
(212) 759-8822 or

Swedish National Tourist Office
655 Third Avenue
New York, NY 10017
(212) 949-2333

Swiss National Tourist Office
608 Fifth Avenue
New York, NY 10020
(212) 757-5944 or

250 Stockton Street
San Francisco, CA 94108
(415) 362-2260

Tahiti Tourist Development Board
7833 Haskell Avenue
Van Nuys, CA 91406
(213) 488-9878

Taiwan Visitors Bureau
One World Trade Center
New York, NY 10048
(212) 466-0691

Tanzania Tourist Corporation
201 East 42nd Street
New York, NY 10017
(212) 986-7124

Thailand, Tourism Authority of
Five World Trade Center
Suite 2449
New York, NY 10048
(212) 432-0433

3440 Wilshire Blvd.
Suite 1101
Los Angeles, CA 90010
(213) 382-2353

Togo Information Service
1706 R Street NW
Washington, DC 20009
(202) 667-8181

Trinidad and Tobago Tourist Board
Forest Hills Tower
118–135 Queens Blvd
Forest Hills, NY 11375
(212) 719-0540

Tunisian Embassy of Tourism
1515 Massachusetts Avenue NW
Washington, DC 20005
(202) 862-1850

Turkish Government Tourism and
Information Office
821 United Nations Plaza
New York, NY 10017
(212) 949-0150

United States Travel and Tourism
Administration
U.S. Department of Commerce
14th Street NW
Washington, DC 20230
(202) 377-0136

United States Virgin Islands
Department of Commerce
1270 Avenue of the Americas
New York, NY 10020
(212) 332-2222

Uruguay Consulate
301 East 47th Street
Suite 19A
New York, NY 10111
(212) 757-3884

Venezuelan Government Tourist
Bureau
450 Park Avenue
New York, NY 10022
(212) 826-1660

Zambia National Tourist Board
237 East 52nd Street
New York, NY 10022
(212) 758-9450

UNITED STATES STATE TOURIST OFFICES

Alabama Bureau of Tourism
and Travel
532 South Perry Street
Montgomery, AL 36104
(205) 261-4169 or
(800) ALA-BAMA

Alaska State Division of Tourism
P.O. Box E
Juneau, AK 99811
(907) 465-2010

Arizona Office of Tourism
1480 East Bethany Home Road
Suite 180

Phoenix, AZ 85014
(602) 255-3618

Arkansas Division of Tourism
Department of Parks and Tourism
One Capitol Mall
Little Rock, AR 72201
(501) 371-7777
(800) 643-8383

California Office of Tourism
1121 L Street, Suite 103
Sacramento, CA 95814
(916) 322-2881

Colorado Tourism Board
1625 Broadway, Suite 1700
Denver, CO 80203
(303) 529-5410

Connecticut Department of
  Economic Development
Tourism Division
210 Washington Street
Hartford, CT 06106
(203) 566-2496

Delaware Tourism Office
99 Kings Highway
P.O. Box 1401
Dover, DE 19903
(302) 736-4271 or
(800) 441- 8846

Washington D.C. Area Convention
  And Visitors Association
1575 I Street, NW
Suite 250
Washington, DC 20005
(202) 789-7000

Florida Division of Tourism
Department of Commerce
107 West Gaines Street
Room 505
Tallahassee, FL 32301
(904) 488-7999

Georgia Tourist Division
Department of Industry and Trade
P.O. Box 1776
Atlanta, GA 30301
(404) 656-3590

Hawaii Visitors Bureau
2270 Kalakau Avenue
Suite 801
Honolulu, HI 96815
(808) 923-1811

Idaho Office of Tourism
Division of Economic and

Community Affairs
State Capitol Building
Room 108
Boise, ID 83720
(208) 334-2470
(800) 635-7820

Illinois Office of Tourism
100 West Randolph Street
Suite 3-400
Chicago, IL 60601
(312) 917-4732

Indiana Tourism Development
  Division
Department of Commerce
One North Capitol
Suite 700
Indianapolis, IN 46204
(317) 232-8860

Iowa Development Commission
Travel Department Division
200 East Grant Street
Des Moines, IA 50309
(515) 281-5536

Kansas Department of Commerce,
  Travel and Tourism Development
400 West 8th Street, 5th floor
Topeka, KS 66603
(913) 296-2009

Kentucky Department of Travel
  Development
200 Capitol Plaza Tower
Frankfort, KY 40601
(502) 564-4930

Louisiana Office of Tourism
P.O. Box 94291
Baton Rouge, LA 70804
(504) 925-3850
(800)-227-4FUN

Maine Division of Tourism
State House Station #59
Augusta, ME 04333
(207) 289-5710

Maryland Office of Tourism
  Development
Department of Economic and
  Community Development
45 Calvert Street
Annapolis, MD 21401
(301) 974-2686

Massachusetts Division of Tourism
100 Cambridge Street

Boston, MA 02202
(617) 727-3201

Michigan Travel Bureau
The Tow Center, Suite F
333 S. Capitol Avenue
Lansing, MI 48933
(517) 373-0670 or
(800) 5432-YES

Minnesota Office of Tourism
375 Jackson, Suite 275
St. Paul, MN 55101
(612) 297-2333 or
(800) 328-1461

Mississippi Department of Economic
  Development
Division of Tourism
P.O. Box 849
Jackson, MS 39202
(601) 359-3414 or
(800) 647-2290

Missouri Division of Tourism
P.O. Box 1055
Jefferson City, MO 65102
(314) 751-4133

Montana Travel Promotion Unit
Department of Commerce
1424 Ninth Avenue
Helena, MT 59620
(406) 449-2654 or
(800) 548-3390

Nebraska Travel and Tourism
  Division
Department of Economic
  Development
P.O. Box 94666
301 Centennial Mall South
Lincoln, NE 68509
(402) 471-3790 or
(800) 228-4307

Nevada Commission on Tourism
1100 East Williams
Suite 106
Capitol Complex
Carson City, NV 89710
(702) 885-4322 or
(800) 237-0774

New Hampshire Office of Vacation
  Travel
Department of Resources and
  Economic Development
P.O. Box 856
Concord, NH 03301
(603) 271-2666

New Jersey Division of Travel
and Tourism
Department of Commerce and
Economic Development
CN 826
Trenton, NJ 08625
(609) 292-2470

New Mexico Tourism and Travel
Division
Commerce and Industry
Department
Joseph Montoya Building
Santa Fe, NM 87503
(505) 827-0291 or
(800) 545-2040

New York State Department
of Commerce
Division of Tourism
One Commerce Plaza
Albany, NY 12245
(518) 474-7712 or
230 Park Ave.
New York, NY 10169
(212) 309-0563

North Carolina Division of Travel
and Tourism
Department of Commerce
430 North Salisbury Street
Raleigh, NC 27611
(919) 733-4171

North Dakota Tourism
Promotion
Liberty Memorial Building
State Capitol Grounds
Bismarck, ND 58505
(701) 224-2525 or
(800) 437-2077

Ohio Office of Travel and Tourism
Department of Economic and
Community Development
P.O. Box 1001
Columbus, OH 43266
(614) 466-8844 or
(800) BUC-KEYE

Oklahoma Tourism and Recreation
Department
500 Will Rogers Bldg.
Oklahoma City, OK 73105
(404) 521-2406

State of Oregon Tourism Division
595 Cottage Street, NE
Salem, OR 97310
(503) 373-1200 or
(800) 547-7842

Pennsylvania Bureau of Travel
Development
Department of Commerce
416 Forum Building
Harrisburg, PA 17120
(717) 787-5453 or
(800) A-FRIEND

Rhode Island Department of
Economic Development
Tourist Promotion Division
7 Jackson Walkway
Providence, RI 02903
(401) 277-2601 or
(800) 556-2484

South Carolina Department of Parks,
Recreation and Tourism
1205 Pendleton Street
Columbia, SC 29201
(803) 734-0128

South Dakota Tourism
Capitol Lake Plaza
711 Wells
Pierre, SD 57501
(605) 773-3301 or
(800) 843-8000

Tennesee Department of Tourist
Development
P.O. Box 23170
Nashville, TN 37202
(615) 741-2159

Texas Tourist Development Agency
P.O. Box 12008, Capitol Station
Austin, TX 78711
(512) 462-9191

Utah Travel Council
Council Hall-Capitol Hill
Salt Lake City, UT 84114
(801) 533-5681

Vermont Travel Division
Agency of Development and
Community Affairs
134 State Street
Montpelier, VT 05602
(802) 828-3236

Virgina Division of Tourism
202 North Ninth Street
Suite 500
Richmond, VA 23219
(804) 786-2051

Washington Tourism Promotion and
Development Division
101 General Administration Building

Olympia, WA 98504
(206) 753-5600 or
(800) 544-1800

West Virginia Travel Development
Division
Office of Economic and Community
Development
1900 Washington Street East
Charleston, WV 25305
(304) 348-2286 or
(800) CALL-WVA

Wisconsin Division of Tourism
Development
123 West Washington Avenue
Madison, WI 53707
(608) 266-8045

Wyoming Travel Commision
I-25 at College Drive
Cheyenne, WY 82002
(307) 777-7777 or
(800) 225-5996

CANADIAN PROVINCIAL TOURIST OFFICES

Travel Alberta
10025 Jasper Avenue
Edmonton, Alberta T5J 3Z3
(403) 427-4323

British Columbia Ministry of
Tourism
865 Hornby Street
Vancouver, BC V6Z 2G3
(604) 660-2861

Winnipeg (Manitoba) Convention
and Visitors Bureau
232–375 York Avenue
Winnipeg, Manitoba R3C 3J3
(204) 943-1970

New Brunswick Tourism, Recreation
and Heritage
P.O. Box 12345
Fredericton, NB E3B 5C3
(506) 453-2444 or
(800) 561-0123

Newfoundland and Labrador
Tourism Branch
P.O. Box 2016
St. John's, NF
(709) 576-2830 or
(800) 563-6353

Northwest Territories
TravelArctic
Yellowknife, NWT X1A 2L9
(403) 873-7200 or
(800) 661-0788

Nova Scotia Tourism
136 Commercial Street
Portland, ME 04101
(800) 341-6096

Ontario Ministry of Tourism and
  Recreation
77 Bloor Street West, 9th floor
Toronto, Ont. M7A 2R9
(416) 965-9991

Prince Edwards Island
Department of Tourism and Park
P.O. Box 2000
Prince Edward Island, Canada
  C1A 7N8
(902) 368-5500 or
(800) 565-9060

Tourism Quebec
P.O. Box 20000
Quebec, PQ G1K 7X2
(514) 873-2015 or
(800) 443-7000

Saskatchewan Tourism
2103 11th Street
Regina, SK S4P 3V7
(306) 787-2878

Yukon Tourism
P.O. Box 2703
Whitehorse, Yukon Y1A 2C6
(403) 667-5429

DOMESTIC TRAVEL ORGANIZATIONS

Air Traffic Conference
1709 New York Avenue NW
Washington, DC 20006
(202) 626-4076

Air Transport Association
  of America
1709 New York Avenue NW
Washington, DC 20006
(202) 626-4000

American Association of Retired
  Persons
1909 "K" Street NW
Washington, DC 20049
(202) 872-4700

American Automobile Association
811 Gatehouse Road
Falls Church, VA 22041
(703) 222-6701

American Bus Association
1015 15th Street NW
Washington, DC 20005
(202) 842-1645

American Hotel and Motel
  Association
1201 New York Ave., N.W.
Washington, DC 20005
(202) 289-3114

American Indian Travel
  Commission, The
10403 West Colfax Avenue
Suite 550
Lakewood, CO 80215
(303) 234-1707

American Society of Travel Agents
1101 King Street
Alexandria, VA 22314
(703) 739-2782

Association of Local Transport
  Airlines
1801 K Street NW
Suite 803
Washington, DC 20006
(202) 638-5600

Association of Retail Travel Agents
1754 Jefferson Davis Highway
Arlington, VA 22202
(703) 553-7777

CHRIE-Council on Hotel, Restaurant
  and Institutional Education
1200 17th Street NW
Washington, DC 20036-3097
(202) 331-5990

Commuter Airline Association
  of America
1101 Connecticut Avenue NW
Suite 700
Washington, DC 20036
(202) 857-1170

Cruise Lines International
  Association
500 5th Ave., Suite 1407
New York, NY 10110
(212) 921-0066

DOT-Department of Transportation
400 7th Street SW

Washington, DC 20590
(202) 366-4000

Elderhostel
80 Boylston Street
Boston, MA 02116
(617) 426-7788

Florida Caribbean Cruise Association
6900 South West 126 Terrace
Miami, FL 33156
(305) 377-2129

Highway Users Federation
1776 Massachusetts Avenue NW
Washington, DC 20036
(202) 857-1251

Hotel Sales and Marketing
  Association Int'l
1300 "L" Street, N.W. Suite 800
Washington, D.C. 20005
(202) 789-0089

Hotel Sales Management Association
  International
362 Fifth Avenue
Suite 1100
New York, NY 10001
(212) 868-3466

Institute of Certified Travel Agents
148 Linden Street
P.O. Box 56
Wellesley, MA 02181
(617) 237-0280

International Association of
  Amusement Parks
7222 West Cermak Road
Suite 303
North Riverside, IL 60546
(312) 442-5866

International Association of
  Convention and Visitor Bureaus
P.O. Box 758
Champaign, IL 61824
(217) 359-8881

International Reception Operators
9601 Wilshire Blvd.
Suite 150
Beverly Hills, CA 90210
(213) 550-8596

National Air Carrier Association
1730 M Street NW
Suite 710
Washington, DC 20036
(202) 833-8200

Natinal Business Travel
  Association, Inc.
516 5th Avenue
New York, NY 10036
(212) 221-6782

National Campground Owners
  Association
c/o Bald Eagle Campsite
Rt. 3, Box 391
Tyrone, PA 16686
(814) 684-3485

National Caves Association
Rt. 9, P.O. Box 106
McMinnville, TN 37110
(615) 668-3925

National Park Service
US Department of the Interior
Washington, DC 22040
(202) 343-6843

National Passenger Traffic
  Association
122 East 42nd Street
P.O. Box 5517
Grand Central Station
New York, NY 10017
(212) 682-0470

National Restaurant Association
One IBM Plaza
Suite 2600
Chicago, IL 60611
(312) 787-2525

National Ski Areas Association
61 South Main Steet
West Hartford, CT 06107
(203) 521-0206

National Tour Association
546 E. Main Street
Lexington, KY 40508
(606) 253-1036

Old West Trail Foundation, The
P.O. Box 2554
Rapid City, SD 57709
(605) 343-7677

Pacific Northwest Travel
  Association
217 Ninth Avenue North
Seattle, WA 98109
(206) 624-9525

Recreation Vehicle Industry
  Association
P.O. Box 204

14650 Lee Road
Chantilly, VA 22021
(703) 968-7722

Society for the Advancement of
  Travel for the Handicapped
26 Court Street
Brooklyn, NY 11242
(718) 858-5483

Society of American Travel
  Writers, The
1155 Connecticut Avenue
Washington, DC 20036
(202) 429-6639

Society of Travel and Tourism
  Educators
12605 State Fair
Detroit, MI 48205
(313) 350-2290

Travel Industry Association of
  America
Two Lafayette Center
1133 21st Street N.W.
Washington, DC 20036
(202) 293-1433

Travel and Tourism Government
  Affairs Council
1133 21st Street NW
Washington, DC 20036
(202) 293-5407

Travel and Tourism Research
  Association, The
P.O. Box 58066
Salt Lake City, Utah 84158
(801) 581-3351

Travel South, USA
Lenox Towers
Suite 703
3400 Peachtree Street, NE
Atlanta, GA 30326
(404) 231-1790

United States Tour Operators
  Association
211 E. 51st Street
New York, NY 10022
(212) 944-5727

United States Travel Data Center
1133 21st Street NW
Washington, DC 20036
(202) 293-1040

United States Tourism and
  Travel Administration

US Department of Commerce
Washington, DC 20230
(202) 377-4028

INTERNATIONAL TRAVEL ORGANIZATIONS

African Airlines Association
P.O. Box 20166
Nairobi, Kenya

Alliance of Canadian Travel
  Associations
75 Albert Street, Suite 1106
Ottawa, Ont., K1P 5E7
Canada

Arab Tourism Union
General Secretary
Amman, Jordan

Association of British Travel Agents
55-57 Newman Street
London, England W1P 4AH

Association of European Airlines
Avenue Louise 350, Bts. 4
1050 Brussels, Belgium

Association of South East Asian
  Nations
6, Jalan Paman Pejambon
Jakarta, Indonesia

Balkan Tourism Association
7, Blvd. Magheru
Bucharest, Romania

Caribbean Hotel Association
18 Marseilles Street
Santurce, Puerto Rico 00907

Caribbean Tourism Association
20 East 46th Street
New York, NY 10017

Caribbean Tourism Research
  Center
Mer Vue
Marine Gardens
Christ Church, Barbados

Central Americans Counsel for
  Tourism, The
Calle Ruben Dario 619
San Salvador, El Salvador

Confederation of Latin America
  Tourist
Organization (COTAL)

Via Monte 640
Buenos Aires, Argentina

East Asia Travel Association
2-10-1 Yurakucho
Chyoda-ku
Tokyo, Japan

Eastern Caribbean Travel
Association
P.O. Box 146
St. Johns. Antigua

European Motel Federation
Woudenbergsweg 44
Maarsbergen, Holland

European Travel Commission
630 Fifth Avenue
New York, NY 10111

Indian Ocean Tourist Alliance
Galarie Remy Ollier
Place Foch
Port Louis, Mauritius

International Air Transport
Association
2000 Peel Street
Montreal, Que H3A 2R4
Canada

International Association of
Convention and Visitor
Bureaus, The
Bloomington Road 702
Champaign, IL 61820

International Council of Monuments
and Sites
75, rue du Temple
75003 Paris, France

International Association of World
Tourism
73 Rue D'Ecosse
B-1060 Brussels
Belgium

International Federation of Tour
Operators
Amaliegade 37, 2 TR
1256 Copenhagen, Denmark

International Federation of Women's
Travel Organizations
4545 North 36th Street
Phoenix, AZ 85018

International Forum of Travel and
Tourism Advocates
693 Sutter Street
San Francisco, CA 94102

International Passenger Ship
Association
17 Battery Place
Suite 631
New York, NY 10004

International Union of Railways
14, rue Jean Rey
75015 Paris, France

Institute of Air Transport
4, rue de Solferino
75007 Paris, France

Organization of American States
17th Street And Constitution
Avenue NW
Washington, DC 20006

Pacific Area Travel Association
One Montgomery Street
San Francisco, CA 94104

World Association of Travel
Agencies, The
37 Quai Wilson
1211 Geneva, Switzerland

World Tourism Organization
Calle Captain Haya 42
E-28020 Madrid, Spain

Glossary

AAA American Automobile Association. Organization that offers a number of travel and motoring services to its members. Through its regional clubs, AAA owns and operates travel agencies, which also provide services for nonmembers.

ABC World Airway Guide An airline tariff used by many international carriers.

Abeam Off the side of the ship, at a right angle to the length of the ship.

ABS The accounting computer, used in conjunction with United Airlines Apollo, to retain all necessary information pertaining to agency sales.

Absorption When a carrier accepts that part of a joint fare that is less than the amount it would have received for the same service without a joint rate.

Add Collect The act of exchanging one accountable document for another, with additional funds due to the supplier. A means by which a ticket of a lesser value may be exchanged for a ticket of a greater value with additional funds supplied by the traveler.

Add On A supplement added to air, sea, or rail fares to raise the total cost to include other services. Often used in reference to international air fares, in addition to the gateway fare.

Adjoining Rooms Rooms or sea cabins that share a common wall, though not necessarily a common door.

ADS (Agency Data Systems) The accounting computer, used in conjunction with American Airlines SABRE, to retain all necessary information relating to agency sales.

Advance Air Tour Tour brought to potential travelers' attention by means of handbills, brochures, magazine and newspaper ads, radio and TV announcements, and direct mail campaigns. In general, a tour must be advertised in a tour brochure

before airlines will agree to pay more than the normal commission on the air travel involved.

Affinity Group An organization, not formed specifically for travel, that may sponsor group travel programs for its members on scheduled or charter aircraft. The travel expenses are shared equally by individual members.

Affinity Group Fare A circle or round-trip fare limited to an affinity group, all of whose members must travel together.

Aft Near, toward, or at the rear of the ship.

Agency
1) In transportation, the place where a retail agent conducts business.
2) An administrative arm of a government; for example, the Federal Aviation Administration.

Agency Data Systems See ADS.

Agency Manager
1) The person who runs an agency, travel or otherwise.
2) Employee of a carrier or hotel who channels sales to wholesalers and travel agents.

Agent A person authorized to act for another in the handling of a contract with a third party.

Air Freight Forwarder Indirect air carrier that assembles and consolidates cargo for transport by a direct carrier.

Airline Codes Abbreviations for airlines, airports, etc., used throughout the world. A two-letter code is used to designate an airline; e.g., the code for Eastern Airlines is EA.

Airline Rep A salesperson for an airline.

Airlines Reporting Corporation See ARC.

Airport Code The three-letter code used to abbreviate an airport; e.g., the code for Newark Airport is EWR.

Airport Ticket Office (ATO) An airline ticket office, located at an airport, where passengers can check in for a flight, check their baggage, and receive their seat assignment.

Air/Sea Travel arrangements that combine air transportation to and from an embarkation port with a cruise. Also called fly/cruise.

Air Taxi Small aircraft operating under fewer restrictive regulations than scheduled carriers, generally within a 250-mile radius.

Air Taxi Agreement Contract between a scheduled airline and members of NATC (National Air Taxi Conference) to deal with requests for ticketing and space to areas serviced by the air taxi operator.

Air Traffic Conference of America (ATC) Once a division of ATA (Air Transport Association of America), ATC's duties were assumed by ARC (Airlines Reporting Corporation) in January 1985. See ARC.

Air Transport Association of America (ATA) Organization of scheduled airlines whose purpose is to promote air transportation, and to further the interests of its members through cooperative efforts to deal with their mutual concerns.

A la Carte Description of separately priced items on a menu.

All Expense Tour An inclusive tour that offers all or most services for a pre-established price. The tour contract specifies exactly what is included in pre-paid tour arrangements.

Alleyway A passageway or corridor on a ship.

Aloft Above the superstructure; in or near the mast of a ship.

American Plan A hotel rate that includes three meals a day. Also called Full Pension.

American Society of Travel Agents (ASTA) Large international trade organization of professional tourism and travel personnel.

Amidships In or toward the middle of the ship.

Amtrak National Railroad Passenger Corporation, a government subsidized company that operates nearly all passenger train service in the United States.

APEX Fare (Advance Purchase Excursion Fare) In international travel, a discounted fare that requires a 21- to 30-day advance purchase, and round trip or open jaw travel. The international equivalent of the domestic supersaver fares.

Apollo United Airlines computer reservations system.

Appointment Official designation in the travel industry to act as a sales outlet for conference groups of carriers. These conferences approve travel agents before their individual appointment by conference members.

Approval Code A multi-digit series used on credit card sales to indicate the credit company's knowledge of the billing.

Arbitrary Fare See Add-on fare.

ARC (Airlines Reporting Corporation) Independent organization under joint ownership of most major United States airlines. Payment for tickets sold by travel agents is collected by ARC and distributed to the airlines. The corporation also establishes the rules that govern the appointment of travel agents to sell domestic air transportation.

Areas One, Two and **Three** Regions into which IATA has divided the world for the purpose of bringing order and cohesion within the international aviation industry. Area One: all of North and South America (the Western Hemisphere), Greenland, Midway Island, Guam, Canton Island, and Wake Island; Area Two: all of Europe, including the USSR east of the Urals, Africa, and the Middle East; Area Three: Southwest Asia east of Iran, Asia, Australia, and all of the Pacific Ocean islands except those included in Area One.

ARNK ARrival uNKnown. Term used in computer reservations systems to account for a missing segment of an itinerary; indicates that the passenger will travel to the departure site by some other means.

ASTA See American Society of Travel Agents.

Astern Beyond the stern.

ATA See Air Transport Association of America.

ATC See Air Traffic Conference of America.

Athwartships Across the ship, from side to side.

ATO See Airport Ticket Office.

Available A conditional status. For example, "space available" means "if the space is available."

Back Haul Fare See One-way Back Haul.

Back Office Automation Refers to systems such as ADS and ABS that allow an agency to collect accounting data and produce reports based on such material.

Back-to-Back Used to describe a series of programs of multiple air charters with arrivals and departures coordinated to eliminate aircraft deadheading and waiting. Thus, when one group arrives at a destination, another is ready to depart from that point.

Backwash Motion in the water caused by the propellers moving in a reverse direction.

Baggage Allowance The weight or amount of baggage a passenger may carry without paying an additional charge.

Baggage Claim Check Receipt issued to a passenger by the carrier for checked baggage.

Baggage Tag Personal identification attached to all pieces of luggage.

Bank Travel Department   Special bank department concerned solely with selling general travel services and passenger transportation. Open to the public for these purposes.

Bareboat Charter   A boat rented without crew or provisions.

Barefoot Cruise   A cruise on which the passengers may help crew the boat. Unlike bareboat charters, a barefoot cruise vessel has a qualified crew on board.

Base Fare   The tariff, not including taxes, charged for a service.

Basing Point   A master point, to and from which fares are established, used to calculate and construct air fares between other points.

Batten Down   To secure the hatches and equipment against inclement weather or an unstable vehicle.

Beam   Width of a ship between the widest points.

Bearing   Compass direction, usually given in degrees, for either steamships or aircraft.

Bed and Breakfast (B and B)   A sleeping room rate, often in a private home, that includes a full breakfast. Also known as Bermuda Plan.

Bed Night   One night spent by one person in a hotel accommodation.

Bedroom   A sleeping room on railroads; a sleeping compartment for two people.

Bedroom Suite   A double room with bath and sitting room.

Bells   A sound used on shipboard to designate the passing/telling of time—one bell for each progressive half hour to a total of eight, commencing at half past the hours of 4, 8, and 12.

Bermuda Plan (BP)   See Bed and Breakfast.

Berth
1) Dock or pier.
2) A bed within a passenger's cabin.

Bilge   Lowest point in a ship's structure.

Binnacle   The ship's compass.

Blocked Space   Reservations that wholesalers or travel agents make with suppliers in anticipation of resale.

Boarding Pass   A document attached to an airline ticket that allows a passenger entry onto a given flight, and which gives the seat assignment.

Boat Train   A service that provides two modes of travel; from boat to train or from train to boat.

Bonding   A security purchased to ensure that, if an agency or carrier declares bankruptcy, all their creditors will receive compensation.

Book   To make a reservation.

Bow   The extreme front of a ship.

Bridge   Navigational control center of the ship.

Britrail Pass   Rail pass used in the United Kingdom that allows unlimited first or second class travel for a specified period of time. A Britrail Pass cannot be used for travel in Europe.

Brochure   A printed pamphlet that describes a specific place, conditions of a tour, etc.

Bulk Fare   Fare carriers make available for resale to tour operators who purchase a specified block of seats at a low, noncommissionable price.

Bulkhead   A vertical partition or wall. All modern passenger ships have bulkheads.

Bulwark   The side of the ship nearest to the main deck.

Bump   To displace or remove a passenger or guest to accommodate someone with a higher priority or who is more important. Depending on the situation, a bumped passenger may or may not be entitled to denied boarding compensation.

Cabana   A hotel room with or without beds, usually located away from the main building and near a pool or beach area.

Cabin
1) A room on a ship.
2) A separate building at a rustic hotel or lodge.

Cabotage Fare   Special rate that applies only to citizens of a particular country, and only within one country or political territory.

Capstan   A vertically mounted motor that winds and unwinds cables.

Carrier   A company that transports passengers or freight.

Carry-on Baggage   Any article a passenger personally takes on board an airline flight. Generally stored in the airline's carry-on compartment, or under the passenger's seat.

Cathode Ray Tub (CRT)   A computer screen that shows what is being entered into the computer and what information the computer is sending. Allows communication with the central computer's data base.

CATM (Consolidated Air Tour Manual)   List of advertised air tours furnished free to ARC appointed agents under cosponsorhip of U.S. and Canadian airlines.

CATO (Combined Airline Ticket Office)   Ticket offices, located in Washington, DC at the Pentagon, the Capitol, and the Departments of State, Navy, and Agriculture, that serve mainly government personnel. These offices are not associated with any individual airline; rather, they jointly represent all airlines serving Washington.

Certified Travel Counselor (CTC)   Designation granted by the Institute of Certified Travel Agents to travel personnel with five or more year's industry experience who have completed a two-year, graduate level program in travel management.

Charter   To hire or lease the exclusive use of a vehicle (aircraft, boat, etc.) for a limited period of time.

Charter Contract   A signed agreement between the charter company and the traveler acknowledging the terms and conditions related to a specifically booked charter.

Charter Flight   A flight hired by and/or for one specific group of people.

Checked Baggage   Luggage carried in the baggage section of an airplane and not available to the passenger during the flight. A receipt is given to passengers for baggage when it is checked in, and the airline assumes some liabilities for the bags.

Check-In   Necessary procedures, such as signing the register, when arriving for a stay at a hotel.

Check-In Time   The time a hotel is ready for occupancy after the previous check-out time.

Check-Out Time   The time a hotel guest is required to vacate a room to avoid additional charges.

Circle Fare   A special round-trip fare that costs less than the total price of the point-to-point rates for a circle trip.

Circle Trip   A journey in which a traveler returns to the point of the trip's origin by a different route, or at a different fare level.

City Code   The three-letter code used to abbreviate a city; e.g., the code for Washington, DC is WAS.

City Pair   The term applied to the departure and arrival cities when combined. For example, Washington to Los Angeles is WASLAX.

City Ticket Office (CTO)   An airline ticket office, not located at an airport, where passengers may check in for a flight, check their baggage, receive their seat assignment, and secure ground transportation to the airport.

Cleat   A horizontal wooden or metal wedge-shaped device to which cables or ropes are made fast.

CLIA (Cruise Lines International Association)   Organization that supplies promotional materials, reference books, training guides, and seminars on behalf of cruise lines. CLIA designates travel agencies to sell cruises and receive commissions for the ship companies that are members of the association.

Client   Person who hires a travel agent.

Coach Service   Class of U.S. passenger airline service at a lower fare than first class, comparable to international economy class.

Coaming   Raised partition around doorways to prevent water from entering.

Co-host Carrier   Applies to an airline reservations system whereby another airline pays for additional information to be housed in the host company's computer.

Colors   A national flag or ensign flown from the mast or stern post.

Combined Airline Ticket Office   See CATO.

Commercial Rate   A fee based on an agreement between a business firm and a hotel or car rental company. Generally, the latter will provide rooms or cars of a certain quality, or higher, at a flat rate.

Commission   The percentage of the total paid that the travel agent receives for selling transportation, lodgings, and other services.

Common Rated   A description of two or more relatively contiguous destinations whose fare from a specific departure point is exactly the same.

Commuter Airline   Scheduled carrier limited to small aircraft, and required to operate with 60 or fewer seats per flight.

Companionway   Interior stairway on a ship.

Computer Reservations System   See CRS.

Concierge   A person or the staff in a hotel that attends to guests' needs, including arranging for theater tickets, making dinner reservations, supplying porterage, and providing general city information.

Conducted Tour   See Escorted Tour.

Configuration   The arrangement of areas, seats, rooms, etc. inside a conveyance, especially an airplane.

Confirmed Reservation   A statement by a supplier who has received a reservation.

Conjunction Tickets   Two or more air tickets, issued together, that form a single contract of transportation.

Connecting City   The city in which passengers must change flights in order to reach their desired destination. For example, if a passenger wants to go from Baltimore to Iron Mountain, MI and the best way to get there is to take two flights, one from Baltimore to Chicago and one from Chicago to Iron Mountain, the connecting city is Chicago.

Connecting Flight   A portion of a journey that requires passengers to change aircraft (but not necessarily carriers).

Connection   Using two or more flights to reach a desired destination. Under IATA regulations, a flight connection becomes a stopover if the passenger is required to wait more than 24 hours for the next flight.

Consolidated Air Tour Manual   See CATM.

Constructed Fares   Fares established by combining published fares with local fares. Local fares are those that may or may not appear in an individual air tariff, but are obtainable from individual carriers' tariffs.

Continental Breakfast   A light breakfast, generally coffee, tea, milk, or cocoa, rolls or toast with butter or jam, and sometimes fruit juice.

Cook's Timetables   Guides published in England by the Thomas Cook Company that provide detailed information on rail schedules, shipping services, and scheduled bus service for Great Britain and Western Europe.

Couchette   A sleeping berth on a European train.

Coupon, Flight   The part of an airline ticket that indicates the route on which passage has been purchased.

Coupon, Passenger   The part of an airline ticket that contains written proof of the carriage contract.

Courier   European term for tour escort.

Course   Direction in which a ship is headed.

Crow's Nest   On a ship, the partially enclosed platform at the top of the mast; used by the lookout.

CRS (Computer Reservations System)   Generic term to describe any automated reservations system, such as American Airlines SABRE, United Airlines Apollo, TWA PARS, etc.

CRT   See Cathode Ray Tube.

Cruise Lines International Association   See CLIA.

CTC   See Certified Travel Counselor.

CTO   See City Ticket Office.

Currency, Basic   Currency, either U.S. dollars or British pounds, on which IATA fares are based, depending on the area or areas where they apply. Dollars are used within Area One, between Areas One and Two, and between Areas One and Three. Sterling is used within and between Areas Two and Three. The industry now uses Fare Construction Units (FCUs) for basing fares.

Currency Conversion   The means by which an agent can convert a given currency to another.

Customer   See Passenger.

Customs   The government agency responsible for collecting duty on certain imported items and preventing the entry of prohibited items. Office where, upon entering a country, passengers must declare foreign-bought articles to government authorities.

Customs Users Fee   A service fee charged for passengers entering the U.S. from foreign countries. There are several exceptions, based on each point of origin, when the fee does not have to be charged.

DATAS II   Delta Airlines computer reservations system.

Davit   A device for raising and lowering a ship's lifeboats.

Day Rate   A specific hotel rate charged for using a room during daylight hours only.

DBLB   Double room with bath.

DBLN   Double room without bath or shower.

DBLS   Double room with shower.

Deadhead   A person who travels on a free pass. More specifically, an airline employee or crew member in transit. Also, a vehicle traveling without a payload.

Debark   To get off a plane, ship, train, etc. Same as disembark.

Delivering Airline   A carrier that is transporting a traveler to an interline point.

Demi-Pension   A hotel rate that includes breakfast and either lunch or dinner. Also called Modified American Plan.

Denied Boarding Compensation   The recommended penalty an airline pays to a passenger if the airline fails to honor a confirmed reservation because of overbooking.

Department of Transportation   See DOT.

Deposit   A partial payment toward a trip. Charter and tour operators often require deposits at the time of booking and at several intermediate intervals.

Destination   Where passengers end their trip. Also called arrival city and termination city.

Differential   Used within international fare calculations to show the fare increase due to a HIP, circle trip minimum, or one-way back haul.

Direct Access   A computer function in American Airlines' SABRE system that allows the subscriber to access last seat availability on co-hosts without leaving the host reservations system.

Direct Flight   A flight that goes from origin to destination without a change of planes. For example, a flight that goes from Baltimore to Myrtle Beach with an intermediate stop in Charlotte is a direct flight—but it is not a nonstop flight. Thus, a journey on which a passenger does not have to change planes, not necessarily nonstop.

Directional Tariff   A discounted fare available to passengers at one end of a route only; usually a seasonal or round-trip fare.

Direct Reference System   See DRS.

Discriminatory   As applied to fares, offering lower rates to certain classifications of persons—military personnel, young people, the elderly, etc. Such promotional fares are constantly under attack—sometimes successfully—on the grounds that they are unfair to those ineligible for them.

DIT (Domestic Independent Travel)   A prepaid, unescorted tour within a country for an individual client or clients.

Dock   Berth or pier.

Domestic Flight   A flight between two points in the same country or territory.

Domestic Independent Travel   See DIT.

DOT (Department of Transportation)   The federal agency that regulates transportation in the United States. On January 1, 1985, DOT assumed the functions and responsibilities of the Civil Aeronautics Board (CAB).

Double   A hotel room with one double bed. Sometimes refers to a hotel room meant to accommodate two guests.

Double Occupancy Rate   The price per person for a room shared by two people.

Double Room Rate   The full price, covering both persons, of a room for two people. Not to be confused with double occupancy.

Downgrade   To move to a lower priced or lesser quality accommodation or class of service.

Draft   Measurement in feet from the waterline to the lowest point of a ship's keel.

DRS (Direct Reference System)   A function within SABRE that allows the user to access information related to the vendors.

DSM   District Sales Manager.

Duplex   A suite with two floors connected by a private stairway.

Duty Free   Not subject to duty or local taxes.

Economy Fare
1) Class of U.S. passenger airline service at a level below coach fare.
2) In international airline service, carriage at a level below first class.

Efficiency   A hotel, motel, or condominium rental room that includes some type of kitchen facilities (stove, refrigerator, etc.).

Embark   To board a ship, plane, train, etc.

Encode   To identify the complete name from a two-letter code, or a three-letter city/airport code.

English Breakfast   Full breakfast, served in Great Britain (including Ireland), that can include fruit or juice, bacon, eggs, cereal, sausage, toast, kippers, butter, marmalade, and tea or coffee.

En Route City   Any city, other than origin or destination, where a flight makes a stop. For example, in a flight that goes from Baltimore to Myrtle Beach with a stop in Charlotte, Charlotte is the en route city. Also called intermediate city.

Escort   A professional travel person, usually employed by the tour operator, who serves as guide, director, troubleshooter, etc. on a tour.

Escorted Tour
1) A prearranged, escorted program of travel, usually for a group
2) A guide-conducted sightseeing program.

Escrow Accounts   Funds placed for safekeeping in licensed financial institutions. Many contracts in travel require that customers' deposits and prepayments be maintained in escrow accounts.

Eurailpass   A discount ticket, purchased outside the European continent, that allows unlimited first class rail travel in Western Europe for a specified period of time.

European Plan   Hotel room rate that does not include any meals.

Even Keel   When a ship is at a true vertical position with respect to its vertical axis.

Excess Baggage   Luggage that exceeds the size or weight specified by the particular carrier.

Exchange   The act of replacing an accountable air ticket for a new document.

Exchange Order   A document issued by a carrier or agent for the exchange of a ticket or other specified services to the person named on the document.

Excursion   A journey, usually of short duration, that returns to its starting point.

Excursion Fare   Round-trip fare that costs less than the combined cost of the component one-way fares.

FAA (Federal Aviation Administration)   The agency of the U.S. Department of Transportation responsible for public aviation. The FAA is mainly concerned with passenger safety, certification of aircraft, licensing pilots, and air traffic control.

Familiarization Tour   A reduced rate trip for travel agents and/or airline employees designed to acquaint them with a specific destination and its accommodations, or with a particular product related to travel.

Family Plan   Discount offered by some airlines, hotels, and resorts to family members traveling together.

Fantail   The rear overhang on a ship.

Fare, Airline   Technical designation describing the types of airline tickets that can be written. These include:

Add-on—An amount arbitrarily appended to international fares to transport passengers from an inland point to a gateway. Always used in conjunction with other air or cruise fares.

Basic—A designated or constructed fare given in U.S. dollars or British pounds according to which IATA area or areas they apply.

Combined—Two or more fares not published as a single rate.

Combination Joint—Fare established by combining two or more published fares.

Joint Interline—Fare, published as a single amount, that allows passage on two or more different airlines.

Normal—Standard established rate.

Proportional—See Add-on.

Special—Fare other than normal; e.g., a discounted fare.

Specified—A fare established in applicable IATA resolutions.

Through—Either a joint fare or a combination of fares from departure point to destination point. See Through Fare.

Fare Calculation   Information on an accountable document showing how the agent arrived at the rate charged.

Fare Construction Unit (FCU)   An imaginary unit of currency designed by IATA to construct and determine international air fares that combine various foreign currencies. Fares constructed in FCU's can be converted to any country's currency.

Fathom   Measurement of distance equal to six feet. Often used to measure depth from sea level to the bottom of a body of water.

Federal Aviation Administration   See FAA.

Fender   Anything that serves as a buffer between a ship and the dock.

Ferry Flight   See Deadhead.

First Class   The costliest and highest level of service in air, rail, and sea travel.

First Refusal Rights   A government policy that permits a particular carrier or class of carrier the right to claim and operate revenue charter flights prepared by other airlines. Some governments do not allow charter airlines to operate in their territory unless certain other airlines are granted the prerogative of claiming the charter.

FIT (Foreign Independent Tour)   A prepaid travel program of many separate components, tailored to the specifications of an individual client or clients.

Flag Carrier   Any carrier, air or ship, designated by a country to serve its international routes.

Flight   A single, scheduled air service from departure point to designated destination point, including any stops in between.

Fly-Drive   A tour that offers air service from departure city to arrival, a rental car to the passenger's next destination, and return air travel, often from other than the original arrival city.

Fore, Forward   Toward the front of the ship.

Foreign Independent Tour   See FIT.

Freeboard   Distance between the waterline and the ship's freeboard deck (the deck below which all bulkheads are made tight).

Freedoms of the Air, Eight   Five freedoms established at the Chicago Convention (1944) as the basis for negotiating air traffic between countries, plus an additional three freedoms that control the transportation of passengers between countries completely different from the airline's domestic affiliation.

1) The right of one country's aircraft to fly through another country's airspace.
2) The right of one country's aircraft to land in another country for non-business purposes (to refuel, change crews, etc.)
3) The right to fly fare-paying passengers from country of origin to another country.
4) The right to fly passengers from another country back to the country of origin.
5) The right of a country to fly passengers from country of origin to another country, then on to other countries, and back again.
6) The right of an airline to fly passengers from one country to another via the country of origin.
7) The right of an airline of one country to fly passengers between two countries, neither of which is the country of origin.
8) The right of an airline of one country to fly passengers between two cities within another country. (For example, Lufthansa German Airlines is permitted to fly passengers from New York to Los Angeles.)

Free Port   A port or place free of customs duties and most customs regulations.

Free Sale   The ability to confirm reservations without advising the carrier. These reservations will be accepted if the carrier is notified within a specified time.

Frequent Flyer Program   Travel benefits, such as standby first-class upgrade, a free international trip, free or reduced rate travel, etc., offered by airlines, car rental companies, and hotel chains to attract frequent customers to their product.

Frequent Traveler's File   See Profile System.

Full Pension   Hotel rate, usually found in Europe, that includes three meals a day. Also called American Plan.

Fully Appointed   Designation of a travel agent who has been officially recognized by the major airlines, steamship companies, and railroad conferences.

Funnel   Smokestack of a ship.

Galley   The kitchen of a ship or airplane.

Gangway   The opening through the ship's bulwarks and the ramp by which passengers embark and debark.

Gap   Portion of an airline itinerary that involves transportation by means other than an IATA or ATA airline.

Garni   Designation for European hotels that serve a continental breakfast but no other meals. These hotels usually have only a small breakfast room and no restaurant.

Gateway   Last city, airport, or area from which a flight or trip departs, or the arrival area from one country to another.

General Sales Agent   Another airline or an agency designated by an airline as its sales agent in a specific country or territory.

GIT (Group Inclusive Tour)   Prepaid travel package, usually round-trip, that offers special air fares to the members of the tour group, all of whom must travel on the same flights.

GMT   See Greenwich Mean Time.

Government Travel   Discount fare available to government personnel on specific carriers that have contracted with the U.S. government for the right to carry passengers engaged in official business. Agents should be aware that government employees are eligible for this special fare only when traveling on official business. Only government approved agencies and the specified carriers may issue government fare tickets, as the sole valid forms of payment are a government-distributed Diners Club credit card or a GTR (Government Travel Request).

Gratuity   A tip. A noncompulsory payment to a service person, such as a waiter, chambermaid, etc.

Greenwich Mean Time (GMT)   The mean solar time at Greenwich, England, used as the reference time for all time zones throughout the world.

Gross Registered Ton (GRT)   One hundred cubic feet of enclosed space on a ship. Measurement used to indicate the size of a passenger ship.

Ground Arrangements   All land services supplied for customers at destinations.

Group Inclusive Tour   See GIT.

GTR (Government Travel Request)   Form government employees must fill out to receive authorization to travel on official business. A government rate ticket is valid only if the GTR number appears on it.

Guarantee   On ships, assured cabin allocation in the class paid for, or higher, but never in a lower class.

Guide   A person licensed or trained to lead sightseeing tours.

Guided Tour   Regional sightseeing trip conducted by a qualified person.

Half Pension   Hotel rate that includes bed, breakfast, and either lunch or dinner. Also called Modified American Plan.

Half Round Trip   Half of a round-trip air charter, sold as a round trip because different seasonal pricing periods may apply to each half. Since the return trip on the same carrier is assured, the half round trip is generally priced somewhat lower than a one-way fare.

Hardcopy   A printout, driven by a CRS to a printer, of whatever can be displayed on a CRT.

Hatch   An opening in a ship's deck leading to a hold.

Hawse Pipe   A large pipe in the bow of the ship through which the anchor chain passes.

Hawser   A rope or chain for towing or securing a ship.

Head Tax   A fee collected by a government from a passenger who enters or departs from that country.

Helm   The ship's steering apparatus, consisting of the wheel, rudder, and their connecting cables.

Hidden City   In determining an international air fare: a city that, though not transited by a passenger, would have afforded the client a lower air fare had it been on that person's route. Thus, provided the maximum permitted milage is not exceeded, the fare may be broken over that location, even though it is not used, in order to save the client money.

Higher Intermediate Point (HIP)   Applies to the rule stipulating that, if an air fare between any two cities on an itinerary is higher, or lower, than the fare between origin and destination, the passenger must pay the higher fare.

Hold   Space within a ship to house cargo.

Host Carrier   An airline that markets its computer reservations system (CRS) to agencies.

Hotelier   Person who owns and manages a hotel.

House Flag   A flag that designates the company that owns a specific ship.

Hull   The frame or body of a ship. Does not include masts, yards, sails, or rigging.

IATA (International Air Transport Association)   Body governing international carriers; based in Geneva.

ICAO   See International Civil Aviation Organization.

ICC   See Interstate Commerce Commission.

ICTA   See Institute of Certified Travel Agents.

Immigration Guide   Reference guide that lists support documents and vaccinations necessary for travel to specific destinations.

Inaugural   First flight on a new route or with new equipment.

Inboard   Toward the center line of a ship.

Incentive Fare   Special airline fare available only to incentive groups.

Incentive Travel
1) A trip offered as a prize or bonus to encourage employee productivity.
2) The business of conducting such travel programs.

Inclusive Tour (IT)   A tour, at a flat rate, that includes air fare, accommodations, sightseeing, transfers, etc., but does not necessarily cover all expenses.

Independent Tour   A tour custom-designed to fit the wishes and specifications of an individual.

Indirect Air Carrier   A travel agent, tour operator, or other person who purchases space from an airline to resell to the public, most often with a tour package.

Infringement
1) The intentional disregard of the cost of a correct airline fare.
2) The intentional disregard of the rules governing a specific fare.

In-Plant Agency   A travel agency, or branch of an agency, located on a company's premises, that provides travel services exclusively for that company.

Institute of Certified Travel Agents (ICTA)   A nonprofit educational organization that grants accreditation (CTC) to qualified travel agents.

Interchange Flight   A single flight number that requires passengers to change flights en route.

Interface   Linkage between various computer systems that permits the systems to communicate with one another.

Interline   Having to do with two or more carriers. If passengers must take more than one airline to reach their desired destination, they are making an interline connection. Also applies to reservations, stopovers, etc.

Interliner
1) An airline employee who travels on another airline.
2) An airline employee who makes reservations for passengers on other airlines.

International Air Transport Association   See IATA.

International Civil Aviation Organization (ICAO)   A special United Nations agency of governments working together for the standardization of aircraft equipment, procedures, training, etc., particularly in developing nations.

International Date Line   An imaginary line in the Pacific Ocean at approximately 180 degrees longitude where, by international agreement, the Earth's day begins. Crossing the line eastward, one calendar day is subtracted; westward, a day is added.

International Flight   Travel between two points, each in a different country.

Interstate Commerce Commission (ICC)   Independent U.S. government agency that regulates the finances and services of specified carriers involved in transportation between states. Surface transportation under ICC authority includes railroads, trucking companies, bus lines, express agencies, and transportation brokers, among others.

Intourist   Official state tour operator in the Soviet Union.

Intraline   See Online.

IT   See Inclusive Tour.

IT Fare   The discounted air fare charged passengers who participate in an inclusive tour.

Itinerary   The travel program devised for a client by a travel agent; the route or travel plans of an entire trip.

IT Number   The code number on a tour approved by ATA or IATA that qualifies agents who sell air travel associated with such tours for an override commission.

ITX Fare (Independent Tour Excursion Fare)   A special air fare that passengers bound for specific vacation destinations are eligible to use.

Jacob's Ladder   A rope ladder used on shipboard.

Jax Fax   A directory of news of the travel industry, including special features and listings of airline charters and scheduled bus tours. Published by Jet Airtransport Exchange, Inc., Darien, Connecticut.

Joint Fare   A less than point-to-point air fare that includes travel on two or more air carriers.

Junior Suite   Large hotel room with a partition dividing bedroom and sitting areas.

Keel   A plate or timber running the length of the ship along the bottom from which all vertical frames are raised.

King Post   A vertical post to which the ship's cargo cranes are attached.

Knot   The unit of speed equal to one nautical mile per hour. A nautical mile is 6,080.2 feet while a land mile is 5,280 feet.

Lanai   A room with a balcony or patio that overlooks or is near water or a garden.

Land Arrangements   See Ground Arrangements.

Latitude   An angular distance measured in degrees north or south of the equator. One degree is approximately 60 nautical miles.

League   A measurement of distance approximately 3.45 nautical miles long.

Leeward   The side of the ship that is sheltered from the wind.

Leg   One part of an entire flight plan. For example, if a flight goes from Miami to Charlotte to Greensboro to Pittsburgh without changing flight numbers, it is a flight with three legs. Also, the portion of a flight between any two consecutive stops.

Lido   On a ship, the swimming pool and adjacent area.

Line   Any rope smaller than a hawser.

Load Factor   Percentage of carrier space actually occupied. If a 100-seat aircraft carries seventy-five paying passengers, it is operating at a 75 percent load factor.

Log   Chronicle, recorded daily, of a ship's speed, activities, course, etc.

Longitude   An angular distance measured in degrees east and west of the prime meridian (Greenwich Mean Time). Due to the curvature of the Earth, each longitude grid equals approximately 60 nautical miles at the equator and zero at the north and south poles.

Manifest   The passenger, crew, and cargo list on any trip by common carrier.

Maximum Permitted Mileage (MPM)   The air miles allowed for every city pair as designated by the IATA. Used when calculating an international air fare based on mileage.

MCO   See Miscellaneous Charges Order.

MCT   See Minimum Connecting Time.

Mileage Surcharge   A penalty excised on a passenger's air fare when the actual mileage flown exceeds the maximum permitted mileage. These additions are based in five, ten, fifteen, twenty, or twenty-five percent charges of the original one-way or half round-trip fare.

Minimum Connecting Time (MCT)   The amount of time a passenger needs to change carriers (to connect). This time is established individually for every commercial airport. If a passenger ticketed with the published minimum connecting time fails to make the connection, the delivering airline is responsible for providing another flight and meals and lodging if necessary.

Miscellaneous Charges Order (MCO)   A document issued by an airline or a travel agency verifying payment for specific services, such as surface transportation, car rental, hotels, land arrangements for inclusive tours, deposits, etc., for the person named in the order.

Modified American Plan   See Demi-Pension; Half Pension.

Mom and Pop Agency   A small travel agency, traditionally run by a husband and wife. Any independently owned small agency.

Moor   To secure a ship to a fixed place with either the hawsers, cables, or the anchor.

MPM   See Maximum Permitted Mileage.

Multi Access Reservations System   A computerized reservations program that allows the user direct access to the data base of more than one carrier or other participating travel supplier.

N/A   Not available.

National Air Transport Association (NATA)   Group that represents air taxi, commuter, and small mail and cargo carriers.

Nautical Mile   Equal to 6,080.2 feet.

Need/Need   A communication that agents with computerized reservations systems use when booking space with an off-line carrier to make sure a seat is available when there is reason to doubt the reliability of the information in the host carrier's computer. The need/need message compels the host carrier to contact the second line, which then must confirm a specific seat for the agency's client, and so advise the first airline. Generally, the host line simply confirms a second carrier's space from a small standing inventory and advises the off-line carrier afterward. See also Sell/Sell.

No Go   A flight that does not take off as scheduled usually because of weather or mechanical problems.

Non Revenue
1) A flight that carries nonpaying passengers.
2) A passenger, generally an airline employee, who has not paid for a ticket.

Nonrevenue Positive Space   The designation given to a passenger, usually an airline employee, who does not pay full fare but can make a reservation on a flight.

Nonscheduled Airline   A charter or supplemental carrier.

Nonstop Flight   A flight that goes from origin to destination with no stops en route.

NOOP   Not operating.

No Show   A hotel guest or an airline passenger who neglects to cancel or to use a reservation.

Official Airline Guide (OAG)   Any of several airline reference manuals, published by Official Airline Guides, Inc., a company of the Dun & Bradstreet Corporation.

North American Edition (NAOAG)—Published twice monthly. Contains information on both direct and connecting flights for all scheduled airlines in Canada, the United State (including Alaska and Hawaii), Mexico, Bermuda, the Bahamas, and the Caribbean. Includes departure and arrival times, types of aircraft, meal service, number of stops, airline flight itineraries, ground transportation available at each airport, tables of information on baggage allowances and rates, acceptance of credit cards, taxes, postal information, aircraft performance statistics, agreements between airlines, and index of scheduled airlines with home office addresses and telephone numbers.

Worldwide Edition (WEOAG)—Published monthly. Contains schedules for flights between and within all countries of the world except the U.S., Canada, Mexico, Bermuda, and the Caribbean; however, it does furnish schedules for flights between these countries and the rest of the world (e.g., New York to Paris). In addition to features also found in the *NAOAG*, the *WEOAG* contains information on international time zones, airport duty-free shops, and exchange rates.

Travel Planner, North American Edition—Mainly a guide to destinations. Also includes hotel listings, climate information, diagrams of airport facilities, maps of airport locations, colleges, universities, and military installations within the U.S. and the closest airport to each, limousine service at major airports, and other valuable travel information.

Travel Planner, European and Pacific Asia Editions—Published quarterly. Contains general facts about countries, hotel listings, maps of hotel locations, airport terminal diagrams, and details of reservations systems.

Official Hotel and Resort Guide   See *OHRG*.

Off-Line   Any carrier employee, function, or facility located or performed at a point not connected with that carrier or its route structure.

Off-Line Carrier   Airline other than that whose computer and automated agency is utilized to make reservations and to obtain information. Also applies to any carrier other than the one the agency is using to make a booking that involves several airlines.

Off Peak   A hotel rate or a fare applicable at the least busy time or season.

Off-Route Charter   A scheduled airline flight to or from a point it is not authorized to serve on a regularly scheduled basis.

OHRG (Official Hotel and Resort Guide)   A hotel and resort reference, frequently updated, that gives statistics on each property.

One Way   Any trip where the passenger travels from origin to destination, but does not return.

One-way Back Haul   Fare check to ensure that a passenger traveling one way who transits a higher intermediate point does not undercut that HIP fare.

Online   Having to do with only one airline. A passenger whose entire trip is on Eastern Airlines is taking an online trip.

Open Jaw   A round trip on which the passenger returns to a point different from the point of origin, or departs for the return trip at a point different from the original destination.

Open Rate   A circumstance in which a carrier is free to set its own rates on certain routes when IATA airlines fail to negotiate uniform rates.

Open Ticket   A valid ticket without a specified flight reservation, which the passenger makes at a later date.

Option Date   Date by which a financial commitment must be made for a plane, ship, or tour reservation.

Option Tour   Side trip offered at no extra cost.

Origin   The location where a flight begins or where a passenger begins the trip. Also called boarding city, "from" city, and departure city.

OSI (Other Service Information)   An entry from the host system to other carriers advising them of additional information that may be helpful in dealing with a specific passenger. An OSI entry relates to information services, not a service that requires a carrier to take action. See also Special Service Request.

OT   On time.

Outboard   Away from the center line of the ship.

Overbooking
1) The deliberate practice of confirming more reservations than there are seats or rooms available, to ensure against cancellations or no shows.
2) The same occurrence due to error.

Override   An extra commission paid to agents by airlines, governments, wholesalers, suppliers, etc. as bonuses for volume and/or productivity, or as incentives to book particular arrangements.

Oversale   The selling of more space than exists.

OW   One way.

Pacific Area Travel Association   See PATA.

Package   A variety of travel arrangements put together and sold at one, all-inclusive price.

Paddle Wheel A wheel with boards about its circumference, often used as the sole means of propulsion for a boat.

Parlor A living room or sitting room not used as a bedroom. Sometimes called a salon.

Parlor Car On a train, a specific type of car with individual swivel seats, food, and bar service.

PARS TWA computer reservations system.

Passenger Any person that any carrier is or will be transporting. Often used to mean "paying passenger."

Passenger Name Record (PNR) Client file, stored in a computer reservations system, that includes such information as name of passenger, flight number, travel times, dates of travel, airline to be used, cost of tickets, etc. Also applies to nonair bookings.

Passenger, Through A traveler continuing a journey on the same scheduled aircraft, train, ship, or bus.

Passenger Traffic Manager An employee who takes care of travel arrangements for other employees of the company.

Passenger, Transfer A passenger scheduled to change vehicles or aircraft.

Passenger, Transit A passenger scheduled to continue the trip without a stopover, or who leaves the aircraft (or other vehicle) during a stop.

Passport A formal document, issued to a citizen by an authorized official of a country, that permits the bearer to exit and reenter the country, and allows the person to travel in a foreign nation.

PATA (Pacific Area Travel Association) Organization of countries whose governments and business groups promote travel to the Pacific and Indian Ocean areas.

Peak Fare, Rate, or **Season** The highest level of prices charged during the year.

PEX Fares Inter-European advance purchase fares. For the agent, these fares are similar to domestic supersaver fares; however, they are subject to extremely high cancellation penalties.

PHASE IV Computer format that allows the agent to enter any fare information that the computer will not automatically quote. Also known as fill-in format in some computer systems.

Pitch
1) Forward/backward motion of a ship at sea.
2) The amount of space between seats on an airplane.

Plates Metal cards resembling credit cards, used in a validator to identify the agency and vendor issuing a document.

Plimsoll Mark Load-line marking on the side of a ship.

PNR See Passenger Name Record.

Point-to-Point A point-to-point fare is the basic charge from one stop to another; a point-to-point sale includes only the cost of the ticket. Applicable to basic transportation only.

Port The left side of the ship, facing toward the bow.

Port Taxes or **Charges** Noncommissionable fees levied by a port on each arriving and departing passenger. Generally, port charges are not included in the cruise cost; the travel agent collects them and remits directly to the cruise line.

Positioning Movement of any transport vehicle to another location where it can perform a revenue service. A positioning cruise may carry passengers, but its primary purpose is to move the ship to another cruising area.

Post-Convention Tour An extension designed to supplement a basic return trip from a convention.

Pre-Convention Tour An extension designed to supplement a trip to a convention.

Prefatory Instructions A computer-related term referring to a stored numeric code that allows the agent to queue a PNR with a specific designation. This tells anyone who accesses the queue what actions must be taken.

Prepaid Ticket Advice (PTA) Request from a carrier or agent in one city to a carrier in another city to issue prepaid transportation to a designated individual.

Profile System Also called Frequent Traveler's File. A list, generally stored in a computer reservations system, of frequent travelers and very important clients, that includes their travel preferences, typical methods of payment, and other information useful in making bookings. With major reservations systems, profile information can be retrieved and transferred intact to the PNR, eliminating the need to reenter the data each time such clients book a trip.

Promotional Fare A fare lower than regular rates, designed to stimulate travel, especially at those times a carrier is not busy. These fares are almost always round-trip, and are always subject to certain restrictions.

Proof of Citizenship Any document that establishes the nationality of a traveler to the satisfaction of a foreign government or carrier. Such a document is necessary to obtain a passport.

Protected Commission Guarantee by a supplier or wholesaler to pay commissions to agents, plus full refunds to clients on prepaid, confirmed bookings, regardless of the subsequent cancellation of a tour or cruise.

Prow   The bow of the ship.

Pseudo PNR   Phrase describing any information stored in an airline computer reservations system using the same format as a standard PNR. Called pseudo because it does not include an air reservation. It can give details of other kinds of sales: car rentals, hotels, package tours, cruises, or travel insurance.

PTA   See Prepaid Ticket Advice.

Public Charter   A form of charter established in 1978 with no restrictions on price, length of stay, land arrangements, or advance booking. Provided that each charter group consists of at least twenty seats, one-way flights and discount prices are permitted at the tour operator's discretion. Bonding and escrow provisions similar to those that apply to other charter types are required for the protection of passenger funds.

Published Fares   Any fare found in a tariff, either as a point-to-point fare, or a point-to-point fare and an add-on together. It is important to remember that any published fare must be used before a constructed fare.

Quay   A term, used mainly in Europe, for dock, berth, or pier.

Queue System   A computer file consisting of as many as 100 queues (a computer's electronic tickler file) furnished as part of an automated reservations system. The system vendor allocates responsibilities to some of the queues, such as providing information on an agency's waitlisted clients, advising agents of any bookings affected by scheduling or fare changes, and as a reminder to print tickets on certain days. Agents can decide what reference information they wish to store on other queues.

Quick-Reference Schedule   The flight schedule that different airlines use to show their flights. These are given away to customers and are a handy reference for regular passengers. Also called a passenger schedule.

Rack Rate   In hotels, the official posted rate for each sleeping room.

Receiving Airline   A carrier that will be transporting passengers upon their arrival at an interline point.

Reconfirm   Action whereby passengers advise an airline that they will be taking the flight for which they have confirmed reservations.

Reconfirmation   State indication by passengers that they intend to use their reservation. Under airline rules, reserved space must be reconfirmed within specified time limits or the space may be resold.

Refund   Repayment to the buyer of all or part of a fare, charge, or rate for unused transportation or accommodations.

Registry   The nationality of a ship according to the country where it has been entered into a register. The ship flies the flag of that country, although its owners and crew may be of a different nationality.

Regulatory Agency   An international or government organization with authority to direct the actions of carriers and carrier conferences.

Rep   An individual or a company representative empowered to act for a principal, generally in the area of sales or reservations.

Res Agent   A person, usually connected with an airline, who takes reservations and/or sells tickets.

Reservationist   A carrier employee, usually for an airline, who accepts, validates, and confirms reservations, but who does not actually write tickets.

Resort Hotel   Lodging that provides recreational facilities and meals in addition to sleeping accommodations.

Responsibility Clause   The part of the brochure that outlines the conditions under which a tour is sold. It should give the name of the company or companies financially responsible.

Retail Agency   The business organization of a retailer; a department of a retail and wholesale travel establishment.

Revalidation Sticker   A notice affixed to a flight coupon indicating that a change has been made on the original reservation.

Rigging   The ship's ropes, chains, or cables that support the ship's mast.

Roll   The movement of a ship from side to side.

Round-the-World   A continuous trip via both the Atlantic and the Pacific Oceans, beginning at and returning to the same point. At no time may travelers on these trips reverse directions or use a surface segment that would place them geographically behind their last known airport city.

Round Trip   A continuing journey in which travelers begin and end their trip in the same city, and use the same route in both directions.

Round-Trip Fare   The rate for a trip to a specific destination, and a return by the same route to the point of commencement; applicable to both direct and indirect routings.

Rudder   A fin-like device attached to a ship's stern which, when moved, will cause the ship to turn.

Running Lights   On a ship, three lights, one on each side, and one on the mast. Required by international law to be lighted from sunset to sunrise when the ship is in motion.

Run of the House   Flat cost for which a hotel offers any of its available rooms to members of a group.

SABRE   American Airlines computer reservations systems.

SAI (SABRE Assisted Instruction)   Self-contained lessons on the daily operations and agent functions in SABRE.

SATO   See Scheduled Airline Ticket Office.

Savings Codes   Function of backroom automation systems that allows the accounting department to produce client reports showing the amount of savings their travelers are allowed.

Scheduled Airline   An airline that offers service in accordance with published schedules.

Scheduled Airline Ticket Office (SATO)   An office at a U.S. military installation operated jointly by carriers. Formerly known as JAMTO, or Joint Airline Military Ticket Office.

Screw   The ship's propeller.

Scupper   An opening in the ship's bulwarks through which water accumulated on deck can flow overboard.

Seat Assignment   The actual seat that the passenger will occupy during the flight.

Seat Rotation   In motorcoach travel, the change of seating that allows all passengers the chance to see out the windows on both sides of the bus, as well as to sit in the front.

Segment   A leg or group of legs, on an air itinerary, from boarding point to deplaning point on any given flight.

Segment Code Status   The two-letter code that designates the status of a given segment in the record. The status shows if the segment is "holding confirmed," "waitlisted," "unable to confirm," "pending action," etc.

Sell/Sell   A communication a host airline uses to confirm a seat on an off-line carrier. It tells the agent using the host line's automated reservations system that space is available on the off-line carrier's flight, based on information that the off-line carrier makes available to the first, or host, carrier. The host line later advises the second carrier of the seat sale without asking for specific confirmation.

Service Charge
1) A supplementary fee frequently charged by hotels to cover additional services (often in lieu of a trip).
2) Charge to a client by a travel agency for non-commissionable services.

Set Address   On a computer system, the ID numbers that identify the line number and the set number of a CRT or printer.

SGLB   Single room with bed and bath.

SGLN   Single room with twin bed, without shower or bath.

SGLS   Single room with twin bed and shower.

Shore Excursion   Land tours of a ship's ports-of-call, sold by cruise lines to passengers.

Shoulder Fare, Rate, or **Season**   Level or prices between high/peak and low/off-peak.

Shuttle   No-reservation U.S. air service in which any passenger showing up before a scheduled departure is guaranteed a seat.

Side Round Trip   On an international itinerary, transit by a passenger of a given city more than once during mileage-based routing, for which an additional fee is charged.

Sine   Set of numbers or initials that form a travel agent's identification signature.

Single Carrier Reservations System   A computerized reservations package made available to travel agencies by one airline, giving the subscribing agency direct access to that carrier's computer.

Single Entity Charter   An air charter sponsored and purchased by one person, company, or organization, on which none of the passengers is charged for any of the travel expenses.

Single Supplement   An additional fee, usually charged by hotels, groups, or charters, for a person who chooses to stay in a private room.

SODA   Eastern Airlines computer reservations system.

Sounding   A means, either by weighted rope or by electronic devices, to determine water depth.

Space   Available seats or accommodations for which reservations are accepted.

Special Interest Tour   Tour designed for clients with a common interest in a particular subject. These tours provide an expert tour leader and visits to places and/or events related to the special interest of the participants.

Special Service Request (SSR)   A request by an airline passenger for a specific service, such as a kosher meal, a wheelchair, or a special seat assignment. The request is kept in the passenger's PNR maintained by the airline.

Special Travelers Account Record System   See STARS.

Stabilizer   A device below a ship's waterline to reduce and eliminate the ship's side to side movement (roll).

Stack   Funnel from which the ship's exhaust gases escape.

Stage   The gangway of a paddle wheel steamboat.

Standard Ticket and Area Bank Settlement Plan   A system, in accordance with ATC rules, under which travel agents report airline ticket sales and remit earnings to various institutions established as area banks.

Standby   A waitlisted passenger. A person with no reservation who remains at the check-in counter waiting for space to become available.

Standby Fare   A promotional charge for a conditional reservation under which the passenger cannot board a flight until all passengers with confirmed reservations have boarded.

Starboard   The right side of the ship, facing toward the bow.

Star Rating System   Five-star system used by some governments and survey groups to rate hotels; five-star hotels are generally considered the best.

STARS (Special Travelers Account Record System)   A STAR contains the important information pertaining to a given corporate account or to a given traveler. Often, for a large account, a Primary (first level) STAR will be built into SABRE, with the company's information. A Secondary (personal) STAR will be used for data on an individual traveler.

Stateroom   A cabin on a ship.

Steerageway   The rate of motion necessary for a ship to respond to the repositioning of its rudder.

Stem   The extreme front of a ship.

Stern   The extreme rear of a ship.

Stopover   The deliberate interruption of a journey, or the right to leave transportation at a regular route stop for a certain period of time.

Stow   Store cargo in a ship.

STPC   The term used when an international traveler must overnight at a foreign point and the hotel accommodations are prepaid by the carrier.

Strand   To abandon a passenger or passengers during or just prior to a prepaid travel program, usually due to the business failure of tour operators or carriers.

Subject to Load   When passengers are advised that their confirmed space for a flight may be withheld due to operating load restrictions.

Suggested Itinerary   Preliminary travel program, including routes, times, accommodations, sightseeing trips, etc., provided by the agent for the client's approval.

Summer Fare, Rate, or **Season**   Depending on the route or destination, the highest, lowest, or middle range prices charged during the year, pertaining to the summer season.

Supersonic Transport (SST)   Type of aircraft that flies faster than the speed of sound.

Superstructure   The structural part of the ship above the main deck.

Supplemental Airline or **Carrier**   An airline that offers passenger and cargo charter service.

Supporting Documents   Supplementary papers required to validate a transaction, such as driver's license, birth certificate, health card, visa, and passport.

SystemOne   Eastern Airlines computer reservations system.

Table d'Hote   Complete menu with no variation in courses, offered at a fixed price.

Tariff   The publication that gives all fare information; a published rate or fare.

Technical Stop   A stop on route to a destination, planned or unplanned, to refuel, change crews, etc., but not to discharge passengers or take on new revenue traffic.

TEE (Trans European Express)   A high-speed train traveling in certain parts of Europe.

Tender   A vessel used to carry passengers from the ship to shore and back when the ship cannot dock.

TGV (Tres Grande Vitess)   A very high speed French train.

Through Fare   An airline term for a fare between two cities. The fare can be published point-to-point, or computed with add-on fares.

Through Flight   See Direct Flight.

Ticket   The completed and validated contract of carriage between an individual, or group of individuals, and the carrier.

Ticket Agent   Person employed by a carrier to take reservations and sell tickets. The federal government applies this term to anyone who sells an airline ticket; for example, travel agents and tour operators.

Ticket Exchange Notice   A nonaccountable document used by travel agents and airline personnel to show that an accountable document has been exchanged for another at either an additional collection, even exchange, or exchange with a refund due the client.

Ticket Stock   Airline ticket blanks, used by carrier employees and travel agents, that become contracts when filled out and validated.

Time Limit   Date, agreed to by the agent and the customer, by which the client must purchase a ticket to avoid loss of the reserved space.

Time Sharing A condominium concept in which clients buy the use of an apartment for a given period of time every year.

Timetable A written schedule of carrier arrival and departure times, flight numbers, stops, and sometimes "remarks."

Tour Any prearranged, generally prepaid, trip to one or more places and back to the point of departure.

Tour Basing Fares A discount rate excursion fare available to customers who buy prepaid tours and packages. Tour basing fares include inclusive tour, incentive group, group inclusive tour, contract bulk inclusive tour, tour basing, and group round-trip inclusive tour basing fares. Any carrier fare on which a travel agent may claim a higher commission if specified ground arrangements are sold at the same time.

Tour Departure The date a person or group begins a trip. The complete operation of a single tour.

Tour Escort The person who accompanies a tour throughout and is responsible for its smooth progress.

Tourism Activities concerned with providing and marketing services and facilities for pleasure travel. All the elements of travel for enjoyment.

Tourist Board City, state, or national government bureau whose purpose is to encourage tourism in its area.

Tourist Card A card, issued to travelers before they enter certain countries, which is sometimes required in addition to a passport or proof of identification.

Tourist Class Generally, accommodations or establishments somewhat below top level. On ships, segregated, less than first class service. On airlines, an unofficial designation for economy or coach service.

Tour Leader An individual with the expertise or special qualifications to conduct a particular travel group. Often used incorrectly to mean a tour escort.

Tour Manager See Tour Escort.

Tour Operator A company that combines travel elements into packages which are then sold through travel agencies. Also known as Tour Wholesaler.

Tour Order An accountable document used to prepay nonair travel arrangements, such as a tour, package, or hotel stay.

Tour Organizer An individual, sometimes a travel agent, who organizes a group of passengers for a special, prepaid tour. An organizer may be an outside salesperson.

Traffic Conferences The three areas into which IATA has divided the world, called TC1, TC2, and TC3.

Transfer Local service provided to transport travelers from the airport, railway station, pier, etc. to their hotel, and vice versa. Cost variables depend upon whether the conveyance is a private, chauffeur-driven car or taxi, and whether the transfer is escorted or unescorted.

Transit Point On the route traveled, any stop at an intermediate point that does not fall into the definition of a stopover as it applies to the fare used.

Transit Without Visa (TWOV) Permission granted to non-U.S. citizens by the U.S. Immigration Service to travel through the United States without a U.S. Travel Visa, when the origin and destination of their trip is outside the United States.

Travel Planner The publication that lists most cities and location of the nearest airport, what hotels are nearby, availability of ground transportation, etc. The *Travel Planner* also lists the nearest airport for numerous colleges, universities, and military installations. See also *Official Airline Guide.*

TRPB Triple room with bath.

TRPN Triple room without bath or shower.

TRPS Triple room with shower.

Tug Strongly built boat, equipped with heavy-duty machinery, used to tow other boats, ships, or any water craft.

Turn-Around Point Place in a round trip where the outgoing journey ends and the incoming journey begins.

Twin A hotel room with twin beds, designed for two people.

Twin Double A hotel room with two double beds, to accommodate two, three, or four people.

TWNB Double room with twin beds and bath.

TWNN Double room with twin beds, without shower or bath.

TWNS Double room with twin beds and shower.

TWOV See Transit Without Visa.

Universal Air Travel Plan (UATP) Air travel credit card system sponsored by U.S. domestic airlines.

Upgrade To change to a better class of service or accommodations.

Uplift Ratio A government system to control the charter actions of foreign airlines by requiring their out-bound charter operations to be balanced by a particular ratio of incoming traffic.

USTTA (United States Travel and Tourism Administration) Government office to promote travel to the United States.

Validation The imprinting of a portion of airline ticket stock with the appropriate stamp that makes it a legal ticket.

Validator
1) A mechanism used to validate.
2) Any of the special airline die plates used in such a mechanism.

Validity of Fare   Whereby normal one-way, round-trip, or circle trip fares may be used to complete the transportation for one year after the commencement of the journey.

Validity of Ticket   Whereby a ticket may be used for one year from the date of issue if no portion of it has been used. Carriage under a ticket must therefore commence not later than twelve months after its date of issuance. Its validity is extended for one year from the date of commencement of travel.

Value Season   A term sometimes used to denote less than peak times.

Video Display Terminal (VDT)   General term describing TV-like display screens that allow the computer user to see what is being entered into the computer and to read the information the computer is sending out. Often used with airline reservations systems and backoffice automated accounting systems in travel agencies.

Visa   Government authorization by a country to permit entry to and travel within that country. Appended to a passport.

Visit USA Fares   Air fares for domestic travel offered at reduced rates to visitors to the United States.

Voucher   Document the client exchanges for services that have been prepaid.

Voucher, Tour   Documents distributed by tour operators to be exchanged for such services as accommodations, meals, sightseeing, etc. Also called coupons.

Wagon Lits   Firm that operates sleeping cars on European railroads; also, the sleeping cars themselves.

Waitlist   Listing of customers waiting for a travel service that has been sold out. As space becomes available, waitlisted passengers are confirmed in the order in which reservations were received.

Wake   The track left in the water by a ship.

Warsaw Convention   The original (1929) agreement in which airline liability for passengers and cargo was established. The per passenger limit of $8,333 was amended to $75,000, waiving the right of defense, in the 1968 Montreal agreement.

WATA   World Association of Travel Agents.

Waterline   The line on the side of a ship that corresponds with the surface of the water.

Weather Side   The side of a ship exposed to wind or bad weather.

Weigh   To raise the anchor.

WHO   See World Health Organization.

Winch   A machine that operates a ship's cranes.

Windward   The direction from which the wind blows.

Winter Fare or **Rate**   The most or least expensive fare, relating to winter, depending on the area.

Working Areas   Areas within a CRT that allow an agent to work on several PNRs at once. Each computer system has its own number of working areas.

World Bank   Special United Nations agency, headquartered in Washington, DC, that makes loans to member nations to facilitate productive investment, encourage foreign trade, and to discharge obligations of international debt.

World Health Organization (WHO)   United Nations agency that studies and provides information on communicable diseases and health problems throughout the world. The WHO instructs governments on vaccination requirements for travelers.

World Tourism Organization (WTO)   Unite Nations affiliated association of national tourism organizations. Formerly, the International Union of Official Travel Organizations.

Youth Hostel   A low-priced, supervised lodging for young people.

Glossary compiled by Leslie Ann Sigrist, currently the owner of Agency Systems Consulting, an advisory firm that specializes in training and office procedures. Ms. Sigrist has taught industry classes at both fully accredited trade schools and community colleges; her background covers all aspects of travel agency operation, from travel consultant and group supervisor to director of product development.

Index

Accommodations, 67–71
    See also Hotels
    effect of airlines on, 69
    effect of meetings and conventions
        on, 70
    employment in, 8, 288–290
    future of, 70–71, 261–263
    influence of automobile on, 68
    post-war growth of, 68
    role of hotel chains, 69
Acculturation, 190
Aeroflot, 55
Africa, 20–21, 190, 198, 256
Aircraft 29, 30, 38–39, 54, 98, 251, 261
Airline Deregulation Act, 31, 39,
    55–58
Airlines, 53–61
    commuters, 58
    employment in, 8, 279–285
    future of, 260–261
Airports, 29, 261
Air Transport
    economics of, 58–59
    employment in, 8, 279–285
    future of, 260–261
    history of, 27–32
    marketing of, 59
Allocentrics, 122
Alternative tourism, 170, 189,
    197–198
American Express, 37, 74
Amtrak, 26–27, 61
Armstrong, Neil, 38
Archaeology, 193
Arts and handicrafts, 193
Attractions, 215–216, 222, 232–241
Automation, 77
Automobiles, 36–37, 213
    future of, 260
    history of, 34–36
Avis, Warren E., 36

Balance of Payments, 161–163
Barriers to travel, 131–132
Benz, Karl, 35
Bermuda Agreement, 29
Blue Ribbon, 24
Broadmoor Hotel, 33
Brown Palace Hotel, 33
Business travel, 3, 6, 75, 132–135,
    137–147, 215, 254, 257

California, 23
Canada, 5, 11, 183, 259
Car rental
    employment in, 8, 294
    history of,   36–37
Caribbean, 68, 165, 192, 193,
    255, 259
Carnival Cruise Lines, 39
Carrying capacity, 168
Cartan Tours, 37
Central Pacific Railroad, 25
Charter tours, 66
Civil Aeronautics Board (CAB), 30, 54,
    55, 57
Colonial Williamsburg, 32
Columbus, Christopher, 21, 22
Community involvement, 196,
    212–213, 222
Concorde, 38, 251
Cook, Thomas, 37, 74
Crompton, John, 125
Cruise lines, 63–66
    employment in, 8, 290–291
    fly-cruise, 64
    growth of, 24, 63, 214
    history of, 23–24
    marketing of, 65
    repeat business, 65
Crusades, 32
Cugnot, Nicolas, 34
Cultural conflict, 184, 202–205

Culture, 154–155, 184–185, 202–205, 232–241
Cunard, Samuel, 23
Cunard Lines, 63
Currency exchange, 122, 215, 256

Da Vinci, Leonardo 27
Daimler, Gottlieb, 35
Demographics, 120, 253
Demonstration effect, 161, 189–190
Deregulation, 30–31
Developing countries, 1, 158–159, 183
Doxey, G.V., 187
Drake, Sir Francis, 23

Economic impact of tourism, 3, 105, 149–182, 210, 219
Egypt, 22
Environmental effects of tourism, 198–200, 219, 276–278
Eurailpass, 63
Europe, 62, 255, 259, 266–275
Excursionists, 4

Federal Aviation Administration, 30, 55
Ford, Henry, 19, 35
Foreign exchange, 99, 158, 165
France, 21, 29, 104, 102, 257
French Lick Hotel, 33
Fraunces Tavern, 32
Frommer, Arthur, 37
Fulton, Robert, 23
Future, 251–264

Gama, Vasco da, 23
Germany, 21, 98, 101, 102, 104, 257
Goeldner, Charles, 127
Graf Zeppelin, 27
Grand tour, 21
Great Britain, 22, 23, 104, 256, 257
Greenbrier, 33
Greyhound Lines, 66
Group travel, 256–257

Hawaii, 22, 100, 198
Henderson, Ernest, 33
Heritage tourism, 154, 192, 210–211, 242–249
Herodotus, 135
Hertz, John, 36
Heyerdahl, Thor, 22
Hilton, Conrad, 33
Holiday Inn, 33, 70
Holland America Lines, 38
Hosting 228–231
Hotel del Coronado, 33
Hotels
    See also Accommodations

classification of, 68
effect of automobiles on, 33, 68
effect of railroads on, 32, 67
employment in, 8, 288–290
history of, 32–34
Hub-and-spoke, 31–32, 57

Ile de France, 24
Imitation effect, 161, 189–190
Incentive travel, 133
Industrial Revolution, 20, 23
Intercontinental Hotels, 34, 69, 263
International Air Transport Association, 29, 54
International Civil Aviation Organization, 30
International Monetary Fund, 2
International tourism, 95, 100–104, 119, 157–159, 184, 218
    border-crossing formalities, 98, 258
    economic impact of, 100–101
    from the United States, 41–51, 104–106, 255–257
    future of, 251–264
    to the United States, 106–110, 213, 218
Italy, 21, 68, 104, 257

Japan, 62, 104, 157, 256

Kosters, Marinus, 127

Land transport, 61–67
Leisure, 3, 97, 100, 119
Lindbergh, Charles, 28

Magellan, Ferdinand, 23
Marketing, 79–93, 97, 122–124, 127, 137–147, 185, 226–228
Matthews, Harry, 194
Mayflower, 23
McAdam, John Loudon, 21
McIntosh, Robert, 127
Mediterranean, 22
Meetings and conventions, 70, 132–135, 215
Mexico, 164, 185, 189, 255, 259
Montgolfier brothers, 27
Motels, 33, 68
Motivation, 97, 119–131
Motorcoach transport, 66–67
    commuter uses of, 66
    employment in, 8, 294–295
    recreational use of, 66
Multiplier, 164–165

National Aeronautics and Space Administration, 55

National Railroad Passenger Corporation, 26–27, 61
Netherlands, The, 23, 157, 257
New York, 24, 123

Olds, R.E., 35
Orient Express, 62

Package tours, 72, 98–99, 185, 212–214
Pan Am, 38, 55
Panhard, Rene, 35
Planning process, 209
Pleasure travel, 6
Plog, Stanley, 122
Ponce de Leon, 33
Polynesia, 22
Portugal, 121
Promontory Point, 25
Psychocentrics, 122
Pull factors, 124
Pullman, George Mortimer, 25
Push factors, 124

Queen Elizabeth, 24
Queen Mary, 24

Railroads
    decline of, 26
    economics of, 61–63
    employment in, 8, 291–294
    future of, 261
    history of, 25–27
Recreation, 135
Ritz, 67
Roads, 21–22
Roman Empire, 21, 32
Royce, Sir Henry, 35

Saturation, 167–168, 187
Savoy, 67
Seasonality, 160, 192, 207
Senior Travel Market, 3, 120, 253
Sheraton Hotels, 33
Six freedoms of the air, 29
Smith, Valene, 130
Social impact of tourism, 183–201
Song of Norway, 64
Spa Resorts, 33
Spain, 68, 102, 104
Spirit of St. Louis, 28
Statler, Ellsworth, 33
Stefan Batory, 63
Suez Canal, 23

Tax revenue, 153, 210
Titanic, 24

Tom Thumb, 25
Tour operators, 37, 71–73, 165–166, 185
Tourism
    components of, 7–8
    cost of, 155–156, 168, 184–185,
        199, 208
    definition of, 3–6, 19, 149
    development of, 158–159, 169–170,
        207–231
    economic impact of, 3, 105, 149–171,
        172–182
    employment in, 1, 151–152, 159–161,
        191–192, 210, 279–298
    environmental impact of, 198–200
    as an export industry, 99, 103, 158
    future of, 251–264
    growth of, 1–3, 95–97
    history of, 19–40, 207
    motivation, 97, 119–131
    planning for, 207–231
    social impact of, 168, 183–201
Tourism development, 168–169,
        186–187, 207–231
Tourism master plan, 223–226
Tourism multiplier, 164–165
Tourism product, 5
Tourist, definition of, 3–6, 19, 149
Tourist information services, 214, 217
Tours, 71–72
Trans-European Express, 62
Transportation, 216
    history of, 19–32
    water, 22–24
Trans-Siberian Railway, 25
Travel. *See* Tourism
Travel agent 73–77, 185
    economics of, 75–76
    employment in, 8, 285–288
    future of, 263
    history of, 74–75

Union Pacific Railroad, 25
United Nations, 2, 193
U.S. Travel Data Center, 4, 110,
    150, 152

Vikings, 22
Visitor services, 228–231

Water transport, 22–24, 63–66
Wholesalers, 71–73
Wilson, Kemmons, 33
World Bank, 2, 38, 95
World Tourism Organization, 95–96,
    103, 184
Wright, Orville and Wilbur, 19, 27